BUSINESS PRACTICES
FOR CONSTRUCTION MANAGEMENT

BUSINESS PRACTICES FOR CONSTRUCTION MANAGEMENT

JAMES J. ADRIAN, PH.D., P.E., C.P.A.
Bradley University

ELSEVIER
NEW YORK/OXFORD/AMSTERDAM

AMERICAN ELSEVIER PUBLISHING COMPANY, INC.
52 Vanderbilt Avenue, New York, N.Y. 10017

ELSEVIER PUBLISHING COMPANY
335 Jan Van Galenstraat, P.O. Box 211
Amsterdam, The Netherlands

Library of Congress Cataloging in Publication Data

Adrian, James J
  Business practices for construction management.

  Includes index.
  1. Construction industry—Management.
  2. Management.   I. Title.
HD9715.A2A34   658'.92'4   75-14999
ISBN 0-444-00169-7

Manufactured in the United States of America

To Chris, Doug, and Kevin

Contents

Preface   xi

Chapter 1
Business Practices: An Introduction
1.1	Introduction	1
1.2	The Study of Business Management	2
1.3	Some Basic Terminology	5
1.4	Decision Making	9
1.5	Summary	11
	Cases	12

Chapter 2
Structure of the Firm: Legal, Organizational, Financial
2.1	Introduction	15
2.2	Types of Construction Firms	15
2.3	Legal Structure of the Firm	24
2.3.1	Proprietorship	25
2.3.2	Partnership	27
2.3.3	Corporation	35
2.4	Organizational Structure	39
2.4.1	The Construction Hierarchical Organization Structure	43
2.4.2	Organic Structure for the Construction Firm	47
2.5	Financial Structure: Leverage and Liquidity	48
2.5.1	Financial Structure of the Construction Firm	53
2.5.2	Financial Analysis of the Firm	58
2.6	Summary	63
	Cases	64

Chapter 3
Marketing: Obtaining and Maintaining Clients
3.1	Introduction	69
3.2	Marketing Environment of the Construction Firm	70
3.3	Planning for Company Operations	71
3.4	Pricing the Firm's Work	77
3.4.1	Pricing Parameters	79
3.4.2	Bid Strategy	81
3.5	Promoting the Firm and Its Work	89

3.6   Placing the Product   95
3.7   Summary   96
       Cases   97

Chapter 4
Business Law: Avoiding Litigation
4.1   Introduction   103
4.2   Constitutional and Administrative Law   104
4.3   Criminal Law   105
4.4   Tort Law   108
4.5   Contract Law   110
4.5.1   Contract Agreement   112
4.5.2   Competent Parties   116
4.5.3   Legal Subject Matter   118
4.5.4   Adequate Exchange   120
4.5.5   Contract Termination   121
4.6   Commercial Paper   126
4.6.1   Checks   129
4.6.2   Promissory Notes   130
4.6.3   Drafts   132
4.7   Employment and Subcontractor Relations   133
4.7.1   Employment Law   134
4.7.2   General—Subcontractor Law   135
4.8   Summary   137
       Cases   138

Chapter 5
Funding: Financing Business Operations
5.1   Introduction   143
5.2   Short Term Financing   144
5.3   Trade Credit   146
5.3.1   Trade Credit and the Contractor   147
5.3.2   The Cost of Trade Credit   149
5.4   Short Term Loans   150
5.4.1   Bank Loans and the Contractors   153
5.4.2   Cost of Short Term Loans   155
5.5   Other Sources of Short Term Funds   157
5.6   Intermediate Term Financing   158
5.6.1   Sources of Intermediate Financing   159
5.6.2   Intermediate Financing and the Contractor   161
5.6.3   Cost of Intermediate Financing   163
5.7   Long Term Funding   164
5.7.1   Long Term Debt   166

5.7.2	The Cost of Long Term Debt	168
5.8	Equity Funds	170
5.8.1	Types of Stock	171
5.8.2	The Cost of Equity Funds	172
5.9	Summary	173
	Cases	173

Chapter 6
Personnel Management: Getting More for Your Money

6.1	Introduction	179
6.2	Construction Industry Productivity Characteristics	180
6.3	Leadership and Directing	183
6.4	Communication	188
6.5	Theory X and Theory Y	193
6.6	Group Behavior	198
6.7	Management by Objectives	202
6.8	Modeling Productivity	204
6.8.1	Traditional Models	206
6.8.2	Method Productivity Delay Model	211
6.9	Applications to the Construction Industry	220
6.10	Summary	223
	Cases	224

Chapter 7
Cost Accounting: Planning and Controlling Costs

7.1	Introduction	229
7.2	Cost Accounting in the Construction Industry	230
7.3	Cost Accounting Terminology	236
7.4	Accumulation of Cost—Bookkeeping	243
7.4.1	Material Costs	244
7.4.2	Labor Costs	248
7.4.3	Overhead Costs	254
7.5	Document Flowcharting	260
7.6	Job Order Costing	265
7.7	Standard Costs	269
7.8	Absorption Versus Direct Costing	278
7.9	Budgeting and Cash Flow	281
7.10	Summary	290
	Cases	290

Chapter 8
Capital Budgeting: Planning Long Term Expenditures

| 8.1 | Introduction | 295 |
| 8.2 | Average Investment Method | 296 |

8.3	Payback Method	298
8.4	Time Value of Money	300
8.4.1	Interest Formulas	301
8.4.2	Annuities	308
8.5	Discounted Cash Flow Analysis	309
8.6	Annual Cost Method	315
8.7	Present Worth Method	318
8.8	Tax Considerations	320
8.8.1	Depreciation	321
8.8.2	Investment Tax Credit	324
8.8.3	Capital Gain Considerations	325
8.9	Summary	326
	Cases	327

Chapter 9
Financial Accounting: Holding the Firm Accountable

9.1	Introduction	331
9.2	The Accounting Cycle	332
9.3	Typical Transactions	344
9.3.1	Initial Investment: Contributed Capital	346
9.3.2	Debt Capital	350
9.3.3	Accounting for Cash	352
9.3.4	Accounting for Fixed Assets	356
9.3.5	Depreciation for Fixed Assets	360
9.3.6	Accounting for Leases	365
9.4	Methods of Recognizing Revenue and Expense	369
9.4.1	Short Duration	370
9.4.2	Percentage of Completion and Completed Contract Methods	371
9.5	Adjustments and Changes	377
9.6	Accounting Errors	384
9.7	Financial Statements	387
9.7.1	Statement of Financial Position	388
9.7.2	Income Statement	391
9.7.3	Statement of Changes in Financial Position	394
9.8	Summary	397
	Cases	398

Appendix A

Interest Tables	405

Index   419

Preface

A large percentage of construction industry financial failures could be prevented by the application of well-founded business disciplines. Better business practices in this area will result in a more stable industry leading to a reduction in unemployment, higher productivity, and less financial risk.

This book covers the skills that are fundamental to the inception and maintenance of a profitable construction business. It emphasizes practical applications of well-founded business disciplines. Each chapter presents a different business skill by means of discussing basic fundamentals of the skill in question and examples of the fundamentals as they apply to the construction industry. The reader is asked to try his hand at applying the business skill discussed by means of solving practical case problems at the end of each chapter.

The business disciplines discussed are presented in an order that is meant to parallel the process of the development of a new firm: early chapters address skills needed to start the firm, following chapters address skills needed to maintain the firm, and the final chapters address skills necessary for the long-term operation of the firm.

The author's firm belief that the construction industry needs to improve its accounting practices has led to a heavy coverage of the accounting discipline as the subject relates to the construction industry. While Chapters 7 and 9 are specifically on accounting, accounting related information is also contained in Chapters 2, 4, and 8.

The need for the business skills discussed is independent of the size of the firm or the type of construction work that the firm performs. As such, the book should be equally applicable to the small or large construction firm as well as the general or subcontracting firm. Architects and engineers will find the book a useful aid in improving their working relationships with the construction industry. Finally, the public accounting firm should find the book valuable in its continuing efforts to offer construction business related management services.

Every book is a conglomerate synthesis of the author's associations and experiences: this book is no exception. My engineering and accounting colleagues have all indirectly influenced the writing of this book. To these individuals I would like to express my appreciation. Finally, and most important of all, I am grateful to my family, for without their inspiration the project would not have been worthwhile.

Peoria, Illinois August, 1975   James J. Adrian

Chapter 1

Business Practices:
An Introduction

1.1 Introduction

Throughout recent years the construction industry has witnessed an increasing number of construction firm financial failures.[1] Although many of the firms that fail are small in regard to their owned assets, there is evidence of business failures among large firms. The potential dollar loss associated with a project is often of such magnitude that it can financially ruin even the more stable, larger firm.

Business failures in the construction industry can be traced to many causes. Some of these are related to excessive competition, unexpected bad weather, national slumps in the economy, and simply bad judgment. In addition, a large number of contractor business failures can be traced to the disuse of proven business practices.

One could justifiably agree that there is no other industry that requires the proper application of business practices as much as the construction industry. The many variables and complex relationships that exist between variables that must be considered in the process of building a construction project necessitate sound business practices and decisions. The coordination and use of the many types of labor skills, materials, and equipment that are used to build a project require daily application of proper business practices. The variable environment surrounding the construction project complicates decisions to be made concerning the use of labor, material, and equipment. In addition, governmental influence and labor union practices have a bearing on business decisions that must be made.

The business practices or disciplines that are a necessary part of a firm's everyday business vary somewhat depending on the size of the firm and the type of work the firm performs. In addition, the need for

[1]"Business Failures," *Duns Review*, 1971, p. 93.

various practices depends on a firm's competition, and the economic environment in which the firm is operating.

The varying necessity or importance of a given business discipline does not remove the contractor's need for certain common business skills. Whereas the firm may be highly competent in regard to the technical aspects of their business, the lack of basic business practices can result in the business failure of the firm. Such basic skills as marketing, personnel management, finance, and cost control are fundamental to the starting and maintenance of a profitable business firm.

Many contracting firms are not large enough in terms of employees to delegate various business practices to company departments or individuals specializing in a given practice. More commonly, a single individual or a few individuals take on the responsibilities for the decisions associated with all of the business practices. It is realistic to assume that an individual can become competent enough in each required business discipline such that he can maintain a profitable firm. The following sections and chapters attempt to aid the contractor in obtaining such skills.

1.2 The Study of Business Management

Business management is both an art and science. It is a science in that there is an organized body of general truths upon which it is based. However, management is more than stated truths. Business management also requires skills to accomplish the desired results. As such it requires creativity. This is, of course, an art.

Business management concerns itself with the efficient accomplishment of stated goals. How this is done is a subject of dispute. Four approaches to business management are generally recognized. These four approaches are as follows.

(1)   Scientific management approach
(2)   Functional approach
(3)   Behavioral science approach
(4)   Systems approach

Frederick Taylor[2] is generally recognized as the founder of the *scientific approach* to management. Observation, measurement, and comparison are the main ingredients of scientific management. Much of the work sampling, time study, and motion analysis techniques in exis-

---

[2]Taylor, F. W., *Scientific Management*, New York, Harper and Row Company, 1974.

tence can be traced to the work of Taylor and his followers. By means of collecting data on the various parameters of a production system (often referred to as motion study) and by applying statistical concepts, standardization and improvement of work production is sought.

The *functional approach* to management study is often traced to Henri Fayol.[3] Fayol suggested that in order for the firm to accomplish its objectives it had to place emphasis on various organizational functions. These functions are identified as follows.

(1) Commercial
(2) Technical
(3) Financial
(4) Security
(5) Accounting
(6) Managerial

Modern day "functional" management theorists might take issue with Fayol's six functions. However, the fact remains that the functional approach to management study concerns itself with the identification of organization functions, the tasks of such functions, and the means of placing personnel in the appropriate functions (including remuneration of personnel).

The *behavioral approach* to management study is an area which has recently been gaining popularity. The approach is not new in that the approach was used in the Hawthorne Plant[4] studies at the Western Electric Company in the 1930s. The behavioral approach to management concerns itself with psychology and sociology as they affect the accomplishment of business objectives. The overall purpose of the behavioral approach is to attempt to make individual worker goals and company goals consistent with one another so that morale and productivity can be improved. Whereas scientific management somewhat ignores the human relations problem in its attempt to increase productivity, the behavioral approach focuses on the relationship of employee satisfaction and productivity. This relationship is often very complex. It will be discussed in Chapter 6. Areas such as leadership and the social system are part of the behavioral approach to management.

The *systems approach* to management (often referred to as the quantitative approach) is a rather new concept. Much of its development can be traced to the operations research work done by Britain during World

---

[3]Fayol, Henri, *General and Industrial Management*, New York, Pitman Publishing Company, 1949.

[4]Committee on Work in Industry, National Research Council, *Fatigue of Workers: Its Relation to Industrial Production*, New York, Reinhold Publishing Company, 1941, pp. 56–57.

War II. The widespread availability of the computer has been a further stimulus to the systems approach. The systems approach to management concerns itself with studying the overall system and its interrelationships. This differs from the functional approach which addresses organizational segments. The systems approach attempts to maxamize the overall objective of the firm by interrelating all of the components or factors that affect the firm. These include social components as well as organizational components. The use of scientific models, mathematics, and computers have facilitated the modeling and processing of the vast amount of interdependent data that is part of an overall systems approach to management.

There are elements of each one of the four management approaches in management study today. Which one is most appropriate when it comes to management and the construction industry? Although one could probably make a case for each, the environment of the construction industry does affect the applications. For example, the strong labor unions that are typical of the construction industry often curtail an all-out application of scientific management principles. Labor is often apprehensive about time studies and work sampling.

There have been several recent contractor efforts in regard to the behavioral approach to management objectives.[5] Such an approach can be made to conform with union objectives. Specific programs and their successes and failures are discussed in Chapter 6.

The construction industry has traditionally been characterized as having a functional approach to management. Functions such as purchasing, planning, and accounting have been singled out and each is addressed individually. While it is inappropriate to totally discount such an approach, the construction industry has often suffered from a lack of personnel qualified to carry out each of the functions. Many contracting firms are small in terms of personnel and therefore an individual is often required to carry out functions with which he is unacquainted or does not have the time to carry out successfully. In addition, this lack of size and knowledge have often resulted in an organizational structure that does not facilitate accomplishing the firm's goals.

The systems approach, being a relatively new concept in regard to business management, is as yet untested in regard to the construction industry. Disregarding this fact, the systems approach to management implies the usage of certain quantitative skills and models (in addition to the possible need for computer implementation). As such, one can-

[5]Schrader, C. R., "Boosting Construction Worker Productivity," *Civil Engineering*, October, 1972, p. 62.

not expect that the systems approach will have an immediate far-reaching effect on the construction industry. However, several large and sophisticated (in regard to the use of models) contracting firms are successfully applying a systems approach to business management.

Throughout the following chapters the reader will be able to identify various applications and references of each of the four approaches to business management. Each has attributes that are lacking in the others. As such, each has its place in the study of business management as it relates to the construction industry.

1.3 Some Basic Terminology

The study of business practices is often addressed by means of a functional approach. Modern management practitioners commonly divide the management process into the four functions of planning, organizing, directing, and controlling.

The degree of emphasis on each of these four management functions in regard to its contribution to the accomplishment of the overall company objective depends on the type of business. In research related business, the planning function is likely to be the most vital function in the firm's business operation. On the other hand, while planning is also important in the construction industry, directing and controlling are equally important in regard to the contractor's overall objectives.

The functions of planning, organizing, directing, and controlling, although not discussed individually in the following chapters, are important in the discussion of the various chapters. The four functions are illustrated in Fig. 1.1.

X Planning is the determining of organization objectives, the recognizing of factors that affect these objectives, and the formulation of activities that are believed necessary to achieve the objectives. Several plans are part of a business firm. These include profit plans, growth plans, and manpower plans. The broadness of the plan depends upon the type of plan. Plans that are financially oriented tend to be very specific, whereas a growth plan tends to be somewhat general and less specific.

Planning should be an integral part of the management decision-making process. It should start with the initial conception of the business firm. Thereafter, the planning function has to be flexible and have the ability to adapt to ever-changing dynamic situations. Planning should be done before actions are taken.

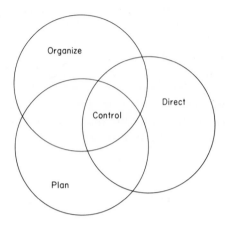

Fig. 1.1. Four management functions.

Because company plans are based on the future, forecasting becomes part of the planning function. *Forecasting* is the prediction of future operations and conditions from the study of available pertinent data. Although forecasting is more of an art than a science, the task can be enhanced by consistently using forecasting procedures and by including the advice of all employees who can contribute to the task. Forecasts are subject to individual opinion and are thus subject to error and variation. However, the intent is to reduce, if not eliminate, such error.

If the objectives determined by the planning function are to be accomplished, the business firm must formulate various activities necessary to this accomplishment. These activities may be separated into policies, procedures, and methods. A *policy* is somewhat general in nature. It states the boundaries and limitations within which the business is to operate. The firm's policies provide the guidelines for each separate classification of its activities. For example, a construction contracting firm might have a policy of training their own people to be project superintendents rather than hire them externally.

A *procedure* is a more detailed part of a plan than is a policy. A procedure lists a sequence of tasks to be accomplished to perform designated work. For example, a procedure for the previously discussed company policy (a company training its own superintendents from within) would clarify the effort and techniques of such a policy. That is, the training of company foreman with three years experience by means of a six week superintendent's course would be a procedure consistent with the firm's policy.

The difficulty of company procedures (especially in a large firm) is that the firm tends to neglect to intermittently review the value of its procedures. As a result, many firms use procedures that are often out-dated and relatively useless.

A *method* is yet more detailed and specific than is a procedure. A method addresses the means by which a stated procedure is to be accomplished. A method for the previously discussed procedure might include the ingredients of the six-week training program and how it is to be implemented and by whom. In addition, specific means of measuring the skills of the applicants to the program might be specified.

In order to determine good methods, a manager must be technically competent and innovative. He must constantly seek better methods of accomplishment.

Company determined plans often result in the setting of standards and the determination of a budget. *Standards* are stated expectancies that the firm seeks in carrying out its plan. They are set to be realistic and are often referred to as norms. For example, a contracting firm might set a profit margin it intends to maintain throughout a given period. Such a desired and expected profit margin can be considered standard. Standards are set consistent with company objectives.

Budgets represent the financial result of planning. A budget is de-termined that will provide for the firm's carrying out its activities to accomplish its objectives. Budgets are prepared for a given period of time. They tend to be all encompassing in that they usually cover the entire operations of the firm. Accuracy and usefulness are the tests of a good planning budget.

Organizing is the grouping of activities that are to be performed by the business firm, and the assigning of managerial authority and re-sponsibility. The performing of the organizing function usually results in the preparation of an *organizational chart*. The organizational chart indicates the grouping of activities, the authority relationships, and the communication channels between the groupings. The overriding goal of organizing is to aid people in working together efficiently.

The grouping of activities of the business firm is often referred to as *departmentation*. This grouping of activities might be done by various means. For example, the grouping might be made by various types of production the firm performs, or by various sales areas.

There are four component ingredients to the task of organizing. These are the environment, the work, the employees, and the relation-ships. The organizational structure that results from these four ingre-dients often determines the success of the firm. The organizational structure includes both vertical and horizontal relationships. These relationships along with the social impact factors of organizing will be discussed in depth in Chapter 2.

The *directing* function can be thought of as the guiding of the efforts of company personnel toward the attainment of the company's objectives. The function of directing includes the subject matter of proper and effective leadership and supervision. Although leadership qualities are somewhat difficult to pinpoint, they most certainly include the ability to gain the confidence and support of the group for which the leadership is to exist. In addition to lending advice to his employees, a leader must also be open to the constructive advice of his employees. Other qualities and types of leadership are discussed in chapter 6.

Much of the function of directing is concerned with the motivation of employees. *Motivation* can be defined as the getting of employees to perform work enthusiastically because they want to accomplish certain individual goals which are made consistent with company goals. Although the task of motivating is often considered an art, there are defined theories concerning the subject matter. For example, one theory (called theory X) assumes that individuals are basically adverse to the performance of work. This type of assumption leads to certain management practices that should be followed to accomplish the firm's objectives. On the other hand, yet another theory of motivation (referred to as theory Y) takes a different view of an individual's approach to work. It assumes that an individual will enthusiastically perform work if he is given the opportunity to accomplish various goals. This approach, which differs from that of theory X, results in other management practices in regard to the accomplishment of firm objectives. These theories of motivation, along with others are discussed in greater depth in Chapter 6.

The fourth management function is that of controlling. *Controlling* can be thought of as the task of establishing various standards (production, financial, etc.), the comparing of actual results to these standards, and the taking of corrective action to reduce or eliminate discrepancies. Thus, the function of controlling consists of three somewhat distinct subfunctions.

The control task is employed for the control of cost, quantity, and quality. Quantity and quality controls are often related to technical disciplines such as engineering and mathematics. For example, statistical testing is often employed as an aid in quantity and quality standards. In addition, engineering method studies are also used. On the other hand, cost standards and controls, although influenced by the scientific areas, are within the realm of financial business practices. For example, cost accounting principles are employed for the purpose of controlling and establishing cost standards.

In addition to using proven business tools and practices for the control task, the controller also has to use his own judgment as an aid in carrying out the function. Controlling should be used as a means of correcting ineffective or inferior performance and as a means of enforcing acceptable performance. Much more will be said about the control function in later chapters. In particular, Chapters 7 and 9 on accounting deal with both operating control and overall company control.

1.4 Decision Making

Business decisions as to each management function are either made by an individual or by a group. When an individual is responsible for a decision it is often characterized as *centralized*. On the other hand, if individuals at several levels of management (including those at lower levels) are included in the decision making as a group, the process is referred to as *decentralized*. Whereas emergency decision making is performed most efficiently by an individual, decentralized decision making has gained in popularity. Business firms are recognizing the advantages of including groups in the decision making process. In addition to obtaining the specialized knowledge of the individuals in the group, group decision making also serves as a motivating force when the individuals who are to carry out a decision are given the opportunity to participate in the decision making.

Even when decentralized decision making is used, the final responsibility for a decision often rests with a single individual. His judgment is often modified by the group, but he must still make the final decision.

Authority for decision making differs from responsibility for decision making. Authority can be delegated, responsibility cannot. One can view *authority* as the power to make decisions and enforce them. A manager can delegate this function to his subordinates. However, the manager remains responsible for the decision made by the subordinate. *Responsibility* is the obligation of an individual to make a decision or to perform assigned activities. Obviously, a single individual might have both the authority and responsibility for a decision. However, an individual might be delegated the authority for a decision, but not have the final responsibility for it. Delegation of authority for decision making is an effective means of developing and cultivating subordinate talent.

Business decision making involves the evaluating of alternatives. The techniques for evaluating the alternatives and reaching a decision vary from sheer guessing to the use of sophisticated mathematical models. Probably the least sophisticated decision making process is characterized as *follow-the-leader decision making*. This type of decision making requires little in the way of management thought or knowledge in that a decision is patterned after the duplication of a decision of a predecessor or recognized leader. Although requiring little in the way of thought or knowledge, this type of decision making is often appropriate and successful.

Decision making by means of *intuition* is another type of process that is not founded on thought or knowledge. This type of decision making is related to an individual's hunch or inner feeling. The process is usually irrational and cannot be traced to a set pattern. One often identifies decisions related to gambling and speculation as being intuition oriented. Contractors seldom rely on intuition as a sole means of their decision making process.

Many of the decisions a contractor makes are *experience* decisions. This type of decision making process is centered around the results of past performances or events. A contractor obtains and retains a vast amount of knowledge by means of his business experience. As a result, he often relies on this practical knowledge to guide him concerning the future. The difficulty is obvious. Things change, and past successes do not ensure future success. Thus, the contractor who relies totally on experience for his decision making process has often met with less than successful results. Experience is an attribute in decision making, but a manager should not be bound to it in making decisions.

Experimentation is yet another decision making process. The concept of trying out the various alternatives on a small scale and seeing what happens is often a useful means of reaching a final decision regarding the alternative to be chosen. However, this process is often expensive and time consuming to implement. This is especially relevant when it comes to contracting decisions. Such decisions often are needed instantly or in a short period of time. When such is the case, decision making by experimentation is inappropriate.

A somewhat more sophisticated decision making process is referred to as *marginal analysis*. This type of decision making involves an evaluation of the extra benefit resulting from a decision versus the cost or effort of implementing the decision. A comparison of this evaluation for the several alternatives that are available is then made, and the most appropriate is determined. Although they are often unaware of the fact that they are performing such a process, individuals commonly use this decision making process. The difficulty however, is that they often fail in their recognition of the benefits and costs of a given alternative, thus leading to a less than desired choice of alternatives.

An increasingly used method of making decisions is referred to as the *systems approach* (Note: The term was also used earlier in the identification of types of approaches to management.). The method involves the making of a decision by means of studying the overall problem and its purpose as a function of the problem's components, their interactions, and the constraints of the problem. Models are used as an aid in the systems approach. This type of approach to making decisions is extremely useful when the problem or decision in question is large and complex in scale. The applying of the systems approach is both an art and a science.

1.5 Summary

Four basic management functions: planning, organizing, directing, and controlling were identified in Section 1.3 as being part of the business management process. Each of these basic functions can be further broken down to include such business management disciplines as marketing, business law, finance, personnel management, cost accounting, etc. Each of these disciplines implies various principles and skills. It is beneficial if not necessary for the business manager of the construction firm to have an understanding of each of the business management disciplines.

The business management disciplines are presented individually in the following chapters. An attempt is made to present the business disciplines and following chapters in an order consistent with the occurrence of the four basic functions of planning, organizing, directing, and controlling. Planning and organizing typically precede directing and controlling. Chapters 2–5 on structure of the firm, marketing, law, and finance, respectively, can be thought of as planning and organizing functions.

Chapter 6 on personnel management is basically a directing function. The remaining chapters on cost accounting, capital budgeting, and financial accounting can be viewed as a control function.

Undoubtedly one can raise issue with the identification of any one discipline as to one of the four identified business management functions. For example, it is common to address capital budgeting as a planning function. In reality most disciplines such as capital budgeting, law, etc., cross over two or more of the functions of planning, organizing, directing, and controlling. The firm will likely plan for a capital expenditure, organize for its payment, and then by means of control procedures attempt to keep the related capital expenditure costs to a minimum.

As such it is difficult to single out a given order of presentation as being most representative of the order of occurrence. However the order of presentation of the following chapters is typical of the order in which the new firm has to make decisions as to its business practices.

Case Problems

After each chapter a series of case problems will be presented. These cases concern themselves with the principles discussed in the chapters. While there may not exist a single best answer for each case, the reader should attempt to use the principles discussed in the chapters in analyzing the cases and determining a solution. In particular, each case should be analyzed through the following steps.

(1)   Identification of the problem to be solved.
(2)   Consideration of the case material relevant to the identified problem.
(3)   Determination and consideration of each of the feasible solutions to the problem.
(4)   The selection and support of the best alternative for solution of the case. This solution should be reached after a careful weighing of the merit of the possible solutions.

While Chapter 1 served as an introductory chapter, and as such few specific principles were presented, a sample case follows so that the reader can become acquainted with the solution process for solving case problems. Each of the following chapters will be followed by several case problems.

**Case 1.1. Training Construction Company:
Improving Business Skills**

The Training Construction Company has been rapidly growing over the five years that it has been doing business. The general contracting firm performed six million dollars of work in its last fiscal year.

The firm has six full-time personnel. They are as follows.

Mr. Edwards: The original owner of the firm. He presently owns 60% of the firm. Originally he was a carpenter. His main function is securing contract work.

Mr. Dely: The bookkeeper for the firm. He has obtained 30% ownership in the firm. A high school graduate, he has taken several correspondence courses relating to bookkeeping and accounting.

Mr. Brown: Serves as company estimator and overall office project manager. He is a graduate of a two-year construction technology program. Over the years he has obtained twelve years of construction related experience.

Mr. Smeja: He owns 10% of the firm. A recently graduated civil engineer, he is viewed as the company's chief job superintendent.

Mr. Mellon: A recently hired project superintendent. He has had nine years of similar experience.

Ms. Jones: A secretary for the firm. Besides acting as a receptionist, she aids Mr. Dely in his bookkeeping function.

A management consultant has recently visited Mr. Edwards and pointed out the need for the firm to improve its business management practices. Included in these practices are better project management, cost accounting, budgeting, and marketing.

Despite increased work volume, Mr. Edwards has witnessed a decreasing profit margin over the past three years. As such, he is convinced that the management consultant is correct in his assessment of the firm's needs. He has decided to take steps to update the business management skills of his firm. His immediate problem is deciding what steps to take.

Naturally the consultant has offered his services to the firm. For a monthly fee of $800 he will put "the house in order." In addition to implementing an information system, he will agree to provide a four hour training session for company personnel twice a month. His normal contract is for six months. At that time the firm has an option to renew his contract.

Mr. Edwards has also determined that other alternatives are available to him.

(1) There is a three day seminar on construction management business practices offered by a national management education company. The cost of the seminar is $400 plus travel and lodging which is estimated at $300 per person. Mr Edwards is considering attending himself, sending Mr. Smeja, or having both attend.

(2) Send Mr. Smeja to business management school for a year. Estimated cost is $8,000 which includes tuition and room and board.

(3) Hire a business management college graduate. Estimated yearly salary is $15,000.

(4) Purchase several volumes of business management books (especially those that relate to construction management). The intent would be to require key personnel to read material relevant to the work they perform. Weekly sessions would be held to discuss readings and to try and apply the material to the business management problems of the firm. Estimated cost of the necessary books is $150.

(5) Require key personnel to attend relevant college courses at a nearby college. While a few of the courses are offered in the evening, most are only offered during the day. The estimated cost of sending each of the six key employees to one course per semester is estimated at $1200 per year.

Like many construction firms, the Training Construction Company is limited as to how much money it can spend to update its skills. Total income after tax for the previous year was $23,500. The firm expects a 10% increase in work volume this year. Because of their inadequate business practices it is difficult to predict this year's income. The firm has total assets of $135,000. It's liabilities are $73,000.

What steps should Training Construction Company take to update their business management skills? Note: Regardless of your solution, please continue in your reading of the following chapters.

Chapter 2

Structure of the Firm:
Legal, Organizational, Financial

2.1 Introduction

A construction firm is one of the easiest businesses in the United States to launch. The use of borrowed funds, the ease of licensing procedures, and the opportunity to rent needed equipment all stimulate entrance into the industry. Approximately 13% of all firms in the industry are new entrants annually.[1]

Whereas the starting of a firm is relatively easy, the starting of a firm that will not eventually fail is difficult. To accomplish this, the individual or individuals starting a construction related firm must be aware of all the factors which will effect the business at the start and in the future. Among these factors are the structure of the firm as to the type of work the firm performs, and its legal, organizational, and financial structure. The relevance of the alternatives available to the firm as to its structure are equally important throughout the life of the firm. Whereas one form of structure may be appropriate for the starting of the firm, another structure may be appropriate as the firm grows in size and volume of work performed. The alternative types of structure of the construction firm and the advantages and disadvantages of each are discussed in this chapter.

2.2 Types of Construction Firms

Among the decisions that the construction firm must relate to in the starting and running of the firm is the type of work it is to perform, the

---

[1]"Business Failures," *Duns Review*, 1971, p. 93.

15

size of its operation, and the contract relationship it is to have with the builder-owner. The decision as to the type of work the firm is to perform is dictated by the skills of the owners and employees of the firm. In the past many construction firms were started by individuals who worked in the crafts. Thus, a worker who was employed as an electrician typically started an electrical contracting firm. Firms that specialize in excavation, plumbing, etc. also were founded in the same manner.

Currently it is becoming more difficult for a single craftsman to start a successful construction firm. There is an increasing tendency for today's construction firm to be larger and have an increasing dependence on management skills. Thus, the decision as to the type of work performed has become less dependent on the physical skills of the founders. In addition, whereas in the past there was a clear line between types of work a firm performed, today's contractor is often expanding his operations to include performing several types of work. For example, in the past more often than not a single firm would perform residential work, another would perform commercial building work, and yet another would perform heavy and highway work. Today several firms, even the relatively small firm, may perform all three types of work. Foremost in the reasoning of the firm in its decision to broaden its markets is to level its workload as a function of the economy. Typically, the amount of residential, commercial, and heavy and highway construction are dependent on economic cycles. During the past decade, heavy and highway construction has been used by the government as a means of stimulating an otherwise stagnant economy. On the other hand, during times of boom in regard to residential and commercial construction, inflation often results and the government has seen it fit to curtail expenditures for heavy and highway construction. It is also true that at times when residential construction is slow (i.e., Fall, 1974), commercial construction expenditures may in fact be strong. The end result is that the firm that can shift its interests as to the type of work it performs tends to be less sensitive to cycles in the economy. These cycles, while occurring at wide intervals in the past, are occurring at shorter intervals thus resulting in difficulty in their prediction, and in the planning for them.

As discussed above, one of the more common classifications of the type of work performed is the recognition of the following types of work.

(1)   Residential
(2)   Commercial
(3)   Heavy and Highway

As pointed out there is the advantage of less sensitivity to the economy for the firm that has skills and performs each of the three types of work. On the other hand, it is not possible for every firm to involve itself in the three types of construction work in that the physical and management skills required differ for the three types of work. Obviously, not every firm can or should thrive to possess all the skills required to enable its performing each of the three types of work.

The decision to specialize in residential, commercial, or heavy and highway construction should recognize the unique characteristics of each of the three types of work. Residential construction is characterized by severe cycles in volume. The residential contractor is subject to the policies of the government. Due in major part to changes in the government's fiscal and monetary policies, new residential housing starts may approach two million units one year and the following year they may be as low as one million starts. Wide variations in housing starts from one year to the next and from one season to the next often create unique managment problems for the residential contractor. His ability to balance his workload and to provide for an adequate cash flow through slack volume periods can make the difference between a continuing firm and a bankrupt firm.

Residential contractors have the advantage of being able to operate on a low volume in that they normally have relatively low overhead versus the commercial or heavy and highway contractors. Whereas the commercial or heavy and highway contractor must compete against above average sized contractors each having relatively sound management practices, the residential contractor competes against much smaller firms who normally have less sophisticated management skills. This is not to say that the residential contractor does not have competition; the opposite is in fact true. However, the size of the average competitor and the management skills of the average competitor allow the residential contractor to actually operate out of his house as a one man show. Because of this, the number of residential contractors is numerous, often leading to excessive competition, low profit margins, and bankruptcies.

Several differences exist between the commercial contractor and the heavy and highway contractor. For one, the commercial contractor is normally less dependent on the need for expensive equipment than is the heavy and highway contractor. Because of its high investment in equipment, the main management task for the heavy and highway contractor centers on the ability to effectively utilize equipment and to minimize idle equipment time. On the other hand, the commercial builder is more dependent on the use of labor. Its management needs

	Building construction	Heavy construction
Current assets to current debt	1.54	1.91
Net profits on sales	1.82	2.26
Net profits on working capital	18.23	16.39
Net sales to working capital	11.73	7.30
Fixed assets to net worth	24.3	57.8
Current debt to net worth	122.5	53.7
Total debt to net worth	198.9	95.5
Funded debt to working capital	42.4	41.6

Fig. 2.1. Financial characteristics—building versus heavy construction firms.

	Variability of work load	Affected by government	Assets	Required management skills
Residential	Very variable	Affected in many ways	Few fixed assets	Emphasis on labor productivity
Commercial	Some fluctuation	Somewhat independent	Depends on specialty	Many required
Heavy and Highway	Somewhat steady	Affected by fiscal policy	Many fixed assets	Emphasis on equipment usage

Fig. 2.2. Characteristics of the types of construction firms.

center on effective personnel management and the ability to control the many materials that flow to the commercial building construction project.

The heavy and highway contracting firm tends to be less subject to bankruptcy than the residential contractor or the commercial building contractor. Perhaps this is due in part to the fact that heavy and highway work (sometimes categorized as *public works* construction) tends to be more stable as to volume as a function of time. In addition, because of the high equipment investment needed to operate, the heavy and highway contractor tends to be a large firm with a relatively sound financial structure. Several of these differences of the types of firms are summarized in Figs. 2.1[2] and 2.2.

[2]"The Ratios of Manufacturing," *Duns Review*, 1973, p. 123.

Within the classifications of residential, commercial, and heavy and highway contractors is a class of contractors referred to as speciality contractors or subcontractors. These types of firms continue to be founded by craftsmen and highly skilled individuals. Typically, the subcontractor is small as to the number of employees and its volume of work. Subcontractors normally have relatively low overhead but are highly dependent on labor and labor productivity. Competition tends to be high and profit margins vary depending on the type of speciality work performed.

Unlike the general contractor, the subcontractor is normally only responsible for his own work. As such, the management skills needed to coordinate the skills of several labor crafts or flows of several types of materials are not vital to the subcontractor's profit on a project or its financial stability. What is needed is an ability to perform a highly skilled type of work and to be able to obtain high productivity while carrying out the work.

The size of the firm and the annual volume of work it undertakes are constrained by the resources available to the firm and its bonding capacity. Perhaps the best measure as to the size of a firm is its bonding capacity. Since the firm is required to submit a bond to the owner before undertaking a project, its bonding capacity limits the size of projects it can undertake and thus plays a role in the annual volume of work the firm performs.

More often than not, the construction firm starts as a small firm. One classification system used classifies a small firm as a firm doing less than one million dollars of work volume annually. The break point between a middle or average sized firm and a large firm can be thought of as an annual work volume of twenty million dollars. Whereas some of the approximately 800,000 existing construction firms started as small firms and have increased their bonding capacity enough to be classified as medium or large firms, many other firms have continued to operate as small firms. Not every firm can or should substantially increase its size or annual volume of work. Many a firm has gone bankrupt trying to carry out its objective of joining the "top 400" firms.

The larger firm does have certain advantages in regard to the construction industry. Foremost among these advantages is the fact that on a percentage basis, the overhead per dollar value of work performed is less than that for the smaller firm. This is evidenced by comparison of income statements for the small and large firms. This ability to operate with a lower percentage overhead results in the larger firm being more competitive and being able to obtain a somewhat higher profit margin. Since the larger contractor can always take on projects that are less than its bonding capacity, it often is in a position to pick and choose from available projects rather than to have to seek to be low bidder on each and every project. The size of the firm relative to its capital structure may also result in the large firm being somewhat less sensitive to economic slowdowns than is the smaller firm.

The small firm is not without its advantages. Normally, it does not have the management problems that are characteristic of a firm that is large and increasing in size. In addition, the rewards of operating successfully are received by the owner and not shared with stockholders or investors as is typical in the case of the large firm. Naturally, the reverse is also true in regard to losses the firm might absorb. However the small firm, because of its relatively low dollar operating overhead, may be in a position to "shut down the shop" during a slowdown. Many a residential home building contractor has seen it fit to being a carpenter for another firm during an economic slowdown only to return to the home building business when the economy recovered.

In general, the size of the firm is not dictated alone by its technical skills. Its growth has to be accompanied by growth in management skills and changes in its financial makeup. While not always the case, a bonding company will consider all three factors of technical skills, management ability, and financial soundness in increasing or decreasing a firm's bonding capacity.

Yet another decision to be made in regard to the type of work the firm is to perform, concerns itself with the degree of responsibility the firm is to enter into with the project owner. In the past its decision was limited to a decision to be a general contractor or a subcontractor. However, the construction industry has witnessed some dramatic contractor-owner relationship changes in the past decade. As such, the question as to the contractor relationship to the owner must recognize the following types of relationships.

(1)   General Contractor
(2)   Subcontractor
(3)   "Spec Builder" *def p. 21*
(4)   Developer
(5)   Design—Build Contractor
(6)   Construction Manager

The general contractor and subcontractor relationships to the owner are the traditional builder-owner relationship in the construction industry. Typically, the general contractor has a contract with the owner for constructing the entire project in question. The general contractor may in fact only construct a portion of the project, say 20%, with his own labor and equipment. The rest of the work is performed by subcontractors whom have contracts with the general contractor. This arrangement has proved to be successful for many years. The owner does not have to deal with several parties in that his contract is limited to a contract with the general contractor. From the contractor's point of view, this traditional contract arrangement has allowed the subcontractor to specialize in his craft and to somewhat neglect the management tasks of scheduling and overall project management. The general contractor is supposedly more skilled in these practices. In addition, the fact that there is one prime contractor and several subs secondary to the prime has reduced potential conflict between the numerous contractors on a project and the owner, that is, contract responsibilities and conflicts are readily singled out in the traditional contractor-owner relationship.

Yet another advantage of the traditional relationship is the fact that in such an arrangement normally the general contractor is the only contractor required to submit a bond. That is, he in effect submits a bond for himself and his subcontractors. The fact of the matter is that several of the subcontractors would likely fail in their attempt to obtain a bond. As such, they would not be eligible to work for the owner on the project in question with the result being a less competitive environment and an overall higher contract price to the owner. The traditional contractor-owner relationship is not without its disadvantages. These will be singled out in the discussion of alternative relationships.

In the discussion of the general contractor and the subcontractor it was assumed that they committed themselves to a dollar value contract with an owner who has a defined project and more likely than not has a set of drawings prepared for the project. An alternative to this arrangement is the case of the *speculative builder*. The so-called "spec" builder is the owner of the project while it is being built. He may in fact be the owner after the project is built if he decides to rent it or has the unfortunate fate of not being able to find a renter or buyer. The advantages of the speculative builder are that he is free to choose his own site and plans, his estimate of cost is not tied to the success of the project in that he "sells" the building after the true cost is determined, it may be easier to build in this manner in that he does not have to compete for a contract to build, and most importantly when the market is receptive his profit margin may be relatively high. Whereas the contract builder may have to settle for a profit margin of about 3%, if the spec builder "moves" his projects after they are built, he may be able to attain a 10% profit margin. Reasons for this higher profit margin for the spec builder stem from profits associated with the land on which the project is built, repetitive type of units which the contractor builds and thus "learns," increased productivity, and a more constant and controlled workload.

However, all these favorable characteristics of the speculative builder are based on the assumption that the builder can immediately rent or sell the project once it is built. The spec builder constructs projects on his money and not the owner's as is the case of the contract builder. As such, the spec builder ties up his money and normally, due to a loan, continues to pay interest during construction and beyond construction if an owner is not secured. Such loans may be purchased through a bank or in the case of a sizeable project through a Real Estate Investment Trust (REIT). The point is that these loans are repayable with interest. The end result is that the spec builder subjects himself to a high degree of risk in that should the cost of money become high such that a potential owner or renter cannot be secured, the spec builder continues to have a cash outflow and no cash inflow. The cash flow problem soon leads to bankruptcy. Typically, in an attempt to resolve the problem, the spec builder sells the project at a reduced price. While this may resolve the cash flow problem for a while, it is only a temporary solution unless the market again turns favorable. The more plausible solution to the potential risk associated with being a spec builder is to have a financial structure that provides for the risk. That is, the firm should maintain adequate cash reserves for potential slowdowns. More will be said of a adequate financial structure in Section 2.5.2 of this chapter.

The *developer* and the speculative builder share some of the same characteristics. In particular, they both build with their own money in anticipation of securing a renter or buyer for the finished project. As to differences between a developer and spec builder, normally the developer does not actually construct a project. He contracts for the construction with various contractors. However, it is not unusual for the developer to be joined by a contractor in a "team effort" on the project. Another difference is that the scale of the project undertaken by the developer is much larger than that undertaken by the spec builder. This often results in the source of funds (i.e., the loan) being obtained from a different outside party. For example, many *developments* are financed through REIT's whereas a more common source of funding for the spec builder is a savings and loan institution or a bank. Chapter 5 deals with the obtaining of funds.

The construction firm's entrance into *design-build* and *construction management* services are becoming common. The design-build concept is merely the merging of the designer and the builder into one team. The builder obtains design expertise or the designer takes on building services by means of merging with a builder or forming a joint venture. The objective of the design team is to offer the owner a design that meets the owner's need and can be constructed economically and in a minimum period of time. For example, the design-build concept can supposedly eliminate expensive steel connections that on paper are adequate but result in excessive field construction costs.

Most industry arguments against design-build concepts focus on the potential colusion of the design-build team. However, this argument is weak, and one can expect that the design-build concept will continue to grow in popularity with project owners.

A firm's entrance into the design-build field obviously requires an expansion of the skills it may have had as a design firm or as a true construction firm. In addition, the management functions that are a necessary part of its business also change. More often than not, the design-build firm obtains its work on the basis of its reputation as to performance. As such, management practices have to emphasize good external relations. Continual awareness of new concepts in design, new materials, and effective cost control systems are means of obtaining and continuing good external relations. Some of these concepts and practices are not typically of great importance to the general contractor or subcontractors.

Construction management is yet another recent change in the traditional building process. Initially, the construction management firm was thought of as the fourth party to the team of the project owner, designer, and builder. Essentially, the construction manager is the agent of the owner. He portrays himself as a professional possessing a high degree of management skills that are aimed at providing the construction owner a project for a reasonable price and within a minimal period of time. The construction manager does this through management skills directed towards effective contract procurements, letting portions of a contract as they are designed (referred to as phased construction), sophisticated financing techniques, effective scheduling, and project cost control.

The firm entering construction management should indeed possess a high degree of construction management skills. Currently general contractors and architect-engineer firms are joining a growing list of construction management firms. Many have not succeeded in that they do not possess the necessary skills required.

From the point of view of the firm entering construction management, the limited project liability has proved to be advantageous, However as competition increases, the construction management firm is being forced to enter into a guaranteed maximum contract with the project owner, and in effect is taking on a degree of risk and liability.

The future of construction management is somewhat uncertain. Not all of its characteristics are favorable. For example, the delegating of responsibility to several contractors (normally in the construction management process all contractors including subs have separate contracts with the owner) can create difficulties as to work jurisdiction disputes.

The point to be made is that the firm contemplating entrance into construction management should know what skills are required and what their responsibilities will be under a construction management contract. This is especially important in that several potential project owners may have a different conception of construction management. The construction management firm can hardly expect to be successful offering construction management services to external parties if it is not first in a position to manage itself.

The construction management business is a service business. Thus, the construction management firm does not need a substantial investment in assets such as cranes or scrapers. On the other hand, a management firm cannot be started without tools. These tools include construction industry experience (i.e., ideally both design and construction) and business and management skills such as those discussed in the chapters of this book.

2.3 Legal Structure of the Firm

The legal structure of the firm affects the everyday operations of the construction firm. The time spent seeking out the best legal form for the business typically pays for itself. The following broad forms of legal structure are available to the construction firm.

(1)   Proprietorship
(2)   Partnership
(3)   Corporation

Additionally, three modifications of the above types are relevant to the structure of the construction firm. These are as follows.

(1)   Limited Partnership
(2)   Joint Venture
(3)   Subchapter S Corporation

Each of these six legal structures, with a few exceptions, are available to each firm when it is started and throughout the period of time it carries out its operations.

The decision as to the legal form chosen should recognize the following factors.

(1)   The effect on the management decision making process.
(2)   The effect on the income tax expense.
(3)   The liabilities of the owners of the firm.
(4)   Provisions for continuance of the firm.
(5)   The effect on the firm's ability to obtain funds.
(6)   The initial cost to form the legal structure.
(7)   The degree of governmental control on the firm.

Other factors are relevant to a lesser degree in that they relate to specific firms. These seven factors as they relate to possible legal structure of the construction firm will now be discussed under the three broad classifications of legal structure.

2.3.1 Proprietorship

The majority of very small construction firms are proprietorships. The arguments for such a legal structure center around retaining ownership and management of the firm for the owner of the firm, and the ease and low cost of taking on such a legal structure. To a lesser degree, the fact that there is little governmental control as to a proprietorship is another plus. On the negative side, the proprietorship is normally unfavorable in regard to tax expense, liability of the owner, ability to raise funds, and continuance of the firm in the case of death of the owner.

Typically, the owner of a construction related firm is somewhat suspicious about "opening up" his books to anyone but himself. This includes keeping his cost data and financial data confidential. In addition, he tends to believe in his own management ability and thus avoids outside help in the form of consultants. Much of this unwillingness to confide in others has no doubt developed from the fierce competition that is characteristic of the construction industry and the competitive nature of the bidding process in itself. The end result is that the construction firm owner often rejects partnership or corporation legal structure on the basis that it defeats his confidentiality of business records and management know-how. It should be pointed out that this confidentiality can work unfavorably as to the contractor. In many cases, his business records and management practices are less than adequate. His confidentiality and ignorance of his failures often go unexposed when the firm is a proprietorship.

More often than not, the construction firm is started under the proprietorship legal structure. This is due in part to the owner's desire to retain the management of the firm. However, an equally or more important factor in the popularity of the proprietorship form of legal structure is its ease of formation. Of all the alternative legal structures, the proprietorship is the easiest to form as to legal requirements or initial cost. Basically, anyone can start a proprietorship. Without the aid of legal counsel, an individual can buy himself a pick-up truck and call himself a general contractor or subcontractor. As to the cost, it is minimal. Whereas it may prove beneficial to consult legal or financial counsel, it is not necessary and this cost can be avoided. Some states require that a firm be licensed in order to be able to contract for construction work in the state. Whereas some states use this license fee as a revenue raising tool, others in fact use it as a means of controlling entrance of nonreputable firms. The point is that if in fact a state requires a license, it is required of the firm regardless of their legal structure. Even when such a license is required, the cost is minimal in that it typically is less than one hundred dollars. If such a license is required, it serves as the only external control on the operations of the proprietorship.

The disadvantages of the proprietorship legal structure grow as the firm grows. However, these disadvantages may in fact outweigh the advantages even when the firm first opens its doors. Perhaps foremost as to these disadvantages are the unlimited liability of the proprietor, and the unfavorable tax position of the proprietor. The liability of the proprietor is such that he risks both his business and personal assets when entering into a business liability. If debtors seek repayment of business loans, should the proprietor's business assets be insufficient to cover these loans, the debtor has a legal right to the proprietor's personal assets. In reality, little difference is attached to the business or personal assets of the proprietor.

The proprietor's income from his business becomes part of his personal income for determination of income tax expense. The disadvantage of this combining of business and personal income for the proprietor is discussed by means of examples in following discussions of alternative legal structures. Finally as pointed out earlier, typically the proprietorship is terminated upon the death of the proprietor. Through legal counsel, steps can be taken to provide for a continuance of the business upon the death of proprietor (e.g., the firm transferred from a father to his son). However, the avoidance of such legal costs is viewed as one of the reasons for forming a proprietorship.

2.3.2 Partnership

A partnership is a business with co-owners organized to make a profit. Approximately 10% of all construction firms are partnerships. The partnership legal structure is merely an extension of a proprietorship to two or more owners. However, because of multiple ownership, several characteristics arise that are unique in regard to each partner and to the external parties dealing with the partnership.

The incentive behind the partnership is "sharing" and "team effort." The belief of the partnership is that the sum of two parts will be more effective than each part taken individually. As such, individuals or firms may form a partnership with the objective of expanding and improving their areas of work and services offered, their management skills, or their financial structure. For example, a general contractor may enter a partnership agreement with an excavation contractor in order to be more competitive as to services offered. Another technically skilled contractor may form a partnership with a management consultant with the objective of offering construction management services. Yet another technically skilled contractor lacking a sound financial statement may form a partnership with a "cash heavy" firm in order to provide financial security and increased bonding capacity. The specific reasons behind two individuals forming a partnership are numerous. In many cases it results merely from the belief that two heads are better than one.

Similar to the proprietorship, the partnership can be formed without detailed procedures or cost. While the partnership agreement does not have to be written, it is often advantageous to do so in that it helps in resolving potential disputes. While not severe, external constraints on the firm are somewhat greater than that of the proprietorship. For example, the partnership must openly disclose the names of the partners when carrying out its operations.

As noted there are several unique operational characteristics of a partnership. These characteristics often lead to disputes among partners and external parties. In particular, confusion and disputes may result as to partnership income distribution, income tax effects on partners, individual partner management rights, liabilities of individual partners, and the effect of dissolution and windup (i.e., termination) of the partnership as to individual partners. Typically, these disputes are resolved by reference to the Uniform Partnership Act (U.P.A.).

Unless otherwise agreed to in the partnership agreement, partnership income is distributed equally to the partners. This is true even if one partner has contributed more capital than the other partner. An agreement to distribute income in an unequal ratio overrides the equal distribution rule. For example, a contractor having a high initial asset contribution may demand and obtain an agreement with a management consultant partner whereby the contractor is to receive two-thirds of partnership income.

It is important to note that the partnership legal structure serves merely as a funnel of income to individual partners. The partnership income is not taxed to the partnership. Rather all income is funneled to partners who are then taxed as individual taxpayers. For this reason there is an internal revenue provision that requires that the income distributions to partners be made in a manner that does not attempt to manipulate tax payments. For example, it is not permissible to distribute all capital gain income (which are taxed at a lesser rate) to a high income partner, and all ordinary income to a relatively low income partner for the purpose of mnimizing total tax expense. Although the internal revenue permits much freedom in regard to partnership income distribution, they are particularly in disfavor of distribution plans that are not consistent from one year to the next.

Individual partner salaries are viewed as distributions of income rather than as partnership expense. In many cases the salary may be used in the calculated total income distribution to the partners. The income of the partnership may be distributed on the bases of capital investment, then salaries, with any remaining income to be distributed equally. For example, two partners A and B may agree to an income distribution plan whereby each is to receive 5% interest on their beginning of the year capital investment, a $12,000 salary for A and a $8,000 salary for B, with remaining income to be divided equally. The income is to be distributed in the order of interest, then salary. Further, the agreement should state what the distribution is to be should there be more income than that required to pay interest but less than that required to pay full salaries. For example, the salaries may be paid on a ratio basis in that case. The actual income distribution, assuming total income of $50,000, beginning of year capital investments of A and B as $60,000 and $100,000, would be as follows.

	Partner A	Partner B
Interest:		
A: (.05) (60,000)	$ 3,000	
B: (.05) (100,000)		$ 5,000

Salaries:	12,000	8,000
Remaining (50,000		
− 28,000):	11,000	11,000
Total	$26,000	$24,000

Because of the almost infinite combinations of possible ways of distributing partnership income, it is absolutely necessary that the agreement be clear and be such that it covers all possible amounts to be
distributed.

As previously indicated, partnership income is distributed to the
partners who in turn include their distributions in their individual tax
returns. Thus the partnership income may be taxed at different rates.

One of the more complex partnership tax transactions that may cause
disputes among partners is the tax implications that arise when a partner turns over a nonmonetary asset to the partnership as part of his
investment capital and the asset is later sold at a profit or a loss. The
difficulty takes place when a partner contributes an asset that has value
(i.e., the tax base) for tax purposes less than or greater than the fair
market value of the asset. During recent inflationary years, the fair
market value has often exceeded the tax base of the asset. For example,
a construction contractor in joining a partnership with another partner
may contribute a piece of construction equipment with a fair market
value of $20,000. However, at the time the construction contractor con-
tributed the piece of equipment, it may have a tax base of $10,000. This
difference in fair market value and tax base may be due to prior accelerated depreciation or merely inflation of equipment prices.

The tax question arises when the equipment is later sold. For example, assume that the partnership later sells the piece of construction
equipment for $30,000. This results in a $20,000 gain as to tax liability.
Typically, the tax expense is identified with the partnership and the
expense is distributed to the partners in the predetermined profit and
loss ratio. The inequity of this procedure is that from the partnership's
point of view, only a $10,000 gain is realized in that the construction
contractor was credited with a $20,000 capital contribution. A more
fair distribution of the tax expense of the gain would be to recognize a
$10,000 personal gain for the construction contractor and a $10,000
company gain for the partnership with the tax expense allocated separately for the two gains. However more often not, the entire gain is
allocated to the partnership. Clearly, the existence of such a tax dis-

tribution and liability is grounds for dispute and should be understood by the partners before the partnership agreement.

When a construction firm enters a partnership it is often not without apprehension as to the future management of the firm. Questions as to who has authority to do what often lead to disputes among the partners and eventual termination of the partnership. Much of this apprehension and dispute could be avoided if the management responsibility and authority of each partner is understood by all when the partnership is formed.

Unless the partners agree to the contrary, each partner has equal rights in the management of the operations of the partnership. When a management decision is made, the majority rules. However, a few decisions need the consent of all of the existing partners.

A partner is essentially a fiduciary. The partner has a duty to the partnership to act with loyalty and to account for his duties. For example, the partner has a duty not to devote excessive time to another business.

A partner has express, implied, and apparent authority. Expressed authority is seldom disputed in that it is set out in the partnership agreement. For example, a partner to a construction firm may have expressed authority to hire and fire personnel. Implied authority is the authority due to his being a partner in a certain type of business. As to a construction firm, implied authority means that a partner would have authority to sign contracts to build projects and purchase material. Apparent authority is the authority that an external party would reasonably assume a person would have because he was a partner in a given type of business. For example, even though a partner of a construction firm may not have express or implied authority to purchase a major piece of equipment, an equipment dealer may reasonably assume the partner has authority and as such the equipment dealer would have legal remedies should the purchase be disputed.

Similar in nature to potential partner management responsibility disputes are questions and disputes that relate to individual partners' liabilities. One of the strongest arguments that can be made against an individual becoming part of a partnership is his subjection to unlimited liability. For all practical purposes a partner is liable for all contracts, torts, and debts of another partner which occur in the normal performance of business. Thus, if a construction firm partner, while trying to collect a business debt, becomes involved in a dispute and physically harms the external party, each partner of the business is liable for the tort of the overly zealous partner. On the other hand, had the partner been attempting to collect a personal debt, no liability for the tort would carry over to the other partners.

Perhaps the most common dispute in regard to its occurrence is the question of liability when a creditor seeks a judgment for the debts of the partnership or the individual partners. The partnership laws that relate to resolving the question of debt liability are referred to as the *marshaling of assets*. Under these laws, each individual partner's personal assets are made available first to his individual creditors, and any surplus is made available to partnership creditors; while partnership property is made available first to partnership creditors, and any surplus remaining that are distributed among the partners are made available to the creditors of each of the individual partners. For example, two parties, A and B, are partners to Dual Construction Partnership, and have the following liabilities and assets.

	Liabilities	*Assets*
Partnership	$80,000	$60,000
A—Personal	20,000	30,000
B—Personal	30,000	25,000

Should three creditors, one for the $80,000 partnership liability, one for the $20,000 liability of A, and one for the $30,000 liability of B, obtain judgments, they would receive the following.

	From Partnership	*From A*	*From B*	*Total*
Partnership creditor	$60,000	$10,000		$70,000
A—Creditor		20,000		20,000
B—Creditor			$25,000	25,000

Somewhat related to the marshaling of partnership assets, is the distribution of partnership assets upon the dissolution (termination) of the partnership. Contrary to any provision in the partnership agreement, any assets remaining after creditor claims are distributed equally. It is possible for the partnership agreement to dictate unequal percentages for profit and loss distribution. Naturally, losses can only be absorbed by a partner equal in amount to his invested capital. That is, once a partner's capital is absorbed, the other partner or partners absorb his

ABC CONSTRUCTION COMPANY
Schedule of Partnership Liquidation

	Assets		Priority claims	Claimants		
					Residual Equities	
	Cash	Noncash		A	B	C
				50	30	20
Profit and loss ratio				50	30	20
Preliquidation balances	$10000	$80000	$12000	$31000	$20000	$27000
Realization of assets and allocation of loss	50000	−80000		−15000	−9000	−6000
Predistribution balances	60000	0	12000	16000	11000	21000
Cash distribution: Priority claims	−12000		−12000			
Partners' residual equities	−48000			−16000	−11000	−21000
Termination	$0	$0	$0	$0	$0	$0

Fig. 2.3. Partnership liquidation schedule.

share of partnership loss (i.e., consistent with the marshaling of assets doctrine).

A schedule of partnership liquidation is illustrated in Fig. 2.3. The schedule assumes that the three partners A, B, and C share profits and losses in the ratio 50, 30, 20, respectively. The somewhat simplified distribution schedule shown in Fig. 2.3 becomes more complex if a partner's capital is not adequate to cover his losses or if one or more partner has loaned or borrowed money from the partnership. Distribution plans for the more complex situations are not discussed here.

As one might conclude from discussion of potential partnership disputes, the disadvantages of such a legal structure for the construction related firm often outweigh the advantages. On the other hand, occupations and businesses such as lawyers, architects, and practicing engineers often choose the partnership legal structure in that one of the alternative forms, the corporation structure, may not be available to them. Clients of these professions require a high degree of trust in that the owners of the business deal in personal services. Under the corporate structure, the actual owners may be unknown to the client and the element of personal trust is absent. On the other hand, the ownership, responsibility, and liability of the partnership are clearly recognized by clients of the partnership. As such, lawyers, architects, and practicing engineers may be forced into forming partnerships in order to gain the trust of clients.

Whereas there are few construction firms that choose the true partnership legal structure, there are several that may take a legal form that approaches such a legal structure. In particular, the limited partnership and the joint venture are legal structures similar to the partnership that are commonly used by construction related firms.

As previously indicated, the construction firm is often reluctant to give up part or all of the management of their individually owned firms. In addition, as will be discussed in a later part of this chapter, many construction firms have an unfavorable cash position as to short term financing and cash for growth. The end result is that the construction firm may be willing to take on a *limited partner*. The limited partner invests cash or a nonmonetary asset in the firm for the right to a percentage of future profits. However, the limited partner has no management input to the firm. This retention of management decisions is compatible with the desires of the construction contractor who is in effect the *general partner* of the newly formed partnership.

From the limited partner's point of view, the arrangement is favorable in that he is offered a share of potential profits with only limited liability. Unlike a general partner, the limited partner's liability is limited to his investment.

In addition to its use by construction contractors, the limited partnership arrangement is very commonly used by real estate investors and developers. Such businesses need a relatively large amount of cash in that cash is their mechanism of operation. Due to the fact that investors often view real estate developments with a high degree of risk, and secondly that the developer may choose to maintain management of developed projects, the limited partnership often proves to be the most favorable means of the developer raising the necessary cash. The compatibility of the limited partnership arrangement to the needs of the real estate investor, developer, and limited partner, in addition to favorable tax laws as to the limited partner, has resulted in an increasing popularity of the legal structure for this purpose.

As is true of any partnership, all parties involved in the general partner/limited partner arrangement should be fully aware of the implications of the agreement. For example, the limited partner has no authority as to signing contracts, making debts, etc., under the limited partnership agreement. As to third parties, it is unlawful to disclose the names of limited partners in the partnership name. Such a disclosure would lead external parties to believe that limited partners are in fact owners and thus fully liable for the debts that may come due to external parties.

The *joint venture* is not legally a partnership. It is an arrangement whereby two firms agree to "join forces" to carry out operations for a relatively short period of time or for a single project. The arrangement is a familiar one in the construction industry. A construction firm may not have the technical capabilities or the bonding capacity necessary to bid successfully on a construction project. Thus, they seek out a compatible firm willing to team up for the project. The arrangement often proves advantageous to both parties (i.e., more than two parties can agree to a joint venture) in that individually neither may be in position to bid or make a profit on a project.

The joint venture is not without its potential difficulties. Foremost is the potential dispute as to who is responsible for completing various work items. In order for the joint venture to be successful, work responsibilities must be clearly defined. In addition, the arrangement must be truly a team effort. That is, each firm must be willing to give and take as to responsibilities, liabilities, and profits.

To the extent that each firm of the joint venture has control over its activities, it is liable for the debts of the joint venture. Individual firms to the joint venture have very limited powers to affect the contractual relations of each other. While typically there is a single contract with the project owner, variations are numerous in regard to the joint venture arrangement. In order to reduce or eliminate possible disputes that occur because of the variations, the construction firm typically enters into a joint venture with a firm that they have had a similar arrangement with on previous projects.

2.3.3 Corporation

A construction firm's decision to incorporate normally centers around potential income tax savings and a more favorable liability position for the owners of the company. Of less significance, but also favorable in the decision to incorporate are the considerations of obtaining capital funds, continuance of the firm, and allowable fringe benefits such as pension plans for officers.

The tax consideration is not favorable for every firm. If a firm is small and thus has little taxable income or the firm wishes to limit its income to single taxation, a corporate structure should not be chosen. In addition, a corporate legal structure implies a decentralizing of company management. While it is possible for a single owner to retain his management responsibility within a corporate structure, the typical corporation is managed by board members acting on behalf of the owners. The corporation is subject to several state laws. However this external control of the states is often insignificant as to the operation of the firm.

While increasing in number, relatively few construction firms are corporations. The smallness of the typical construction firm is no doubt one of the reasons for the nonuse of the corporate structure. However, the ignorance of the construction firm as to the potential benefits of a corporate structure is likely another reason for the relatively few construction firm corporations.

Corporations are licensed by the state in which corporate structure is sought. Licensing procedures vary from state to state. For example, whereas a single individual can form a corporation in Illinois, other states require two or more incorporators. In addition, some states have rigorous requirements whereas other states are quite liberal as to fees and regulations. The state of Delaware has long been known to bend over backwards to businesses that incorporate. In addition to state laws governing corporations, certain types and sizes of corporations come within the jurisdiction of the Securities Exchange Commission (S.E.C.). Among other requirements, corporations governed by the S.E.C. must openly publish their financial statements.

In addition to a license fee of approximately $100, costs of incorporation include legal costs that may run from $100 to $1,000 depending on the state and the size of the business in question. For a construction related firm, the cost of incorporating typically sums to approximately $500. To a very small firm, the incorporation cost is sometimes prohibitive.

Upon incorporating, a firm must issue at least one class of stock. If the corporation is *closed*, the stock issuance is limited to a restricted number of select individuals. On the other hand, if it is *open* the stock is traded openly in a market and any individual has the opportunity to become part owner of the firm. The stockholders of the firm are the legal owners of the firm. On the basis of the number of shares they own, they obtain voting rights which entitle them to elect board members and also have a right to retain their percentage ownership through the *preemptive right* of buying new shares when issued. The board members in effect manage the firm and are responsible to the stockholders (i.e., the owners) of the firm for their performance. The board members make decisions related to the firm's financial structure and whether or not dividends are to be paid to stockholders. As is true of the stockholders, board members of the firm may change. However, the change comes about by election rather than by selling one's shares as in the case of the stockholder. Theoretically the life of the corporation is infinite. However, it can be terminated by the failure to pay the annual state corporation fee, by agreement of stockholders, by merger, or by bankruptcy.

The motivating force behind most proprietors changing to a corporation legal structure is a potential reduction in income tax expense. When one considers the fact that the income tax expense of doing business may exceed 40% of pretax income, even the slightest percentage reduction in tax expense can mean a significant dollar savings. While it is not the purpose of this chapter to fully discuss taxation, it is meaningful in the comparison of corporate structure to other legal structures to note a few different income tax implications. As discussed previously, the income tax expense for a proprietorship or a partnership is funneled through the tax returns of the individual owners. On the other hand, the corporation pays income tax as a separate entity. In addition, income that is distributed to owners is again taxed to each owner as an individual tax expense.

At first glance, this double taxation for the corporation may seem to be unfavorable and in fact it may be. However, two points are noteworthy before judgment is passed. For one, the income tax rate differs for the proprietorship and the corporation. For the individual, the rates vary from 15% to 70% (i.e., 50% is the maximum rate on nonpassive earned income). As to the corporation, the first $25,000 of taxable income is taxed at a rate of 22% and an additional tax of 26% is charged on taxable income over and above $25,000.

For relatively small taxable incomes, the tax rate is less for the individual versus the corporation. As the taxable income increases, the effective tax rate becomes smaller for the corporation versus the individual. For example, for taxable income of $10,000, the tax liability for the single taxpayer is $2,090 or 20.9%. This compares to a corporate tax of $2,200 or 22% on a corporate taxable income of $10,000. On the other hand, for taxable income of $44,000 the tax liability for a single taxpayer is $16,590 or 37.7%. The corporate effective tax rate is less for this income in that the corporate tax liability for taxable income of $44,000 is $14,620 (i.e. .22 × 25,000 plus .48 × 19,000) or 33.2%.

A second point has to be recognized in the comparison of the tax liabilities of the corporation versus the proprietorship or partnership. In the example described above, in addition to the $14,620 corporate tax liability calculated for the corporation, any income distributed will again be taxed to the individuals to whom it is distributed. The point to be made is that only the income that is *distributed* is taxed twice. The corporation can shelter income from double taxation by retaining the income for corporate growth and operations and thus in effect pay a smaller tax rate than it would had it been a proprietorship or a partnership.

In addition to different tax rates that relate to a corporate legal structure versus a proprietorship or partnership, the tax "formula" including what is deductible from revenues in the calculation of taxable income differs for the alternative legal structures. These differences and a more rigorous treatment of the determination of tax liability for alternative legal structures of the firm are not discussed here.

A longstanding argument for choosing the corporate structure is centered around the issue of ownership liability. As noted previously, the owners of a proprietorship or partnership have virtually unlimited liability for the debts of the firm. This often proves unfavorable in that should the firm fall on hard times, the owners may loose their house, car, and other personal assets. On the other hand, the liability of the owners (i.e., the stockholders) of the corporation is normally limited to their initial investment. In addition, they may be liable for the difference between the stated face value of their ownership stock and the value for which the stock was issued should the stated face value be greater than the cost. However, stock is seldom issued below its face value removing this potential liability.

In the case of the construction related firm this limited liability as to the corporate legal structure is often overemphasized. Due in part to the relatively high financial risk associated with a construction firm, few creditors are willing to lend money to construction firms unless the loan is secured. If the construction firm is a corporation, the creditor will likely require the owners to secure the loan by pledging their personal assets. Thus, the limited liability of the corporate legal structure loses its significance.

Less significant in importance but also relevant to the decision to incorporate are the considerations of fringe benefits for company personnel and the ability to raise cash for the firm. Pension, annuities, and profit sharing programs for individuals and businesses are governed by governmental and internal revenue guidelines. In the case of individuals (i.e., proprietorships and partnerships) the guidelines are rather restrictive. For example, a self-employed individual can currently only shelter $7,500 of income from tax for purposes of providing a pension. On the other hand, liberal pension and annuity programs in addition to stock option plans are available to corporate owners and personnel.

Although it is difficult to generalize as to the availability of cash to alternative legal structures, the corporate structure does provide the best mechanism for raising cash. Corporations tend to be larger firms with more assets which they can use to secure loans. Thus, the larger size of the corporation distorts a comparison of legal structures as to ease of raising funds. However, it can be stated that large creditor's relatively favorable attitude towards the corporate legal structure results in the corporation being in a favorable position as to raising equity capital or issuing debts. However, being realistic, the construction related firm remains risky in the eyes of investors or creditors regardless of whether the firm is a proprietorship, partnership, or corporation.

Whereas the smallness of the construction firm has limited the number of construction firms turning to a corporate legal structure, an increasing number of construction firms are recognizing the benefits of a *subchapter S corporation*. A subchapter S corporation (sometimes referred to as a *tax option corporation*) is actually a form of a corporation. The subchapter S corporation offers many of the benefits of the corporation and in addition can be used to avoid double taxation. Rather than the firm being viewed as a separate entity as to the tax liability, both distributed and nondistributed income can in effect be funneled for tax purposes to the individual owners of the firm. The internal revenue imposes several guidelines on the subchapter S corporation as to its income distributions. For example, any income distributed from the firm's retained earnings in the first two and one-half months of its fiscal year is considered income earned and taxed in a prior year. Such rules are aimed at eliminating possible manipulation of tax liability.

In order to be eligible to be a subchapter S corporation, a firm must not have more than ten stockholders, must have only one class of stock, and not more than 20% of gross receipts of the firm can be passive income such as income from rents, royalities, dividends, and interest. However, there is no limit as to the dollar value of work the firm performs. The fact that most construction related firms have less than ten owners results in the subchapter S corporation structure being readily available and often advantageous to the construction firm.

2.4 Organizational Structure

The basic task of *organizing* is performed to amass and arrange all required resources, including people, such that the objectives and required work of the firm can be accomplished effectively. Organizing is primarily a people problem. The need for organizing is created because work to be done is too much for one person to handle. Thus it follows, that as a firm grows in regard to its workload, the need and complexity of organizing increases.

The product of organizing is an organization structure. The organization structure determines the flow of interactions within the organization. It determines who decides what, who tells whom, who responds, and who performs what work. If the organization structure is effective it should accomplish the following.

(1)   Aid coordination
(2)   Expedite control
(3)   Emphasize human relations
(4)   Provide benefits of specialization
(5)   Pinpoint responsibility

Coordination is a fundamental requirement of an effective organization structure. Coordination enhances communication. Unless procedures, orders, and objectives can be communicated through coordination, individuals will perform their various functions in a less than optimal manner. The running of any firm, including a construction related firm, is a team effort. Very few teams can operate successfully without the coordination of the team members. An estimator cannot accurately price a work item unless he has the aid of past project data from a project manager. A construction planner needs the aid of an expeditor in determining a feasible schedule for a project. Viewing each function of the firm as being isolated from others defeats effective coordination.

Whereas planning provides the potential for a profitable operation, control is the mechanism by which profits are realized. As such, ignorance of the control function in the organization structure eliminates the potential for an effective organization structure. Much of effective control centers around operative cost accounting and its relation to various individuals and functions in the firm. While this section will somewhat relate to this relationship of cost accounting to the overall organizational structure, Chapter 7 in its entirety is devoted to cost accounting.

An organization structure should focus on the long term as well as the immediate future. An organization structure that fails to recognize and promote human relations is normally short lived in regard to its effectiveness. Failure to recognize "people problems" results in worker resentment, poor worker morale, low worker productivity, embezzlement and theft, and high worker turnover. A people oriented organization structure can facilitate personnel management effectiveness. More is said of personnel management practices in Chapter 6.

While assignment of work functions to specific individuals is aimed at overall coordination, a secondary benefit should be higher productivity through specialization. One of the distinct advantages that the large construction firm has over its smaller competitor is that the individuals within the large firm can specialize as to their work functions. Whereas the single owner-employee of a construction firm may have to keep the books, find work, and manage the work; a single individual or group of individuals may be assigned a single function within the large firm. That is, one individual may be responsible for estimating, another for accounting, another for finance, another for material procurement, another for project management, etc.

The benefit of specialization is that it provides the potential for learning, which can lead to added productivity and quality in regard to the work function. There are potential difficulties associated with specialization that have to be weighed against potential benefits. Overspecialization sometimes leads to isolation and lack of communication. In addition, worker specialization can lead to worker dissatisfaction. In fact, some firms have found that an effective personnel management technique is to rotate workers among work assignments. Other firms tend to have production people specialize, whereas trying to expose management personnel to variable work tasks as a means of personnel development and motivation. The concept behind these two different philosophies is that the "inner needs" (see Chapter 6) differ for production and management personnel. The end result is that while specialization can prove beneficial, a fine line exists between effective specialization and inefficient specialization. Thus the difficulty of structuring an organization structure.

An organization structure can provide for two extreme types of decision making. *Centralized* decision making focuses on decision making by an individual or small group of individuals. Other organizational structures are aimed at *decentralized* decision making that focus on decision making by groups with each member of the group having somewhat equal contribution in the process. Centralized decision making is characteristic of small firms that are individually owned. On the other hand, the large amount and varying types of expertise that are part of a large firm are best utilized through a decentralized decision making process.

The point to be made is that regardless of whether a centralized or decentralized process is emphasized in the organization structure, the structure should enable the pinpointing of responsibility for operations, planning, control, etc. The pinpointing of responsibility is necessary if good performance is to be awarded, poor performance corrected, and management objectives evaluated.

The three basic functions of sales, production, and finance have to be carried out by almost every type of profit oriented firm. As the firm grows in size the required functions grow in number and those in existence are often divided into several functions. For example, the basic function of finance is divided into bookkeeping and finance. In the case of a construction firm it may divide the production function into project estimating and project management.

The functions of the firm and relationships of the functions within the organization structure are illustrated by means of an *organization chart*. Such a chart is drawn to help visualize what activities are performed and by whom, the work grouping of activities, and their relationships. An organization chart and structure may appear as a *chain* (sometimes referred to as a hierarchy) or appear *circular* (alternatively referred to as organic). The two alternatives are shown in Fig. 2.4. Chart lines joining the organization functions indicate the normal flow of communication and decision making. The chain structure is characterized by centralized decision making where each individual or function is subordinate to that above it. Communication typically proceeds from the top down although the chain structure does at least provide the potential for communication from bottom upwards. The circular structure emphasizes decentralized decision making. The channels of

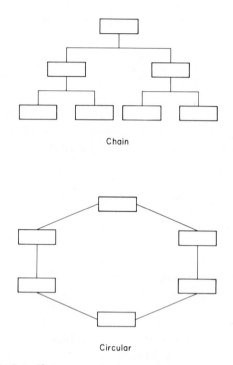

Chain

Circular

Fig. 2.4. Chain versus circular organization structure.

Communication characteristic	Chain	Circular
Speed	Fast	Slow
Accuracy	Good	Poor
Stability of leadership position	Firm	None
Average morale	Low	High
Flexibility to problem change	Low	High

Fig. 2.5. Communication and organization structure.

Fig. 2.6. Organization chart—small sized firm.

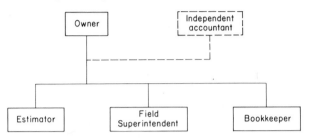

Fig. 2.7. Organization chart—medium sized firm.

communication of the two alternative structures are summarized in Fig. 2.5.[3] Characteristics and utilization of the two organization structures as they relate to the construction firm are discussed in the following two sections.

2.4.1 The Construction Hierarchical Organization Structure

More often than not, the organizational structure of the construction firm appears as a chain structure (i.e., hierarchy). While the structure increases in complexity as the firm grows in size, the chain structure remains characteristic of the firm.

The smallest of construction firms is made up of a single individual. The individual assumes all of the management duties of the firm. He is responsible for sales or marketing, finance and accounting, and production, which entails project estimating, planning, and project supervision. The organizational chart of such a firm is extremely simple and appears as is shown in Fig. 2.6. The restricted time considerations of the sole manager typically limits the annual volume of work of the one man operation to a million dollars or less.

As the firm grows in regard to work performed it is necessary to employ more personnel to carry out the management functions of the firm. Perhaps the next level of organization complexity and size as to the construction firm is shown in Fig. 2.7. The owner of the firm is

---

[3]Kazmier, L. J., *Principles of Management*, New York, McGraw-Hill, 1969.

primarily responsible for the sales and marketing function. The amount of financial paperwork of the firm necessitates the employment of an individual to handle the financial concerns of the firm. At this level of organizational size, the finance function is typically characterized by a high degree of bookkeeping with little time spent on financial analysis. More often than not, two individuals will be employed to carry out the production function of this relatively small firm. In particular, one will be responsible for project estimating with perhaps additional responsibilities of material procurement and cost analysis. Yet another production oriented individual will be given project supervision responsibilities and be singled out as a project superintendent. As is true of the estimator, he likely will be responsible for several on-going projects at the same point in time.

As an alternative to having two individuals, one for estimating and one for project supervision, a firm with a size characteristic of the one illustrated in Fig. 2.7 may have the estimating function carried out by the owner as part of the sales and marketing function, or have it carried out by the project superintendent. The size of firm characterized by the organization structure illustrated in Fig. 2.7 typically has an annual volume ranging from one to two million dollars of work.

The organizational structure shown in Fig. 2.7 is characterized as one having *horizontal growth*. This is evidenced by the addition of horizontal dimensions to the structure. The establishment of new functional assignments results in horizontal organizational growth. Growth in the very small firm is typically horizontal.

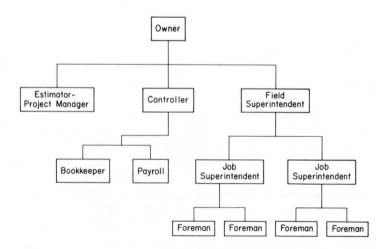

Fig. 2.8. Organization chart—large sized firm.

As the firm grows in size, some horizontal growth continues. In addition, vertical growth is evident. As to the construction firm this growth pattern is shown in Fig. 2.8. As can be observed, several job superintendents are part of the structure. Each is subordinate to a field superintendent who is responsible for all field construction. The addition of several job superintendents is *vertical organizational growth*. The addition of subordinate estimators and individual job accountants are other examples of vertical growth. Such growth is typical of the relatively large firm.

Horizontal growth can also be observed in the organizational structure of the relatively large construction firm shown in Fig. 2.8. The procurement function is separated from the estimating function. Another example of horizontal growth is the dividing of the financial function into an accounting or controllership function and the treasurership function. Whereas the individual duties of the company controller and treasurer vary from firm to firm, typical duties and responsibilities of the two functions are singled out by the Financial Executives Institute[4] as follows.

Controller	*Treasurer*
1. Planning for control	1. Provision of capital
2. Reporting and interpreting	2. Investor relations
3. Evaluating and interpreting	3. Short term financing
4. Tax administration	4. Banking and custody
5. Government reporting	5. Credits and collections
6. Protection of assets	6. Investments
7. Economic appraisal	7. Insurance

The type of firm illustrated in Fig. 2.8 has both horizontal and vertical growth as it continues to grow. More likely than not, horizontal growth predominates as the firm increases its annual volume in the range of ten to twenty million dollars. Firms with volume greater than this have to consider the feasibility of including branches within their organization structure.

Functions within the organization structure are classified as being *line* or *staff* functions. Whereas line functions are directly related to the production of the firm's product such as the construction project, staff

[4]Horngren, C. T., *Cost Accounting: A Managerial Emphasis*, Englewood Cliffs, Prentice-Hall, 1972, p. 12.

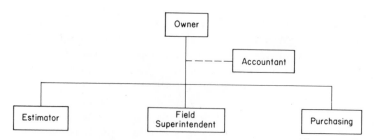

Fig. 2.9. Staff function in an organization structure.

functions are only indirectly related to production in that such functions support line functions. This is not to say that support functions should be viewed with less importance than line functions. The fact of the matter is that such functions may prove more vital to the accomplishment of company goals than do some line functions. Perhaps the best example of a vital staff function in the organization structure is that of accounting. While accounting personnel do not physically construct the construction project, the cost data they provide to line personnel such as project estimators and project superintendents provide these latter individuals the potential to build the project in an efficient manner that controls project time and cost.

Staff functions in the organization chart of the firm are sometimes singled out by means of either connecting the function to others by a dashed line, or by attaching the function horizontally to the chart, or both. Both procedures are used in Fig. 2.9. Theoretically, staff personnel have no control over line functions. However, in that they are to provide support to line functions, their advice and support is usually accepted by line personnel. Distinct personnel management practices for line versus staff personnel are discussed in Chapter 6.

The chain or hierarchy type of organization structure that has been discussed in this section is characterized as pinpointing responsibility and authority. Things get done. Decisions are typically made by a single individual or individuals and the resulting procedures and policies funneled down to subordinates vertically. On the other hand, functions tend to become isolated horizontally from one another within such a structure. Information is not totally passed from one function to another, and as such, is not input to many important decisions that are made within the firm. This unfavorable isolation of information and centralizing of decision making is especially noteworthy in regard to the construction firm. The management and building process that are characteristic of the construction industry results in a need for the recognition of the strong relationships that exist between the management functions. The traditional chain organization structure of the construction firm is not totally compatible with the recognition of the relationship of the management functions and as such is often less than optimal as to facilitating effective management. The problem can be somewhat alleviated by providing links of communication between dependent functions and promoting the usage of such links.

2.4.2 Organic Structure for the Construction Firm

The organic or circular organization structure is aimed at a sharing of infomation, ideas, and feedback. It is based on the theory that there is a set of information and data that are common to decision making as it relates to several management functions. The sharing of the information and data are to facilitate optimal decisions and provide an efficient and effective organizational structure.

Much of the management of the construction firm relates to project management. One of the strongest relationships between management functions is evident in project management. Relationships between various project management duties and functions are illustrated in Fig. 2.10. The key to the relationship of the functions shown in Fig. 2.10 is an information system based on past project data. As projects are performed cost and productivity data are funneled into the accounting functions where the data is structured for used by the payroll function, project supervision function, the estimating function, the planning and procurement functions, and further use by the accounting function. Each of these functions are related and relevant information is funneled back and forth to the individuals and departments responsible for the functions. For example, cost and productivity data are funneled from past projects to the estimating individual in charge of pricing a future project. The completed estimate serves as the basis for the work carried out through the project planning and procurement functions. In addition, past project data are quickly structured and analyzed and compared to the project plan and estimate. The project superintendent uses this comparison as the basis of project control.

The point to be made is that a properly designed information system that enhances communication between the project management functions results in each function aiding the optimization of another. In order for such an information system to be effective, the organizational struc-

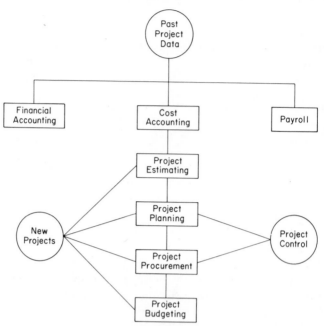

Fig. 2.10. Project management relations.

ture has to be compatible with the system. The organic or circular organizational structure has the potential for such compatibility.

An organic organization structure as illustrated in Fig. 2.11 is not without potential difficulties. The success of the structure is dependent on the total cooperation of each individual that is part of the structure. In addition, when one decentralizes decision making as is a characteristic of an organic structure, the potential for confusion and lack of strong leadership and decisive decision making increase. On the other hand, given the cooperation of all, not only is a better and more complete decision enabled, but morale tends to improve in that individuals and groups within the organizational structure become part of a team effort.

2.5 Financial Structure: Leverage and Liquidity

The success of a profit oriented firm is often measured by the firm's earning power. The earning power is the ratio of the firm's net opera-

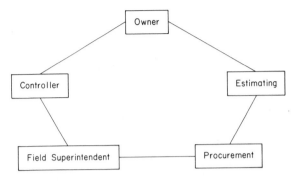

Fig. 2.11. Organic organization structure.

ting income divided by its net operating assets. In effect, it is a measure of the firm's ability to maximize its return on its investment.

The firm can increase its earning power or return on investment through operations. This is evident from inspection of the following formula for earning power.

Earning power   =   Margin   × Turnover

or

$$\frac{\text{Net operating income}}{\text{Net operating assets}} = \frac{\text{Net operating income}}{\text{Sales}} \times \frac{\text{Sales}}{\text{Net operating assets}}$$

As to the construction firm the *margin* is merely the ratio of project profit to project contract value. The *turnover* relates to the volume of work the construction firm performs versus the dollar value of assets of the firm. By means of increasing their volume of work performed, reducing their expenses, or decreasing their assets, the earning power of the firm can be increased. Unfortunately, this increasing or decreasing of factors that influence earning power does not linearly affect earning power. For example, if the firm decreases its invested assets, it will likely result in less volume of work. In addition, increased volume of work may add to overhead expenses and thus lower the profit margin. The end result is that the increasing of earning power through variations in operations is complex and the output of a given management adjustment may not be known until after the fact.

An equally important aspect of maximizing a firm's rate of return on its investment relates to the financial structure of the firm. In particular,

the assets of the firm can be obtained through issuance of debt to creditors or by means of investment of equity capital by the owners of the
firm. This invested capital is sometimes referred to as owner's equity,
or residual owner's equity. In the following discussion the terms debt
and equity will be used to represent the two segments of the capital
aspect of the financial structure of the firm.

The previous discussion of earning power assumed that the assets
of the firm were in fact obtained through equity investments. However,
the firm may in fact be able to generate profits through the purchase of
assets that are obtained by the issuance of debt. Assuming that the
interest rate associated with such debts is favorable, the resulting earn-
in power will be increased. For example, let us assume for simplicity
purposes, that $10 of assets are purchased through issuance of $2 of
debt and investment equity of $8. Should the firm earn $1, the rate of
return (i.e., the nonadjusted earning power) on total assets is $1/$10 or
10%. On the other hand, realizing that only $8 has been invested (i.e.,
the net assets) the true earning power (i.e., the return on equity) is
$1/$8 or 12.5%. Thus, the earning power is in fact increased due to the
financial structure. The difference between the earning power of 10%
and the return on equity of 12.5% is produced by financial *leverage*. If
we let the return on equity be designated as R, earning power (i.e.,
nonadjusted) as EP, and the leverage factor as L, then

$$R = EP \times L$$

or

$$L = R/EP = 12.5/10$$

Thus the earning power is magnified by 1.25 to produce the rate of
return on investment capital.

The above calculation of the leverage factor ignored the effect of
interest which the owners of the firm have to pay creditors when issuing debt. The presence of a high interest cost may in fact negate the
positive effects of earnings obtained through the issuance of debt.
Looked at another way, the leverage factor L represents the ratio of the
earnings actually received by the residual owners to the amount they
should have received based solely on their proportionate contribution
of funds to the business. Let T equal the proportion of total assets
financed by the investment equity (i.e., 80% in the previous example),
and Y equal the total earnings. The earnings the owners should receive
based on their proportionate share is TY. However, they also receive

earnings due to the issuance of debt. The additional earnings they receive is equal to the difference between what the creditor's share would be (i.e., $Y - TY$), and what the creditors *actually* receive in interest I, where I is the annual interest paid to the creditors. Thus, the bonus earnings to the owner are

$$(Y- TY)- I$$

or

$$(1- T)Y- I.$$

As long as $(1 - T) Y$ is greater than I, the leverage is favorable. The actual leverage factor, considering the interest effect, can be calculated as follows.

$$\text{Leverage} = \frac{\text{Owners' proportionate earnings} + \text{Bonus earnings from debt}}{\text{Owners' proportionate earnings}}$$

$$\text{Leverage} = \frac{TY + ((1-T)Y - I)}{TY} \quad \text{or} \quad \frac{1 (Y-I)}{T(Y)}$$

Assuming an annual interest charge of 5% in the previous example, the leverage would be calculated as follows.

$$L = \frac{.80 (\$1) + ((1-.80)(\$1) - \$.10)}{.80 (\$1)} = \frac{.80 + .10}{.80} = 1.125.$$

This would result in a 12.5% increase in earning power. Note that as long as the annual interest charge is less than $.20 (i.e., 10% interest rate on the $2.00 debt) the leverage is favorable in that the leverage factor is greater than one. If the interest charge is $.30 the unfavorable leverage factor would be as follows.

$$L = \frac{.80 - 10}{.80} = .875$$

This would result in a decreasing of the unadjusted earning power of the firm. The end result is that leverage tends to multiply a positive earning power or negative earning power. This multiplication effect can be observed in Fig. 2.12.

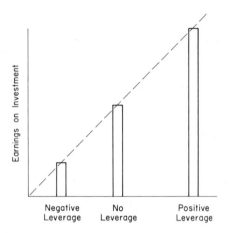

Fig. 2.12. The effect of leverage.

One other consideration can result in a slight modification in the determination of the leverage factor. Interest is a deductible expense to the firm and thus a benefit of issuing debt. This added benefit can be recognized in the leverage formula. However, because the modification is slight as to the leverage factor it will be ignored here. Ignoring any tax effects and assuming a given income, the two factors that influence the determination of the leverage are interest and the percentage ownership by equity versus creditor debt. Assuming a favorable leverage factor (i.e., greater than one), the smaller the interest charge the more favorable the leverage factor. Naturally, a zero interest charge would be ideal. Unfortunately for the firm, creditors are not willing to lend money without a charge for their money to cover their risk of loss of repayment.

From inspection of the formula for the leverage factor, it can be observed that the percentage ownership of the firm through investment equity also effects the determination of the value of the leverage. Assuming a favorable leverage, the smaller the proportionate investment ownership of the assets the more favorable the leverage factor. In fact, the determination of the value of the leverage is much more sensitive to the ownership percentage than it is to the interest charge.

The question might be raised, "Why not decrease the proportionate equity ownership of the firm relative to the debt ownership?" Theoretically, the proportionate equity ownership can be reduced to a percentage that approaches zero (i.e., admittedly it would be difficult to continue to get creditors to increase their lending percentage). From the previous discussion it follows that such a decrease in equity ownership would provide substantial earning power benefits to the owners. However, it is noteworthy that only the issue of return to the owners has been raised in the discussion of leverage and financial structure. An important factor that has been neglected is the issue of risk.

Two somewhat independent points should be recognized when considering the leverage and financial structure of the firm as they relate to risk. In order to obtain leverage, debt has to be issued and this debt implies an interest charge. An interest expense is a fixed cost to the borrower of money. It comes due regardless of the amount of income obtained through operations. It can create a *liquidity* problem for the firm in that it reduces the amount of liquid assets (cash or assets readily transferable to cash) available to the firm. In more cases than not, bankruptcy problems start with the unavailability of cash and other liquid assets such as receivables. Ideally, a firm that is high leveraged should have high liquidity such that they are in a position to pay interest when it comes due. Specific adequate liquidity values as they relate to leverage are discussed in a later section on financial ratios.

A second relevant consideration of leverage and risk relates to possible decreases in income. As income decreases, a favorable leverage factor greater than one can decrease to an unfavorable value less than one. This is evident from the fact that as the value of Y decreases, $((1- T) Y- I)$ becomes smaller and can become negative, thus resulting in a leverage factor less than one. In addition, the leveraging effects tend to multiply the negative effects as income continues to decrease. The end result is that return has to be balanced with risk when considering leverage and the financial structure of the firm. Consideration of expected income, interest expense, liquidity, and to a lesser degree taxes, are necessary to the financial structure decision. The uncertainty of some of these factors such as income, increase the complexity of the analysis. However, recognition of the relevant factors can go a long way in generating profits and decreasing profits through financial structuring of the firm. More will be said of leverage and liquidity of the construction related firm in the following sections.

2.5.1 Financial Structure of the Construction Firm

Leverage and liquidity are two important aspects of the financial structure considerations that relate to the financial soundness, income,

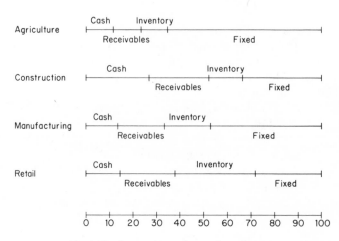

Fig. 2.13. Composition of assets by industries.

and growth of the construction firm. In addition, the actual makeup of the balance sheet items of the firm relate to the overall strength of the firm.

Unique external factors tend to shape the total financial structure of the firm. The inability to raise equity capital, the operating on short term credit, the large amounts of receivables on the books because of the owner's retention of part payment, and the dependence of some firms on large dollar values of equipment all dictate the financial structure of the construction firm. Some of these industry characteristics result in a less than favorable structure that contains an undue amount of risk for the firm.

The primary assets of any firm are its cash, receivables, inventory, and fixed and other assets. In comparison to all other industries, the construction firm has a high percentage of its assets in receivables. In addition, compared to the manufacturing industry (of which construction is a part), the construction firm has a relatively small percent of fixed assets. These characteristics can be observed from inspection of Fig. 2.13.[5]

The construction firm's high dependence on receivables results from the billing and payment retention procedures that are characteristic of the industry. Upon completing various work items, the construction firm bills the owner. However, actual payment may be slow depending on who is the owner. Delays of a month or more are common. In addition, when in fact the payment is made, the owner may choose

[5]Johnson, R. W., *Financial Management*, Boston, Allyn and Bacon, p. 89.

to retain part of the payment (typically 10%) until the construction project is substantially completed. Considering the fact that projects may have a contract value exceeding $100,000, this 10% retention can amount to a substantial dollar value receivable.

Receivables are troublesome assets. For one they do not provide the construction firm an asset that can be used for operations and growth. It is true that the firm can convert them to cash by means of assignment or factoring (these procedures are discussed in Chapter 5), however such procedures are not readily available to the construction firm and when they are they are relatively unfavorable as to interest cost. As such, receivables typically do not aid the firm in resolving any cash flow problems. In fact a large buildup of receivables is often characteristic of a cash flow problem leading to bankruptcy.

Unlike receivables in other industries, the construction firm seldom receives interest from the project owner. As such, the owner is in fact using the construction firm's money to finance his project.

The uncertainty and risk associated with receivables are other unfavorable financial considerations. Many a construction firm has had to enter court in order to collect its receivables. Other construction firms have been less successful in their attempts to "get what was coming to them."

Various construction related associations have continued their efforts to somewhat aleviate the difficulties that are part of the process in which the construction firm is paid. However, by itself the individual construction firm can do little to change the process. As such, the firm has to pay special attention to control its receivables. This control entails adequate accounting records, adequate collection procedures, and an adequate and realistic provision for bad debts.

Inspection of Fig. 2.13 also yields the fact that the construction firm has a relatively large percentage of its assets in cash. The construction firm continually has to have cash on hand to pay for varying amounts of labor and material expenses. While an adequate amount of cash for this purpose is necessary in order to avoid cash flow problems, the fact remains that cash is not a good *income producing asset*. Cash heavy firms tend to be nongrowth firms in that income and growth are generated by means of investment in nonmonetary assets such as plant and equipment. The construction firm has to be cautious as to using its cash for nonmonetary investments due to its need to have a large amount of cash readily available for operations.

It is difficult to generalize as to the construction firm's investment in fixed assets. The amount of such assets within a given construction firm varies from relatively high for the heavy and highway firm to

Assets

Current Assets
Cash	$103,991
Notes and accounts receivable	233,100
Cost of uncompleted contracts	92,528
All other inventory	37,834
Other current assets	28,531
Total current assets	495,598
Fixed assets	32,166
Other assets	11,134
Total assets	$539,284

Liabilities

Current liabilities
Notes, accounts, and other payables	$151,667
Billings on uncompleted contracts	139,468
Total current liabilities	291,135
Noncurrent liabilities	26,699
Total liabilities	317,834
Net worth	221,450
Total liabilities and net worth	$539,284

Fig. 2.14. Balance sheet—one million volume construction firm.

practically nothing for the specialty subcontracting firm. However as
can be observed from Fig. 2.13, the typical construction firm has less
fixed assets than its counterparts in the manufacturing industry. While
this smaller dependence on fixed assets frees cash for other purposes, it
is also true that firms with relatively large amounts of investment in
such fixed assets tend to be more financially stable. More will be said of
investment in various types of assets in the discussion of financial
ratios in the following section.

As to the capital side of the construction firm's balance sheet, the
firm is characterized by a high degree of debt. Whereas typical manufacturing firms have approximately the same amount of debt capital
and equity capital (i.e., invested capital plus retained earnings), the
construction firm typically has liabilities in excess of their equity capital. As can be observed from Fig. 2.14,[6] which illustrates the typical
balance sheet of the construction firm, for a firm with an annual volume
of one million dollars of work, the liabilities may be one and one-half

[6]"1973 Annual Statistical Survey," Mechanical Contractors Association of America,
Washington, D.C., 1974, p. 10.

times the equity capital. This higher dependence on debt is not unexpected when one considers the difficulty that the construction firm has with raising investment capital. Typically, the construction firm is relatively small and not in a favorable position to issue stock that provides equity capital.

Inspection of Fig. 2.14 also illustrates the fact that of the construction firm's liabilities, a large percentage of them are current liabilities. Normally this means that they are liabilities that must be repaid within a duration of a year versus long term liabilities that typically can be repaid in periods of ten or twenty years or more. The lack of significant long term liabilities relates to several factors. For one, similar to investment capital, third parties viewing the construction firm with risk, are reluctant to commit funds to the firm on a long term basis. Secondly, many construction firms lease their construction equipment by means of a long term contract. While recent accounting rules will force the recognition of these long term leases as long term liabilities (which in effect they are), most balance sheets including the one illustrated in Fig. 2.14 have not recognized the lease as a liability.

The nature of the construction firm's business operations also result in the firm being much more dependent on current liabilities than on long term liabilities. Short term loans provide the firm the means of financing material purchases and meeting the weekly payroll. These needs are often compounded by slow payment from the project owner. The developer and spec builder are greatly dependent on the so-called *construction loan* which in effect is a current liability even though the loan may cover a period somewhat greater than a year. (Note: By definition a current liability is one that is to be repaid in the normal business operating cycle.)

The construction firm's high dependence on current liabilities places it in a position of high financial risk. By definition, current liabilities come due in a relatively short period of time. Should the firm have difficulty making payment due to a slump in its operations or poor cash flow planning, it in effect defaults and becomes subject to bankruptcy proceedings. In order to operate and to reduce some of the financial risk of current liabilities, the construction firm should seek a sound and flexible credit line with a lending institution. While it is the purpose of Chapter 5 on financing to discuss a credit line, it should be pointed out here that the flexibility and willingness of a lending institution in its dealings with a construction firm can often mean the difference between the construction firm's success or failure. The lending institution's willingness to extend the time of payment or waive a loan agreement such as the required working capital the firm must retain, can extend the life of the construction firm. On the other hand, this extension or waiver of loan clauses may be merely delaying the inevitable failure of the firm. Ideally, the firm should never find itself in a position where its livelihood is dependent on the good graces of its creditors. Wishful thinking indeed!

2.5.2 Financial Analysis of the Firm

Numerous financial ratios can be developed by dividing one of the many different items in a firm's income or balance statement by another item. The firm can then compare the values of its ratios to the average values of the ratios for its industry, and perhaps decide to make an adjustment in its financial structure. Ratio analysis is also used by external parties in evaluating the financial structure and risk of a firm. As to the construction firm, sureties and bankers will typically concentrate on what they view as key financial ratios when determining the feasibility of bonding the firm, or lending money to the firm.

The user of financial ratio analysis should be aware of the limitations of such analysis. For one, each industry and each firm is somewhat unique as to its product, its objectives, and its financial structure. It follows that each firm is somewhat unique as to the values of its ratios. A firm's policies based on a specific growth objective may result in a variance of its ratios from those accepted as average for the industry. However, the firm may have a very sound financial structure.

When one compares a given firm's financial ratios to industry wide average ratios, the source and reliability of the average ratio comes into question. Numerous services and associations publish such ratios. Among these are Dun and Bradstreet, the Small Business Administration, Robert Morris Associates, and various trade associations. The variance between values of specific ratios published by different firms raises the question of reliability. Yet another point as to the source and reliability is the fact that published ratios represent historic data. The optimal financial structure for a firm or industry can change over a period of years. What was ideal as to various financial ratios ten or five years ago, may not be ideal today. Changes in interest rates, accounting practices, and tax laws are a few of the external factors that can justify changes in the financial structure and financial ratios of the firm.

Perhaps the greatest difficulty related to ratio analysis is the fact that a firm can greatly manipulate its financial ratios through transactions that are for this purpose alone. For example, should a firm be in need to improve its short term position as to current assets versus current liabilities, it can issue long term debt and thus either raise cash (i.e., a current asset) or use the cash to reduce its current liabilities. Similarly, the selling of fixed assets such as plant or equipment will provide cash that will improve the value of the current ratio that might be analyzed by a potential creditor.

A difficulty somewhat unique to the construction industry in its use of financial ratios relates to the alternative accounting methods used by construction firms. The uses of alternative accounting methods such as the completed contract method versus the percentage-of-completion method results in different values for certain financial ratios. Accounting methods are discussed in Chapter 9.

Regardless of the problems associated with financial ratio analysis, such ratios continue to be used by the firm and external parties. Particular values of the ratios are not as important as what the ratios are supposed to indicate. Knowing that a given ratio is indicative of a firm's ability to meet payment on its current liabilities is more important than trying to memorize specific acceptable values of the ratio. In addition, observation of the trend of the value of a given ratio is useful in that it may flag a future potential financial problem. The observation of the ratio as a function of time will also aid in the detecting of any attempt on the firm to manipulate its ratios.

Whereas certain financial ratios are useful for evaluating the short term soundness of the financial structure of the firm, others are more relevant to the evaluation of the long term soundness. Thus, potential creditors considering the lending of short term loans may be interested in one set of ratios, potential creditors considering the lending of long term loans and potential investors of equity capital may be more concerned with a different set of financial ratios. Let us first consider some of the more commonly used financial ratios that relate to short term financial analysis.

While not truly a financial ratio, the measure of a construction firm's working capital to its dollar value of work being performed is indicative of its ability to meet committments as to material purchases and labor payroll. Working capital refers to current assets that are readily transferable to cash. For the construction firm, this consists primarily of cash and current receivables. As a general rule, the construction firm should maintain a 10% to 15% ratio of working capital to its dollar work load.[7] A value less than this enhances cash flow problems.

---

[7]Wolkstein, H. W., *Accounting Methods and Controls for the Construction Industry*, Englewood Cliffs, Prentice-Hall, 1967, p. 95.

The four most commonly used financial ratios for short term analysis are as follows:

Current Ratio	=	$\dfrac{\text{Current assets}}{\text{Current liabilities}}$
Quick Ratio or Acid Test Ratio	=	$\dfrac{\text{Quick assets}}{\text{Current liabilities}}$
Receivables Turnover	=	$\dfrac{\text{Credit sales}}{\text{Average receivables}}$
Inventory Turnover	=	$\dfrac{\text{Cost of projects}}{\text{Average inventory}}$

As to creditors these financial ratios center on the relation of current assets to current liabilities and the rapidity with which receivables and inventory turn into cash in the normal course of business. Short term creditors are concerned with the immediate and short term ability of the firm to generate cash for the payment of the loan principal and interest. The four ratios that focus on this availability of cash are developed primarily from the firm's balance sheet. Whereas short term analysis focuses on the balance sheet, as will be discussed later, long term analysis primarily focuses on the income statement.

The current ratio is by far the most recognized short term financial ratio. It is a test of the solvency of the firm. It indicates the ability of the firm to meet current obligations. Typically lenders of money prefer to see a current ratio of 2 to 1 or even 2.5 to 1. However, it is difficult for even the most financially sound construction firm to maintain such a high ratio. The construction firm's high dependence on short term credit results in a current ratio of about 1.5 to 1 being realistic. Any deviation lower than a 1.5 to 1 ratio should be viewed as an indicator of future solvency problems.

Theorectically, the acid test is even a more severe test of a firm's solvency. Whereas the current ratio includes inventories in the determination of assets, they are excluded in the determination of quick assets. Unlike cash, current receivables, and temporary investments, it is sometimes difficult to-transform inventory into cash without absorbing a loss on the transaction. As to the construction firm, the difference between the current ratio and quick ratio loses some of its significance due to the fact that the construction firm is not heavily invested in inventories. This contrasts to other manufacturing industries such as the automobile industry which has a high inventory investment in raw materials. A quick ratio for a construction firm that is less than 1.25 to 1 or even more critically 1 to 1 should be viewed with alarm.

The receivable turnover and inventory turnover ratios are indicative of a firm's ability to convert receivables and inventory into cash. Both ratios are not as meaningful in the construction industry as they might be in other industries. The billing and payment process typical of the construction industry dictates the construction firm's collection of receivables. However should the firm deal in credit sales such as small repair jobs, then the receivable turnover ratio may be indicative of the soundness of the firm's accounting practices as to receivables, and its collection procedures. For the most part, the construction firm's receivable turnover is mainly dependent on the type of owner for which the firm performs work, and the duration of projects the firm undertakes. Perhaps the most meaningful use of the receivable turnover ratio for the construction firm is for the firm to observe changes in the value of its own ratio with the goal of implementing procedures that increase the value of the ratio.

Similar to the receivable turnover ratio, the inventory turnover ratio is distorted by the fact that the typical construction firm has a relatively small investment in inventory. Since each project is somewhat unique it is often unwise for the construction firm to build up an inventory of raw materials. However, it should be noted that in effect, a project which is not completed is in fact inventory to the construction firm. In this context, the inventory turnover ratio can be used to analyze the firm's ability to complete projects on schedule and turn them into cash. However it should be noted that the value of the ratio will be significantly different depending on what type of accounting method is used to recognize project income and project work in progress. Alternative accounting methods are discussed in a later chapter.

Although the long term creditor or investor has to be concerned about the firm's ability to meet its current obligations, it is also concerned about the long range profitability of the firm. Expected income growth, ability to pay future dividends, and the ability to raise long term funding are of upmost importance to the long term financial success of the firm. In great part, these long term success factors are reflected through the firm's income statement.

Of the many financial ratios used for evaluating the long term financial soundness of the firm, perhaps those most used and most relevant to the construction firm are illustrated in Fig. 2.15. The average value of

	Average for construction firm	Range for construction firm
Net profits / Annual volume	1.48	0.85–2.98
Net profits / Net worth	11.5	5.7–20.1
Net profits / Net working capital	18.8	8.4–41.5
Annual volume / Net worth	7.5	4.4–12.2

Fig. 2.15. Financial ratios—long term considerations.

the ratios along with a range as determined by a survey of construction firms conducted by Dun and Bradstreet[8] are indicated in Fig. 2.15.

The net profits on annual volume, net worth, and net working capital ratios relate to the earnings rate of the firm as a function of annual volume, net worth, and net working capital, respectively. The net worth equals the owner's invested capital plus any retained earnings. The value of the net profit on annual volume shown in Fig. 2.15 is relatively small for construction firms versus other industries. On the other hand, the values of the net profit on working capital ratio and net profit on net worth ratio shown for the average construction firm in Fig. 2.15 are higher than the values for the corresponding ratios in other industries. However, the relatively large values of the ratios are due to the relatively small amount of working capital and net worth of the construction firm rather than a large dollar net profit.

The ratio of annual volume to net worth measures the number of times net worth is "turned over" in workload. It is indicative of the utilization of owner's equity and too low of a value may indicate over-capitalization in relation to volume of work performed. Because of the widely varying dollar values associated with types of work performed by different construction firms, the ratio of annual volume to net worth can vary substantially from one firm to the next. As such, as is true of the other financial ratios discussed, the most meaningful use often centers around the firm's comparing the value of the ratio as a function of time. Such a comparison can often flag needed corrective financial adjustments.

In addition to the short term and long term related financial ratios discussed, numerous other ratios have been used with less frequency to

[8]Clough, R. H., *Construction Contracting*, New York, Wiley, 1969, p. 173.

analyze the financial soundness of the construction firm. Included in these are the ratio of fixed assets to net worth, the ratio of net income to project direct costs (i.e., profit margin on cost), and various ratios that are aimed at analyzing the contents of the overhead of the construction firm. The profit margin ratio of construction firms has been discussed in other sections. Other less used ratios are left for the reader to pursue if interested.

2.6 Summary

The ease of entrance into the construction industry has resulted in numerous new entrants annually. More often than not, little thought and effort is used in the structuring of the firm. Instead entrants "play it by ear" with the result being that the structure of the firm is shaped by the environment of the firm. The end result is a structure that is not optimal as to legal consequences, liabilities, tax benefits, organizational operation, and financial soundness and stability.

The first step on the road to a long lasting financial successful construction firm is a thorough analysis and selection of the type of work the firm is to perform; and its legal, organization, and financial structure. The decision to be a general contractor, construction manager, proprietorship, partnership, etc., is a decision that plays as an important role in generating future profits as other management functions such as personnel management, and project cost control. Equally important is the decision as to the firm's organizational structure and financial structure. The organization structure provides the means of efficient management communication, effective personnel management practices, and required company project control.

The construction industry is affected by unique external factors that in part dictate the financial structure of the firm. The inability of the construction firm to raise equity capital, its high dependence on short term credit, its low investment in raw materials, and the large amount of current receivables on its books owing to the process by which it receives payment from project owners, all place constraints on the financial structure of the firm. Within these constraints the firm has to strive to build a sound financial structure such that it remains solvent, and to enable itself to be in a favorable position in its dealings with potential creditors and investors.

Case 2.1 Aloma Construction Company:
Legal Structure of the Firm

Steve Aloma is the owner of the Aloma Construction Company. Although he is the sole owner of the proprietorship, the business is very dependent on the skills of two of Steve Aloma's colleagues. One is Rich Younger who is a recent engineering graduate who is a designer and planner. Since the Aloma Company is now very active in design-build, Richard Younger is a valuable asset to the Aloma Company. He has been with the firm 2 years. John Busman is a business college graduate who has been with the firm 3 years. His responsibility has included the financial, accounting, and cost control functions of the firm. Since over the last five years Aloma's annual volume of work has increased from 5 to 12 million dollars, the business aspects of the firm have become more complex and more important.

Steve Aloma started the Aloma Construction Company 12 years ago. Prior to starting his firm, he was a carpenter for 8 years. As such, although he has little formal education he has had 20 years of practical construction building experience.

This past year Aloma Construction Company had 12 million of sales and after expenses of 11.6 million (including a $21,000 salary to Richard Younger and $19,000 to John Busman) left Steve Aloma with a taxable income of $400,000.

The average cost of the projects in which the Aloma Company engages in has increased from $500,000 to $1.0 million in the last three years. In addition, the firm has increased liability in that they are the designer of many of the projects they build. Steve Aloma has become convinced that he might lose the service of Rich Younger in that he has asked for a 25% raise and increased benefits.

These facts, along with the high rate of taxes Steve Aloma has paid the last year has led him to consult you about the legal structure of his firm. Given the above information and the fact that Mr. Aloma expects sales and expenses to increase at an annual rate of 4%, what legal form should the Aloma Construction Company have. Steve Aloma's estate is estimated at $900,000, whereas the estates of Rich Younger and John Busman are estimated at $110,000 and $55,000, respectively.

Case 2.2 Rucks Construction Company:
Organizational Structure of the Firm

Steve Rucks, the president of Rucks Construction Company, is faced with a problem within his firm. His problem is centered around the purchasing function and its relation to the other management functions of the firm.

As the Rucks company grew in size, all company managers along with Steve Rucks decided that the firm's purchasing function should be centralized and that a specialist, Dick Goodson, should be hired and placed in charge. This centralizing of the purchasing function took place three years ago.

When the purchasing function was established, Mike Stoner the overall project superintendent in charge of all project superintendents, stated that the creation of the position would free his superintendents from the detailed ordering duties. As such, he believed his superintendents could spend more time performing their main duties of managing their assigned projects. The two other company managers, Doug Banks head of marketing and finance, and Kevin Brooks head of accounting, had also agreed that the centralizing of the purchasing function would facilitate the performance of their individual functions.

Within the last year there has been increasing confrontations between the purchasing department manager and the other managers of the Rucks Construction Company. These confrontations have recently been brought to the attention of Steve Rucks.

Mike Stoner has become dissatisfied with Dick Goodson and the purchasing department. He has stated that instead of simplifying his job as overall project superintendent by taking care of purchasing for him, the purchasing department has developed a formal set of procedures that has resulted in as much time commitment on his part as he previously spent in placing the orders himself. In addition, Mike Stoner and his project superintendents have been increasingly irritated by the fact that their needs for particular items are constantly being questioned by Dick Goodson. Mr. Stoner believed that Dick Goodson was to fill his needs, not question them.

Doug Banks had always believed that the marketing, purchasing, and finance functions were a unified process. His being assigned both the marketing and finance responsibilities was the result of the lack of qualified personnel to fill one of the positions and his argument that both positions were compatible. When the purchasing function was centralized, Doug Banks saw the opportunity to unify the purchasing function with his existing two functions. However, according to Doug Banks, Dick Goodson has been carrying out the purchasing function without regard to the marketing and finance functions. As such, Doug Banks believed that his job was made more difficult in that marketing strategy became more difficult.

Kevin Brooks, head of accounting, has had several confrontations with Dick Goodson. Most of these confrontations were the result of personality conflicts between the two managers. Both individuals were dominating types of individuals and as such often did not accept one anothers ideas. The end result was that the purchasing function and the accounting function tended to be independent in regard to management of the firm.

Dick Goodson previously was the purchasing manager of a manufacturing firm considerably larger than Rucks Construction Company. Through the acquaintance of a friend, Steve Rucks had met Dick Goodson. He offered him a 10% salary increase to join the Rucks Construction Company as the purchasing manager.

Dick Goodson has his own view of the current problems. He views himself as a professional, hired to do a professional job. However, he believed that Stoner, Banks, and Brooks thought that he was subordinate to each of them, which he believed not to be the case.

While acknowledging the fact that he required detailed reports and requisitions, Dick Goodson had documented proof that construction materials were now being purchased more economically than they were under the previous decentralized purchasing system. In addition, he sees no strong relationship between purchasing and the marketing and finance functions. Therefore, he is confused as to why Doug Banks is disturbed with the current operations. As to his confrontations with Brooks, Goodson sees him as unwilling to acknowledge the purchasing function.

Steve Rucks has always believed that some conflict between the firm's managers to be beneficial. However, since the confrontations now seem to be disrupting overall company morale and taking more of his time, he feels he has to take the appropriate action. What should this action be?

Case 2.3 Expand Construction Company: Financial Structure of the Firm

The Expand Construction Company has been operating as a building contracting firm for over twenty years. While it is legally a corporation, ownership is limited to Ed Swartz head of accounting, Jim Michaels who is responsible for production, and Steve Ofken who handles estimating and purchasing. Several others are employed on a full-time basis.

In planning for the future, the three owners have decided to expand into the performing of heavy and highway work. Such an expansion should prove beneficial as to being less susceptible to fluctuations in the economy. In addition it should provide substantial growth for the firm. Because of the elder ages of two of the owners there is some thought of building the firm to an annual volume of about fifty million dollars of work versus the current level of ten to fifteen million. Hopefully such growth can be obtained within three years such that the owners may sell out to outsiders by selling stock of the firm in an open market.

In order to be able to perform heavy and highway work, the Expand Company will find it necessary to have available a substantial amount of equipment. In particular they estimate they will need equipment costing about one million dollars. Currently they own $200,000 of equipment.

The balance sheet (i.e., statement of financial portion) for the firm as of its last reported ending fiscal year is summarized as follows.

Assets		Capital	
		Liabilities	
Current assets		Current liabilities	$400,000
Cash	$150,000	Long term liabilities	200,000
Accounts receivable	250,000	Total liabilities	$600,000
Total current assets	$400,000	Net worth	
Fixed assets	$200,000	Stockholders investment	$100,000
Investments	400,000	Retained earnings	300,000
Total assets	$1,000,000	Total net worth	$400,000
		Total capital	$1,000,000

The firm has a credit line at a local bank for $800,000. However should the firm's total debt to net worth exceed a ratio of two, this credit line is reduced to $500,000. Currently the firm has $300,000 borrowed on this credit line and all of it is a current liability.

The personal estates of Mr. Swartz, Michaels, and Ofken are $120,000, $45,000, and $85,000, respectively. These values include the investment of $40,000, $10,000, and $50,000 of Swartz, Michaels, and Ofken, respectively, in the Expand Construction Company.

The three owners are faced with finding means of financing the added $800,000 of equipment. Alternatives available to the firm are as follows.

(1)   Obtain a 12% long term loan from a bank and secure the loan with the personal assets of the owners.

(2)   Obtain the required $800,000 by taking in two new owners. These potential owners will invest this amount for a 75% ownership of the firm.

(3)   Lease the needed equipment at an annual cost of $150,000 a year. The firm has an option of signing this lease for 10 years or signing a three year lease at $200,000 per year.

(4)   Purchase the equipment through a loan from the equipment manufacturer. Such a loan will be for 15% for ten years. At the end of any year the company has an option of purchasing the equipment with 70% of their investment in principal applying to the initial $800,000 cost.

In evaluating the alternative means of financing the equipment, the three owners recognize that their decision will affect yearly earnings, return on investment, and financial ratios. Given the external constaints on the firm, and the long range objectives of the owners of the firm, determine the financing alternative that the owners should select.

Chapter 3

Marketing: Obtaining and Maintaining Clients

3.1 Introduction

It is common to think of marketing as selling. If one accepts this definition, the construction firm's involvement with marketing is minimal in that the firm does not have to "sell" its product in that the firm typically either wins or loses a project contract in the competitive bidding process. There are two fallacies with this conclusion that one might reach. For one, negotiated contracts whereby the construction firm obtains work on the basis of its promotional efforts, its ability to perform, and its overall "selling" efforts, are becoming increasingly common in the construction process. Secondly, contrary to the beliefs of many who think of marketing as only selling, the study and application of marketing encompasses much more than the selling of one's product or service.

Marketing is the planning, pricing, promoting, and distribution (distribution is also referred to as placing) of one's product or service. Thus, reference to the four P's (planning, pricing, promoting, and placing) is common when a broad and complete definition of marketing is given. The selling function that was referred to earlier is more properly referred to as the promoting aspect of marketing.

The construction firm, similar to an automobile manufacturer, produces a product that it must market to a purchaser. Although its means of marketing its product differ from that of other manufacturers such as the automobile manufacturer, the construction firm has to perform the same functions of planning, pricing, promoting, and placing. As will be discussed in this chapter, the construction firm's emphasis on each of the four marketing tasks may vary from that of other producers of manufactured goods. This change of emphasis is a result of the differences of the environment of the construction industry from that of other industries.

It has been correctly stated that the marketing business function is fundamental to the necessity of all other business functions. That is, there would be no need for such business functions as business law, financing, or personnel management unless a product or service is marketed by the firm. With this in mind, this chapter focuses on marketing terminology and practices as they relate to the construction firm.

3.2 Marketing Environment of the Construction Firm

Required marketing practices differ for the construction firm depending on whether the firm engages in competitive-bid contracts or negotiated contracts. In the past, negotiated contracts were limited to small construction projects. However, an increasing number of large negotiated contracts are being entered into by the construction firm. The end result is that many firms are finding themselves entering into both types of contract agreements.

The construction firm is basically marketing cost in the competitive-bid process. Much of the firm's efforts center on submitting a bid on a project that has a cost low enough to be the low bid yet large enough to provide the firm a profit. On the other hand, the construction firm seeking negotiated contracts, while concerned with cost, has to pay added attention to external relations. As such, special care must be directed to turning out quality work and keeping and obtaining personal contacts with potential owners through associations, social clubs, and in some cases providing free work or donations to charitable organizations.

As to its type of operation, most business services and the government classify the construction firm as a manufacturing industry. However, in reality the construction firm is somewhat of a combination of a manufacturer and a service oriented firm. It is true that the traditional construction firm manufacturers a construction project. However the project is not truly the construction firm's product in that the project is built for an owner and the project has in fact been designed by the owner through his architect/engineer. In one sense the construction firm is providing a service function in that it is providing management and technical skills to the owner such that the owner's project can become reality.

In that the construction firm is not normally responsible for the conception of a project, its marketing tactics do not have to concentrate on customers' needs and satisfaction and pricing practices such as markups, markdowns, etc. On the other hand, because the construction firm has some of the characteristics of both manufacturing and service industries, its marketing tactics have to recognize both physical commodities such as concrete and service attributes such as ethics and professional external relations. The latter attributes of ethics and professional external relations are becoming increasingly important with the increasing popularity of negotiated contracts, design-built, and construction management contracts.

Most of the unique marketing aspects of the construction firm relate to the fact that each project the firm builds is somewhat unique. Much of marketing study, research, and publications relate to the marketing of a product that is produced and sold several times. Because this is not a characteristic of the construction product, many of the traditional manufacturing principals are not applicable to the construction industry. This fact complicates the study of planning, pricing, promoting, and placing as it relates to the construction firm but it does not follow that the construction firm can pass over these marketing functions.

3.3 Planning for Company Operations

The first step in a successful marketing process is that of planning. By definition, *planning* is the selection of objectives and their means of attainment. As it relates to construction firm marketing, planning addresses the determination of the type of work the firm is to perform, the decision as to where it is to perform work, the determination of the organizational structure for the marketing of the firm's product, and the means by which the firm is to construct its product (i.e., the construction project) such that the firm can price, promote, and place the product with an owner in a manner that satisfies the firm's profit oriented objectives. This later planning task entails many of the traditional construction management functions such as project method analysis and improvement, and overall project scheduling. Yet another planning oriented function, one that is often overlooked, is the determination of growth objectives and the corresponding policies and procedures.

In the discussion of organizational structure in the previous chapter, the three basic business functions were defined as sales or marketing, production, and finance. It was also pointed out the owner of the small or medium sized construction firm performed the marketing

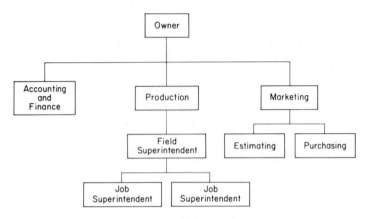

Fig. 3.1. Marketing within the organization structure.

function himself. However as a firm grows in size, several individuals are required to carry out the function. In fact the owner or president may see it fit to remove himself from the function entirely in favor of setting up a distinct marketing department as shown in Fig. 3.1. In fact several large construction firms have created two marketing related departments, one referred to as *marketing* and one referred to as *sales*. While not typical of the construction related firm, some businesses will expand the marketing function to yet a third department referred to as *research*.

As is true of all management functions, the marketing function should not be isolated from other functions. The organizational structure should be such that it facilitates communication between marketing, production, and finance. For example, past project data from the production function provides planning data for marketing. In addition, in order to properly finance operations, the finance function must have marketing plans available for evaluating alternatives. Examples of additional functional relationships are numerous.

Alternative types of work that are open to the construction firm were discussed in the previous chapter. As noted in that chapter, the newly formed construction firm often chooses its area of work concentration on the basis of the skills of the founders. While this seems logical, it also is true that more attention should be given to the market for the type of work being considered. Many a company founder has commenced operations as a residential home builder in his home city only to later find that the demand for housing is short lived.

The point to be made is that the construction firm should have knowledge as to the potential construction expenditures in its area of speciality. While the dollars spent in different categories vary some-what from one year to the next, substantial changes are unlikely. Various government services keep records as to various types of construction expenditures. The records are readily available to individual firms through publications and charts such as that illustrated in Fig. 3.2.[1]

Perhaps more important than the concern for the breakdown of total expected construction expenditures, is the concern for expected expenditures as a function of geographic locations. The fact that residential expenditures are 36% of all construction expenditures is not totally relevant to a construction firm doing work in a town where residential work is only 5% of construction expenditures in the community. Variations in the makeup of construction expenditures occur from one part of the country to the next due to environmental differences, variations in local economics, population growth patterns, and to a lesser degree material availability. This interaction is illustrated in the model of a business system shown in Fig. 3.3.

The process by which the firm seeks to determine potential construction expenditures in a given geographic location is referred to as *marketing research*. Marketing research can embrace several somewhat independent activities such as the following.

Market Analysis—the study of the size, location, and characteristic of markets.
Volume Analysis—an analysis of past sales such as volume and type of construction expenditures.
Consumer Research—concerned with the analysis of consumer attitudes, reactions, and preferences.

By carrying out one or more of these marketing research activities, the construction firm can take out some of the guesswork as to expected construction expenditures in a given location. While it is unrealistic to think that the typical construction firm will or can engage in extensive personal surveys, less extensive marketing research can be carried out with little effort or expense. For example, by merely consulting published governmental data, existing and projected population growths in various geographic locations can be determined. Information such as

---

[1]"Value of Construction Contracts in the United States" *Construction Review of the U.S. Department of Commerce*, Volume 20, December 1974.

(Millions of dollars)
Building construction

| Period | Total construction | Total bldg. construction | Residential bldgs. | | | Nonresidential bldgs. | | | | | | Non-bldg. construction | Dodge index of construction contracts seasonally adjusted 1967=100 |
			Total	House-keeping residential bldg.	Non-housekeeping residential bldgs.	Total	Commercial bldgs.	Mfg. bldgs.	Educ. and sci bldgs.	Hosp. and other health treat. bldgs.	Public bldgs.		
1966	51,510	38,580	19,187	17,767	1,420	19,393	5,835	3,623	4,939	1,721	939	12,930	94.8
1967	54,514	41,294	21,155	19,715	1,440	20,139	6,080	3,701	5,216	1,873	959	13,220	100.0
1968	61,732	47,350	24,837	23,345	1,492	22,513	7,645	3,768	5,347	2,114	1,112	14,382	113.2
1969	68,294	51,583	25,634	24,018	1,616	25,950	9,786	3,915	5,543	2,817	1,154	16,710	123.7
1970	68,294	49,293	24,837	23,439	1,398	24,456	9,056	3,664	5,253	2,811	1,007	19,001	123.1
1971	80,188	60,304	34,714	33,190	1,524	25,590	9,610	2,619	5,649	3,188	1,493	19,883	145.4
1972	90,979	71,996	44,975	42,882	2,093	27,021	11,369	3,005	4,760	3,516	1,490	18,983	165.3
1973	99,304	77,230	45,696	43,137	2,559	31,634	12,846	4,841	5,061	3,324	2,014	22,074	179.9
1974	93,076	68,034	34,174	32,559	1,615	33,859	12,117	5,578	6,452	3,996	2,093	25,042	168.6

Fig. 3.2. Construction expenditures.

74

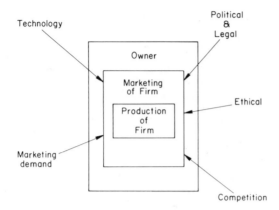

Fig. 3.3. Model of a business system.

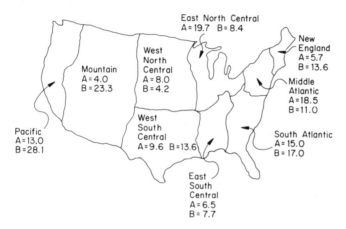

Fig. 3.4. Distribution of population.   A = 1969% distribution
B = 1968-1980% growth distribution

that illustrated in Fig. 3.4[2] can be useful to the construction firm in choosing a location, and in determining what type of work it is to perform. For example, projected population growth in the western states should result in favorable markets for firms located in these states that construct residential units, and outdoor recreational facilities such as swimming pools.

More often than not, geographic factors (i.e., hometown considerations) dictate the location of the construction firm. When this is the case, more attention has to be given to local projections versus projections

[2]Stanton, W. J., *Fundamentals of Marketing*, New York, McGraw-Hill, 1971, p. 80.

such as those illustrated in Fig. 3.4. However, marketing research can still prove useful to the firm fixed to a given location. Observation and analysis of various markets and common attitudes within a given location can lead the construction firm into new markets such as entrance into residential work or heavy and highway work. Analysis of planned public construction expenditures, analysis and projections of industrial capital expenditures, recognition of current and projected interest rates (i.e., residential construction being very sensitive to interest rates), and an awareness of existing and expected competition from other construction firms in the geographic area are all worthwhile marketing research practices. Daily reading of a business publication such as the *Wall Street Journal* or local financial institution economic publications are other means of carrying out marketing research.

The firm's marketing plans have to recognize the firm's objectives as to growth. Different pricing and promoting procedures and policies are justified given different growth objectives. For example, a growth objective aimed at increasing company work load may justify lowering of the firm's profit margin such that it can be more competitive as to obtaining new work. In addition, such an objective may justify an escalated advertising effort, and the added overhead expense of branch offices. On the other hand, should the firm have a growth objective that centers on a constant work volume but an increased profit margin, different pricing and promoting procedures and policies may follow. For example, emphasis on productivity and obtaining clients more interested in quality than low cost may be part of the firm's pricing and promoting policies.

In addition to the firm's marketing plans as to volume of work, is the consideration of its future product line. As to the construction firm, this marketing decision centers on the feasibility of a residential contractor entering the commercial marketplace, the commercial contractor taking on heavy and highway services, etc. These types of decisions and their consequences were discussed in the previous chapter.

The planning aspect of marketing can also be thought of to include the more specialized construction project management practices of project planning, scheduling, material procurement, etc. These practices, along with project estimating border between the planning and pricing aspects of marketing. While emphasis is not given here to project management tools such as networks, optimization, work analysis and improvement, etc.; these tools are important elements of marketing planning. For example, the ability to utilize work improvement techniques enables the construction firm to competitively price certain types of work which in part dictate the type and amount of work the firm undertakes.

3.4 Pricing the Firm's Work

Pricing is considered by many to be the key activity within the capitalistic system of free enterprise. The pricing aspect of marketing dictates both the profit margin of the firm and its volume of work performed. As to the construction industry, pricing takes on added importance. Construction contract specifications almost totally dictate the degree of quality the construction firm is to attain when building the construction project. As such, quality of work somewhat loses its significance in regard to obtaining new work. This is especially the case when the competitive bidding process is used to secure a construction firm.

Typically, the construction firm is basically selling price to the construction project owner. Assuming quality is determined by the owner through his architect/engineer, time is the only other variable the project owner is in effect purchasing. However, time to construct projects can be expressed monetarily. That is, time is money in that rent is lost when an apartment complex remains unfinished, fees are lost when a recreational facility is not ready for use, etc. The end result is that the construction firm's ability to serve up the construction project to a owner within budgeted cost and time is the best marketing technique available to the construction firm. Naturally such a cost should provide the construction firm with a reasonable profit.

Profit considerations have to be foremost in the pricing aspect of marketing. While a company's operational objectives may somewhat vary, it is unusual to find a profit oriented firm that has objectives that do not relate directly to profit. Whereas some firms will have an objective of attaining a specific profit margin such as three percent after taxes, other firms may strive for maximization of total profits. The important point is that both objectives relate to profit and as such the pricing of work.

Because of the construction firm's type of product, it is in a rather unique position as to pricing. As noted earlier, the construction firm can be categorized as being somewhere between a manufacturing firm and a service oriented firm. *Sales volume* pricing theories for manufacturing firms do not totally hold true for the construction firm in that the firm does not sell repetitive types of units that are subject to demand price sensitivity factors. On the other hand, like other manufacturing firms, the construction firm has fixed expenses and variable expenses that vary with the volume of work performed. In this sense, profit volume curves such as the one illustrated in Fig. 3.5 are relevant to the construction firm. The profit volume curve indicates that profit increase as volume increases.

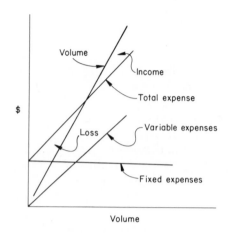

Fig. 3.5. Profit volume relationships.

While linear variable expenses are shown, the fact of the matter is that such expenses in addition to fixed expenses may defy the theoretical graph presentation as volume increases.

In the sense that the construction firm contracts with an owner to build the owner's project, the construction firm is providing a service. The pricing theories of such service businesses focus on expected volume of work performed. That is, fixed expenses of service industries are often considered to be insignificant in pricing procedures and policies.

The business environment of a service firm or industry is often characterized as being *perfect competition* or a *monopoly*. In reality no industry finds itself in either of the two extreme environments. However, the construction industry approaches perfect competition more closely than any other industry. This is especially the case in large cities where several firms participate in the construction industry. The presence of several firms prevents any one firm from dictating the contract price and profit margin. Rather the contract price and profit margin result from the competition of all firms active in the geographic area.

Even in an area of limited population, the fact that firms outside the geographic "come in" to bid work results in somewhat perfect competition. The number of geographic areas where a single firm or a very few number of firms bid construction work is decreasing. When in fact a firm does find itself in the position of being able to dictate the contract price it is characterized as operating in a monopoly.

The large construction firm competing against much smaller firms may sometimes be able to use price strategy characteristic of a firm operating in a monopoly. The large firm's ability to lower its profit margin, or its smaller percentage overhead may allow them to dictate project contract price. The large firm may settle for little or no profit in the short run with the objective of eliminating long term competition from other firms.

The ease of entrance into the construction industry, the mobility of the construction firm, and the bidding process which is used in the industry typically results in policies based on a monopoly being short lived. The end result is that regardless of whether the construction firm obtains work through competitive bidding or negotiated contracts, its pricing procedures and policies will eventually have to recognize competition.

3.4.1 Pricing Parameters

Competition is one of several variables the construction firm has to recognize in its pricing of construction projects. The variables to be recognized can be classified as long term or short term considerations. Long term considerations or variables include the following.

(1) Historical pricing practices and profit margins of the industry.
(2) Price required to generate capital for growth.
(3) Price and profit margin required to facilitate raising of debt and equity capital.

These and perhaps other long term considerations should shape the overall pricing aspect of marketing for the construction firm. For example, it is unrealistic to think that a given construction firm's pricing practices can completely ignore the profit margin of the overall construction industry. The near perfect competition characteristic of the industry prevents a single firm from isolating itself as to the marketplace.

Short term variables may cause a need for short term adjustments in the pricing procedures and policies of the construction firm. Some of these variables are as follows.

(1) State of present and expected future economy
(2) Need for work
(3) Dollar value of project being considered

(4) Duration of project being considered
(5) Expected project risk
(6) Expected bidding competition on project being considered

The first two variables noted are related. That is, the state of the economy, both nationally and locally, will likely affect the individual construction firm's need for work. The point to be made is that should the firm be in need for work, it may be satisfied with a short term pricing policy that provides for a lessening of the long term desired profit margin. Such a policy would aid the firm in covering its fixed expenses illustrated in Fig. 3.5. The same type of policy might be used when the firm foresees a future slowdown in construction activity. Again, in order to cover fixed expenses, taking on work with little or no profit margin included may prove to be a financially sound policy.

The dollar value and duration of a project being considered may also effect the pricing of the construction project. In particular, some construction firms have a pricing policy of somewhat decreasing their profit margins as the dollar value of a project increases or the expected duration of a project decreases. Such a policy is based on the fact that a smaller profit margin on a large dollar value project (i.e., all other factors being equal) will still yield a considerable total dollar profit. In addition should the duration of a project be short, a small profit margin or total dollar profit will still yield a favorable rate of return due to the short period of time for which the firm ties up its assets.

Expected project risk is yet another short term project pricing variable. While risk is difficult to measure, surely a firm's pricing procedures should attempt to account for varying amounts of risk that are characteristic of individual projects. Such risk may be in the form of expected weather difficulties, problems in coordination of subcontractors, labor union difficulties, etc. One justifiable pricing policy would be merely to avoid such projects. At the very least, an upwards adjustment in profit margin is needed.

Perhaps of all the short term variables noted, the one that has received the most attention as to pricing policies is that of expected bidding competition. There is an increasing amount of study being directed towards the modeling of pricing as it relates to expected bidding competition. More likely than not, the increased interest in this area is generated by the fact that a quantitative solution can be formulated for the modeling of pricing as a function of expected competition. The fact remains that all of the short term variables are important in the pricing aspect of marketing. In fact, if one was forced to weigh the factors as to importance, the need for work would certainly be on top or near the top.

The efforts aimed at structuring the pricing function to recognize expected bidding competition have resulted in a so called bidding strategy model. Let us now consider the bidding strategy pricing model.

3.4.2 Bid Strategy

The optimal profit that a contractor should add to his bid proposal is partly determined by the contractor competition for the project. This is particularly true in the competitive bidding procedure. A contractor's winning or losing a project contract often depends on how well he has formulated his information about his competitors. A contractor must always search for ways to gain an advantage over his competitors. This includes using new and cheaper construction methods and management practices. One of the ways a contractor might gain an advantage over his competitors is to formulate bidding information about their past performances. The contractor can formulate this information into some type of bid strategy. For our purposes, we will consider bid strategy as a combination of various bidding rules a contractor follows for bidding, based on a formulation of information. In our case, the information will be past bids of contractors. Formulating the information is often referred to as determining a bidding model.

The profit in a contractor's bid for a particular project is the amount of money he intends to make on the project. For purposes of discussion, let us assume that the contractor's estimated cost of bidding a project is indeed accurate and is equal to his actual building cost. Therefore, on a particular project for which a contractor submits a bid, he will either receive his desired profit (assuming he receives the project), or will receive zero profit (assuming he does not receive the project). It becomes clear that a contractor's long term profit (average profit over a long period of time) will not only be a function of the profit within his bids, but a function of how many projects he receives from the number of projects for which he submits bids.

Owing to the possibility of two levels of profit (depending on whether a contractor wins or loses the contract for a project), it is necessary to define two different types of profit. A contractor's *immediate profit* on a project is defined as the difference between the contractor's bid price for the project and his actual cost of building it. Assume a contractor's bid is equal to X. If we let A represent the contractor's actual cost of building the project, then the contractor's immediate profit on the project (I.P.) is given by the following formula.

I.P. = X − A

If a contractor submits a high bid (a large profit included), his chance for receiving the contract in a competitive bidding environment is very small. As he reduces his profit, and therefore his bid, his chance for receiving the contract increases.

If we assign probabilities of receiving the contract to the various bids the contractor considers feasible, we can calculate an *expected profit* for the various bids. The expected profit of a particular bid on a proposed project is defined as the immediate profit of the bid for the project multiplied by the probability of the bid winning the contract. In a competitive bidding procedure, winning the contract implies that the bid is the lowest responsible bid. If we let p represent the probability of a particular bid winning the contract for a project, then the expected profit of the bid (E.P.) is given by the following formula.

E.P. = p(X − A) = p(I.P.)

Assume a contractor is interested in a certain project, a project the contractor estimates to cost $20,000 to build. The contractor has a choice of submitting 3 different bids for the project. These bids and their probabilities of winning the project contract are as follows.

Bid name	Amount	Probability of winning contract
B_1	$30,000	0.1
B_2	25,000	0.5
B_3	22,000	0.8

The probabilities shown are estimated from the contractor's evaluation of the chance of being the lowest bidder. Of course, bid B_1 has the highest immediate profit ($30,000 − $20,000, or $10,000). However, because of B_1's low probability of winning the bid, it may not be the best bid to make to maximize overall profits. The calculation of the various bid's expected profits is as follows.

Bid name	Probability x Immediate profit	Expected profit
B_1	0.1 (10,000)	$1,000
B_2	0.5 (5,000)	2,500
B_3	0.8 (2,000)	1,600

It is observed that bid B_2 has the highest expected profit. Expected profit may be conceived as representing the average profit a contractor can expect to make per project, if he were to submit the same bid to a large number of similar projects. Expected profit does not represent the actual profit the contractor expects to make on a project. In the problem described, the contractor would either make a profit of 0 or a profit of $5,000 if he submitted bid B_2, whereas the expected profit is calculated to be $2,500. Immediate profit does not recognize the probability of a bid winning a contract. Expected profit recognizes the objective of maximizing total long term profits. Thus expected profit calculations are more meaningful than immediate profit calculations, and should be used to determine the optimal profit and bid. In the example described the contractor should submit bid B_2.

By using the discussed expected profit concepts in addition to information concerning the past bids of his competition, a contractor can develop a bidding strategy which he may use to optimize his profits. At a competitive bid letting it is common practice to announce openly all the bids of the respective contractors. The intelligent contractor can record the bid prices of the contractors, along with his own bid and his own estimate of the project's cost. If it is possible for him to learn the actual cost of the project (either through building it himself or through information obtained from others), he should also record this information. The intelligent contractor should also be aware of any special conditions, such as knowledge about a particular contractor's need for work. Having recorded the past bidding information about his competitors, the contractor should also take note of any special conditions, such as knowledge about a particular contractor's need for work. Having recorded this past bidding information about his competitors, the contractor may formulate the information into a bidding strategy for future projects. Naturally, the more information the contractor has available, and the more accurate his information, the better is his chance of having his strategy prove successful.

When a contractor is bidding on a project in a competitive bidding atmosphere, he generally finds himself in one of the following states regarding his competition. In the most deterministic or ideal state, the contractor knows who each of the competitors will be on an upcoming project. A somewhat infrequent situation occurs when the contractor knows how many competitors there are for the project, but does not know who they are. Since there is less information available in this case than in the case of known competitors, the bidding strategy will be less deterministic and therefore less reliable than the bidding strategy for known competitors. A less deterministic and less desirable situation occurs when the contractor knows neither who the competition is, nor how many competitors there are. The bidding strategy for this situation will be less reliable than the previous two cases, owing to the lack of more complete information. Rubey and Milner[3] address all of the cases in their presentation of bidding strategy.

Consider the case in which the contractor knows who his competitors will be for a competitive bid project letting. In particular, let us assume that the contractor knows he is only going to be competing against one contractor (contractor XYZ). Assume the contractor has bid against contractor XYZ many times in the past and has kept records of contractor XYZ's bids. For each of the projects the contractor has also recorded his estimated cost. Having this information, the contractor can calculate the ratio of contractor XYZ's bid price to the contractor's cost estimate for the various projects. The contractor's recorded information is summarized as follows.

Contractor XYZ's bid/ Contractor's estimated job cost	Frequency of occurrence
0.8	1
0.9	2
1.0	7
1.1	12
1.2	21
1.3	18
1.4	7
1.5	2
	Total = 70

Having the frequency table of the various ratios, the contractor can calculate the probability of each bid ratio by dividing each bid's frequency of occurrence by the total number of measured bid occurrences. For example, the probability of a ratio of 1.0 is 7/70, or 0.10. Probabilities of the other ratios are as follows. The probabilities are rounded off to two decimal places.

[3]Rubey, H., and Milner, W. W., *Construction and Professional Management: An Introduction*, New York, Macmillan, 1966, Chapter 15.

Contractor XY's bid/Contractor's estimated job cost	Probability
0.8	0.01
0.9	0.03
1.0	0.10
1.1	0.17
1.2	0.30
1.3	0.26
1.4	0.10
1.5	0.03
	Total= 1.00

Having calculated the probabilities of the various ratios, the contractor can calculate the probability of his various bids being lower than contractor XYZ's bids. To eliminate theoretical bid ties, it will be assumed that the contractor will bid different ratios than the computed ratios for contractor XYZ. For example, to be lower than contractor XYZ's bid-to-cost ratio of 1.10, the contractor might make a bid with a bid-to-cost ratio of 1.05. Let us assume that the contractor decides upon the following bid-to-estimated-cost ratios as being feasible.

Contractor's bid/ Contractor's estimated job cost	Probability that contractor's bid is lower than bid of XYZ
0.75	1.00
0.85	0.99
0.95	0.96
1.05	0.86
1.15	0.69
1.25	0.39
1.35	0.13
1.45	0.03
1.55	0.00

The calculated probability of being the lowest bidder, or winning the contract, for any particular bid ratio is found by merely summing all the probabilities of contractor XYZ's ratio being higher than the particular bid. For example, if the contractor is to make a bid with a bid-estimated-cost ratio of 1.35, the probability of winning would be the sum of 0.03 (the probability that the ratio of XYZ's bid to the contractor's estimated cost is 1.5), and 0.10 (the probability that the ratio is 1.4). Thus, the probability of a contractor bid with a bid-to-estimated-cost ratio of 1.35 winning the contract is 0.13.

The contractor may now use this information to form a bidding strategy for bidding against contractor XYZ. He may do this by calculating the expected profits of his possible feasible bids. Expected profit of a bid was defined as the immediate profit of the bid multiplied by the bid's probability of winning the project contract. Immediate profit for a bid was defined as the bid price minus the actual cost of the project. Let us assume that the contractor's estimated cost of the project is equal to the actual cost. Ideally the contractor would like his estimator to estimate the actual cost correctly, but this is not always the case. However, owing to the lack of information about the actual cost of the project, let us assume that the estimated cost of the project is the actual cost. The immediate profit for each of the contractor's possible bids then becomes equal to the bid price minus the estimated cost of the project. The bid prices are given in terms of the estimated cost of the project. Letting c equal the estimated cost of the project, the immediate profit of the contractor's possible bids may be stated in terms of c. The immediate profit of the bids may be found by merely subtracting $1.0c$ (the estimated cost of the job) from the respective bids. For example, for a bid of $1.35c$, the immediate profit is $1.35c - 1.0c$, or $0.35c$. The expected profit of the possible bids may then be found by multiplying their immediate profits by their respective probabilities of winning the project against contractor XYZ. For a bid of $1.35c$, the probability of winning against contractor XYZ was calculated as 0.13; therefore, the expected profit is 0.13 multiplied by $0.35c$, or $0.0455c$. The expected profits for the contractor's feasible bids are as follows. They are rounded off to 3 decimal places.

Contractor bid	Expected profit of bid when bidding against contractor XYZ
0.75c	$1.00 (-0.25c) = -0.250c$
0.85c	$0.99 (-0.15c) = -0.149c$
0.95c	$0.96 (-0.05c) = -0.048c$
1.05c	$0.86 (+0.05c) = +0.043c$
1.15c	$0.69 (+0.15c) = +0.104c$

1.25c	0.39 (+0.25c) = +0.098c
1.35c	0.13 (+0.35c) = +0.046c
1.45c	0.03 (+0.45c) = +0.014c
1.55c	0.00 (+0.55c) = +0.000c

It is observed that the bid of 1.15 multiplied by the estimated cost of the project yields the maximum expected profit of 0.104c. This implies that when bidding against contractor XYZ, over a period of time it would be most profitable for the contractor to submit a bid with a bid-to-estimated-cost ratio of 1.15. For example, if the estimated project cost was $100,000, the bid proposal should be $115,000. Considering the possibility of not winning the contract, the contractor's expected profit for such a bid would be $10,400. Of course, the contractor should keep his bidding information about contractor XYZ current. The best bid ratio for the contractor to use in a future project against contractor XYZ may change, depending upon contractor XYZ's future bidding performances.

If a contractor was bidding against several known competitors rather than only contractor XYZ, he could formulate his bidding strategy in a similar manner. Let us assume that a contractor knows he will be bidding against two known competitors on an upcoming job, contractor XYZ and contractor UVW. Assume the contractor's information about contractor XYZ is the same as in the previous example. Let us assume that the contractor has also gathered information about contractor UVW's bidding performances, and has calculated the probability of his bids being lower than contractor UVW's. This information along with the probabilities of winning versus contractor XYZ are as follows.

Contractor's bid/Contractor's estimated job cost	Probability of contractor's bid winning versus:	
	XYZ	UVW
0.75	1.00	1.00
0.85	0.99	1.00
0.95	0.96	0.98
1.05	0.86	0.80
1.15	0.69	0.70
1.25	0.39	0.60
1.35	0.13	0.27
1.45	0.03	0.09
1.55	0.00	0.00

To calculate the expected profit of the feasible bids, the contractor must determine the probability that his bid is lower than both contractor XYZ's and contractor UVW's bids. Both of these events are independent. The probability of being lower than XYZ is independent of the probability of being lower than UVW. From probability theory, one may show that the probability of the occurrence of joint events, which are independent, is given by the product of their respective probabilities. For example, the probability that the contractor's bid of 1.15c wins (is lower than XYZ's and UVW's bids) is the product of 0.69 and 0.70, or 0.483. Having found the bid's probability of winning the contract, its expected profit is calculated as 0.483 multiplied by its immediate profit of 0.15c, resulting in an expected profit of 0.07245c. The expected profits for all the bids are calculated as follows. They are rounded off to 3 decimal places.

Contractor's bid	Expected profit
0.75c	$1.00(1.00)(-0.25c) = -0.250c$
0.85c	$0.99(1.00)(-0.15c) = -0.149c$
0.95c	$0.96(0.98)(-0.05c) = -0.047c$
1.05c	$0.86(0.80)(+0.05c) = +0.034c$
1.15c	$0.69(0.70)(+0.15c) = +0.072c$
1.25c	$0.39(0.60)(+0.25c) = +0.059c$
1.35c	$0.13(0.27)(+0.35c) = +0.012c$
1.45c	$0.03(0.09)(+0.45c) = +0.001c$
1.55c	$0.00(0.00)(+0.55c) = +0.000c$

Note that the contractor should submit a bid which has a ratio of bid cost to estimated project cost of 1.15. Thus, the contractor should make the same bid he should have made when bidding against only contractor XYZ. However, the expected profit of 0.072c when bidding against the two contractors, is less than the expected profit of 0.104c when bidding against the single contractor. This is because of the added competition. The more competition a contractor has, the less likely he is to receive the contract. The problem of more than two known competitors is handled in a similar manner. We should not conclude that the optimal bid remains unchanged with increasing competition. In general, the optimal bid will have a tendency to decrease with an increasing number of competitors.

The bidding strategy model can be extended to more complicated applications. While such extensions are not discussed in detail here, other applications include the handling of an unknown number of competitors and the including of uncertainty in the cost of the project.

The bidding strategy model implies a competitive bidding construction contract letting procedure. A growing number of construction contracts are being awarded to construction firms through a negotiation process. The potential construction project owner approaches one or more construction firms and negotiates a contract price for which the construction firm will build the project. Although price may not be the only factor in the owner's selection of a firm (i.e., quality of work, financial reputation, and ability to perform within a budgeted time constraint may be other factors), it is difficult to find an owner who isn't operating within a dollar budget. As such, pricing and bidding strategy models are relevant to the negotiated contract process as well as the competitive bidding process.

In reality, pricing procedures and policies differ little for the construction firm participating in the competitive bidding process or the negotiated contract process. It is in the promoting aspect of marketing that distinct differences exist as to the two means of securing construction work. These differences are emphasized in the following section.

3.5 Promoting the Firm and its Work

The term *promoting* is more commonly referred to as *selling*. In fact some definitions of marketing limit themselves to selling or promoting. Before the firm can "sell" its product, it must first plan its product and price its product. As to the construction firm, the firm must first determine what type of work it is to construct and where it is to operate. In addition, it must cost or price its services. However, the marketing process is only half complete upon pricing. The construction firm must now sell its plan and price to a potential project owner if it is to complete its operational cycle.

The ability to find work through promotion of the firm and its product is the key to free enterprise. Unfortunately the technical skills of the owners of a firm are wasted unless the selling or promoting function is accomplished.

Numerous books have been written and theories developed as to how to "sell." The fact remains that selling can only in part be learned. Personalities, motivation, and verbal skill, while difficult to learn, are vital to selling one's product.

The selling of one's product starts with the searching out of potential clients. As to the construction firm this involves the finding of potential project owners. The means by which the construction firm becomes aware of construction projects are referred to as *bird dogging*. Included in these means are the following.

(1) Membership in technical associations

(2) Subscription to services

(3) Attention to public announcements

(4) Personal contacts

(5) Advertisements

(6) Direct mail

(7) Publicity

As is true in most professions, several construction related associations are readily available for the construction firm to become a member. National associations such as the Associated General Contractors (A.G.C.) are available as well as local city and county associations. While the objectives of the many construction associations are numerous and somewhat vary from one association to the next, many serve as a "clearing house" for the disclosure of upcoming construction projects to their membership. This service in itself can in many cases justify the membership dues that the construction firm pays to the association.

Subscription to construction related services can also aid the construction firm in the finding of projects. While services such as the Dodge Service concentrate on providing its subscribers cost data, and management services; information relating to upcoming projects in various geographic regions is also made available to the subscribing construction firm. The benefits of any one service must be weighed against its costs. The point is that while a service may have benefits as to finding work, the cost of the service should not result in such a high overhead cost for the firm that it prevents a reasonable profit margin on the projects the firm in fact obtains and builds.

In many cases the least cost and most effective means of searching out work are through attention to announcements and through personal contacts. Municipal, state, and federal construction projects are *openly* advertised through newspapers, and bulletins. State boards such as the Illinois Capital Development Board notify registered contractors within their state of all upcoming construction within the jurisdiction of the board.

As is true in obtaining work in any business (i.e., especially in service oriented businesses), personal contact is in many cases the key to finding construction projects. Contacts through country clubs, church organizations, and charitable organizations can lead to a contract for work. The key to securing work through personal contact is the followup. Many times a construction firm has lost a potential project because of its failure to follow up a lead. In the absence of the construction firm following up its initial contact, the owner may be approached by yet another firm or the owner may be influenced by others in its evaluation of the feasibility of the project.

Unlike several service oriented businesses, the "code of ethics" of the construction industry do not prevent the construction firm from openly advertising for work. Yellow page telephone directory advertisements are the most common form of construction firm advertisements. However several firms place a regularly appearing advertisement in a local newspaper, church related publication, or local news magazine. Others advertise in more widely circulated technical magazines such as *Engineering News Record,* or a country wide newspaper such as the *Wall Street Journal.*

Many a construction firm has seen fit to sponsor local sport teams such as a little league baseball team or a bowling team. While this practice may stem merely from the firm's interest in the sport or the participants, in many cases the motivation for the sponsorship is advertising. While it is difficult to measure the dollar benefit associated with having the name of the sponsoring team on the uniforms of the team, surely (assuming the team does not discredit itself—everybody likes a winner) such publicity contributes to the marketing of the firm. The benefit of the type and amount of advertising varies depending on the type of work the construction firm performs. Local advertising through telephone directories, newspaper, and sponsorship of teams proves very effective for residential construction firms. The majority of the clients of the residential firm are individuals within the community of the firm.

The returns for advertising are probably the least for the heavy and highway contractor and the middle sized commercial and industrial firm. These firms obtain most of their work through open advertisements of the project owner. In particular, government and industry are the main clients of these types of construction firms. While advertising such as that gained through sponsorship of a team may favorably influence this type of potential project owner, it is unlikely that the advertising is the reason the owner is drawn to the construction firm.

The pendulum shifts back to relatively large benefits when one considers the large construction firm. These firms often operate throughout a large geographic radius. In fact the larger firm may be receptive to performing a construction project anywhere within the country or even overseas. When this is the case, advertising provides the communication link between the construction firm and the distant potential project owner. The type of communication needed results in a different type of advertising versus that used by the small residential firm. In particular, the large firm seeking work in distant locations will get the largest returns from advertisements in publications distributed to these locations. An advertisement in *Constructor* (i.e., the magazine of the A.G.C. that is distributed nationally) may result in benefits many times the cost of the advertisement.

Similar to the use of advertisements for finding clients, is the use of direct mail. In fact the use of direct mail can be viewed as a form of advertising. The only difference is that direct mail represents a concentrated effort aimed at known individuals or firms whereas the type of advertising discussed previously was aimed at the general public. Obviously direct mail proves advantageous when in fact the recipient is contemplating the building of a construction project. The fact of the matter is that seldom will an individual or firm initiate a construction project due to the direct mail of a construction firm. There are exceptions as in the case of a homeowner being "sold" on the need to make some home repairs or remodeling through an advertisement or direct mail of a construction firm. Nonetheless, direct mail can prove an economic means of having one's firm added to the list of firms considered when an owner's future construction plans become reality.

Other than personal contacts, direct mail provides the firm with the most personal means of communication with future clients. However the direct mail communication has to be well worded and in fact be aimed at the needs of the client. A poorly written form letter may not only prove nonpersonal but it will likely be discarded as another piece of time consuming mail.

There is a degree of risk associated with direct mail. Its very existence may lead the recipient to believe the sending firm is hard pressed for work due to unfavorable characteristics of the firm. The end result is that direct mail advertising has to be well written and well directed if it is to result in benefits.

A firm's success has a way of generating good publicity. If this is recognized, and the publicity is properly utilized, the publicity can become part of the firm's marketing program to ensure future success. As to the construction firm, good publicity can develop from several facades of the firm's operations. The building of a unique structure, or the use of new construction techniques can aid the firm through favorable publicity. Other recognized favorable activities include completing a project well before the forecasted completion date (i.e., especially noteworthy when it is a project that has public attention such as a recreational facility or highway), the receiving of professional awards as to individual firm members or the entire firm, the election of members of the firm as officers in professional organizations, and the firm's contribution to community or charitable projects.

The firm should not go out of its way to prevent favorable publicity. Regardless of how humble the individual firm members are, publicity should be as much as a part of a construction firm's marketing program as any bird-dogging practice. Seldom if ever will good publicity hinder the firm's marketing. And best of all it is free. Free in the sense that its distribution is free. Naturally it is not free in the effort generated that in fact causes the publicity.

Publicity outlets may be through the local press, trade publications, and professional magazines. While it is gratifying to have these outlets come to the firm there is nothing wrong with the firm initiating the communication to the publicity outlet. The preparation of news releases is the responsibility of the marketing function within the firm. An effective communication link with the local press can prove to be an inexpensive means of obtaining construction work through publicity.

Just as good publicity can aid in the finding and securing of construction work, bad publicity can hinder such efforts. Years of sound business practices, and success in building projects to specifications and within an allotted time schedule can be forgotten by the public through a single news release citing an unfavorable activity of the construction firm. An unfavorable suit stemming from the injury or death of an employee, failure to meet project specifications or a project completion time, and the involvement of company personnel in bid fixing or bribery efforts can virtually ruin a firm as to its marketing efforts. In fact it is fair to say that a single bad publicity news release has a much more unfavorable impact on the firm's marketing than the favorable impact of a good publicity news release. As is true of many areas of reader interest, bad news seems to get more attention than good news. The fact that a construction firm completes construction of a highway before the forecasted completion time often goes unnoticed. However, the public is up in arms should the highway project be delayed. Such is the difficulty of obtaining and maintaining marketing benefits from publicity.

Needless to say the construction firm can not spend unlimited time and money on each of the means noted for finding construction work. Too much effort and cost expended defeat the very purpose of doing business. The end result is that the firm must weigh the expected benefits versus the cost for each and every means considered. Models such as dynamic programming have been structured to aid the firm in its evaluation of its total work finding efforts.[4] However the fact remains that it is often difficult to quantify benefits from individual marketing efforts. However this difficulty should not prevent the firm from attempting to analyze its efforts as to returns. Such an analysis may pinpoint wasted efforts as well as pinpointing where more effort should be directed.

The promoting or selling aspect of marketing does not terminate with the finding of potential construction project owners. The promoting aspect of marketing is only complete upon the forming of a contract by the construction firm with an owner in which the firm agrees to build the owner's project in return for monetary rewards for its services.

In the competitive bidding process, once the potential project owner is found, the rest of the promoting process is straightforward. Assuming the construction firm meets the qualifications stated by the owner (i.e., usually expressed in a bonding capacity requirement), the construction firm submits its bid which is evaluated as to dollar value by the owner. Normally the low bid is selected as the bid awarded the contract. The end result is that once the firm finds the potential project owner, and satisfies the owner's stated qualifications, its success in the competitive bidding process is dependent solely on its pricing practices.

The success of the construction firm in securing a project contract in a negotiated contract environment is typically dependent on an extended list of owner considerations. That is, the project owner may recognize factors in addition to the cost for which the construction firm will build the owner's project. Included in these factors are the following.

(1) Prior dealings with the construction firm.
(2) Reputation of the construction firm as to ability to perform type of work being considered.
(3) Reputation of the construction firm as to ability to perform work within budgeted time.
(4) Social acquaintances of owner with members of the construction firm.
(5) Hiring practices of the construction firm (e.g., affirmative action program of the firm)
(6) Recognition of "home location" of the firm (i.e., an owner may choose to deal with a local firm)

[4]Adrian, J. J., *Quantitative Methods in Construction Management*, New York, Elsevier, 1973, pp. 40–48.

(7) Recognition of the current work load of the construction firm.

(8) The construction firm's willingness to "give and take" with owner as to current and future work negotiations.

Other factors might be present in isolated cases. The point to be made is that the negotiated contract process more clearly pinpoints the need for marketing considerations by the construction firm. Neither the construction firm or the owner is locked in to a predetermined structured bidding process. Construction firm external relations are fundamental to securing work in the negotiated contract awarding process.

3.6 Placing the Product

The marketing process is completed with the placing of the firm's product. As to the construction firm, the *placing* of its product entails the completion of the building process in a manner consistent with the plan and price previously determined. In this sense the placing aspect of marketing is part of a complete cycle starting with planning, continuing with pricing and promoting, and finishing with placing.

The placing aspect of marketing is aimed at satisfying two related objectives. First of all the placing or building of the construction project has to be carried out according to plan and price such that the firm realizes a profit. This profit is vital to the overall objective of a profit oriented firm. Secondly, the placing or building of the construction project has to proceed in a manner that meets the satisfaction of the owner. As discussed in the previous section, the ability to carry out the future promoting aspect of the marketing of the firm is dependent on the reputation of the firm as to past performances. Satisfied customers are the best marketing asset available to the firm. Goodwill is often priceless.

In a number of cases it may prove wise to weight the placing objective of satisfying the customer above that of profit. A construction firm's willingness to absorb added costs associated with an owner's change order may result in the securing of future contracts with the owner. Naturally the construction firm can not always give and not take. Profit remains its vehicle for successful operations. However a short term loss that creates owner satisfaction may in fact lead to long term profits. Each project and individual circumstance is unique as to each give and take decision. The important point is to recognize the long term as well as short term effects of each project and individual circumstance.

Placing of the construction project consistent with the predetermined plan and price entails the utilization of sound project management tools and practices. Economic material procurement and project material flow, effective equipment utilization, productive use of labor, recognition of weather as to resource scheduling, the training and utilization of management personnel, and the ability to coordinate project subcontractors are all necessary to placing the construction project.

Tools such as optimization models, network techniques, economic decision models, and cost accounting can all aid in the accomplishment of placing the construction project. It is not the purpose of this book to elaborate on the know-how or use of these tools and models. These tools and models are well documented in other books including one by the author.[5] It should be pointed out however, that these tools by themselves will prove inadequate unless experience and common sense are assets of the individuals responsible for the placing aspect of marketing.

Planning, pricing and promoting provide the construction firm the potential for the carrying out of its profit oriented objective. It is the placing aspect of marketing that provides the firm the realization of such an objective. To this end, the firm's marketing and overall organization structure should fully recognize the importance and interrelationship of placing relative to the more commonly thought of aspects of marketing.

3.7 Summary

Of all the business functions that are necessary to carrying out a profitable firm, marketing is perhaps the most difficult to learn and quanitify. Marketing is a people problem; a communication problem. The firm with all the technical and management know-how in the world will not generate profits unless it can market its product or service.

The complexity of marketing as to the construction firm is increased by the fact that the construction industry is somewhat unique as to its

[5]Adrian, J. J., *Quantitative Methods in Construction Management*, New York, Elsevier, 1973, Chapter 5.

type of business and product. The construction firm is somewhere between being a manufacturer of a product and being a service oriented business. The firm builds a product, but it is not truely its product in that it is constructing a predetermined design of the owner. Typically the construction firm will build a given type of product only once in that each construction project is somewhat unique. The end result of the uniqueness of the construction industry's product is that many of the marketing theories and practices that apply to other industries are incompatible with construction firm marketing.

The marketing function is more than that of selling. In particular, marketing consists of planning, pricing, promoting (more commonly referred to as selling), and placing. These four aspects of marketing make up a complete cycle. Absence of any of the four results in an ineffective marketing program.

Planning consists of determining the type of work, location, and amount of work the firm would like to perform. Pricing quantifies the profit oriented objective of the firm such that the firm is more than doing work for the sake of doing work.

Promoting or the selling aspect of marketing provides the link between plans and reality. The construction firm must "sell" its plan and price. Finding work is of upmost importance. Numerous means such as personal contacts and advertising are available to the firm for the purpose of finding work. Once an owner is found, promoting efforts differ depending on the contract awarding procedure. Low cost is the key in the competitive bid process. While low cost remains important, external relations increase in importance as to securing a contract with an owner in a negotiated contract environment.

Once a project contract is secured, the marketing function should see to it that the project is placed consistent with the predetermined plan and price. This aspect of marketing focuses on project management. Planning, pricing, and promoting provide profit potential. Placing realizes it.

Case 3.1 Searo Construction Company:
Locating the Firm

Jeff and Mike Searo are in the process of starting a construction firm that is to specialize initially in building residential single family homes. Jeff has been a carpenter for three years and Mike is a recent graduate of an architectural engineering program.

As the firm grows in experience and financial strength, the brothers would like to fully utilize Mike's skills and branch into commercial work with a ten year objective of doing fifteen to twenty million dollars of work a year.

One of the initial decisions Jeff and Make have to make regarding the Searo Construction Company is where to set up their company headquarters. Because of the closeness of four different cities, Northo, Easto, Southo, and Westo, each is a candidate for their company headquarters. The geographic locations of the four cities are shown on the following grid (each square is five miles by five miles).

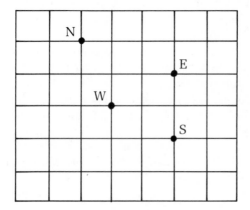

N= Northo
E= Easto
S= Southo
W= Westo

The current and projected ten year populations of the four cities are as follows.

	Current	10 Year Projection
Northo	140,000	150,000
Easto	85,000	70,000
Southo	20,000	60,000
Westo	40,000	45,000

Housing starts are currently about proportional with current population. The only exception is in Southo where the recent building of a community college has spurred several new subdivisions.

The large population of Northo is due to the existence of a large auto parts plant being located in the outskirts of the city. The high wage rate paid by the plant has resulted in a relatively high wage rate for labor in the city.

Easto is by far the oldest of the cities. Very few new buildings are present and there seems to be a trend of some of its population shifting to Southo. Southo while growing has little industry.

Many of the people that live in Westo actually work in Northo. Westo differs from the other cities in that much of the construction, especially residential, in recent years has been performed by nonunion workers.

Westo is in a different county than the other three cities and as such its union labor belong to a different local union. About 50% of all its construction labor belong to a union. This compares to one hundred percent for the three other cities.

Because of its industrial environment numerous material supplies are located in Northo. With the exception of a lumber yard company in Easto and a ready mix plant in Westo, few suppliers of materials are presently located in the Easto, Southo, or Westo.

The grid lines shown for locating the cities approximate the location of roadways connecting the cities. While the plans have not been finalized, there has been some talk of an expressway running through Northo and Easto.

Jeff and Mike were born and raised in Northo. Jeff is single and has an apartment in his hometown. Mike, his bride of two years (an out of state girl by birth) and his 3-year-old twins recently bought a new home in Southo.

Jeff and Mike have obtained a loan to locate their headquarters. They have no desire to initially operate out of their residences. Where should they set up shop?

Case 3.2 Biddo Construction Company:
Pricing Work

Biddo Construction Company has specialized in building commercial projects for which the typical bid price is $1,000,000. However consistent with their objective of growing and due to the unavailability of other types of projects, the firm is contemplating submitting a bid for a project that the architect has estimated at $5,000,000.

Biddo has typically determined their bid price by calculating their direct cost of doing a project and adding 30% of this direct cost to the direct cost. Such a procedure has typically resulted in a 5% profit

margin. The firm recognizes that while such a procedure can be justified for projects of approximate equal dollar amount and type of work,
such a procedure for covering overhead and establishing profit may be
too gross and approximate for a unique project.

Biddo has been informed that a total of five bids will be submitted
for the $5,000,000 project. The project is to be awarded to the lowest
bidder. Two of the firms, Ace Company and Build Company are also
bidding on this scale of project for the first time. In fact these two firms
have repeatedly been competitors of Biddo Company. Biddo Company
has gathered bidding data on these firms from its past bids. This data is
as follows.

Competitor's bid Biddo's direct cost	Ace (Frequency)	Build (Frequency)
.9	2	1
1.0	3	0
1.1	8	5
1.2	12	5
1.3	18	20
1.4	10	4
1.5	1	0
1.6	1	0

The two other firms expected to bid on the project are larger firms
and each has repeatedly bid on projects of the scale being considered.
Little is known of their past bidding practices. However it is known
that one of the firms has already over extended itself and is likely
submitting a bid merely to satisfy the owner's request.

Biddo has estimated its direct costs for building the project being
considered at 3.75 million. While Biddo would really like to win the
project, it also recognizes that there is substantial risk in that the scale
and scope of work is new for the firm. While it is difficult to predict
future bidding volume, it is likely that within three or four months one
or two $1,000,000 projects will be announced and a $5,000,000 school
project is scheduled for letting in six months.

Biddo is in the final month of finishing its only current project, a 1.2
million dollar project. The $5,000,000 project is scheduled to start in
three weeks and Biddo estimates its duration to be fifteen months.
Assuming Biddo is not in a position to pinpoint their overhead costs,
what if any bid should they submit for the project being considered?

Case 3.3 Tradition Construction Company:
Marketing the Firm

Tradition Construction Company has been in the general contracting business for over twenty years. While they are located in a large city with a population of 500,000 people, they have performed work throughout the state in which they are centrally located.

Approximately eighty percent of their current annual volume of twenty-five million is obtained in a competitive bidding procedure. The remainder of their work is typically obtained from local industry through negotiated contracts.

Tradition Construction Company has five key personnel. Mr. Fingo, Ms. Alta, Mr. Pred, Mr. Eddy, and Mr. Marky are primarily responsible for finance, accounting, field production, estimating, and contract procurement respectively.

Mr. Marky's role essentially centers on coordinating bidding dates, checking bidding instructions, and assuring that the firm is aware of projects to be let and checking that the projects are such that they fit the firm's resources and time schedules. Mr. Marky is the son of the founder of the firm who is deceased. Mr. Marky while experienced as to dealing with present clients, is not learned in the practices of a salesman. By education, he is a civil engineer.

Mr. Pred has convinced other company personnel that an increasing number of owners are building projects by means of a construction management contract. Such a practice has resulted in several of Tradition's general contractor competitors offering construction management services. Tradition has thus decided that it is in their best interests to offer such services. On the bases of Mr. Pred's predictions, the company has estimated that in order to keep on their past growth plans of 15% increase in volume a year, that within five years 50% of their work will be through a construction management arrangement.

Tradition Company has recognized that the obtaining of construction management contracts involves a great deal of successful external relations. Whereas low bidding cost is the key to obtaining competitive bidding work, the ability to make contacts and sell the skills of the firm is the key in securing construction management work.

Tradition's current problem is how to start marketing construction management. Currently they have a good reputation of performing general contracting work. Because of this reputation, they have not found it necessary to do any advertising.

While they want to grow rapidily in the area of construction management, they also recognize that many owners, including several of their clients, prefer the traditional owner, architect/engineer, general contractor process. As such they don't want to over sell their entrance into construction management.

Based on the fact that most projects for which construction management contracts are warranteed are large, Tradition has recognized that many of their future construction management clients may be located throughout the state and perhaps throughout a five or six state radius.

Develop a specific marketing plan for Tradition Construction Company in its efforts to change the type of work it is to perform. Such a plan should include determination of personnel, duties, and marketing techniques. The plan should cover a five year period.

Chapter 4

Business Law: Avoiding Litigation

4.1 Introduction

The subject of law is of such vastness that no one—literally no one—could possibly know all there is of it. A dictionary containing only definitions of legal terms is a substantial volume. Undoubtedly, one cannot expect the construction contractor or manager to be knowledgeable regarding all of the subdivisions of law such that he can consider himself a lawyer capable of seeing to all of his own legal interests. The services of a lawyer are sometimes necessary to the financial success of the contractor. However, the contractor may often avoid the need for services of a lawyer or the costs of a law suit by means of a general knowledge of circumstances that often lead to legal liabilities or suits. Such knowledge can reduce, if not eliminate, his very involvements in legal disputes and law suits.

The construction contractor receives no financial gain as a result of becoming involved in a law suit or dispute. At best, the suit or dispute is resolved in favor of the contractor, and he is placed in a position equal to that that would have existed had the dispute not arose. Obviously, the contractor would be just as well off had the suit or dispute not arisen. Not all law suits or disputes in which the contractor becomes involved are resolved in his favor. In addition to having to perform unexpected tasks or incur unexpected costs when a suit or dispute is resolved against him, the contractor will also be liable for court costs and legal fees associated with the judgment.

The various types of laws in existence in the United States can be classified as either common law or statute law. Common law consists of doctrines which have their origin in court decisions. These laws are the result of the judicial process. Statute law consists of rules of conduct enacted by authorized individuals. These laws represent the will of

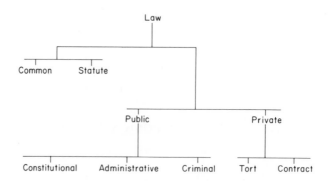

Fig. 4.1. Classifications of law.

the lawmaking power and rendered authentic by enforcement of legal authority.

The subject of law is often divided into *public* law and *private* law. Private law is alternatively referred to as *civil* law. The public law pertains to the public as a whole. Private law concerns itself with the relations between individuals within society. Public law is divided into *constitutional, administrative,* and *criminal* law. Private law is divided into *tort* and *contract* law. Contract law is undoubtedly the single most important field of law in regard to construction contracting. However, contractor knowledge of his liabilities in regard to all fields of law can reduce his risk of being involved in a law suit. The various fields of law are shown in Fig. 4.1. These various fields of law, as they affect construction contracting, are discussed in this chapter.

4.2 Constitutional and Administrative Law

Constitutional and *administrative* law are part of public law. Constitutional law deals with the power of Congress, the legislature, and the federal and state governments. Two constitutions are in force in each state—one is the state and the other is the national constitution. Constitutional law concerns itself with such matters as the power to tax, bankruptcy laws, and the establishment and regulation of currency.

Administrative law concerns governmental bodies which are created by the Congress or state legislatures for the purpose of enacting what amounts to further legislation. One of the distinguishing characteristics in American law in the last half century has been the growth in number and importance of administrative law and administrative bodies and commissions. An example is the National Labor Relations Board. Congress enacted a law creating the board and granting it certain powers. The board in turn makes laws.

The board was created to administer the National Labor Relations Act which was passed by Congress in 1935. The purpose of the act can be summarized by the following excerpts from the act.

"The denial by employers of the right of employees to organize and the refusal by employers to accept the procedure of collective bargaining lead to strikes and other forms of industrial strife or unrest, which have the intent or the necessary effect of burdening or obstructing commerce . . . "[1]; "Experience has proved that protection by law of the right of employees to organize and bargain collectively, safeguards commerce from injury, impairment, or interuption, and promotes the flow of commerce by removing certain recognized sources of industrial strife and unrest by encouraging practices fundamental to the friendly adjustment of industrial disputes arising out of differences as to wages, hours, or other working conditions and by restoring equality of bargaining power between employers and employees".[2]

These excerpts from the act show that the government became aware that the mere statement of its wish to have collective bargaining carried out on an equal footing for all parties was not sufficient stimulus to bring it about. As such they passed an administrative law.

The National Labor Relations Act (also known as the Wagner Act) has been somewhat changed by the passage of the Labor Management Relations Act of 1947, and the Labor Management Reporting and Disclosure Act of 1959. However, the board created by the National Labor Relations Act, the National Labor Relations Board, has stayed intact and its obligations have remained somewhat unchanged. In particular, the creation of the board (by administrative law) was for the purpose of hearing complaints of unfair labor practices against employees' rights.

4.3 Criminal Law

Criminal law is another important phase of public law. Here certain actions by individuals and groups are prohibited and penalties are

---

[1]United States Statutes at Large 1935–1936, Vol. 49, Washington, Government Printing Office, 1936, p. 449.

[2]Ibid., p. 449.

enforced in the name of the public as a whole. Proceedings may be instituted by a public official or body such as a grand jury or a police officer or some individual not personally affected, in the name of the public as a whole. Suppose that Jones murders Smith. Jones will be proceeded against by the state. If the crime takes place in Illinois, an *indictment* (written complaint) will be entitled "The People of the State of Illinois versus Jones." The indictment after reciting the facts will end with the assertion that the killing was "against the peace and dignity of the People of the State of Illinois." The case is not entitled "The orphaned children of Smith versus Jones" and it does not allege that damage was suffered by such children due to the loss of the father. Crimes may be punished by imprisonment, fine, removal from office, or the deprivation of the right to hold public office. A recent Supreme Court ruling has virtually eliminated death as a punishment for a crime.

Crimes are subdivided into two large classes, felonies and misdemeanors. Felonies are serious crimes, punishable by imprisonment. Among these are murder, rape, robbery, and burglary. Misdemeanors are crimes of a less serious nature such as traffic violations, drunkeness, trespass to real estate, vagrancy, and other offenses of a similar nature. Punishment is usually by fine only or short sentences in such corrective institutions as local jails or work houses.

Whereas a contractor may often become involved in a contract law dispute due to his ignorance of the law, his involvement in the violation of criminal law is somewhat intentional. Examples of such criminal acts include the defrauding or misleading of the public, embezzlement, and the receiving of stolen goods.

Contractors are guilty of *defrauding and misleading the public* when two or more contractors collude in their fixing of their bids to be submitted to an owner for the building of the owner's project. Such a practice is commonly referred to as "rigging" the bids.

Embezzlement is the fraudulent conversion of money or property of another party by a person to whom the money or property has been entrusted. As a result of statutes in several states, contractors have been ruled guilty of a crime when an owner gives a contractor money which is intended to be used in paying labor for work done in connection with the building of the owner's project, but the contractor does not use the money for that purpose. This form of embezzlement is referred to as misapplication of trust funds.

A contractor may be given or he may purchase at a discount, material or equipment that has been stolen. Regardless of whether the material or equipment has been stolen by the individual from whom they are received, or from an individual who was not the individual who stole them, if the contractor is aware that it is stolen material or equipment he is guilty of *receiving stolen goods*. It is immaterial that the contractor does not know the owner or the thief.

A contractor who obtains material from a supplier by means of a worthless check may be guilty of obtaining goods by false pretenses. The question that determines guilt is whether the contractor intended to defraud the supplier that the check had value when he knew in fact that it did not. If such is the case, the contractor is guilty of the crime.

Forgery differs from the crime of obtaining goods by false pretenses in that it consists of the material alteration of an instrument which creates or changes the liability of another party. The most common form of forgery is the fraudulent making of a check by means of signing a false signature. The construction project building process usually initiates the production of many checks. The contractor may receive checks from project owners, architects, engineers, or even material suppliers. When such a check is lost or stolen, the contractor may be victim of forgery. To eliminate this possibility, the contractor upon receiving a check, should immediately place his bank endorsement stamp on the back side of the check.

A continuing struggle exists in the construction industry as to a contractor's use of nonunion labor versus using union labor. *Open shop* contractors (those who use nonunion labor) have been the victims of disruptive and destructive actions of outside parties. Such actions are often crimes in that they may result in *larceny* or *arson*. In addition, as a result of *antiriot statutes*, the very act of assembling as a riotous group and engaging in civil disorders is generally a crime in itself.

Several states have statutes requiring contractors doing business within the state to be licensed. Some states require this licensing merely as a revenue raising measure, whereas others use the licensing procedure as a means of requiring that the contractors meet certain qualifications. There is an important difference in these two licensing objectives. If the license is used as a means of requiring certain qualifications, a contractor operating without a valid license can be ruled to be guilty of a misdemeanor. In addition, if he is *operating illegally* the contractor cannot enforce contracts to which he is a party. Thus, he may not be in a position to force payment from an owner who refuses to pay for work performed by the contractor. If a license is required solely for revenue raising, the contractor operating without it is not committing a misdemeanor. In addition, his contracts are enforceable.

The crimes discussed to this point are the result of an intentional act of an individual. There are circumstances that may result in the contractor being guilty of a crime due to his ignorance or lack of action. For example, a contractor may be guilty of the felony crime of manslaughter when a worker is killed as a result of the contractors failure to install or maintain safety equipment that is required by statute. The enactment of the Occupational Safety and Health Act (OSHA) of 1970 has resulted in the prosecution of many contractors who have been judged to be guilty of violation of safety requirements. Such crimes have resulted in fines ranging from $50 to $10,000. It is obvious that "crime does not pay."

4.4 Tort Law

Tort law along with contract law make up private law. Tort means "wrong," in this case a "private wrong." As a result, tort law is sometimes referred to as *civil* law. It is possible, indeed, it is true more often than not, that a wrong inflicted upon an individual not only wrongs the individual but society as a whole. Hence, a crime is usually a tort, and a tort may be a crime which is the subject of public law in the form of criminal law.

Let us go back to Smith's murder by Jones. We have already seen that Jones's action was an offense against the peace and dignity of the People of the State of Illinois. Jones's action was also a wrong to Smith and Smith's family. Hence, although Jones may be tried, convicted, and executed under criminal law, a branch of public law, he may not have heard the last of the consequences of his wrongful action. Smith's widow and children may sue Jones or Jones's estate under private law in what is called a tort action for damages suffered by the loss of support furnished by the deceased husband and father. Jones's action was not only murder under the criminal law; it was also a trespass to the person of Smith. Trespass may take the form of an unlawful invasion of the person ranging from murder to simple assault, trespass to real estate resulting from unlawful entry thereupon, or even injury to one's reputation by slander or libel.

The construction contractor is likely to become involved in a tort due to either an intentional act or due to his failure to recognize his legal responsibilities. A tort can arise when the contractor violates an obligation or duty created by law. When the contractor is guilty of a *breach of contract* that causes a wrong or injury to other parties of the contract, he is guilty of a tort. Thus, the contractor's act can be both a breach of contract and a tort.

To be guilty of a tort, it is usually required that the person committing the tort had intent to cause harm. However, this is not the case when it comes to torts resulting from *absolute liability*. For example, when a contractor uses dynamite in an excavation operation and debris from the explosion is hurled onto the land of another, the contractor is usually (depending on the state law) guilty of a tort. The fact that the contractor used due care in handling the dynamite is not relevant as to his guilt. Several states have ruled that such activity is so dangerous to the public that liability is imposed regardless of intent. Similar practices such as the contractor's creation of harmful noise or pollution often are within the realm of absolute liability.

A difficult question arises when it comes to an accident occurring to a child when the child trespasses onto the contractor's building project. In general, the contractor is under no obligation (no absolute liability) to make the construction site safe for infant trespassers. However, he is liable for the injuries to these trespassers if his building site is ruled to be an *attractive nuisance* to the infant trespasser.

Most torts are the direct cause of an individual's *negligence*. In torts of this type the question of guilt is centered around whether the defendant acted with less care than a *reasonable man* given the circumstances. The definition or description of a reasonable man is for the courts to determine. Thus, when a contractor trespasses the land of a land owner when transporting material to his building site, the courts have to decide if he acted as a reasonable man would have given the circumstances.

Torts resulting from negligence are of numerous types. Defamation by libel, infringements of patents or trademarks, unfair competition, interference with contract, nuisance, violence, trespass to land, and wrongful interference with business relations are all torts.

Examples of torts of which the construction contractor has been accused include the tort of unfair competition, trespass to land, and nuisance. A contractor is guilty of the tort of unfair competition when he becomes involved in the practice of "fixing" bids with other contractors. Use of someone's private property to haul construction materials without permission constitutes the tort of trespassing of land. When building a construction project with noisy equipment that disturbs the residents of the nearby area, the contractor may be judged to be guilty of the tort of nuisance.

4.5 Contract Law

By far the most frequent involvement of the contractor in a legal conflict occurs in the branch of law referred to as the *law of contracts*. The contractor enters into contracts with building project owners, material suppliers, equipment manufacturers and lessors, subcontractors, and labor. The complexity of contracts, especially contracts with the building project owners, enhances the possibility of contract disagreement, a breach of contract, and a law suit. The complexity of the construction contract with a project owner is due in part because of the unique nature of every project, the many types of work involved in a single contract, and the large dollar value of the single contract.

As is true of other conflicts of law to which the contractor is a participant, the contractor is almost always better off if the conflict had never arisen. The contractor's awareness of contract law as it relates to his everyday making and carrying out of his contracts can often result in the savings of money associated with project expenses, breach of contract, and law suits.

A contract can be defined as an agreement between two or more competent parties for a legal subject matter, whereby one party exchanges an act for the promise or the act of another party. A contract between two parties creates legally enforceable obligations on each of the parties. Upon one party's failure to perform his obligation, the other party can sue and receive damages from the party who is guilty of *breach of contract.*

A contract that is binding and enforceable on both parties of the contract is referred to as a *valid* contract. A *voidable* contract is binding and enforceable on both parties but because of certain circumstances such as one party being a minor, the contract may be rejected by one of the parties. A *void* contract is not binding or enforceable on either party of the contract.

Although it is best to make contracts in writing since this helps to eliminate misunderstandings of the participating parties, most contracts can in fact be made orally. Certain types of contracts as dictated by the statute of frauds must be in writing. The contracts that must be in writing are contracts to sell interest in property, contracts that cannot be performed within one year after the contract is made, a contract made in consideration of marriage, a contract for the selling of goods with a value in excess of $500, a contract to pay the debt of another, and a contract by the executor of a decedent's estate to pay a claim against the estate from his personal funds. The statute of frauds affects the form of the contract that the contractor makes with a building project owner in that the duration of the work involved often exceeds a year duration. Thus, the contract must be in writing. It should be noted that even if the contract is for a duration less than one year, it is rare to find a contractor-owner construction contract that is not in writing.

Most contracts to which the contractor is a participant are *expressed* contracts. These are contracts whereby each of the parties of the contracts have made oral or written declarations of their intentions. A contract does not have to be an expressed contract to be enforceable. An *implied* contract is enforceable if one party offers services to the other party indicating that he expects to be paid for the services, and the other party accepts the benefits of the services. Implied contracts are often the rule for several professional services such as those offered by an engineer, physician, or lawyer. A contractor may become involved in an implied contract when he is forced to perform work for which the actual scope of the work is not completely determined and the cost of his services can only be determined upon completion of the work. Such a contract is referred to as a cost plus contract.

In addition to express and implied contracts, the courts may also enforce the obligations of a party when in fairness and good conscience a party has received goods or services for which he should pay or return. This is referred to as a *quasi contract*. An example of a quasi contract is the performing of house improvements by a renter. If the owner of the house was aware of the fact (perhaps by seeing them) that the improvements were being made and he did not prohibit the renter from making them, the courts will likely require the owner to pay the renter for the improvements.

A contract is classified as a bilateral or unilateral contract. The more common contract, the *bilateral* contract, is one where one party, the *offerer*, makes a promise to do something in exchange for a promise from the offeree to do something. Thus, when a contractor promises a potential building project owner to build the owner's project for a promise from the owner to pay the contractor a defined amount, they have entered into a bilateral contract.

A *unilateral* contract is one where one party, the offerer, makes a promise to do something for an act from the other party, the offeree. There is no mutual agreement in an unilateral contract in that the party who may perform the act is not legally required to perform the act. Thus, when a potential building project owner promises a contractor $30,000 if the contractor will build his project, the contractor can claim the $30,000 upon building the project. However, the contractor does not have to build the project in that he has not legally entered into an agreement to build it. Unilateral contracts tend to be "weak" contracts in regard to the offerer's legal remedies. Thus, such contracts are rare except if the circumstances necessitate such a contract. For example, a person upon losing property, finds it is necessary to enter into an unilateral contract when he promises a reward for the return of the property.

4.5.1 Contract Agreement

In order to be a valid contract, there must be both an offer and an acceptance. An agreement is initiated when one person, the *offerer*, makes an offer to another person who is referred to as the *offeree*. An offer may be expressed in writing, by words, or it may even be implied.

In order to qualify as a legal offer, the offerer must intend to create a legal obligation. If there is no contractual intention, there is no legal offer. A project owner's advertisement for contractor bids is merely an invitation to negotiate. Because of the lack of intention the advertisement does not constitute an offer. On the other hand, a contractor's bid for the project is an offer. However, the bid by itself is not a contract until there is an acceptance by the owner.

One is not legally obligated to carry out an agreement to make a contract at a future date. Thus, there is no legal contract when a contractor promises to enter into a contract at some future date to build an individual a construction project.

An agreement to enter into a contract at some future date differs from an *option contract*. An option contract is a promise to keep open an offer for a stated period of time or to a specific date. For example, a construction contractor may give an equipment finance company $100 for the option of purchasing a certain piece of equipment from the company within a 30-day period. The equipment finance company cannot revoke its offer to sell the equipment during the option period. The $100 the contractor paid for the option generally goes toward the payment of the asset upon purchase. If the contractor decides not to purchase the asset, a portion or all of the $100 is forfeited to the equipment company.

Whereas, an offer usually has to be definite and certain in substance in order to constitute a valid offer, there are exceptions. For example, a cost-plus construction contract is valid even though the offer made by the contractor is not certain in regard to the dollar value of the cost of the work. Such contracts are ruled valid in that the type of work involved (uncertain work quantities) necessitates such a contract. The courts acknowledge the fact that to require a definite dollar amount (a lump sum contract) would result in the contractor bearing an excess amount of financial risk associated with work and cost uncertainties.

An offer to contract can be revoked by the offerer before it is accepted by the offeree. Of course, this privilege does not hold in regard to an option contract. If an offer is accepted by an offeree before he is notified that the offer has been revoked, the contract is valid. Thus, if a contractor mails his acceptance of an owner's offer to pay the contractor $50,000 for the contractor's building of a project, the contract is valid even if the owner mails his intent to revoke the offer before the contractor mails his acceptance. The owner's letter of revocation must be received by the contractor before the contractor's acceptance if the offer is to be legally revoked.

An offer is terminated upon a counteroffer by the offeree. Thus, an offer by a contractor to an owner to build the owner's project for $50,000 is terminated when the owner replys he will give the contractor $45,000 for the building of the project. The counteroffer becomes an offer made by the owner. It is now up to the contractor (now the offeree) to accept or reject the offer, or to make yet another counteroffer.

An offer may or may not include a date on which it expires. If a date is included, the offer terminates on the stated date. If there is no stated date, the courts will rule that the offer is for a "reasonable time." A reasonable time is the time a reasonable man acquainted with the type of proposed contract would assume it to be, given the circumstances. For example, a contractor's offer to build an owner's project would be judged to terminate at the letting of a project.

In addition, to requiring an offer, a valid agreement must contain an acceptance by the offeree. The offer can only be accepted by the person to whom it is intended. The acceptance by the offeree can be in any format which expresses the intent to accept. Thus, a contractor's acknowledgment by saying okay over the telephone to an offer constitutes an acceptance. Although either the offer or acceptance can be made in such a haphazard manner, it is advantageous to have a more formal acknowledgment in order to avoid disputes.

An acceptance must be unconditional. If a change of the offer is made by the offeree, a new offer is in effect made. An offeree's failure to respond to an offerer's offer does not constitute an acceptance. Thus, an owner's failure to respond to a contractor's offer to build a project for a stated sum of money does not result in any owner legal obligations.

The validity of a contract may be affected by a mistake by one of the parties involved in the contract. A mistake in a contract may be a mistake of fact or a mistake of law. It may also be a unilateral or a bilateral mistake.

If there is a mutual mistake of fact by the parties the contract is normally ruled to be void. For example, if a contractor enters into agreement with an owner for the remodeling of the owner's building for a stated sum of money, and the building has burnt down and neither party is aware of the fact, the contract is void.

Ordinarily a unilateral (one party) mistake of fact does not affect any of the legal obligations imposed by a contract. However, there are exceptions. For example, a contractor may mistakenly add his bid items resulting in him submitting a very low bid price to an owner. If the mistake is so apparent to the owner that he should be able to recognize the understated price, the courts will usually rule that the owner cannot hold the contractor to the bid price. Even though the courts recognize that negligence of the contractor is not grounds for invalidating the contract, they also recognize that the owner should not take undue advantage of the contractor. This reasoning is stated in the court's judgment in regard to the case of *Geremia v. Boyarsky*.[3]

An agreement is not valid if one of the parties concealed information that would have influenced the other party not to enter the agreement. However, if the complaining party should have been aware of the concealed facts, it is not the obligation of the other party to bring them to his attention. A party to a contract is expected to know information available to a reasonable man. Thus, it is not the responsibility of an owner to inform a contractor of the soil conditions underlying a proposed building. However, if the soil is of extremely abnormal condition such that the contractor would not be expected to know of its state, the owner has the responsibility of informing him of the conditions. His concealment of the fact may be grounds for judging the contract void or voidable (the contractor may choose to accept the contract regardless of the concealment).

[3]Dunham, C. W. and Young, R. D., *Contracts, Specifications, and Law for Engineers*, New York, McGraw–Hill, 1971, p. 38.

Fraud is yet another reason for a contract not being valid. *Fraud* occurs when a person misrepresents a fact, known or believed by him to be untrue, with the intention of causing another party to enter into a contract. Besides being grounds for making a contract invalid, fraud is a tort. The injured party can recover money damages resulting from the fraud of another.

The validity of a contract is removed if one party causes another party to enter a contract under *duress*. Duress relates to the depriving of an individual's free will as a result of a threat of violence. A threat of economic loss is not grounds for duress. Thus, a threat from an owner not to provide building material credit from the owner's supply subsidiary is not considered duress in influencing a contractor to build a project for the owner.

A contract which involves concealment, fraud, or duress is considered to be a voidable contract. The offended party may choose to accept the contract or he may choose to avoid it. If he accepts it, the contract is then valid. If he avoids the contract (referred to as *rescinding* the contract) he is required to restore the other party to his original position. That is, he cannot take financial advantage of the other party. Of course, if he has been the victim of fraud, he has a claim to damages.

As mentioned earlier, certain contracts have to be in writing. A construction contract agreement for which the work is to take more than one year is such a contract. If the contract violates the requirement that it be in writing, it may be judged void or voidable, depending upon the statute of the state in which it is made.

In many cases disputes arise as to what was offered and agreed to in a contract. Usually the courts will decide the dispute by means of studying the written agreement. If there is a written agreement, the courts will not allow contradictory testimonies of one of the parties. This type of testimony is referred to as *parol evidence*. Parol evidence is only permissible when there is evidence of fraud, or the contract is not complete and therefore needs clarification.

The courts will interpret an agreement as it is stated or implied. Clerical errors and omissions are ignored and the contract is interpreted as the courts judge its intent. If there are contradictions between what is written and what is typed in an agreement, the written part is ruled to prevail. A conflict between a numerical quantity that is written in words and written in figures is resolved in favor of the amount stated in words. When a contractor makes a contract in one state and performs the work stated in the contract in another state, the contract is often written with a clause indicating the state to which laws are to apply.

4.5.2 Competent Parties

One of the requirements of a valid contract is that the parties to the contract are legally competent parties. The most common examples of parties lacking authority to enter into a valid contract are minors, intoxicated persons, and corporations acting beyond their legal powers (*ultra vires act*).

When a contract is signed between a legal party and a party lacking the legal capacity to enter into a contract, the agreement is normally a voidable contract. In the case of a corporation acting beyond their powers, rather than rule the contract invalid, the courts will neither enforce the contract nor hold either party liable for any breach of contract.

The party lacking legal competence to enter a contract has the option of avoiding the contract (referred to as *disaffirmance*) or he may perform his voidable contract (*ratify* it). The competent party does not have the right to disaffirm the contract. The person lacking competence (e.g., a minor) upon disaffirmance of the contract usually has to set things back to their original position. That is, he must return what he has received as a result of the contract. This act of returning consideration received is referred to as *restitution*.

Many of the states have statutes that require certain professionals to obtain a license in order to practice their profession. This license may be required in order to protect the public from individuals who are unqualified. On the other hand, several states impose a license requirement merely as a means of raising revenue by requiring a fee for the license. If the license is required for the purpose of protecting the public, a party practicing without a license is in fact entering a voidable contract when making a contract for such services. For example, if a contractor does not have such a required license when entering an agreement to build an owner's project, the contractor may find it difficult to win contract disputes against the owner. The owner has the option of avoiding or performing such an agreement. However, once the owner indicates that he is going to carry out his contract obligations, the voidable contract becomes a valid contract.

If the license is required for the purpose of raising revenue, the contractor's failure to obtain the license has no legal bearing on the validity of his contracts. Obviously, it is not always clear whether a license is required for public protection or merely for raising revenue. For this reason and for reasons of maintaining good external relations, it is rare to find a contractor who practices without a required license.

In regard to the parties of a valid contract, more than two parties can be involved. That is, two or more parties may make a contract with one, two, or more than two parties. When two or more parties jointly promise to perform an obligation, or when two or more parties are jointly the recipient of benefits from an agreement, the contract is referred to as a *joint contract*. The construction contractor enters into such a contract when he combines his labor force and equipment with those of another contractor for the purpose of building a construction project. Such an arrangement is referred to as a *joint venture*. Such an arrangement is somewhat similar to a partnership. The main difference is that the joint venture is usually for a single project, whereas a partnership is formed for the carrying out of business for an unstated period of time.

Both of the parties to a joint contract must be legally competent parties. Any court action on a joint contract must be brought against all of the joint parties.

Two competent parties may also enter into a *several contract* with another party. In such a contract, each of the two parties are separately liable for their agreement even if they both agree to the same contract obligations.

A *third party beneficiary contract* is a contract where two parties enter into an agreement whereby one of the parties is to perform an obligation for a third party. Such a contract is a valid contract. An example of such a contract is where a contractor signs an agreement with an owner where the owner promises to pay the contractor a sum of money for the promise of the contractor to build a project for a creditor of the owner. The third party, the creditor, has a right to sue the contractor for breach of contract upon the contractor's failure to carry out his obligations.

Not all contract beneficiary parties have the right to sue for breach of contract. Such is true in the case of an *incidental beneficiary*. For example, a landowner does not have the right to sue a contractor upon the contractor's failure to properly pave a city street along which the landowner's property lies.[4] Only the city can sue the contractor for his lack of carrying out his obligation.

The question as to whether the third parties harmed as a result of a party's negligent performance can sue the party is a difficult one to answer. In several states, only the parties directly involved in a contract can enter a breach of contract suit. Thus, if a contractor negligently fails

[4]Anderson, R. A. and Kumpf, W. A., *Business Law*, Cincinnati, South-Western Publishing Company, 1972, p. 209.

to take measures to make a project safe for which he has contracted with a potential owner, a third party injured because of that failure cannot sue for breach of contract. However, it should be noted that a third party injured due to a contractor's negligence can often succeed in obtaining damages in a tort action centered around the contractor's absolute liability.

A competent party to a contract can transfer his rights from the contract to another party outside of the contract. Such a transfer is referred to as an *assignment* of contract rights. The party to the contract who makes the assignment is referred to as the *assigner*, and the recipient of the rights is referred to as the *assignee*.

A contractor can assign his right to receive payment from a building owner to the bank. This is often done for the purpose of providing security to the bank for a loan. The contractor is the assigner and the bank is the assignee.

Certain rights or obligations to a contract cannot be assigned regardless of whether the parties involved are legally competent or legally incompetent. A right to have an employee work for oneself cannot be assigned. If one enters into a contract for the unique services of an individual (e.g., the services of a well-known architect), the individual cannot assign his obligations to perform. An assignee of a contract can sue for breach of contract as if he were a party to the contract.

When a construction contractor who is a party to a contract to build a project for an owner is subjected to grave financial difficulties, the owner may agree to release the contractor from the contract. The owner will then seek another contractor to take the place of the original contractor. This type of contract change is referred to as a *novation*. The old contract is substituted with a new contract.

4.5.3 Legal Subject Matter

In order for a contract agreement to be valid, the formation and the performance of the agreement must be legal. Thus, the agreement must be for legal subject matter. If it is not, the resulting contract is usually void. However, if the circumstances of the agreement are such that an innocent party to the contract is subjected to an unfavorable position as the result of the illegal act of the other party, the contract may be voidable. In this case, the innocent party may choose to avoid the contract or he may choose to have the contract performed.

There are several types of agreements that do not meet the requirements of being for legal subject matter. Included in these are agreements calling for an act that is a crime, an agreement that involves a conflict of interest (e.g., government officials are prohibited from entering contracts that relate to their public position), and agreements requiring public service (e.g., the payment of a public official for something he is required to do).

In regard to agreements which the contractor may enter, several practices may constitute illegal subject matter. In some cities and states there are laws that regulate the business activities of certain businesses. For example, in the previous section the licensing of contractors was discussed. The issued license often regulates the activities of the contractor. If the contractor violates the stated regulations he may be subject to a fine or criminal prosecution.

A contract in restraint of trade is another type of contract that is not valid due to illegal subject matter. A contractor cannot enter a contract with other contractors to create a monopoly on the construction market, or to "fix" bid prices on a given project. In addition to making the contract void, such practices are subject to civil and criminal penalties. Such contracts violate fair trade agreements. A similar violation occurs when the contractor performs below cost for the purpose of harming or eliminating his competition. Although several states have statutes against such a practice, the vagueness of the term below cost results in the statutes being relatively ineffective. In addition, the laws are hard to enforce in the case of the construction competitive bidding procedure in that the very procedure promotes such an "undercut competition" practice.

Certain contracts which the contractor enters into with a project owner may also be invalid due to illegal subject matter. For example, a contract to build a project which violates a city zoning law is an agreement that is not valid because of the illegality of the subject matter. Such contracts are ruled to be void.

A contractor is often involved in the borrowing of money for the payment of project and equipment expenses. State statutes regulate the maximum interest rate which a person or lending institutions can charge borrowers for the use of their money. If the person or institution charges an amount in excess of this specified amount they are guilty of usury. If a party is guilty of usury, the loan agreement is not valid due to the lack of legal subject matter. The remedies that are open to the borrower as a result of the lender's usury vary from state to state. Some states require the borrower to perform the loan agreement, adjusted to a legal interest rate. Others declare the entire loan agreement void and require that both lender and borrower be placed in their original position before the loan. Still other states penalize the lender who is guilty of usury by allowing the borrower to keep the borrowed money without requiring him to pay the money (principle or interest) back to the lender.

4.5.4 Adequate Exchange

In addition to the agreement, legal parties, and legal subject matter requirements of a valid contract, there must also be an element of exchange. Each of the parties to the contract must exchange something with the other party. This exchange is often referred to as the providing of *consideration*. Consideration is what one promises or does for the promise or act of the other party. This promise or act may be in the form of money, physical property, a service, or even a promise not to do some act (referred to as *forebearance*).

If only one party offers consideration while the other party does not, there is no valid contract. For example, if a contractor merely offers to build a owner's project there is no contract in that the owner has not offered consideration.

The validity or the enforceability of a contract is not affected by the inadequate nature of one party's consideration. For example, if a contractor offers to build an owner a project for $20,000 from the owner, the fact that it will cost the contractor $25,000 to build the project does not make the contract invalid.

A difficult question in regard to a contract's requirement for consideration arises when a contractor requests and obtains additional money over and above the amount stated in the original contract. This requesting of additional money is often related to work covered by the original work. For example, a contractor may contract with an owner to build a project for $20,000. Upon completing 75% of the work and having absorbed $20,000 of costs, the contractor might inform the owner that because of high costs he will require another $5,000 to complete the project. The owner may agree to the extra $5,000. However, upon further thought the owner may decide not to pay the additional $5,000. His defense is based on the fact that his $5,000 promise was in exchange for work covered in the original work and he therefore received no consideration for his $5,000 promise. Technically the owner is correct and the courts may rule in his favor. However, several courts have ruled in favor of the contractor (entitling him to the additional $5,000) on the grounds that the original contract was rescinded [done away with] when the owner agreed to the additional $5,000.

It should be noted that if the owner had not agreed to the additional $5,000 that no legal dispute would have arisen in that the contractor would have to absorb all the costs, whatever they may be, as part of the risk of the contract. It should also be noted that if the reasons for the contractor absorbing added costs were not in the control of the contractor (e.g., extremely unseasonal weather) the courts may also rule that the contractor is entitled to extra money regardless of whether the owner agreed to the claim. Such a ruling is centered around the fact that the conditions that prevailed during the construction were not those implied in the contract. However, there is a difficult question here as to what conditions the contractor should expect. In many cases, the courts rule that the unforeseen conditions are part of the risk of contracting and costs associated with them are to be absorbed by the contractor. The fact that the contractor cannot obtain additional payment can also be explained by the fact that the courts do not enforce extra payment merely because a party did not obtain what he expected.

A different situation arises when the contractor agrees to accept $950 before it is due in payment of the $1,000 in full. In this case, the owner does give new consideration in that he makes early payment. Such an agreement does meet the requirements of a valid contract.

4.5.5 Contract Termination

The majority of contracts are terminated by the performance of the terms of the contract. However, circumstances may arise that result in a contract being terminated by impossibility of performance, by agreement, or by acceptance of breach of contract.

The construction contract is normally terminated when the contractor finishes building the owner's project according to specifications and in return receives final payment from the owner. If a dispute arises as to whether each of the parties has performed his obligations, the party claiming his performance must show that he has in fact performed.

The construction contract may or may not state a time period for performance. If it does state the time period, then performance should be made within the time period. If the performance is not completed within the time period, the courts may rule it a breach of contract. However, if it can be shown that the other party did not incur harm due to the delay in performance, the courts will often ignore the performance time period clause of the contract.

The contract may stipulate that a certain amount of money is to be paid by the party guilty of not meeting a performance date. This is often true in the case of construction contracts. The amount of money is referred to as *liquidated damages*. These liquidated damages should not be construed as penalty costs. That is, liquidated damages are enforced only to the extent of the costs the innocent party incurs as a result of the other party's lack of performance by the stated date. Penalty clauses are void, liquidated damage clauses are valid.

If a stated time period for the performance of a contract is not stipulated, the courts generally rule that performance must by made within a "reasonable time." A reasonable time is defined as the period of time in which the type of contract in consideration is normally performed.

The rule of *substantial performance* often applies to construction contracts. This rule states that if the contractor performs all of his obligations, except for a slight defect in his performance that he did not make willfully, the owner cannot hold back the entire payment from the contractor. The contractor is ruled to have made substantial performance and is entitled to the entire payment due on the contract minus the amount it will cost the owner to cover the defect. Theoretically the rules of contract would hold that the contractor is entitled to no payment in that he has not performed his contract obligations. However, the courts recognize the unfair nature of such a performance rule in regard to the building of a construction contract. Thus, if a contractor contracts to build a project for $50,000 and performs his obligations except that the quality of a certain phase of the work is unacceptable and will cost the owner $500 to repair, the contractor is in fact entitled to $49,500 on the grounds that he has completed substantial performance. If it can be shown that the contractor intentionally performed negligently in regard to the $500 of unacceptable construction he has no claim on the owner. It should be noted that intent is often difficult to prove. Thus, the courts usually rule in favor of substantial completion.

The acceptance of the contractor's performance of a construction contract is often subject to the approval of an architect or engineer who is hired by the owner. Unless it can be shown that the architect or engineer is guilty of fraud, the acceptance or rejection of the performance of the contractor by the architect or engineer is final and binding on both the contractor and the owner. When the contractor deals directly with the project owner, the contract is often written that the contractor's performance is subject to the satisfaction of the owner. In such a case, the courts rule that the owner must pay the contractor according to the contract if the contractor's work would be acceptable to a reasonable man.

A contract is not discharged on grounds of impossibility of performance merely because one party finds it an economic burden to perform. Impossibility of performance is grounds for termination of a contract only when it is indeed impossible to perform. For example, if a contractor contracts with an owner of a building to repair the building for a stated sum of money, and the building burns down before the contractor's performance, performance is deemed impossible. In such a case, the contract is ruled to be void.

Changes in laws which result in the contractor's performance being more expensive are not grounds for his nonperformance. For example, a new safety law may require the contractor to provide additional shoring for a building project. The fact that the law was nonexistent at the time the contractor entered into an agreement to undertake the work is not grounds for the contractor's nonperformance.

If a party to a contract is constrained in his performance of the contract then the innocent party is relieved of his obligations on the grounds of impossibility of performance. Thus, a subcontractor is relieved of his obligations of a contract with a general contractor when the general contractor does not perform the work precedent to the subcontractor's performance.

Impossibility of performance on grounds of bad weather (referred to as acts of God) is no defense. That is, bad weather is part of the risk of contracting. Modern day construction contracts often provide for extra time for the contractor when he is subjected to such conditions. Even when such a stipulation is not in the contract, when abnormal conditions persist the courts sometimes rule that there is no breach of contract and extend to the contractor extra time to perform.

The two parties to the construction contract may terminate a contract by agreement. For example, a project owner may find it difficult to raise the money needed to initiate construction, and the contractor realizing that he may get future work from the project owner if he cooperates, may decide to agree to terminate the contract agreement. The government often reserves the right to terminate a construction contract at any time during its performance. An agreement of this type with a contractor usually provides for liberal termination benefits for the contractor should the owner decide to terminate the project.

Because of changes of work units, the contractor and the owner may agree to a different performance than that stated in the original agreement. Such an agreement is referred to as *accord*. When the new agreement is performed there is *accord and satisfaction* and the original contract is disregarded. To avoid the requirements for an entire new contract everytime work changes occur, construction contracts are usually written to provide for *change orders*. The contract states that the contractor will be paid an amount in addition to the stated contract sum for work changes that occur. Usually this is in the amount of the contractor's cost plus a stated profit.

When one party to the contract fails to perform his obligations of the contract, he is guilty of *breach of contract*. Upon the breach of contract of one party, the other party is relieved of his obligations. However, if the contract term broken is not a sufficiently important part of the contract, the innocent party is not relieved of his contract obligations.

If the innocent party does not take action when the other party commits a breach of contract he is said to have *waived* the breach. In such a case, the innocent party cannot at a later date take action because of the other party's breach of contract. For example, if a contractor commits a breach of contract as a result of performing work that does not meet specifications, and the owner accepts the work, the owner cannot seek remedies at a later date for the contractor's breach.

An injured party is entitled to sue for damages upon the other party's breach of contract. If the injured party does not actually sustain a loss because of the other party's breach he is still entitled to *nominal damages*. Nominal damages are a small sum of money, such as a dollar of two.

If the innocent party to the contract sustains damages because of the breach of the other party, the innocent party can recover the damages. These damages are referred to as *compensatory damages*. If a contractor is guilty of breach because of inferior work, the owner is entitled to compensatory damages from the contractor equal in amount to the costs the owner incurs to hire someone to repair the work such that it meets specifications.

The courts will usually not require the breaching party to pay *punitive damages*. These would be damages in excess of those actually incurred by the innocent party and imposed for the purpose of punishment.

An innocent party is required to *mitigate damages* when he becomes aware of the other party's breach. This means that he cannot let damages increase if he can prevent them. If he does, he is not entitled to sue for such damages. Thus, a contractor cannot be entitled to those damages that he incurs on a building project after he is informed by the owner that the owner will not be able to meet further financial obligations.

In addition to being liable for damages to the owner when he fails to perform his obligations, the contractor may also be liable for a tort to a third party when he commits a breach of contract. Thus, when a third party is injured due to the negligence of the contractor when breaching a contract with an owner, the third party may bring a tort action suit against the contractor. Tort was discussed in an earlier section of this chapter.

Related to the performing of a contract and the breach of contract is a legal device referred to as a *lien*. A lien is a legal claim against the property of another for the satisfaction of a debt. There are many types of liens that are used in regard to the building of a construction project. These liens that are drawn for use in the construction industry are often referred to as *mechanics liens*. All lien laws are statutory laws.

In regard to the performance of the project owner and the construction contractor, the contractor may obtain a personal property lien or a real property lien. Thus, upon nonperformance of the owner's payment of the debt owed to the contractor, the contractor may state claim to the personal property or real property stipulated in the lien. In the case of a construction project lien, the real property involved is usually the project itself. As is true in any legal dispute, the project owner has a right to defend himself in a lien dispute.

The first step in the establishment of the mechanic's lien is the filing of a notice of mechanic's lien. It is filed with the clerk of the county in which the property is located. The notice gives the name of the lienor (i.e. the contractor), the name of the project owner, a description of the labor performed, and the materials furnished to the project. In addition it states the contract price, the amount unpaid, the date of commencing the work, and a description of the property. The time in which a notice of lien must be filed by the contractor varies from state to state. A typical time is three months. Once the lien is filed it must be acted on by the contractor within a stipulated period of time. While the time varies from state to state, a typical maximum time in which the contractor must act on his filed lien is three years.

The lien rights of contractors and subcontractors are dependent on whether the state in which the work is performed abides by the "New York System" or the "Pennsylvania System". Under the New York System a subcontractor is limited in the amount he can collect by the amount due the general contractor from the owner. Let us assume that a project owner enters into a contract with a general contractor for $20,000, and the general contractor hires a subcontractor to do some of the work for $4,000. Under the New York System, if the subcontractor gives the project owner notice as to the amount of money that will become due on his contract with the general contractor, then the project owner is entitled to withhold that sum from any payments to the general contractor. If no notice has been given from the subcontractor to the project owner and the project owner pays the entire contract sum of $20,000 to the general contractor, the subcontractor cannot collect his $4,000 from the project owner but must look to the general contractor.

Under the Pennsylvania System the subcontractor has a right to file a mechanic's lien for his labor and material even though the entire contract price has been paid by the project owner to the general contractor. Thus the owner may be forced to pay for the contract work twice should the general contractor fail to make payment to the subcontractor. To avoid this possible double payment, the owner will usually require a *waiver of lien* when making payment on the work performed. Once the contractor signs the waiver of lien, he no longer has any claim to ownership of improvements.

A contractor's lien on the project owner is not the only type of lien that is used in the construction industry. Others include a materials supplier's lien on the contractor, and a subcontractor's lien on the contractor.

4.6 Commercial Paper

Commercial paper plays a role in the everyday business of the construction industry. Commercial paper consists of written promises or orders to pay money that is transferred by negotiation. Written promises to pay are usually in the form of promissory notes. Checks and drafts are examples of written orders to pay a stated amount of money.

Seldom does today's businessman pay his bills and receive revenue in the form of cash. He is much more likely to handle business transactions by means of commercial paper. Commercial paper serves as a substitute for cash. Commercial paper transactions often prove to be more convenient and safe in regard to the possibility of loss than are cash transactions. This is especially the case in regard to the construction contractor. Daily he engages in the writing and receiving of checks, and the writing of promissory notes and drafts.

Commercial paper transactions are similar in structure to contract agreements. However, the assignee of commercial paper is subject to less risk and given more rights than those given the assignee of contract rights. That is, commercial paper can be more easily assigned and rights transferred from one individual to the next. Commercial paper law is dictated by the Uniform Commercial Code.

A person who holds commercial paper that is payable to the individual holding the paper (his name does not have to be on the paper) is refered to as the *bearer*. This type of commercial paper is referred to as *bearer paper*. On the other hand, some commercial paper is payable to an individual only if the individual's name appears on the paper. Such paper is only payable to the *order* of the individual designated.

An owner of commercial paper can assign his paper to another individual by means of signing his name to the back of the paper. The person who transfers the paper by means of his signature is referred to as the *endorser*. The person to whom the endorser assigns the commercial paper is referred to as the *endorsee*.

An endorser can transfer commercial paper by means of one of several types of endorsements. A *blank endorsement* contains only the name of the endorser. There is no designated endorsee. As such, any individual who might find the paper holds bearer paper and can in effect cash the paper. Thus, while the blank endorsement remains the most commonly used endorsement, it is also the most dangerous in regard to risk of loss.

A less risky form of endorsement takes place when the endorser designates an endorsee. He would do this by writing "Pay to Jim Smith" on the back of the commercial paper. This type of endorsement is referred to as a *special endorsement*.

An even less risky endorsement is one where the endorser signs his name and adds the words "without recourse." Such an endorsement is referred to as a *qualified endorsement*. The effect of a qualified endorsement is that it relieves some of the liabilities of the endorsement in regard to the default of the drawer of the paper.

A *restrictive endorsement* is one that states the purpose of the endorsement. For example, a member of the ABC Construction Company would endorse commercial paper by means of a stamp that might read:
                     For Deposit Only
                ABC Construction Company
The effect of such an endorsement is that the paper can only be transferred to the account of ABC Construction Company. However, a restrictive endorsement does not prohibit further transfer of the instrument.

A person who adds his signature to commercial paper and adds a statement that he will pay the value of the paper if the maker does not pay is referred to as a *guarantor*. This may often be done to add strength to the maker such that he can negotiate the paper. However, the guarantor places himself in a state of risk in that upon the maker's inability to pay (i.e. he is ruled to have insufficient property to cover the debt), the guarantor becomes liable.

In order to be negotiable (i.e. be transferrable from one individual to the next), commercial paper must conform to certain format requirements. A fundamental requirement is that the paper be in writing and signed by the maker. The paper may be handwritten, typed, or printed. The maker usually signs his name to the lower right-hand corner of the commercial paper. However, this is not a requirement in that the paper is negotiable as long as his signature appears on the paper. In absence of a statute that forbids it, the initials or a symbol which identifies the maker is a substitute for an individual's full signature.

Commercial paper must be unconditional in order to be negotiable. Thus, when an owner writes a check to a contractor and stipulates on it that it is payable upon the contractor's completion of construction work, the paper is not negotiable. The same is true in regard to the contractor's writing a promissory note to a bank for a loan in which he promises to make payment of the note upon winning a certain construction contract.

The amount of payment indicated on commercial paper must be certain in order to be negotiable. If the stated amount in writing on the paper differs from the amount printed on the paper, the written amount is ruled to be the amount due. Commercial paper must also be payable in money in order to be negotiable.

The paper should indicate a date or a time interval in which payment must be made. If it states that it is payable when a certain event occurs, it is nonnegotiable in that the event may never occur. Certain types of commercial paper are payable on demand.

In order to be negotiable, commercial paper must be payable either to a stated individual or to any holder of the paper. When it is payable to a given individual it is referred to as *order paper*. If it is payable to any holder it is referred to as *bearer paper*. The paper may stipulate that it is payable to both order and bearer. For example, it may state "Pay to Jim Smith or Bearer."

In addition to the general formal requirements for negotiability, there are additional legal terms and obligations that relate to specific types of commercial paper. These will now be discussed.

4.6.1 Checks

The most used type of commercial paper in the construction industry (or any other industry) is the check. A check is an order by a depositor of a bank upon the bank to pay a stated sum of money to another individual. The individual who writes the check is referred to as the drawer. The individual to whom the check is addressed is referred to as the payee. The depositor's bank upon which the check is drawn is referred to as the drawee.

A check is in effect a kind of draft. However, it differs from a draft (as one commonly refers to a draft) in that the drawee of a check is always a bank, whereas in a draft the person to whom the draft is given is the drawee. In addition, due to state bad check laws, a violator of check laws may be subject to criminal action as well as being civilly liable as in the case of a draft.

Although several banks' checks vary in style, most allow space for the drawer to note the purpose for which the check is written. It is beneficial for the drawer to place the purpose of the check in that the courts will recognize the written notation should the purpose be later questioned. In addition, the drawer can use the notation space to indicate that the check is for "Payment in Full." Upon the drawee's acceptance of the check, the corresponding debt is discharged regardless of whether or not the payment is really in full.

Checks are demand paper. Thus, when a drawer's check is presented to the bank, the bank has an obligation to make payment on the check. However, this obligation is removed once the drawer's funds in the bank are exhausted. If the bank fails to meet its payment obligation it is liable to the drawer. However, the payee of the check cannot seek damages from the bank. The bank may refuse to make payment on the check if it is presented to the bank more than six months after the date on the check. In regard to a dispute as to whether a check is still negotiable, the Uniform Commercial Code states that a check should be negotiated within thirty days.

A depositor's bank has a duty to stop payment on a check if informed by the depositor before the check is received by the bank. This practice is commonly followed when a check is lost or a question of payment dispute arises shortly after the drawer writes the check. The drawer's notice to stop the check is referred to as stop payment order. This order can be oral or written. If it is oral it is only good for fourteen days whereas if it is written it can be in effect six months and then renewed. Should the bank mistakenly make payment on a check that has properly been stopped by the drawer, the bank is liable for payment of the check out of its own funds.

One cannot stop payment on a *certified check*. A certified check is one that the bank certifies by means of setting aside funds for its payment when it is written. The certified check protects the individual to whom the check is addressed (the payee) in that the question as to whether the drawer has sufficient funds in the bank for payment of the check is removed.

Yet another type of check is the *cashier's check*. The drawer of a cashier's check is the bank. Upon receipt of payment by the depositor, or upon charging the amount against the depositor's account, the bank issues a check on its own funds to the depositor or to the person designated by the depositor. The purpose of the cashier's check is to increase the strength and the ability of the depositor to negotiate the check.

When a person writes a check and does not have sufficient funds in his bank to cover the check, he may be subject to criminal as well as civil action. He is usually ruled to be guilty of fraud. If an individual signs the name of the drawer to a check in order to negotiate the check he is guilty of *forgery*. The depositor's bank is liable to the depositor for the amount of the check if they make payment on a forged check.

It should be noted that in order to relieve himself of liability in the case of forgery, the drawer must exert reasonable care to prevent his name from being forged. Thus, if a contractor negligently always uses a mechanical writer for signing checks and it comes into the hands of another, he becomes liable for the checks signed with it. In addition, in order to relieve himself of liability of forged checks, the drawer must inform the bank of the forgery within a reasonable time after receiving his bank statement.

If the bank makes payment on a check on which the stated sum of the check has been altered, the bank is liable to the drawer for any amount over the amount stipulated on the check by the drawer. However, as in the case of forgery of signature, the liability of the bank is removed if the drawer contributes to the alteration by means of his negligence.

4.6.2 Promissory Notes

The second most widely used type of commercial paper by the construction industry is the *promissory note*. Usually the contractor is the *maker* of such a note. A promissory note is a written promise by the maker to pay money to the recipient of the note. The recipient, who in effect is a lender of money, is referred to as a *payee*. Promissory notes differ from other types of commercial paper in that only two parties, a maker and a payee are involved in the paper.

Promissory notes are used when an individual obtains a loan from another party. A contractor often has to sign a promissory note when obtaining loans to finance material, labor, and equipment. To provide the payee (who is often a bank) security, the maker often has to put up property or collateral in the form of stocks or bonds. If property is put up as security, the note is referred to as a *mortgage note*. If stocks, bonds or another type of collateral is provided, the note is referred to as *collateral note*.

A promissory note may be either payable on demand of the payee, or it may be payable on a stated date. If the note is payable on a given date, the maker's liability to make payment on the note is not removed if the payee does not present it to him on the due date. The maker's liability continues until it is relieved by the statute of limitations.

A note will often state that it is payable within a certain period of time. For example, it may state that it is payable within 30 days. When such is the case, it is payable within 30 days of the day after the stated date on the note. If the last date due falls on a holiday, the note is payable the following business day. If the maker does not make payment by the due date, he is subject to legal action. His action of non-payment results in the note being *dishonored*. However, if his delay in paying is caused by circumstances beyond his control, he is granted a delay and must then make payment within a reasonable period of time.

Even when a note is not payable until a stated date, the payee may have the right to *accelerate* the payment of the note. If the note is such that the maker is to make installment payments on the note, the failure of the maker to meet a payment is grounds for the payee making immediate claim to the entire amount. A note also may be written such that even though a future date is stipulated as the payment date, the payee reserves the right to demand full payment at any time. This is done to protect the payee should it become apparent that the maker is having financial difficulties. For example, a bank may reserve such a right when entering into a promissory note agreement with a contractor. If it becomes apparent to the bank that the contractor is not meeting his financial committments such as paying his project labor costs, the bank may accelerate its claim on the note.

In regard to acceleration clauses, the maker may also have the right to make early payment. These early payments are referred to as prepayments. They are made to reduce or eliminate interest costs that are associated with the corresponding loan and note. In many cases, the making of prepayments initiates a small charge to the maker. Such charges are not ruled by the courts to be penalty charges and therefore are ruled to be legal.

Like any other type of commercial paper, the payee (the holder) of a promissory note may endorse the note and transfer it. An individual who receives the note from the endorser is refered to as a secondary party. All succeeding parties to which the note is transferred are referred to as secondary parties. If informed of dishonor of payment by the maker, secondary parties can be held liable to the present holder of a note. The holder has a choice of suing any of the former holders to the note. Obviously he will usually make a claim against the party whom he believes is most capable of making payment.

4.6.3 Drafts

A third type of commercial paper is a *draft*. A draft is sometimes referred to as a *bill of exchange*. A draft is a written order of one individual to another demanding an amount of money. The person who issues and signs the draft is referred to as the *drawer*. In issuing the draft the drawer usually demands that the person to whom he issues it, who is referred to as the *drawee or debtor,* pay the stated amount to a third party. This third party, who is referred to as the *payee* is commonly a bank at which the drawer has an account. The purpose of a draft is to require the debtor (the drawee) to pay the money he owes to the creditor (the drawer).

Drafts may be either sight drafts or time drafts. A *sight draft* is one that is payable on demand. Thus, the drawee has to make payment upon receipt of the draft. A *time draft* is one that is payable within a stipulated period of time. A certain type of time draft, referred to as a *trade acceptance,* is commonly used in the construction industry. A construction material supplier will often send a trade acceptance to a contractor when he sends material to him. Such a trade acceptance usually is payable within thirty days. Besides the legal remedies that the material supplier has upon the contractor's acceptance of the draft, the material supplier can often use the issuance of trade acceptances for the purpose of obtaining loans. He may also actually sell the trade acceptances as accounts receivable to a finance company.

A drawee does not have to accept a draft. However, his nonacceptance of the draft does not eliminate any claim that the drawer has against the drawee. In order to receive material or services, the drawee may have to accept a draft. This acceptance has to be in writing. Upon accepting the draft, the drawee admits to the debt and thus, becomes liable for its payment. The drawee's acceptance of the draft may be either a *general acceptance* or a *draft varying acceptance*. A general acceptance is one in which the drawee accepts the draft and does not impose any restrictions on it. On the other hand, a draft varying acceptance is one whereby the drawee imposes a restriction or change on the draft as stated by the drawer. For example, the drawee may stipulate that he will make payment within 60 days rather than 30 days as stipulated on the draft. Naturally, the drawer has the right not to accept the varied condition. However, if he accepts the variation, he is then bound by the changed conditions.

As is true of all commercial paper, the draft can be endorsed and transferred. A drawer might transfer his right to payment from a drawee to another party. If this occurs, the drawer becomes secondarily liable. That is, if the drawee, who is primarily liable, fails to make payment of the draft, the drawer becomes secondarily liable to the party who holds the draft.

4.7 Employment And Subcontractor Relationships

Besides criminal and tort law, contract law, and commercial paper law, several other areas of law affect the construction industry. Included in these areas are company legal organization law, tax law, and laws pertaining to employment and contractor–subcontractor relationships.

The legal structure of a firm is dicussed in Chapter 2, and tax laws are discussed intermittently throughout various chapters. The purpose of this section is to discuss various legal aspects of employment practices and the contractor–subcontractor relationships.

In the normal contractor–owner relationship the contractor is ruled to be an *independent* contractor rather than an agent of the owner. The legal difference is that an independent contractor is ruled to be acting free from the control of the owner, whereas an agent works under the control of the owner. An agent can make contracts with third parties on behalf of the owner. As a result, the owner can be held for various types of liabilities in an owner–agent relationship that he cannot be held liable for in a owner–independent contractor relationship.

The employee of a contractor may be one of several types. He may be a union laborer in which case the laborer is neither an agent or an independent contractor. Yet another contractor employee may be a job superintendent who has legal authority to be an agent of the contractor. On the other hand, the contractor–subcontractor relationship is often of the type such that the subcontractor is an independent contractor.

Similar to the distinction between an agent and an independent contractor is the distinction between an ordinary laborer or material man and a subcontractor. The Miller Act defines a subcontractor to mean one who performs for and takes from the prime contractor a specific part of the labor or material requirements of the original construction contract.[5]

4.7.1 Employment Law

When an employee of a contractor is a laborer, both parties have traditionally been guided by the various employee laws in determining the benefits that the laborer is to receive. Minimum wage laws require a certain minimum wage. In addition, the Davis Bacon Act requires that labor on a federal construction job is to be paid the prevailing wage rate of the immediate area.

Recent years has seen enactment of several employment acts and programs that affect the relationship between the construction firm and its employees. These employees include union craftsmen.

The most widely publized of the employment acts is the Civil Rights Act of 1964. In effect this act makes it unlawful to fail or refuse to hire or to discharge any individual, or otherwise to discriminate against any individual with respect to his compensation terms, and conditions or privileges of employment because of such individual's race, color, religion, sex, or national origin. In addition it is unlawful to limit, segregate, or classify employees in any way that deprives any individual of employment opportunities because of such individual's race, color, religion, sex, or national origin.

These discrimination laws do not only apply to the construction firm in its employment of labor. In addition it is unlawful for a labor organization, such as a construction craft union, to exclude or expel

---

[5]Colby, E. G., *Practical Legal Advice for Builders and Contractors*, Englewood Cliffs, Prentice-Hall, 1972, p. 191.

from its membership, or otherwise to discriminate against, any individual because of race, color, religion, sex, or national origin.

If a court finds an employer, such as a construction firm, guilty of an intentional violation of the Civil Rights Act, it has a wide range of potential remedies including injunction, damages, required hiring, and the awarding of back pay. This last remedy can be particularly burdensome to the employer.

The construction firm is under increasing pressure to hire minorities. Through an *Executive Order*, government contractors and subcontractors are required to maintain detailed *affirmative action programs*. It is not sufficient that the contractor shows the intention to comply with both the letter and spirit of the equal employment opportunity program. As a practical matter, the contractor is forced to be "Quota conscious" in hiring.

Numerous other employer–employee labor acts are on the books. Included are the Equal Pay Act and the Age Discrimination in Employment Act. Most of these acts are widely publicized to the point where noncompliance is usually intentional. The labor unions have a way of policing the construction firms for possible violation of any employer–employee act.

Construction labor injuries are almost universally covered by workmen's compensation statutes. The first of these state laws was passed in 1913 in Wisconsin, and today almost every state has workmen's compensation laws. The effect of these laws is that the question of who is negligent, the worker or the employer, is removed in regard to payment for the worker's injuries. That is, compensation for the worker's injury is paid by an independent fund which is financed by employers' payments. A complete discussion of workmen's compensation laws is beyond the scope of this book.

4.7.2 General Contractor–Subcontractor Law

The legal relationship between a project's prime contractor and subcontractors is often complex and may vary from one project to the next. Part of this variation in legal relationship is due to the fact that in some projects the prime contractor selects the subcontractors whereas in other projects the subcontractors may have to meet the approval of the project owner or may be even contracted directly by the owner. The complexity and variability of the contractor–subcontractor relation-ship makes it difficult to cover the entire legal area in detail. As such, only a few somewhat general legal contractor–subcontractor liabilities and relationships are discussed.

The most normal contractor–subcontractor relationship is one in which the prime contractor enters into a contract with a subcontractor to perform part of the work of a construction project. Upon performing his contracted work, the subcontractor is paid the contracted amount of money. As in the case of the payment from the owner to the prime contractor, the subcontractor normally receives payment from the prime contractor in relation to the percentage of his work completed.

Unless the owner directly hires the subcontractor by such a means as *separate-but-equal contracts*, only the prime contractor is said to be *in privity* with the owner. Privity of contract is a term that denotes a legal right of contracted duties or subject matter. When a project's subcontractors are hired by the prime contractor, there is no privity of contract between the project owner and the subcontractors. As such, the subcontractor usually cannot sue the owner when the owner causes a delay in the project work. Only the prime contractor (commonly referred to as the general contractor) has legal remedies against the owner if such a delay occurs. Naturally, the subcontractor has privity of contract with the prime contractor when he is hired by the prime con-tractor.

When the subcontractor contracts with a prime contractor, the con-tract liabilities of each of the parties are similar to those that exists when a prime contractor contracts with a project owner. However, whereas there is seldom a conflict between the owner and prime contractor as to what work the contractor is to perform, the problem as to who is to do what is a common prime contractor–subcontractor legal dispute.

Typical functions and responsibilities that often are disputed as to whether the prime contractor or subcontractor is to perform are as follows.

(1) Who is responsible for various phases of project cleanup.
(2) When are progress schedules due and to whom are they to be given (that is, is the subcontractor to make such reports to the owner or to the prime contractor).
(3) Who is to provide various project storage facilities.
(4) Who is responsible for obtaining permits and licenses.
(5) Who is to provide various required safety facilities and pro-grams.

The responsibilities and liabilities of each of the parties should be clearly stated in the contract agreement. A well-written contract is often worth many times the expense of a lawyer's fee for aiding in the writing of the contract. When in fact there is a dispute as to whether the prime contractor or the subcontractor is to perform various work items, the provisions of the contract prevail.

The prime contractor might fail to perform a certain aspect of his project work resulting in the subcontractor not being able to perform his contracted work. When such is the case, the prime contractor is held liable for damages suffered by the subcontractor. In addition, if the subcontractor is delayed in performing his work due to an act of the prime contractor, the courts usually rule that a stated time of completion clause is negated.

In regard to worker injuries, the prime contractor is responsible for keeping the project site in a safe condition for the use of the employees of any subcontractor who are working on the project site. This rule is only in effect when the general contractor is in possession and control of the premises awarded to him by the owner. If he is, then he is liable for the worker's injuries if he is negligent. Obviously, if a worker is injured due to the subcontractors negligence then the subcontractor, not the prime contractor, is liable. If the prime contractor makes workmen's compensation payments for such a worker, the subcontractor is liable to the prime contractor for such payments.

A prime contractor might receive compensation from a subcontractor for allowing the subcontractor to use his equipment on the prime contractor's project. If such is the case, and an employee of the subcontractor is injured while using the equipment as a result of the prime contractor's failure to keep the equipment safe, the prime contractor is liable for the injury. On the other hand, the subcontractor might use the prime contractor's equipment without receiving permission from the prime contractor. When this is the case, the prime contractor is no longer liable for injuries resulting from the contractor's failure to maintain the equipment. The courts rule that the subcontractor using the equipment is a *licensee* and is not entitled to damages occurred as a result of negligence of the owner of the equipment.

4.8 Summary

This chapter has attempted to relate business law to the everyday business of the construction industry. The reader should not come to the conclusion that upon reading this chapter that he is now a competent lawyer totally capable of handling all his legal affairs. Law is a very large, complex, and changing field of study. Law cases and court judgments concerning the construction industry alone would fill thousands of volumes of books.

However, the fact that the contractor is not capable of handling all of his legal matters does not eliminate the urgency for his knowledge of law fundamentals as they effect his everyday business. Such knowledge can often prevent his involvement in legal disputes and therefore eliminate his need for expensive legal advice and representation. Such legal costs have to be absorbed as an overhead cost and therefore cut into the contractor's profit margin.

Law that affects the nonbusinessmen also affects the contractor. That is, the contractor is not exempt from criminal and tort actions such as negligence, forgery, and fraud.

More frequent in occurrence in the contractor's everyday business are legal disputes arising as a result of his contracts, commercial paper transactions, and relationships with other industry parties such as the subcontractor. A contract must have four legal requirements in order to be valid. It must contain an agreement, competent parties, legal subject matter, and exchange (consideration).

There are several types of commercial paper which the contractor may negotiate. The most widely used commercial paper is a check. Other types include drafts and promissory notes.

The legal relationship between a prime contractor and his employees and project subcontractors varies somewhat from one project to the next. The written contract provides the means by which the relationships of the parties is determined. When a dispute arises, the written documents prevail.

Case 4.1 Newcon Construction Company: Contract Liabilities

The Newcon Construction Company has decided to join an increasing number of general contracting firms that have started to offer construction management services. Such services center around providing the owner his project in a short period of time and a low if not minimum cost.

In the past the Newcon Company has signed the traditional owner-general contractor contract whereby the construction firm agreed to build the owner's project for a stipulated lump sum of money. When forced to, Newcon would also agree to a stated completion time and in several cases agree to a liquidated damage clause.

One of the reasons Newcon Company decided to start offering construction management services centered around the potential of limited liability. Several firms offering construction management services, especially architects, typically have no liability to deliver to the owner the project at a specific price or time period. On the other hand, many general contracting firms providing construction management services do contract for a specific cost and time in which to deliver the project.

Naturally Newcon was free to determine what they wanted to agree to in offering its services. While it was not afraid to take on some liability as to its services, its objectives were to reduce the liability it had in its typical owner–general contractor contract. The firm did recognize that in order to obtain clients it would likely have to bend to many of the owners' demands as to liability. Perhaps after it builds a reputation, the firm could be more selective in limiting its liabilities.

Contract cost and time are not the only considerations that must be analyzed as to what Newcon will commit itself to as to liabilities. Additionally the construction management contract should be clear as to liability for possible violations of safety acts (i.e., OSHA), labor disputes, who has final say so as to substantial completion of the project (i.e., the construction manager or the architect), etc. In general, the Newcon Company has to decide what specifically should be included in its contract for construction management services.

In order to avoid costly lawsuits, you are asked to aid the firm in being precise in stating what liabilities the firm will have and what it promises to do as its part of the bilateral contract. The ability to obtain clients should be considered in structuring such a contract.

Case 4.2 Signa Construction Company:
Commercial Paper Procedures

The Signa Construction Company has had an increasing number of disputes arising with its bank and third parties as to checks it has written and checks it has received. These disputes have centered on discrepancies between amounts written on checks signed by Signa and what was entered into the firm's disbursement book. Additionally some checks that have been written by the firm seem to have become lost, and forged by a party other than the intended payee.

As to checks received by the firm, several times the firm has endorsed the check, only to later lose the check before depositing it at the bank. The end result has been that several of these checks have been found and cashed by an outside party.

Signa is a relatively small firm with an annual volume of around two million dollars of work. The firm is made up of three owners. Jim Payco is president and serves as office manager. Mr. Fields and Mr. Esco are in charge of project estimating and project supervision respectively.

Mike Fields' wife serves as a part-time bookkeeper working on Tuesdays and Thursdays. She typically is responsible for making the payroll, and signing checks for amounts of invoices. She is not particularly well versed in construction field operations or in numerous payment terms available from material suppliers. While Mrs. Fields does not endorse incoming checks, she does deliver them to the bank for deposit every Thursday afternoon.

Occasionally in the absence of Mrs. Fields, Mr. Esco has had to write checks for material purchases. While some of these checks are mailed directly to the material supplier, they are occasionally left at the main desk of the firm when it is known that a given material supplier will be visiting the office.

Both Jim Payco and Mr. Fields endorse incoming checks. Typically Mr. Payco merely places his signature on the back of the check. Because he is often out of the office, he typically endorses the checks upon receipt such that they can be later deposited by Mrs. Fields.

You are asked to aid the Signa Construction Company in eliminating its difficulties as to incoming and outgoing checks. Your advice should include specific routes for both incoming and outgoing checks, pinpointing authority for signing and endorsing, and specific terminology and wordings used in signing and endorsing the checks.

Case 4.3 Employ Construction Company:
Employment Practices

Employ Construction Company is considering bidding more government work. The company has become aware of strict employment laws governing government construction work.

The company has been in business for over five years. It has enjoyed substantial financial success. Much of this success has been based on the type of employer–employee relationship that the firm has been able to obtain.

Employ has employed nonunion construction workers. While paying these workers about one dollar less than the union scale rate in the immediate geographic area, the firm has continued to obtain higher than average productivity by offering the workers fringe benefits and in several cases, a guaranteed number of work hours per week.

Many of the craftsman that the firm has hired have been in their thirties or late twenties. Employ has found that workers at this age are the most productive.

Employ's craftsman are with one exception caucasian. One black man, age forty-eight was hired within the past year. He is a skilled ironworker. However because of some recent racial problems between the other ironworkers and the minority worker, Employ has found it necessary to have the minority worker work with the laborers. While performing laborer type work, he is paid the higher ironworker wage rate.

Employ is concerned in keeping the minority worker happy. Basically he was hired to satisfy some of the demands of the local affirmative action board in the community. The local union hall consists of about 12% minority workers. To keep the minority worker happy and to discourage him from wanting to join the union, Employ has repeatedly overlooked his tardiness and nonproductive characteristics.

As to office personnel, they consist of seven individuals. Two of these individuals are assigned to the bookkeeping and accounting function. One of the two, a young female accounting graduate, was hired at the same time as her male counterpart. She is paid an annual salary of $8,000 versus the male's salary of $11,500. The firm knew she would accept the lower salary in that her husband is employed in the city and jobs for female accountants are scarce in the city.

Within the last six months, the firm has had to terminate one office worker. While he was productive at his position, an estimator, he was in a continuous dispute with the other office workers and company owners over his nationality and religion. He was of Polish birth and a Roman Catholic. Office personnel were all of German backgrounds, and each and every one was a Lutheran. It is no coincidence that the three owners of the firm are also German and Lutheran. The constant ribbing of the Polish worker finally led to an uncontrollable situation and the worker resigned under pressure.

Employ Company never has been concerned with its employment practices. It's main concern has been productivity, and it has been successful in obtaining higher than average productivity. What types of practices will Employ have to eliminate in the future. Specifically set out a program of hiring and promotion that will be consistent with labor law.

Chapter 5

Funding: Financing Business Operations

5.1 Introduction

Financing for projects and operations is one of the contractor's greatest concerns. Historically, contractors operate on a small profit margin with little working capital to carry them from job to job. This is the case because of retainages carried through a job that may last several years, large payrolls that must be met every week, and receipts that generally occur only once a month. Most contractors find, because of these factors, that it is necessary to obtain some sort of short term financing from time to time. The tasks of budgeting, cash flow, and determining financing are needed by the contractor.

In addition to the need for cash for financing of project costs, the contractor may need cash for the financing of equipment purchases and for financing planned company growth. Cash for these purposes is usually required for a longer period of time than cash required for project cash flow.

The term *fund* has several different meanings in the business world. As is noted in Chapter 9 on accounting practices the term fund is often used to mean the net working capital of the firm. As is explained in this latter chapter, net working capital is merely the difference between a firm's current assets and its current liabilities. As such in this context, the term "fund" relates to such items as cash, accounts receivable, and accounts payable.

To the nonaccountant, the term "fund" generally has a more limited meaning. That is, the term "fund" is often used merely as a substitute for cash. This is consistent with the use of the term in this chapter. As such, the use of the words cash and funds can be interchanged in reading this chapter. Similarly, the term *funding* will be used to refer to the obtaining of cash or funds.

Funding requirements are often classified as to the period of time for which the funds are obtained. Thus, funding is often classified as to short term, intermediate term, or long term. There really is no clear-cut line between what is a short term funding and what is an intermediate term funding or as to what is an intermediate term funding and a long term funding. However, for purposes of discussion it is useful to differentiate funding as to short, intermediate, or long term. For our purposes we will consider short term financing to be of less than one year duration, intermediate financing to be of duration from one to ten years, and long term financing to be of duration greater than ten years.

The contractor may have a choice of several types of funding for the various periods of time for which he needs them. In this chapter, the availability of various types of financing, the extent used, and the most desirable types of funding for various situations are discussed.

5.2 Short Term Financing

Short term financing is usually identified with a contractor's need for funds for the payment of costs associated with the building of a construction project. Typically the construction firm receives payment for its work from the project owner after the construction firm has incurred the costs of doing the work.

Many project owners finance their projects by means of two loans: a *construction loan* and a *long term mortgage loan*. A construction loan typically provided by a bank, provides money for the owner to pay costs of construction during construction. Once the project is complete, the owner obtains a long term mortgage loan that is used to cover the construction loan. Such a mortgage loan will typically cover a period of twenty to thirty years and can be obtained from a savings and loan company or in some cases a bank. Typically the construction loan is more difficult to obtain and has a high interest rate in that the lending institution bears a risk of owning an incomplete asset should the owner default on a mortgage loan. On the other hand, upon borrower default the long term lending institution becomes owner of the completed building. Such an asset can usually be sold without any financial burden to the lending institution.

The construction loan provides the project owner the means of paying the construction firm for its services. When a payment is due, the payment is made by means of a *draw* account on the construction loan. Should the project be a residential unit, the determination of the amount and timing of the payments to the construction firm are somewhat standard. For example, once the foundation work is judged complete, the construction firm may be entitled to 20% of the cost of the residential unit.

The payment to the construction firm for projects other than residential usually are based on regularly occurring progress reports and a owner *retainage clause*. For example a contract may read that the construction firm is to be paid at the end of every month for the work judged to be completed at the end of the previous month. However the owner is to retain 10% of each payment until the project is completed. This "holding back" of a part of the payment is intended to ensure that the project is completed according to specifications.

Regardless of whether the construction firm is involved in building a residential unit or performing commercial, industrial, and heavy and highway construction, the firm typically receives its revenue after the incurrence of a cost liability. This liability may in fact have to be paid before the revenue is received. The end result is that the firm has a need for short term financing.

The analysis of a contractor's costs versus his revenues throughout the building of a project is often identified as a *cash flow* analysis. Cash flow is discussed in Chapter 7. In this chapter we are assuming that there is a cash flow shortage and the discussion centers around how to obtain the needed cash, not why the cash shortage occurred. Thus, in the following sections we will be concerned about the sources, and appropriateness of types of short term financing. The common types of short term financing include trade credit, and loans from a bank or other commercial lending institutions. Other sources of obtaining short term financing include the use of a credit line at a bank, the sale of accounts receivable, loans from officers, friends, customers, or suppliers, or loans from the Small Business Administration.

It should be noted that short term financing as it relates to the construction industry is used for financing associated with the building of a construction project. The financing relates to current assets and current liabilities. The conversion of the current assets, in particular cash, into construction projects are the means by which the contractor generates profit. Because of its relation to the exchange of current assets, short term financing is sometimes referred to as *working capital* financing.

5.3 Trade Credit

Probably the major source of short term financing available to the contractor is the credit extended by material suppliers. This form of financing is referred to as *trade credit*. Although it is difficult to document the actual usage of trade credit it would indeed be a rare event to find a contractor who did not take advantage of some sort of trade credit.

Trade credit is the credit extended by a seller to a buyer of goods that the buyer will ultimately resell. This definition excludes the credit given to a contractor for the purchase of equipment, in that the intent of the contractor is to use the equipment, not resell it. In addition, trade credit does not include common credit in that this form of credit relates to goods for consumption rather than resale.

Trade credit is especially relevant to the construction contractor in that the contractor is a major purchaser of material when building a construction project. In addition, the relatively small size of the average contractor is related to the wide usage of trade credit in the construction industry. It has been shown that smaller firms make a greater usage of trade credit than larger firms. This is evidenced by the fact that a study has shown that firms with assets of less than $1 million financed 17.4% of their assets with trade credit, whereas firms with assets greater than $1 billion used trade credit to finance only 6.9% of their assets.[1] Whereas large firms usually only borrow under favorable conditions, small firms including the average contractor, often have to rely on trade credit when short term money is too expensive to obtain.

Trade credit differs from other means of financing, such as bank loans, in that one may not have to pay added costs associated with its use. If all available cash discounts are taken, the use of trade credit adds no cost. For this reason, it is desirable to take advantage of this form of credit. One pays something extra only upon failure to take advantage of the discount.

The arrangement between the purchaser of material and the supplier does not always allow for a cash discount. For example, the trade terms may be Cash Before Delivery (C.B.D.) or Cash On Delivery (C.O.D.) Cash terms usually allow an extension of several days for payment. A typical extension is seven days. This in effect is a means of credit.

[1]Federal Trade Commission and Securities and Exchange Commission, *Quarterly Financial Report for Manufacturing Corporations*, 1st quarter, 1970, pp. 12–33.

A more common trade arrangement between a contractor and a supplier is referred to as *ordinary terms*. Such an arrangement provides for a cash discount if the bill is paid within a stated number of days, such as 10 days. The payment must be paid before another stipulated period, such as 30 days, or else a penalty interest charge is imposed. Such an arrangement, assuming a 2% cash discount, is designated as 2/10, n/30. If the material is shipped from a distant location or the shipment is slow, the terms may be 2/10, n/30 A.O.G. (arrival of goods).

Another somewhat frequently used form of trade arrangement is the use of *monthly billings*. This arrangement is especially advantageous when it is difficult or uneconomical to keep track of the cash discounts on each transaction. The monthly billing arrangement allows the purchaser to take advantage of a cash discount for all his purchases in a given month, if the payment is made by a given date of the following month. For example, the terms 2/10, E.O.M. n/30 provides for a 2% discount on all material purchased in April, if the bill is paid by the 10th of May. In addition, the entire bill must be paid by the end of May or a penalty charge is imposed.

Less widely used trade arrangements (especially in the construction industry) are the use of seasonal dating or the use of consignments. Seasonal dating trade arrangements pertain to the terms resulting from a supplier's intent to encourage purchasers to send in orders for seasonal goods before the period of peak sales. Consignment trade arrangements refer to the supplier's willingness to grant the purchaser credit for the entire period that the purchaser holds the goods before the purchaser sells the supplies or receives money for their usage.

5.3.1 Trade Credit and the Contractor

The relationship between the contractor and the material supplier should be one of trust. This is because each depends on the other for their making of a profit; therefore, it cannot be one of untrustworthy actions. There has to be a great deal of mutual understanding with much give and take on both sides.

Most material suppliers, regardless of the outward appearance, are rather large dollar volume sized with an annual gross volume of around one million dollars or more. A substantial percentage of their sales are to governmental agencies such as the city, county, and state, for their construction projects; but with 55% to 60% of their sales to private contractors on private jobs. Also reported in their sales figures are what is called "supplier intersale." Supplier intersale is used if a particular supplier is caught short of material and is forced to purchase a similar product from a competitor. There is nothing illegal about selling a specified product to a contractor which was purchased from another supplier. Also as far as competition goes, one does not have to sell to another supplier. If this is done and the supplier's underrun is very serious, a supplier could possibly attract his customer to its side, but as far as many suppliers are concerned, they do not need his business nor do they want it, they are often busy enough themselves. Plus if one supplier helps another, the one supplier will often come to the other's aid at another point in time.

The financial arrangements between a contractor and a material supplier are very much standardized throughout the industry. The more common arrangements consist of ordinary credit and monthly billings. Generally as far as actual numbers are concerned, most suppliers give a 2% discount for cash payment. Cash here does not mean greenbacks over the counter at delivery, but payment of the debt within fifteen days from the date of delivery. This practice is commonly called two in fifteen and is a very widely used instrument to attract early payment of the balance due. It should be noted here that this 2% is from the quoted price and not from the list price of the material in question. A word later on the difference of the list price to the quoted price. On any unpaid debt left on the books after fifteen days and paid before the thirtieth day there is no difference from the quoted price. This again is used as an inducement to pay the debt early for after thirty days, a 1.5% service charge per month is levied against the unpaid balance. This service charge is not used for the cost of carrying the debt on the books for there is hardly any expense in that, but is used in consideration of the time value of the money game. It works something like this: After a large order has been shipped, the supplier must replenish any depleted stock. This takes money for materials, labor, and overhead. To get this money the supplier may be forced to borrow money which must be paid back with interest. Another alternative may be for him to use his own capital which he must remove from some other area which is providing him with some opportunity interest which he now forfeits. To make either of the above methods economically practical a service charge must be raised to provide some security and financial gain to the supplier for either risking his own money and forfeiting his interest gain or having to borrow money at some interest rate.

There are exceptions to every rule and the supplying business is no exception. If a contractor has dealt regularly for some time with a certain supplier and paid his debts on time, the supplier, relying on previous experience, may take over some of the risk of the debt and waive the 1.5% charge in an expression of good faith while also hoping to keep the customer for many years to come. The supplier rationalizes this action by stating that the loss of the 1.5% is more than compensated for by having this person become or stay a repeat customer. This practice is not a "seat of the pants" decision for before any contractor is extended credit or given a 1.5% waive he must have on file at the suppliers office a completed credit approval form. This is to give the supplier some security in extending credit.

Other typical terms of material suppliers are as follows: A lumber company: 5% discount if paid within 10 days, net in 30 days, 1% per month is charged on the unpaid balance. A concrete material supplier: material delivered between the 1st and the 15th, accounts due the 25th of the month. Material delivered the 16th thru the 30th, accounts due the 10th of the following month, 1.5% per month interest is charged on the unpaid balance. A steel corporation: 5% discount if paid in 10 days, net in 30 days, 6% per year interest on unpaid balance.

As can be seen, material suppliers do extend some free credit, varying from ten to thirty days. The contractor is wise to take advantage of this free credit as much as possible to keep his working capital at a maximum. The actual dollar value savings received from taking advantage of trade credit are discussed in the following section.

As was previously mentioned there is a difference between the quoted and list prices of a supplier's materials. A *trade discount* is used for many varied reasons under many different conditions. The discount ranges anywhere from 5% to 40% off the list price. Therefore the price given with the discount is the seller's quoted price. The primary reason for the discount is that among suppliers of the same material the list prices are almost exactly the same and so to compete for business the discount method is used. The amount of the discount varies with the time a contractor has been with a particular supplier; with the highest discounts being given to the oldest customers with good financial backing. The important aspect of the mutual understanding relationship is that these discounts can often spell the difference between a profitable or unprofitable construction project.

5.3.2 The Cost of Trade Credit

The failure to take trade discounts results in an interest rate associated with the use of trade credit. The effective interest rate varies depending on the terms of the supplier, and the time at which the payment is made. For example, let us assume a contractor purchases $1,000 of plumbing materials from a supplier on terms of 2/10, n/30. If the contractor pays the bill on or before the 10th day he only pays $980, thus, saving $20. However, if paid after the 10th day the contractor has to pay the extra $20. Let us assume that the contractor pays the $1,000 on the 30th day (thus avoiding a further penalty cost). In effect the contractor is using the supplier's money for 30 days. The effective interest rate for the last 20 days is 20/980, and there are 365/20 20-day intervals during the year. The true annual interest rate of missing the cash discount and paying the bill on the 30th day is

$$\frac{20}{980} \times \frac{365}{20} = 0.3724 \text{ or } 37.24\%$$

If the contractor were to miss the discount (pay after the 10th day) but paid before the 30th day his effective interest rate would in fact be more than the rate previously computed. This should be obvious in that the contractor is paying the $1,000 prior to when it is due. Thus, the contractor is losing an opportunity to use the money, which results in a higher interest rate. The effective interest rate for payment on any day after the discount day and before the penalty date can be calculated by multiplying the effective interest rate for the total period, 20/980, by the ratio determined by 365 days divided by the number of days beyond the discount date. For example, let us assume that the contractor paid the $1,000 bill on the 20th day, 10 days after the discount date. The effective interest rate associated with not taking advantage of the discount is calculated as follows:

$$\frac{20}{980} \times \frac{365}{10} = 0.7448 \text{ or } 74.48\%$$

Note that this effective interest rate is double the rate associated with paying the bill on the 30th day.

It should also be noted that if the contractor pays a bill before the discount date, he is in effect paying an added cost in that he is providing his cash to the supplier before it is due. Thus, the contractor should either pay his supplier on the discount date or on the day before a penalty charge is imposed. Of course the discount date is preferable.

5.4 Short Term Loans

Next to trade credit, short term bank loans are the most widely used short term financing for a business firm. Short term bank loans are used extensively by the manufacturing industry. Typical manufacturing firms who make abundant use of short term bank loans are construction contractors, the apparel industry, and leather product firms. On the other hand, large manufacturing firms such as steel companies use very little short term loan bank credit. This is mainly due to the fact that such large firms are less dependent on the need for current assets, in particular cash.

Short term bank loans are often unsecured. However, the borrower may have to pledge or sell some of his assets as security, in which case the loan is *secured*. Commercial banks are the major source of secured and unsecured short term loans. Finance companies are another source of these loans. Finance companies may be of several types. A consumer finance company usually only gives small loans to individuals. Commercial finance companies give loans to a company in return for the company's pledge of accounts receivable or inventory. Factors are finance companies that deal only in granting loans for accounts receivable security.

The security that banks or finance companies require companies borrowing money to pledge may be cash, inventory, or accounts receivable. Banks may require a borrower to provide cash security by means of having the right to *offset* against any deposits the borrower has in the bank. The bank's advantage from having a right to offset are explained by the following: Let us assume that after having obtained a $10,000 short term loan from a bank, a contracting firm has the following balance sheet.

Cash in bank $ 5,000	Bank loan $10,000
Fixed assets 35,000	Accounts payable 10,000
$40,000	Capital 20,000
	$40,000

If the contractor is forced to liquidate and the fixed assets bring $5,000, the bank's claim would be $5,000, calculated as follows.

Available	*Distribution*
Cash available $ 5,000	Bank loan $10,000 × .5 = $ 5,000
Cash from $ 5,000	Accounts payable $10,000 × .5 = $ 5,000
liquidation $10,000	$10,000

$$10,000/20,000 = 0.5$$

However, if the bank had the right to offset, upon contractor liquidation the bank would receive $6,667, calculated as follows.

| *Available* | | *Distribution* |

$$\text{Bank loan } \$\ 5,000 \times .333 = \$\ 1,667$$
$$+5,000$$

Cash from $5,000   Accounts receivable $10,000 × .333 = $\underline{\quad 3,333}$

liquidation $5,000 $\overline{\$10,000}$

$$5,000/15,000 = 0.333$$

Thus, upon the contractor's inability to repay the loan, the bank receives $1,667 more with the right to offset versus the situation where such a right does not exist.

When inventory is required as security for a short term loan, the amount of money loaned is often a percentage of the inventory. For example, a lender may have a policy of lending up to 70% of the inventory value of the borrower. The inventory that is used as security may be kept in the possession of the borrower, or it may be held by a third party. The difficulty associated with an agreement whereby the borrower keeps possession occurs when the borrower manipulates the inventory in a manner that reduces the required security inventory. Such a situation places the lender in a weak position. For this reason the lender may require the borrower to place the inventory in the possession of a third party where it is controllable and under the supervision of the lender.

A borrower may also provide security for a loan by assigning accounts receivable to the lender. The lender, as with the inventory, will usually only loan a percentage of the value of the assigned accounts receivable. This percentage is usually higher for commercial finance companies than it is for commercial banks. For example, a typical commercial finance company may loan 80% of the accounts receivable, whereas a typical commercial bank would more likely loan about 75%.[2]

Other forms of collateral used for security include securities, mortgages on the borrower's residential property, and passbooks on savings accounts. Stocks and bonds are other sources of collateral. To be used as security, they must be marketable. Banks will usually borrow no more than 75% of the market value of quality stocks, and 90% on Federal municipal bonds.[3] Life insurance may also be an acceptable form of collateral. Banks normally will lend up to the cash value of such a policy.

Because of their weak financial condition, a borrower may get another individual to sign a loan note to strengthen the borrower's

---

[2]Johnson, R. W., *Financial Management*, Boston, Allyn and Bacon, 1971, p. 293.
[3]Ibid., pp. 297–298.

credit. The individual who signs such a note is referred to as an endorser, and he becomes contingently liable for the note. An endorser may be a co-maker of a note, or he may be a guarantor. A *co-maker* is an individual who creates an obligation jointly with a borrower. He becomes equally liable with the borrower for the loan. A *guarantor* is one who guarantees payment upon default of the borrower.

In addition to requiring collateral, a bank upon making a loan to a borrower, may place restrictions on certain management practices of the borrower. For example, the lender may limit the dividends that a borrower can pay out to stockholders while the loan is outstanding.

As previously noted, short term loans are referred to as short term financing in that the loans are obtained for a period of a year or less. Yet another description of short term loans is that they are repaid within the normal course of business. For most industries these descriptions are consistent in that the normal business cycle is usually one year or less. However, in the case of a building project that takes several years to construct, the business cycle (the project duration) will be a period greater than one year. In such a case, the financing for the project is referred to as short term financing.

A short term loan from a bank may be in the form of a single loan or it may be a result of an arrangement referred to as a *credit line*. A credit line is an informal agreement between a bank and borrower as to the maximum amount the bank will lend the borrower at any point in time. The agreement is not legally binding on the bank. The bank often imposes a fee for a firm committment to keep a credit line for a borrower. This is especially the case when money is tight.

A credit line is usually reviewed annually by the bank. In addition, many commercial banks require borrowers to keep some percentage of the credit line as a deposit in the bank. This deposit is referred to as a *compensating balance*. The compensating balance requirement has the effect of increasing the borrower's effective interest rate associated with his bank loans. Finally, several commercial banks require a borrower to annually reduce his debt to zero in order to maintain a credit line for the next year. This annual elimination of debts is referred to as *cleaning up the credit line*.

5.4.1 Bank Loans and the Contractor

The first and foremost avenue for the contractor to consider for a short term loan is his local bank. Initially, a contractor is wise to do business through his various accounts with a large bank. The bank and the contractor need to have a mutual trust and familiarity for each other. A contractor will do well to have his business all in one bank and to build a good reputation with his particular bank.

Short term contractor financing through a bank may be secured with collateral or unsecured. Banks are extremely careful about lending money to contractors. One reason is that contractors, in general, have been found to be bad risks. Because of the many variables involved with a large project, it is difficult to determine whether a loan may be considered safe by the bank. Another reason for the reluctance of banks to make loans on large projects is because of the uniqueness of the product. Most new construction, excluding homes and most warehouses, are unique products that do not have a readily large market. A large office building, for example, might need modifications and would cost a bank a large amount of money if they had to sell it. A bank that gets involved in the financing of large projects may very well have more invested in the project than the contractor. If, for some reason, there is a default on the loan, the bank not only incurs losses in trying to sell the product, but also opportunities lost because of the large amount of money invested in the project. In general, banks, as well as savings and loan associations, are more interested in housing loans with a 20% down payment and the home being a readily marketable product.

When a contractor goes to a bank or commercial lending institution for a loan, the bank will base its analysis on several factors. Factors that the bank may consider are: risk involved with the particular project; reputation of the contractor; type of job and who the owner is; other types of similar work going on in the area; examination of documents, such as take–off sheets, CPM, profit percentage; current financial statements of the contractor; the workload the contractor is presently engaged in; and the ability of the contractor to perform the work involved. Before extending any type of financing to a contractor, a bank will do an analysis involving the above-mentioned factors. The process of financing should not be viewed as trying to "trick" the institution into lending the money. The contractor should present his needs and reasoning, as well as showing the safeness of the loan, to commercial lending departments in a professional manner. Financing should be viewed as an exchange of information and resources the contractor showing potential with the banker showing his available dollars. A bank will base its decision on fairly reliable concrete facts. A large lending institution will be involved in what is going on in the area and will probably have more facts available to them than the contractor in their financial decision analysis. A refusal for a loan for a particular project may, in the long run, save the contractor problems, as well as money.

In evaluating the feasibility of giving a loan to a contractor, a banker may also evaluate the firm by means of financial or *operating* ratios. These ratios were discussed in Chapter 2. A working capital ratio of 2 to 1 and a quick ratio of 1.25 to 1 are usually considered acceptable.[4] Ideally, the contractor should have on hand working capital that is 10% to 20% of the value of his ongoing projects.

The most common form of short term financing from a bank is the 90 day loan. A bank may be willing to loan up to the net worth of a company. A typical rate might be 9.5% interest, plus direct costs involved with the loan. Construction loans do carry a higher interest rate than other commercial loans. A contractor is wise to take advantage of the short term financing from material suppliers and then to borrow from insurance policies before going to a bank, because of the high interest rate.

A contractor may obtain a credit line from a bank of $100,000 or more. Many contractors can only obtain a credit line which is a small percentage of this value.

5.4.2 Cost of Short Term Loans

The interest rate charged by banks for short term loans is very dependent on the prime rate of interest and the availability of money. The *prime rate* is the interest rate banks pay for money. When money is tight, the spread between the prime rate and the interest rate charged to borrowers from banks increases. Commonly, the interest rate for short term loans is about 1% in excess of the prime rate.

The interest rate on short term loans is also dependent on the size of the loan. The smaller the loan, the higher the rate; the reason for the higher interest rate for small loans is related to the fact that the bank has certain fixed costs associated with making a loan. For a small loan, these fixed costs make up a larger percentage of the loan, resulting in the banks charging a higher interest rate.

[4]Wolkstein, H. W., *Accounting Methods and Controls for the Construction Industry*, Englewood Cliffs, Prentice-Hall, 1967, pp. 96–97.

The effective interest rate actually paid by a borrower is dependent on the loan agreement. The simplest form of agreement is one where the borrower pays the lender an interest rate on the unpaid balance of the loan. Thus, a borrower upon making payment on a loan one year after receiving $5,000 at 8% a year would make a payment of $5,400. The 8% interest rate is in fact the effective interest rate.

A more common loan agreement used by banks is the *discounted* loan. The borrower signs a note promising the bank to pay $5,000 to the bank one year from now. The bank, assuming an interest rate of 8% takes out the interest charge in advance and thus gives the borrower $4,600 ($5,000−5,000 (.08)). The effective interest rate for this discounted loan is $400/$4,600 or approximately 8.7%.

Yet another common loan agreement is the installment loan. This type of loan is often combined with a discount agreement. For example, a borrower upon borrowing $5,000 at 8% a year would receive $4,600. The bank would then require the borrower to repay back the $5,000 in equal twelve month payments. Thus, at the end of each month the borrower would pay the bank $416.67. The effective interest rate for such a loan is considerably higher than the 8%. For one the loan is discounted. Secondly, the borrower does not have the use of the $4,600 for the entire year in that he repays it in twelve installments. An approximate effective interest rate for the loan can be calculated by dividing the interest charge by the average amount of money the borrower has from the loan. Thus, the approximate effective interest rate for the loan in question is $400/$2,300 or approximately 17.4%. A more accurate method of calculating the effective interest rate is given by the following formula,

$$i = \frac{2mD}{P(n + 1)}$$

where i is the effective annual interest rate, m is the number of payments in one year, D is the interest charge in dollars, P is the cash advance, and n is the total number of payments. For the example in question the effective annual interest rate is calculated as follows.

$$i = \frac{2(12)(400)}{4,600(12 + 1)} = 16.1\%$$

Regardless of whether the approximate or theoretically correct method is used, it can be seen that the effective interest rate is much greater than the 8%.

5.5 Other Sources of Short Term Funds

In addition to trade credit, and bank loans, other sources of short term funds available to the business firm include the sale of the firm's accounts receivable; loans from relatives, friends, customers, and suppliers; and loans from the Small Business Administration. These methods of obtaining funds are not looked upon highly in that they are often costly, and often result in bad public relations. However, in the absence of funds from other sources, a firm including a contractor may often turn to these less widely used sources of funds.

Several firms, rather than providing their accounts receivable as security, actually sell their accounts receivables to companies called *odd line factor* companies who purchase the accounts at a discount. The purchasing company then has the ownership and responsibility of collecting the accounts receivable. Obviously due to the effort and risk associated with making the collections, the factor charges a rather high interest and service charge for these services.

The construction contractor is usually not active in the selling of his accounts receivable. This practice is more widely used in an industry such as the textile industry which has wide seasonal variations in volume and accounts receivable.

Contractors often rely on loans from relatives and friends when starting their firm. However, as they become established they become less dependent on this source of loans. Loans from customers and suppliers are yet other sources. Trade credit is in fact a form of a loan from a supplier.

Another form of short term financing that is available to the small contractor is the loan from the Small Business Administration (SBA). The SBA was created by Congress in 1953. It was established to aid and stimulate small business. In regard to the construction industry, a contractor is classified as a small business if the annual receipts of the firm are not more than $5 million, averaged over a three year period. Because of the small size of most contractors, many of the existing firms are eligible for aid from the SBA. This aid often comes in the form of loans for working capital (short term loan).

Usually loans from the SBA are only available when other sources have been shown to be unavailable. The SBA is involved in giving out two types of loans. For one a borrower may be able to obtain a *direct loan* from the SBA. This type of loan is obtained directly from the SBA. A second and more frequent type of loan which a firm can obtain from the SBA is a *participation loan*. In a participation loan the SBA shares the loan with a bank or guarantees the portion of the loan provided by the bank. Thus, the small firm that is unable to provide security and thus cannot obtain a bank loan, by means of a guarantee from the SBA may find that such a loan becomes accessible. The SBA's interest rate for its position of a loan is set at a maximum.

Because of the contractor's inability to provide security for bank loans, SBA financing is often used by the construction industry. In addition to providing working capital loans, the SBA involves itself in loans for business expansion and for the purchasing of equipment. These loans are discussed in following sections.

5.6 Intermediate Term Financing

Intermediate term financing was previously described as financing that was arranged for a period of more than one but less than ten years duration. Intermediate term financing is frequently referred to as *term financing* or *term loans*. Because of the longer duration of the financing, intermediate loans are used for a different purpose than are short term loans. In particular, intermediate financing is associated with the purchase of machinery and equipment, and for the permanent increase in the firm's current assets such as material inventory. Unlike many short term loans, term loans are almost always secured by collateral of the borrowers. The required types of collateral are similar to those discussed for short term loans.

Term loans are repayed by means of monthly, quarterly, or yearly installment payments. They are *amortized* in the same manner as home mortgages, That is, the initial payments are almost entirely interest, resulting in little reduction in principal. Latter payments go more to reducing the loan principle. When a firm takes out a term loan it expects to repay the loan from profits generated from the usage of the newly acquired assets. Thus, the lender has to evaluate the firm's ability to generate these profits when determining the feasability of making such a loan. An evaluation of several consecutive income statements and balance sheets of the firm becomes a means of evaluating the risk of the loan.

One may question why term loans are chosen rather than short term loans when purchasing equipment. The most obvious reason is that the firm has to be certain of the availability of the funds. The firm cannot be assured of receiving continual short term loans from a bank. In addition to the changing financial structure of the firm, the bank's cost of making several loans rather than one, and the bank's uncertainty as to the availability of money would make future short term loans uncertain. In addition, the term loan often affects a firm's balance sheet in a more favorable manner. A term loan appears as a long term liability on the balance sheet, thus it doesn't totally influence the firm's current liabilities and this does not affect the firm's current ratio (current assets /current liabilities). A low current ratio often is a constraint to the firm's ability to obtain financing, especially term financing.

The sources of intermediate financing are somewhat different and more in number than the sources of short term loans. These sources are discussed in the following section.

5.6.1 Sources of Intermediate Financing

Banks do not play as dominant a role as a source of intermediate financing as they do for short term financing. Banks favor the giving of short term loans in that the giving of intermediate loans results in constraints upon the bank's deposit liabilities. However, the advent of the Federal Deposit Insurance Company has somewhat relieved the constraint, resulting in an increase in the frequency of banks supplying term financing.

Banks almost always require the term loan to be secured by assets. Because of the duration of the loan, the bank has to make safeguards against the borrower's use of the assets. This is done by placing a constraint upon the borrower which prevents him from selling certain fixed assets. In addition, the borrower is prevented from pledging the assets to another lender for the procurement of a loan.

In addition to constraints placed upon the borrower's assets, the bank also takes steps to ensure itself that the borrower will meet his installment payments on the term loan. This is often done by means of prohibiting the borrower from making withdrawals or paying dividends in excess of the amount that reduces the firm's net working capital or current ratio below a stated minimum.

A bank usually reserves the right to collect the entire loan before it is all due if the borrower fails to make an installment payment that is due. This is done by means of an *acceleration clause* in the loan agreement.

Although savings and loan associations do not make unsecured short term loans, they do provide term financing along with long term financing. Financing by savings and loan associations require real property as collateral. As such, savings and loan associations seldom aid in equipment financing.

A savings and loan is restricted by its national charter as to how much money may be invested in construction. A typical example is: they may invest 5% of savings in land development, 5% of assets in housing for the elderly, and 20% of their assets in apartments. A large savings and loan association has a tremendous amount of assets and is a good source of money for a contractor. However, since real property is required for collateral, loans are somewhat limited to owner—developers or contractors that are in some sort of legal partnership with the project owner.

As with banks, savings and loans have found contractors to be bad risks. As with the banks, savings and loans have found that most contractors do have the need for financing from time to time. These associations are less inclined to loan money for construction for two reasons: (1) higher risk, and (2) more work for the lender. The associations send out inspectors to see if the work is progressing as it should. The savings and loan associations require and check many of the same factors that a bank does before extending a loan. A typical savings and loan may consider these factors: audited financial statements, reputation, Dunn and Bradstreet report, credit reports, and risk of the particular project. The types of construction that most savings and loans may be involved in are: sales and service buildings, industrial, motels, churches, specific purpose (bowling lanes, etc.), medical and office, warehouses, mobil home parks, and nursing homes.

Savings and loan associations have maximum term loans of 25 years, with 15 to 20 years being their preferred amount of time. They may loan up to a maximum of 75% of appraised value of construction with this being raised to 80% if the construction is apartments that are finished and ready to lease. The rate typically varies from 8% to 10%.

As mentioned in a previous section of this chapter, the small sized contractor can turn to the Small Business Administration (SBA) for loans. In addition to supplying loans for use as working capital, the SBA is a source of loans for the purchasing of equipment. Thus, the SBA is yet another source of intermediate financing. However, as in the case of SBA working capital loans, equipment loans from the SBA are usually only available when it can be shown that other sources are not available.

Although not as abundant a source of term loans as are commercial banks, intermediate financing is also available from insurance companies. However, insurance companies tend to give few loans to small firms, especially small contractors. In addition, loans from insurance companies tend to be long term rather than intermediate term. Sometimes a bank and an insurance company combine their financing in giving a loan. In such a case the bank provides the intermediate term funds and the insurance company provides the long term portion.

A unique source for intermediate term financing, and a source widely used by the construction industry is equipment financing from finance companies. Equipment can be financed through a finance company by means of purchasing the equipment on installment or by leasing the equipment. In addition to differences in the format of the arrangement, the accounting methods for each of the two procedures differ. As such, the impact of purchasing, whether installment or leasing, differs on a firm's financial statements. The different accounting methods for handling equipment finance loans is discussed in Chapter 9.

The main difference between purchasing equipment on installment from a finance company and leasing the equipment from the finance company lies in who owns legal title to the assets. Under the purchase agreement, the purchaser (the borrower) obtains title of the asset upon payment of all the purchase installments. Under the lease agreement, the user of the equipment (the lessee) never obtains title to the asset. However, he is in effect financing the asset in that he is using it for payments of money. A lease agreement may be written such that the lessee is liable for repairs and maintenance costs, or it may be written such that the finance company (the lessor) is liable for such costs.

Yet another arrangement by which a firm can obtain funds through a finance company is by means of a *leaseback* arrangement. In such an arrangement the firm exchanges its owned assets to a finance company for cash. The firm then repurchases the assets by means of installment payments. Thus, in effect, the firm sells title to its assets and repurchases the asset by installment payments. Obviously the finance company charges the firm for providing the financing. The effective interest rate in a leaseback arrangement is usually quite high. However, in absence of available sources of funds to the borrower, such an arrangement becomes feasible. The tax and accounting effects of a leaseback arrangement are discussed in following chapters.

5.6.2 Intermediate Financing and the Contractor

The contractor's need for intermediate term financing is centered around his need for equipment financing. Unlike entrepreneurs in many other manufacturing industries, the contractor has little need for financing for a permanent increase in inventory.

Due in part to the nature of the use, and the inability of the contractor to provide security, a common source of a contractor's intermediate term financing is obtained from an equipment finance company. This financing is obtained by means of purchasing installment agreements or lease agreements. The past ten years has seen a twofold increase in the number of construction equipment finance companies and leasing companies. Financing for equipment from a finance company is available to many contractors, including those that may not be able to obtain financing from another source due to their inability to provide security.

The inability to provide security loses its value to the lender in the case of an equipment finance company in that the finance company legally holds title to the equipment until the contractor has completed total payment for its purchase. If the contractor fails to meet installment payments, the finance company is not left holding a useless and unsellable asset in that they are in the business of selling and leasing such equipment.

Contractors are less active in the practice of obtaining funds by a leaseback arrangement than are other manufacturing industries. This is probably mainly due to the fact that the contractor seldom owns much of his equipment and therefore cannot provide it as owned collateral.

Next to equipment financing through a finance company, commercial banks provide the largest source of term financing to the construction contractor. The availability of these loans to a contractor varies depending on the interest rate on money at a given point in time, the bank's available funds, the ability of the contractor to provide security, and the bank's evaluation of the firm's ability to repay the loan.

Unlike a short term loan where the interest rate in the banking system remains relatively unchanged throughout the period of the loan, the interest rate may change substantially during the duration of a term loan. As a result, a bank may be unwilling to commit funds at a low interest rate to a contractor for the purpose of term financing. If the interest rate increases substantially the bank may have to pay a higher rate for obtaining cash than the rate it is collecting on its loan. The willingness to lend money at a given rate also depends on the bank's available money. If money is readily available from the banking system, the interest rate consideration lessens in value. A low interest rate and sufficient available cash often occur simultaneously in our banking system.

If money is "tight" the bank may charge the contractor money over and above the current interest rate when making the loan agreement.

This extra charge is in the form of *points* which add to the contractor's effective interest rate. For example, during the credit crunch of 1974–1975 it was not uncommon for a bank to add 1% to the interest rate as a cost of making a loan.

Intermediate term loans to a contractor from a bank usually require security. As a result these types of loans are more readily available to larger contractors who have more assets which they can put up as security.

The bank's evaluation of a contractor's ability to repay a term loan is centered around the firm's ability to generate profits over a period of years. Thus, in addition to working capital considerations, the strength of the firm's management and the firm's market capabilities become important considerations. The small contractor is often put at a disadvantage when these factors are evaluated.

The SBA is yet another widely used source of financing to the contractor. However, this source is limited to contractors who do an annual volume of work less than $5 million, averaged over a three year period. In addition, the firm must also be able to show that other sources of money are not available.

Insurance companies and savings and loan companies are not major suppliers of term loans to the construction industry. These sources are more readily available to owners and developers of projects who can put up the proposed project as security. In regard to funds available to the building owner, a lender upon making a loan for a building may require a certain ownership share in the project. For example, the lender may make an arrangement whereby they receive 10% of all rent from the owner's renting of his building. Such an arrangement is most common in periods of tight money.

5.6.3 Cost of Intermediate Financing

A bank will normally charge a higher interest rate for an intermediate term loan than a short term loan. This is due mainly to the uncertainty of the interest rate of the banking system as a function of time. It should be noted that when the interest rate is high, the gap between the interest rate of intermediate and short term loans narrows. The stated interest rate is also dependent on the size of the loan. Normally, the larger the loan the smaller the stated interest rate. In respect to the actual interest rate charged by the bank for term loans, it should be remembered that these loans are normally repaid in installments. Thus, the effective interest rate is much higher (often double) the stated interest rate. The stated interest rate for the term bank loan is closely related to the prime rate. For example, if the prime rate is 7%, the stated interest rate may be 8%. The effective interest rate is much higher, the actual rate depending on the duration of the loan. On large term loans that extend for a rather long duration, banks may make an arrangement with a borrower to adjust the stated interest rate as a function of changes in the prime rate.

The effective interest rate associated with term financing from finance companies normally exceeds the effective interest rate of secured term loans from banks. The effective interest rate often ranges from 10% to 25%. Term loans for equipment are normally for a duration of one to four years. Knowing the duration of the financing, and the stated interest rate, the effective interest rate can be calculated.

Equipment finance companies have to charge an interest rate high enough to cover their expenses associated with the possibility of buyer default and subsequent reselling of the equipment. If the finance company is in the business of leasing equipment, the interest charge or rent must be high enough to allow for replacement cost, maintenance and repair costs, and provide a reasonable profit.

The question as to whether it is cheaper to purchase equipment or to lease it involves an economic analysis comparison of the alternatives. This economic analysis comparison requires the use of present value calculations. Economic analysis comparisons, including comparisons of purchasing versus leasing are discussed in Chapter 8 on capital budgeting.

The effective interest rate associated with leasebacks normally exceeds that of purchase loans. Such a means of obtaining funds is unfavorable to the borrower and is normally only sought after failure to obtain the funds from other sources.

By law, the maximum interest rate for SBA loans is set. However, because the SBA often participates with a bank (which charges a higher interest rate) when making a loan, a higher than maximum interest rate results. The SBA is not in the business of undercutting financial institutions in the lending market. Its objective is to supply funds to small firms who could not otherwise obtain needed funds.

5.7 Long Term Funding

As previously defined, long term funding is financing that is intended to be used for a period of ten years or more. Long term funding can be separated into two sources, long term debt and equity funding. Yet another source of long term funding is the obtaining of long term leases on property or equipment. However, this source is similar to intermediate term financing by means of leasing and will not be discussed further.

Because of the risk to the lender long term debt and equity funding is usually only available to the large, established firm. This type of firm is usually a corporation. As a result, sources of long term funding are not often available to the contractor in that he tends to be small in size in regards to owned assets. However, as a contractor grows, as many do, long term debt and equity funding become possible. Although one thinks of going to an outside lender when speaking about financing, a proprietor upon starting a firm by means of investing several hundreds or thousands of dollars for the purchase of assets is in effect providing long term funds for the firm. This is in fact the purpose for obtaining long term funding, that is, long term funds are obtained for the purchase of assets and for the capital structure that will permit the firm to operate over a long period of time, in particular for more than 10 years.

The reasons for obtaining long term funds versus attempting to obtain continuous short term or intermediate term funds are centered around the uncertainity of obtaining several continuous loans, and the large dollar value of funding involved. Upon implementing a plan to increase capacity by means of building new plant facilities, a firm has to be assured of being able to have the funds available to meet the large financial committment. In addition, it is not likely that they will be able to repay the financing (if it is debt financing) in a period of less than 10 years because of the large dollar value of the financing. Even if the firm were capable of repaying it in a shorter period, say 5 years, it may be better to defer the payments over a longer period in that large payments over the 5 years will have a substantial adverse affect on those year's earnings. It is usually better financial management if the assets are paid for as the revenue is generated from the usage of assets. Thus, long term funding is often consistent with matching the firm's revenues against expenses. This is consistent with accounting practices discussed in Chapter 9.

Long term debt and equity funding are quite different. Long term debts are paid back by a borrower to a lender in a fashion similar to that of an intermediate term loan except that the duration is longer and the payment of the principal often is made in a single payment at the end of the duration of the loan. Equity capital is never repaid. It is money obtained by selling a part of the interest in the business. In addition to the differences in maturity, other differences between debt and equity include the claim on assets and income, and the effects on management.

The large dollar amount of money involved in long term funding has given rise to specialized institutions that arrange the funding agreement between the borrower and the lender or investor. This is particularly the case in obtaining of equity funds.

5.7.1 Long Term Debt

Long term debt is obtained by means of selling *bonds* to lenders. The interest charge and provisions of how the principal is to be repaid is determined by means of intensive bargaining between the borrower and the lender. The final terms are set forth in an *indenture* which is a legal contract. The bondholders are often represented by a *trustee* who sees to it that terms agreed to in the indenture are enforced. If the borrower (usually a corporation) fails to meet its agreement, they are ruled to be in default. The trustee can then take legal action against the borrower. The interest rate the bondholder receives is referred to as his *yield*.

The time at which the lender receives his principal depends upon the loan agreement. In the normal situation, the money loaned by the lender is returned at the maturity date of the loan. For example, it may be 10, 15, 20, or 30 years. The bonds are often negotiable bonds and can be sold by the lender to other lenders (investors).

The lender may also have a right to require the borrower to speed up payments or make installment payments to a third party in order to ensure that the borrower has the funds available for repayment. This may be done by means of a *sinking fund* agreement whereby the borrower must make periodic payments to the trustee for retirement of the bonds. In a *serial bond* agreement, part of the total loan is repayable every year. This arrangement is similar to an installment loan. Obviously, a borrower would prefer to repay a loan by a single payment at maturity. In a sinking fund or serial bond agreement, the effective interest charge exceeds the stated interest charge.

The borrower might also reserve the right to retire the loan payment before its maturity. For example, if the initial bond is negotiated in a period of tight money such that the bond is sold at a discount or a high interest rate, say 9%, the borrower may choose to *refund* the bonds at a later time when interest rates are lower. Refunding would mean the repurchasing of the sold bonds and the reissuing of a new bond issue. Obviously, the lender has to be compensated for this right to repay the bonds before their maturity. This compensation may be in the form of a higher discount on the original issue, a higher interest rate, or a call premium. A *call premium* is a penalty fee for calling the bonds. For example, a bond with a face value of $100 may be callable at $106 after a stated number of years. The borrower's right to redeem bonds earlier than the maturity date is referred to as a *call privilege.*

The question as to when it is financially sound to refund a bond issue involves the analysis of the interest rate at the time of original issuance and the current interest rate, the legal fees, and other expenses, and the call premium involved in the refunding. The analysis can be made mathematically by calculating the present worth of the alternatives.

Refunding should not be confused with another common loan practice referred to as *funding.* Funding is the repayment of several loans with the issuance of a bond. This practice if often followed by the owner of a construction project. Rather than issue a bond to raise capital from which he pays a contractor for a project as the project is being built, it is often more profitable to pay the contractor by means of several loans as they are needed, and finally repay the loans by issuance of a bond.

Yet another form of bond agreement includes a *conversion privilege.* Under this arrangement the lender (the bondholder) has a right to convert his bond into common stock of the borrowing corporation. The price of the stock at which the bond is convertible is referred to as the *conversion price.* The number of shares of a stock obtained from the conversion is determined by dividing the face value (the maturity value) of the bond by the conversion price. For example, a bond with a face value of $1,000 is convertible into 20 shares at a conversion price of $50.

A borrower may be willing to put a conversion privilege into the bond agreement in that he may be able to issue the bond at a lower effective interest rate. In addition, the conversion privilege indirectly offers the borrower a means of raising equity capital (discussed in a following section). From the lender's point of view, a conversion privilege offers the potential of capital gains in that the price of the common stock may rise above the conversion price in which case he can make profit from converting. Even if the common stock price never exceeds the conversion price, the bondholder still holds his bond.

The major disadvantage of issuing long term debt by means of bonds is that the borrower is committing himself to the payment of interest for a long period of time. If it would turn out that the borrower is unable to meet these payments, he is placing himself in a position of possible insolvency. The bondholder can accelerate the loan upon default of interest payments. In addition, the bondholders, by means of the loan agreement, may require certain management practices such as requiring the borrower to keep a stated amount of working capital on hand.

Bond creditors have a claim on the borrower's income prior to that of the owners of stock of the borrower's firm. In addition, they usually have a prior claim on the borrower's assets. It is in the best interests of the borrower to make a bond agreement that places the lender in equal ranking with unsecured lenders in regard to the borrower's assets. This will facilitate the borrower's obtaining short term and intermediate term loans. Obviously, it is best to make an agreement that requires no claims on the assets. Such a bond is referred to as a *debenture*. Debentures can be arranged only if the borrower's credit position and income generating potential are strong.

5.7.2 The Cost of Long Term Debt

The effective interest rate associated with long term debt by means of issuance of bonds is dependent on the stated interest rate, the face value of the bonds, the discount or premium associated with the bonds, and the tax adjustment. Bonds often sell at a discount (less than the face value) or at a premium (more than the face value) in that lender's demand for the bond is affected by the loan agreement, the financial strength of the firm, and the competition for the lender's money. For example, if a borrower seeks to sell a $1,000 bond at an interest rate of 5% and a lender of funds can currently obtain a similar agreement with an interest rate of 7%, the $1,000 bond is going to sell at a discount, say $960.

The effective interest rate of a bond (referred to as yield) can be calculated approximately or by means of introducing present worth concepts (discussed in Chapter 8) the effective interest rate can be calculated accurately. The difference between the approximate and accurate methods are usually small. If we let C equal the actual cash obtained from the issuance of the bond, F equals the face value of the bond (referred to as *par value*), n equals the number of years to maturity, and L is the annual dollar amount of interest paid on the bond, the effective interest rate can be computed approximately by means of the following formula.

$$\text{Approximate effective interest rate} = i = \frac{L + [(F-C)/n]}{(C + F)/2}$$

For example, if a $1,000 20 year bond is sold for $950 at an interest rate of 5% ($50 interest per year), the effective interest rate or yield is calculated as follows:

$$\text{Approximate effective interest rate} = i = \frac{50 + [(1,000 - 950)/20]}{(950 + 1,000)/2} = 5.38\%$$

A more accurate calculation of the effective interest rate is determined by solving the following equation for i.

$$C = \frac{L}{(1 + i)} + \frac{L}{(1 + i)^2} + \ldots + \frac{L}{(1 + i)^n} + \frac{F}{(1 + i)^n}$$

The solution to this equation is facilitated by means of the use of present worth tables. For the example discussed, the use of such tables results in a calculation of an effective interest rate of 3%. Table 5.1 which is referred to as a bond table, can be used for calculating the effective interest rate.

The effective interest rate associated with a borrower issuing debt by means of bonds should be adjusted for taxes in that interest paid on the bonds is a tax deductible expense. Assuming the borrower is making profit, the effective interest rate of the bonds should be adjusted downward. For example, if the borrower is a corporation and therefore

Table 5.1 Typical Bond Yield Table

Bond table for values of a bond for $1,000,000
at 5% interest, payable semiannually

Yield	3 Years	4 Years	5 Years
4.00	$1,028,007.85	$1,036,627.41	$1,044,912.93
4.85	1,004,141.48	1,005,394.84	1,006,589.56
4.90	1,002,758.67	1,003,592.72	1,004,387.36
4.95	1,001,378.18	1,000,794.45	1,002,190.85
5.00	1,000,000.00	1,000,000.00	1,000,000.00
5.25	993,143.53	991,084.91	989,130.25
5.50	986,344.08	982,264.21	978,399.81

subject to a 48% tax rate, a pretax interest rate of 5.4% is adjusted to an after tax rate of 2.8% (5.4 × 0.52).

5.8 Equity Funds

Proprietorships and partnerships raise equity capital by means of the investment of the individual proprietor or the investments of the individual partners. Corporations raise their equity capital by means of selling shares of stock, which represent certificates of partial ownership to investors. The funds obtained from these investors do not have to be paid back to the investor as they do when the funds are obtained from the purchasers of bonds.

Because of the small size of the construction contractor, obtaining funds by the selling of stock is not readily available to most of the firms. This is also true of the obtaining funds by the issuance of bonds. The firm, due to its lack of size in regard to its assets and its operations, finds it difficult to locate individuals or firms who are willing to invest their capital in the firm. In addition, the contractor may be unwilling to sell stock as a means of obtaining equity funds in that the contractor is unwilling to sell part ownership of his firm. It is also true that the contractor usually does not have the same demand for long term financing as he does for shorter duration financing. He usually does not require large amounts of cash, such as those negotiated in long term loans for the building of a plant. The contractor is more in need of cash for working capital and equipment purchasing.

On the other hand, large contractors such as Bechtel, Turner, or Brown and Root, may find that raising funds by issuance of stock is advisable. Their need for large sums of money for the building of plant facilities or for the formation of a more optimal company capital structure may lead them to the issuance of new stock.

Because he is better able to market the securities, and better able to determine a fair price for the securities, a corporation hires an *investment banker*. The investment banker, for a fee (usually a fee of about 1% is charged) will market the securities for the corporation. The initial investment banker hired for the marketing of the securities is referred to as the *originating house*. It is common for the originating house to work with several other investment houses in marketing the securities.

If the securities are to be sold interstate they are governed by the Federal Trade Securities Act of 1933. This act requires the firm that issues the stock to file a registration statement and to issue a *prospectus* which describes the firm and the issuance in detail.

When a firm is considered a good sound investment, and the economic conditions are healthy, the investment banker will *underwrite* the issuance of the firm's securities. This in effect guarantees the firm that the investment banker will pay the firm the amount of cash that the securities are to be issued at. A more risky issuance of security would be sold on a *best efforts* basis, and the investment banker would only be liable to the firm for a dollar value in proportion to the securities actually sold.

A new issuance of securities may be sold to the public or it may be sold privately to an individual or investment firm. In addition, if shares of stock in the firm are already held by individuals, they have a legal right, called a *preemptive right*, to buy shares of a new issuance such that they can maintain their proportionate share in the firm. This is done by issuing the existing stockholders a certain number of *rights* which allow them to buy a certain number of shares of the new issuance.

5.8.1 Types of Stock

Equity ownership by means of holding stock in a firm differs greatly from being a creditor of a firm by means of holding a bond of the firm. The creditors have first claim on the income of the firm, and they have first claim on the assets of the firm upon insolvency. On the other hand, creditors, other than constraints that they may place upon management in the loan agreement, have no voice in the management of the firm. Stockholders have a voice in management in proportion to the percentage of the number of shares of stock they hold. In addition a firm does not have a legal obligation to pay dividends to stockholders as it does have an obligation to pay interest to bondholders.

In addition to differences between debt and equity, there are differences between different types of equity ownership. Securities issued by a corporation may be either preferred stock or common stock. The major difference between the two types of stock is that preferred stockholders have a prior claim to dividends before dividends can be paid to the common stockholders. On the other hand, common stockholders often have a larger share in the voice of management.

Preferred stock may be either cumulative or noncumulative. If it is cumulative, dividends not paid in a given year must be paid before common stock dividends are paid. Preferred stock may also be *participating*. In this case after the stated amount of dividends are paid to the preferred stockholders, excess dividends are shared by the preferred and common stockholders.

Issued stock may be either par value or no par value stock. There is little difference between the two because the actual value of the stock is determined in the market place. There are differences in the manner in which accounting practice handles par value versus no par value stock. These are discussed in Chapter 9.

Although it is not the intent of the firm to repay equity funds raised by the issuance of stock, they may in fact do this by means or repurchasing previously issued stock. This repurchased stock is referred to as *treasury stock*. A firm may repurchase its own securities for one of several reasons. Included in these reasons are its beneficial effects on the company's earnings per share, its reduction in the number of owners who have a voice in management, or because the firm has to legally have shares on hand to satisfy company employee stock option programs.

5.8.2 The Cost of Equity Funds

The calculation for determining the interest rate or cost of capital for the issuance of stocks is quite simple and determinate for preferred stock, but more difficult and uncertain for common stock. The market price at which preferred stock can be sold is usually reliably predicted by comparing the issuance to competing issuances. In addition, unless the firm is not being profitable, it will issue regular yearly dividends of a known amount to the preferred stockholders.

The calculation of the interest rate is not complicated by taxes in that dividends on preferred stock is not a deductible expense. Thus, if a firm receives $50 for the issuance of a share of preferred stock and pays an annual dividend of $3 to the stockholders for each held share, the interest rate or cost of capital to the firm is calculated as 6% ($3/$50).

The calculation of the interest rate or cost of capital for issuing common stock is complicated by the uncertainty concerning the market value of the stock, and the uncertainty of the frequency and amount of annual dividends paid. The market value at which the common stock will be purchased by investors is affected by the investor's prediction of the firm's future earnings and dividends, and investor speculation concerning the overall value of securities. The uncertainty is made more difficult by the fact that the issuance of new shares dilutes the existing shares in regard to earnings per share of outstanding shares.

The interest paid (dividends) by the firm is subject to the uncertainty of future earnings, plant investment, and management practices. In absence of precise information, one has to estimate both the market value and the predicted dividends (which likely will vary as a function of time) in order to estimate the cost of capital for issuance of common stock. It should be noted that in the calculation of the cost of capital for both preferred and common stock, the expenses (including those of the investment banker) must be recognized.

5.9 Summary

It is a rare event to find a contractor who is totally self-sufficient on his own funds for the operation of his firm. More than likely, he will find that at some point in time he is in need of financing for use as working capital or for the purchase of equipment.

Financing arrangements can be classified as short term, intermediate term, or long term. The contractor is usually involved in short term and intermediate term financing. This is usually in the form of the use of trade credit, loans from banks, or equipment finance arrangements from finance companies.

Long term financing by means of the issuance of bonds or stocks is seldom used by contractors. This is especially true in the case of the small contractor. His lack of size and the nature of his business operations are usually not consistent with long term funding agreements.

The contractor, in seeking funding, should be able to compute the effective interest rate associated with the using of the funds. The effective interest rate often differs from the stated interest rate because of discounts, required compensating balances, and installment agreements. In addition to the cost of capital implied in a funding agreement, the firm has to be aware of the agreement's affect on its management practices and ownership of its assets. A good funding arrangement is the result of much searching and negotiation.

Case 5.1 Ineed Construction Company:
Seasonal Financing

The Ineed Construction Company is confronted with building up a seasonal expansion of inventory of $80,000. This seasonal expansion is in anticipation of the spurt in summer building. You, as the manager in charge of financing, find that the necessary funds will be available through any of the following sources.

(1) Borrow from a commercial bank at 8.5% for a year.

(2) Borrow from a commercial bank at an annual rate of 8% discounted.

(3) Buy on terms of 2/10, n/60; plan to pay on the 60th day.

(4) Borrow on accounts receivable from a finance company at a rate of 1/20 of 1% per day on the outstanding face value of the accounts receivable pledged, the loan value of the accounts to be 90% of their face value.

(5) Borrow on a warehouse receipt from a commercial finance company. Terms are 10% interest per year, with the loan value equal to 75% of the value of the goods. Additional inventory is available to provide the needed collateral. The warehousing charge is a fixed yearly charge of $500 plus a flat charge of 1.5% of the value of the inventory warehoused.

Assuming that the Ineed Construction Company anticipates that their billings will be such that they can repay the $80,000 after a five month period, what means of financing should they use to finance their seasonal expansion?

Case 5.2 Trade Construction Company:
Using Trade Credit

Trade Construction Company specializes in placing concrete. Much of their work involves the placement of residential foundation walls. On the average they order and place fifty cubic yards of ready mix concrete each working day throughout the year. On the average a cubic yard retails for $25 to the walk-in customer.

In the past Trade Company has purchased their concrete from numerous ready mix plants. Little attention has been given to trade discounts or actual purchasing terms in the decision as to where to purchase material. Instead the firm has left it up to project superintendents. More often than not the superintendent has ordered the material from the closest located ready mix firm.

Recently, Ed Estimate, the head of Trade's estimating department has suggested that the firm may be able to save a substantial amount of money if they negotiate an agreement with a single ready mix plant. The large amount of concrete Trade Company purchases should put them in a favorable position as to obtaining a favorable price per cubic yard.

Through Mr. Estimate, the firm has contacted four different ready mix firms. Each has a retail price of $25 per cubic yard. However each firm has offered a different discount. These are as follows.

Firm A: A 20% trade discount from the retail price. All purchases must be made C.B.D. (cash before delivery).

Firm B: A 8% trade discount and ordinary terms of 2/10 n/30 with a 1.5% monthly interest charge for overdue accounts.

Firm C: A 10% trade discount. All amounts due ten days after delivery.

Firm D: A 5% trade discount. Ordinary terms are 5/5 n/60. No penalty charge is stated with the assumption that payment will be received before sixty days.

In weighing the alternatives it has also been brought to the attention of the Trade Company that in the past most of their concrete has been purchased from Firm C in that its location was normally closest to the firm's building sites. Additionally it is known that several of Trade's job superintendents have voiced dissatisfaction with the drivers of Firm A. This dissatisfaction stems from disputes as to the drivers' willingness to properly maneuver their trucks to facilitate job productivity.

Based on both financial and nonfinancial considerations where should Trade Company purchase its concrete?

Case 5.3 Finance Construction Company: Project Finance Costs

As is true of most construction firms, the Finance Construction Company is often paid for their services from an owner after they have in fact paid for their expenses of doing work. This coupled with the fact that Finance Company, like many construction firms, has little cash available results in a need to obtain short term financing in order to perform its services.

Up until the present time, a $10,000 reserve of cash has allowed Finance to pay their material and labor bills without securing short term financing. This has been true mainly because of the small dollar value of the projects in which Finance has engaged.

Finance Company is now considering expanding through the submission of a bid for a considerably larger project than they have been accustomed to bidding. The project in consideration is to take one year's duration and is estimated by the architect/engineer to cost $1.75 million dollars.

Because of the scale of the project being considered, Finance Company has decided that should they receive the large project being considered, it will be forced to direct all of its efforts toward the completion of this single project.

Based on a budget of cash flows (the preparation of such a budget is discussed in Chapter 7) for the project, Finance Construction Company has determined that its need for short term financing for the project to be as follows (i.e., these do not recognize the availability of the $10,000 cash).

Month	Average amount of financing needed
March	$ 8,000
April	12,000
May	21,000
June	21,000
July	35,000
August	12,000
September	15,000
October	28,000
November	31,000
December	16,000
January	15,000
February	2,000

The amounts are not cumulative, that is, a total of $20,000 is not needed for the first two months of the project. Rather $8,000 is the maximum level of financing needed in March, and $12,000 is the maximum amount needed in April. A loan of $25,000 would be sufficient to pay bills in any given month throughout the project.

Finance's immediate problem is one of determining the best means of financing the needed cash and determining the dollar value of interest expense to include in its bid. While it wants to recognize this interest expense in it's bid in order to cover its costs, Finance Company expects competition in obtaining the work and as such would like to keep the interest expense paid and recognized in the bid to a minimum.

Finance Company has visited several lending institutions (i.e., primarily banks) and has found that the following are available.

(1) It can obtain sixty day interest bearing notes in multiples of $10,000 at an effective interest rate of 16%.

(2) It can obtain quarterly noninterest bearing notes in $1,000 amounts discounted at 5% quarterly. The maximum amount of interest or noninterest bearing notes it can obtain is $15,000 in that a value in excess of this is ruled to reduce its current ratio to a point of high risk.

(3) It can negotiate a $20,000 credit line at an annual interest rate of 15% of the average of each month's borrowing. A compensating balance equal in amount to half the amount loaned is required. This balance earns 5% annual interest compounded daily.

(4) It can obtain a ten year loan of $10,000 with 10% annual interest payable on each six months unpaid principal (i.e., payments are made each six months). Should the firm decide to pay off the entire loan in a period of time less than ten years, a prepayment cost of 4% of the initial loan is charged to the firm.

The alternatives of the financing methods are from different lending institutions. As such, Finance can use any combination of the alternatives. How should Finance Company finance the project being considered and what finance cost should they include in their estimate?

Chapter 6

Personnel Management: Getting More for Your Money

6.1 Introduction

Traditionally productivity has been defined as output per man-hour of input. The United States has had increases in productivity averaging approximately 3.3% annually over the past 25 years. The United States ranks eleventh in productivity gains among the world's eleven most industrialized nations.[1] The effects of limited increases in productivity relate to several national economic concerns. Productivity is related to a country's ability to be competitive with developing nations, to increase capital investments, to provide jobs and limit unemployment, and to restrict inflation and increase the "real wage" of the worker.

Disregarding the impact of limited increases in productivity on the national scale, limited productivity has direct effects on the individual firm. A lack of productivity results in a firm's inability to compete with firms in regard to cost, time, and quality of work or services performed.

When one looks at specific industries in regard to annual increases in productivity, evidence indicates that the rates vary substantially from one industry to the next. The construction industry is characterized as having one of the smallest annual increases in productivity of all industries. Typically, the construction industry has less than a 1% annual productivity increase.[2] The lack of substantial increases in construction industry productivity has come under attack from both the private and public sectors of the economy. These attacks have recently been intensified by evidence of significant increases in the cost of construction labor, material, and equipment.

[1]Grayson, Jackson, "Man with a Plan," *Constructor*, February, 1973, pp. 37–41.

[2]Kendrick, J. W., *Productivity Trends in the United States* (a study by the National Bureau of Economic Research), Princeton, Princeton University Press, 1961, pp. 464–498.

There are many factors that affect productivity in the construction industry. The industry is somewhat unique in its type of product, the construction project is built in a variable environment, and many types of resources are used to build the construction project. These unique characteristics are discussed in the following sections.

When one considers means of measuring and improving productivity, several factors must be taken into consideration. The study of productivity requires the study and identification of many factors that relate to many different disciplines: psychology, sociology, and economics. Psychology necessitates the study of human needs, perception, attitudes, etc. Sociology requires the study of culture (norms, values, and changes, etc.), positions, and roles. Economics requires the study of organizational goals, allocation of resources, rate of return on investment, and determination of output rates.

No single individual can manipulate more than a limited number of factors at a time as possible determinants of productivity. As such, the result is that many individual pieces of research are produced, but there is no comprehensive treatment of the overall problem.

In addition to the labor consideration, such other factors as equipment, material, and the environment affect productivity. However for the most part, many of these other factors can be related to the labor consideration. Therefore, discussions concerning productivity usually focus on the labor input to production. In this context the terms motivation, job satisfaction, leadership, and direction are used to characterize the labor input to productivity. In particular, the obtaining of higher productivity and the term motivation are often used somewhat interchangeably. The motivating of labor is both an art and a science. Whereas certain theories are well founded, much of the ability to increase productivity by motivation can still be considered an art. In this chapter basic principles, theories, practical considerations, and applications of personnel motivation and management are presented as they apply to the construction industry.

6.2 Construction Industry Productivity Characteristics

Before discussing principles and application of motivation and various personnel management business tools, it is appropriate to briefly discuss some of the unique characteristics of construction industry productivity. By so doing, the reader will be in a better position to evaluate the various tools and skills presented as they may or may not apply to the construction industry.

As indicated earlier, the construction industry has witnessed only small (1%) annual increases in productivity. Several characteristics of the construction industry are unique in regard to how they affect the industry's productivity. Unlike most industries, the industry's product is for the most part immobile. As such, the product usually has to be manufactured at its final destination which often means that the product is manufactured in a less than ideal environment. This nonideal environment (i.e., variations of temperature, precipitation, and humidity) reduces productivity in that it adversely affects labor and equipment productivity.

The flexibility and variability of the type of construction product often results in management's inability to rigorously plan the work to be performed. The unpredictable environment adds to the difficulty of preplanning. This inability to rigorously plan results in nonoptimal productive use of labor and equipment. It is not unusual for a laborer to spend his last hour or two of a day filling in time so that he receives pay for a full day's work. Equally typical is the stretching of less than an 8-hour day's amount of work to 8 hours by slowing down (reducing productivity). The end result is that planning continuous work is often difficult to accomplish in the construction industry.

Yet another factor that is somewhat unique in regard to construction productivity is the existence of variable building codes in the industry. The builder often has to construct the same type of project using two different techniques due to the fact that the projects are built in two different locations with different required specifications. This lack of uniformity of required specifications restricts productivity since it does not permit duplication of the use of methods and materials. Such duplication, consistent with learning curve principles, decreases production time per unit of output. In addition to being variable, construction building codes have been cited as being outdated in that they restrict the implementation of modern day technology.

Undoubtedly all of the factors cited do adversely affect construction productivity. However, the most common adverse productivity element cited is labor. There are several reasons why labor comes under attack when viewing the need for improved construction industry productivity. Construction labor unions tend to be very organized with strong bargaining powers. They have been successful in bargaining for wages and working conditions. The end result is that labor is getting more money and often does not have to perform certain work functions that would have been normally assigned to it in the past.

The increases in construction labor wages and restrictions as to working conditions has resulted in several contractors turning to the use of nonunion labor. Although the comparison of union versus nonunion productivity is as of yet not fully documented, there is evidence that the union contractor sometimes finds it difficult to compete with the nonunion contractor in regard to costs and productivity. However, even if this is the case, one would have to consider the quality of work performed before one could justifiably make a case for nonunion versus union labor.

The question arises as to how much productivity can be increased by incorporating more productive labor practices. A recent survey among construction contractors (union and nonunion) has indicated that low labor productivity wastes from 14% to 40% of every construction dollar.[3] Since construction currently has an annual volume in excess of $115 billion and the total labor factor is about 40% of the cost of the construction product, Americans (including the contractor) are spending about $14 billion a year on wages for nonproductive hours.

Several studies have been undertaken to identify the sources of nonproductive construction time. The author undertook such a study and concluded that approximately one-third of all nonproductive construction time was directly related to nonproductive labor time. Other major factors include poor method planning, the environment, and inefficient use of equipment. Similar studies and results have been carried out by various agencies such as the National Association of Home Builders.[4]

Not only has the rate of construction productivity not kept pace with increased construction labor wages, but there are cases in which evidence indicates that productivity has actually decreased with an increased labor wage. For example, a construction contractor has stated that in 1926 when masons were receiving $1.50 per hour, one mason could lay 600 blocks a day. In 1972 with masons getting about $9.00 per hour, two men average only 100 blocks a day.[5]

Needless to say, not all accusations made in regard to construction

[3]"Now Building Unions Offer More Work for the Money", *U.S. News and World Report*, January 15, 1973, p. 59.

[4]"Pilot Study of Productivity in the Residential Building Trades", *NAHB Research Foundation*, Rockville, 1972, p. 32.

[5]"Low Productivity: The Real Sin of High Wages", *Engineering News Record*, February 24, 1972, pp. 18–23.

labor productivity are valid. In many cases labor can counter with arguments of their own. However, the mere fact that labor costs make up around 40% of the total construction industry product justifies focusing on means of improving overall productivity by increasing labor productivity. The ratio of the industry's material to labor cost varies from values of 1 to 2.[6] This compares to a 5 to 6 material to labor cost ratio for many other manufacturing industries such as the automobile industry. This means that the construction industry approaches a service type industry. Such industries can greatly improve their overall productivity by increasing their labor productivity. It is with this in mind that following sections present personnel management and motivation principles.

6.3 Leadership and Directing

If the construction manager is to obtain a high level of productivity from his workers, he must have the ability to lead and direct them. Modern leadership theory defines leadership as interpersonal influence toward the attainment of specific goals in specific situations.[7] The objective of leadership behavior is aimed at accomplishing company goals. A leader's behavior and communicative ability dictate his ability to influence his workers. As is indicated in the definition of leadership, leadership must relate to specific situations. A specific act of a leader may have one effect in one situation and a different effect in a different situation.

Leaders exhibit different qualities and styles in obtaining their objectives. Such characteristics as vitality, persuasiveness, intellectual capacity, decisiveness, and responsibility, make up the style of leadership employed by different managers. The degree to which each of these qualities is used by a given manager results in a classification of his leadership style. Generally four types of leadership styles are recognized.

The *authoritarian* leader is characterized by stern, factual qualities. The autocratic leader centralizes power and decision making in him-

---

[6]U.S. Department of Commerce, "New Facts of Construction: The 1967 Census of Construction Industries", *Construction Review of the U.S. Department of Commerce*, 1970, No. 10.

[7]Stanford, Aubrey, C., *Human Relations: Theory and Practice*, Columbus, Charles E. Merrill Publishing Company, 1973, p. 139.

self. As such, his workers have little influence on decisions. The authoritarian leader determines all policy himself and assigns specific work tasks to each worker. Because of the high degree of control over the workers by the authoritarian leader, a high degree of worker discontent is sometimes characteristic of this type of leadership. On the other hand, because of the control that is part of this style of leadership, a high level of productivity is often identified with this style of leadership.

A second type of leadership style is referred to as *participative* leadership. This type of leader shares responsibility with his subordinates. As a result, authority is decentralized and the individual workers have an input to decision making. However, subordinates are not given equal authority as their leader. They are only included in decision making when their superiors feel they are needed.

A *democratic* leadership style emphasizes even more decision making decentralization than a participative style. The democratic leader seldom uses authority. Instead he delegates authority to groups of workers. The workers' interests and initiative are emphasized. As such, a high degree of worker expression and originality are characteristic of a democratic leadership style. In addition, this type of leadership usually results in a high degree of friendliness among the workers. It should be noted that while all policies are a matter of worker decision, the democratic leadership style still results in the leader providing active assistance.

When complete worker freedom is given in the decision making process, the type of leadership style is referred to as *free-rein*. This type of leadership results in maximum decision making decentralization. This type of leadership style is usually not preferred in that a high degree of disorganization, nonproductive time, and play-oriented behavior result from the leader's failure to lead. This is especially the case when the workers are unskilled and not self-motivating.

The question arises as to which leadership style is preferred. Unfortunately there is not a single most effective style. The best type of leadership style is dependent on the work situation and most of all on the personal characteristics of the individual who is attempting to lead. A good amount of research has been performed to try and determine what personality traits are associated with effective leadership. For example, a few years ago *Fortune* magazine conducted a survey in an attempt to identify leadership qualities.[8] Among the qualities indicated are the following.

[8]Stryker, Perrin, "On the Meaning of Executive Qualities", *Fortune*, June, 1958, p. 189.

   (1) Thoroughness, steadiness, reliability
   (2) Does complete job
   (3) Honest, trustworthy, conscientious, keeps promises
   (4) Uses good judgment in decision making
   (5) Meets schedules
   (6) Accepts full responsibility
   (7) Inspires confidence
   (8) Cooperative
   (9) Considers others
 (10) Good personal habits

The list goes on to list a total of 21 qualities. Similar research by others has resulted in focusing on yet other qualities. It should be noted that some of the qualities listed are in fact overlapping one another. In summary, many of these leadership qualities can be classified as to the personal traits of intelligence, maturity, initiative, and objectivity toward human relations and behavior.

Intelligence above all other personal traits is a necessary leadership quality. In order to be an effective leader, a manager's intelligence must be respected by his subordinates. In general, a manager's ability to manage increases with his level of intelligence. On the other hand, a high level of intelligence does not assure effective leadership. If the manager does not demonstrate other required personal traits, his high level of intelligence might in fact be resented by his subordinates.

The effective leader must also demonstrate *maturity*. In particular he must portray a high level of emotional maturity. In order to gain and maintain the respect of his workers he must portray self-respect and self-assurance. He must be mature to the point where he can share the interests and acknowledge the beliefs of others.

The effective leader must possess and portray *initiative*. That is, the leader must want and constantly try to achieve certain goals. If the manager desires initiative on the point of his workers, he must first demonstrate initiative himself.

A fourth and important leadership personal trait is the leader's ability to be *objective* toward human relations and behavior. He must be unbiased and unemotional in his dealings with his workers. He should not prejudge a situation or a worker. Having made an objective decision he must have the ability to convincingly communicate his decision to his workers. His personality should be such that he is approachable by his workers and can cooperate with their suggestions when they are valid.

In summary, the effective leader must possess personal traits and a leadership style that relate to both a concern for company production goals and a concern for workers as individuals. The objective is to properly address these two somewhat seemingly opposite objectives. The leader who concentrates merely on production goals in his leadership style may in fact obtain high productivity for a short period of time. However, over a long period of time his lack of concern for the needs of the workers will result in less than desirable worker productivity.

In reality it is possible for the manager to address both production and the needs of the worker. The effect of the various degrees of concern for production and the workers as individuals is illustrated by way of a *managerial grid* that was developed by Blake and Mouton.[9] The managerial grid is shown in Fig. 6.1.

Five leadership approaches are shown in the managerial grid illustrated. The numbers shown with each approach indicate the extent of leadership concern for production and workers, respectively. Each of these is on a scale of 9. For example, a "2, 8 style" would indicate a relatively low concern for production and a relatively high concern for workers.

We might look at the extreme points shown on the managerial grid in Fig. 6.1 and discuss the implications. The (1, 9) approach describes a very low concern for production and a high concern for workers. This type of approach is somewhat similar to the previously discussed "free-rein" type of leadership style. This type of approach emphasizes the eliminating of worker conflict and has a tendency for goals to be determined by the workers themselves.

In contrast, the (9, 1) approach is characteristic of a high degree of concern for production and a low degree of concern for the needs of workers. This approach views workers as tools for high production. However, one should not conclude that the (9, 1) approach will always have a negative effect. This approach may in fact be very effective leadership when the educational level of the workers is somewhat low and submissive.

The (9, 9) approach shown on the managerial grid assumes that a concern for production and a concern for the needs of a worker are not incompatible. It assumes that workers have a need to be involved and committed to productive work. Undoubtedly, the reaching of the point (9, 9) on the managerial grid should be the goal of the manager. However, being realistic, the manager may have to settle for something less, such as point (5, 5) on the managerial grid shown.

The construction manager has traditionally been viewed as an au-

[9]Blake, R. R., and Mouton, J. S., "Managerial Facades", *Advanced Management Journal*, July, 1966, p. 31.

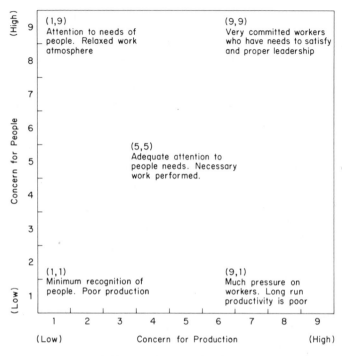

Fig. 6.1. Managerial grid.

thoritarian type of leader or manager. The type of work the construction worker performs and the lack of innovative skills required on the behalf of the construction worker have usually made the democratic type of leader rather ineffective. In addition, the rather well-defined type of work to be done, and the somewhat noncompany attitude of the construction worker would result in a free-rein leadership style resulting in chaos.

The construction industry is rather unique in regard to the relationship between the individual construction worker and his employer. Unlike the factory worker, the construction worker normally works for several employers within a short period of time. A given worker may work for one firm one day and yet another firm the following day. The end result is that it is difficult for the manager to get the total cooperation and initiative of the workers as to company goals. Thus a participating, democratic, or free-rein leadership style will often prove somewhat inappropriate as a stimulus to higher worker productivity. This is not to say that a complete authoritarian style is the answer.

There is evidence (cases discussed in a later section) where providing the construction worker the opportunity to participate in decision making has in fact resulted in higher productivity and worker morale. Although a (1, 9) or even a (9, 9) approach is not being suggested, the industry is starting to recognize that construction worker needs are not totally incompatable with production concerns.

Even if one is to accept the fact that the authoritarian style of leadership is the most appropriate construction manager leadership style, the need for strong leadership personal traits does not diminish. A construction manager who is incompetent as to construction drawings, construction methods, and work schedules will soon lose the respect of his workers. This type of attitude will result in the workers being nonproductive and having a low morale. Even in the rather "harsh" and "rough appearing" environment of the construction industry and project, workers must have a degree of respect for the leader. Lack of respect often leads to too casual of an environment which, in turn, can lead to less than desirable productivity. In addition, a "noninitiative" construction manager will not be respected by his workers. The appearance of laziness and "taking it easy" on the behalf of the manager will soon have a negative productivity impact on his workers. The construction manager's almost constant input to construction productivity requires a high and constant degree of leadership qualities. The strong leader is worth his weight in gold to the construction firm.

6.4 Communication

Every manager must be able to communicate effectively. This is especially true in the case of the construction manager. His ability to effectively communicate work tasks and company objectives to his workers dictates construction productivity. The detailed and nonrepetitive type of work performed as part of a construction project makes it necessary that the construction manager continuously communicate with the labor foremen and craftsmen during the building of a project. The communication process between the construction manager (possibly the project superintendent) and the construction worker is made more difficult by the fact that there often is a gap in the educational and communication skills of the two parties.

In addition to having to communicate between the construction manager and his project foremen and craftsmen, there is a need for

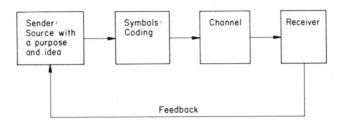

Fig. 6.2. Communication process.

communication between the owners of the firm and project managers, between the owners and potential clients, between the owners and labor unions, and between the builder and material suppliers.

Every individual has participated in some form of communication. However, many persons participate in communication without recognizing the process that is taking place. *Communication* can be defined as the transferring of information and understanding from one person to another. It cannot occur unless there is both someone to trasnfer the information and someone to receive the information being transferred.

The communication process can be viewed as consisting of four elements. These are as follows.

(1) Sender
(2) Symbols
(3) Channel
(4) Receiver

The process in which these four elements come together to form the communication process is shown in Fig. 6.2. The process begins with a person who has reasons for communicating. He is referred to as the *sender*. The objective of the communication is to influence individuals (the receivers) to accept the idea of the person sending out the communication. For example, the construction manager upon recognizing the need to provide strength to vertical forming has to communicate this to craftsmen in a manner such that the craftsmen provide adequate required bracing.

In order to communicate his idea to another individual, the sender of the message has to use *symbols*. The study of communication symbols is included in the study of *semantics*. Words and their meanings are the symbols by which the sender of a message communicates with the receiver of the message. One of the difficulties of obtaining effective communication is that words do not necessarily have commonly understood meanings. Many words are likely to have ambiguous meanings. For example, the word "management" is one that has different meanings to the owner of the firm, the construction manager, and the construction worker.

Words are often classified as concrete or abstract. *Concrete* words such as rebar, wall, and slab are words that stand for an object with a physical reality. On the other hand, *abstract* words such as strength, compact, tall, and progress are words that represent concepts. In general, concrete words enable more effective communication than do abstract words. Although it is sometimes necessary to use some abstract words, the sender of messages in the construction industry will not find it difficult to emphasize the use of concrete words. The construction industry concerns itself with well-defined physical objects. Specifications are generally written very precisely and in terms of concrete words such that the freedom of interpretation is held to a minimum.

Abstract words can be further classified as being either connotative or denotative. *Connotative* words point to an individual's inner feelings or reactions. Such words as fearful and cleverness are connotative. These types of words are usually very ambiguous. *Denotative* words point to external events outside the individual. For example, management, profit, and compaction are all denotative. These words while being less preferred than concrete words, are preferred to the use of connotative words in regard to being ambiguous. On the other hand, connotative words are often more effective as to motivation versus the use of denotative words.

The proper symbols to use in coding a message to a sender is somewhat dependent on who is to receive the message. Obviously the construction manager may not be able to effectively communicate with the construction worker if the manager uses very scientific concrete design oriented words. On the other hand, poetic type abstract words will also prove very ineffective in such an environment.

Once the sender has chosen his symbols for communicating his message he than has to use the proper *channel* for sending the message to be transferred. The simplest type of communication channel is that which exists when only two people are involved. This type of channel is sometimes referred to as *circuit* communication. A more complex channel of communication exists when several individuals or departments are involved in the transfer of the message. This type of channel involves the study of company organizational structure. Organizational structure as to facilitating communication was discussed in Chapter 2.

Communication channels can be classified as downward or upward communication, formal or informal communication, or oral or written communication. Downward or upward communication is somewhat self-explanatory. Typical construction communication is downward, that is, management relate company objectives to project superintendents who in turn communicate to project foremen. These foremen in turn communicate work tasks to labor. Although the characteristics of the industry often curtail upward communication (e.g., labor does not work for a single employer and will often refrain from making rewarding suggestions), such upward communication can often prove financially rewarding to the firm. As such, the construction firm should, when possible, encourage this type of upward communication.

The line of difference between formal and informal communication is not totally clear. Generally, formal communication is considered to be done in a rather structured environment. Such formal communication normally takes place when using established company communication channels. In addition to formal meetings, such communication takes place via telephone calls, posters, and letters. For example, a company meeting in which company management relates company goals to project managers would result in formal communication. In addition, a project manager's field instructions to an ironworker as to the placement of steel would be considered formal communication.

Informal communication exists because of the personal and group interests of people. This direct and fast means of communication is sometimes referred to as the *grapevine*. An example of this type of communication is the communication that occurs when laborers see an end of a project coming and start to discuss among themselves the possible laying off of workers. Although informal communication takes place in an unstructured channel, it is often a very effective communication channel. The only danger is that information communicated in such a channel is sometimes unfounded or distorted.

Much of the communication that exists between the parties involved in the construction process is oral communication. Written communication occurs when contracts need to be written (as is the case of contracts covering performance that takes longer than a year's duration), when purchase orders are made, or anytime it is advantageous to put communication in writing. On the other hand, much of the communication between the construction manager and labor is oral. This oral communication has the advantage of enhancing face-to-face exchange and encouraging questions and a friendly spirit.

The channel of communication used by the sender is not independent of the symbols used by the sender and vice versa. Formal and written communication is often accompanied by the use of more concrete words. On the other hand, informal and oral communication make more use of abstract words. Regardless of the situation involved the sender should always keep in mind the following when choosing his symbols or communication channel.

(1) Know what he is trying to communicate.
(2) Communicate adequately; no more, no less.
(3) Realize that his communication may be altered in its distribution.
(4) Seek to clarify his ideas before communicating.
(5) Consult with others where appropriate in planning communication.
(6) Follow up the communication.
(7) Seek not only to be understood, but to understand—be a good listener.

We have now considered three of the elements (sender, symbols, channel) of the communication process. The fourth and final element, the *receiver*, is probably the most important element to effective communication. The success of the communicative effort is based on the extent of the new information and understanding achieved by the receiver, and what it means to the receiver dictates the effectiveness of the communication.

The receiver of communication interprets it on the bases of his background and experience. A construction worker who is told to brace a wall form will rely on his experience for determining what the sender of the message intended and how he responds in bracing the wall. However, his experience may be such that it is not in conformance to what the sender of the instruction had in mind. Clearly, the construction worker (the receiver) cannot be held totally responsible for the failure to carry out the less than completely defined instruction. It is true that the construction manager should be able to make some assumptions as to the level of understanding and experience of his workers. However, he is responsible for knowing this level of understanding and experience.

The communication sender must be sensitive to the level of understanding of the receiver. For example, not all construction workers have the same level of experience or intelligence. As such, two different laborers will have different degrees of understanding from a single instruction from a project superintendent. A sender's tendency to categorize his receivers rigidly is referred to as *stereotyping*. This type of attitude impedes communication or leads to miscommunication. A construction manager's "talking down" to a rather informed worker will cause resentment from the worker. In such a case it is probably better if there had been no communication in the first place.

The sender of instructions should be sensitive to the reactions of the receivers. The behavior of the receiver upon hearing an instruction often can be used as a means of judging the level of understanding by the receiver. A simple facial gesture or body movement can indicate the degree of understanding. Often a *communication gap* exists between what the sender is trying to say and what the receiver interprets him as saying.

The sender and the communication channel should provide for communication feedback. *Feedback* is the observation by the sender of the effect of the communication on the behavior of the receiver. As such, the processing of information and understanding in the reverse, that is from receiver to sender, is feedback. The success of communication efforts cannot be evaluated without providing for feedback. In addition, feedback facilitates modification of the sender's future efforts at effective communication. Feedback will often bring to light a potentially unprofitable mistake, or may bring to surface a profitable course of action. For example, early detection of a worker's failure to understand an instruction as to the proper height of placing reinforcing may eliminate the erroneous placement of the reinforcing plus several cubic yards of concrete. By the same token, even upon properly receiving and understanding an instruction, by means of feedback, a worker might communicate a time saving construction method which came to mind when informed of the current procedure to be followed. This type of feedback, in addition to being profitable to the communication sender, often satisfies a worker's inner personal needs and serves as a production motivating force.

Effective communication that recognizes all four identified elements should serve to motivate both management and labor. Sharing information of mutual interest and benefit aids in motivating personnel. Explaining plans and policies, encouraging suggestions, and asking questions almost always have positive motivational effects.

6.5 Theory X and Theory Y

How does the construction manager motivate his employees to be productive? There are in fact several tools or gimmicks he may employ and a few of these are discussed in Section 6.9. However, ignoring specific programs or actions, two contrasting sets of assumptions can be cited that dictate the proper practices of the manager. Theory X and theory Y are the two widely regarded assumptions as to motivation theory. These two assumptions are brought out and argued by the famous social scientist Douglas McGregor.[10]

Theory X takes a dim view of human beings and their work behavior. It assumes that the average human being has an inherent dislike for work. If possible he will avoid work. Related to the assumption that the human being dislikes work is the assumption that he avoids responsibility, has little ambition, and desires a high degree of security.

There are several motivational management approaches that follow from the acceptance of theory X. For one, it implies that leadership must be strong and responsibility should be concentrated with the manager. That is, the individual worker merely wants to be directed. How then does one motivate the individual worker given theory X assumptions? The answer is to coerce the worker. One can either use the *positive motivational approach* or the *negative motivational approach*. That is, in order to motivate the theory X worker the manager might offer extra pay (the positive approach), or the manager might threaten the worker with punishment such as the possible loss of his job.

Theory X states that a human being works in order to satisfy his physical needs. Physical needs are only one of several types of human being needs that are identified by social scientists. In particular, Maslow[11] identifies five types of needs. These are shown in Fig. 6.3. The physiologic needs shown in the illustration include the need for food and shelter. These physiologic needs and the safety and security needs shown are often referred to as *physical needs*. On the other hand, the social activity needs, the esteem and status needs, and the self-realization and fulfillment needs shown are often referred to as *personal satisfaction needs* (sometimes referred to as "inner" needs or "higher-order" needs). Theory X assumes that personal satisfaction needs are not the motivating force behind a human being's work production. Instead, the theory assumes that a worker is influenced by only physical needs. As such, management has to address these needs using either a positive or negative approach. Although either of these approaches is consistent with theory X motivation, the negative motivational approach is much more commonly associated with the theory X assumption.

[10]McGregor, Douglass, *The Human Side of Enterprises*, New York, McGraw-Hill, 1960.

[11]Maslow, A. H., *A Theory of Human Motivation*, New York, McGraw-Hill, 1969, p. 657.

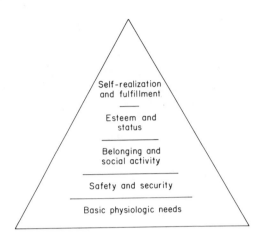

Fig. 6.3. Maslow's hierarchy of needs.

Contrasted with theory X, *theory Y* assumes that the human being may receive both external and internal satisfaction from the performance of work. It assumes that the average human being does not inherently dislike work. Theory Y indicates that if a worker is committed to the objectives of the work, he will in fact accept work as he does play or rest. The key is to make the worker's objectives consistent with the firm's objectives. Unlike theory X, theory Y assumes that the human being can learn to accept responsibility. In addition, it assumes that the worker has the capacity to be creative and imaginative in solving company work objectives.

Theory Y relates the performance of work to the satisfying of the personal (higher order) needs of the human being. If man can satisfy these inner personal needs in performing work, he will in fact find satisfaction in his work and as a result be productive.

Theory Y assumptions imply different management techniques for motivating a worker than does theory X. Theory Y plays down the need to coerce workers by threatening them with lower pay or loss of their jobs. Instead, this theory indicates that management can motivate workers by making an effort to get goal congruence between the workers' objectives and the company objectives. That is, in order to obtain high work productivity organizational goals and worker goals must be integrated. Workers must be encouraged to develop and utilize their knowledge and creative skills in accomplishing organizational goals. For example, the worker might be given added pay or promotional benefits if he can find a better way of manufacturing a segment of the firm's product. By enhancing the worker's opportunity to be creative, one is providing the potential for the worker to satisfy his inner personal needs.

The more traditional view of motivational theory is theory X. However, modern day personnel management is founded more on theory Y. Perhaps this recent acceptance of theory Y by the social scientists is the result of the strong arguments for its use that were set out by McGregor. In addition, acceptance of theory Y assumptions result in giving the social scientist greater opportunities for utilizing motivational methods.

Theory Y is often difficult to apply when the production process utilizes unskilled employees. Such circumstances tend to create motivational problems because there is a limited opportunity to satisfy personal inner needs. Given this type of situation, the manager is forced to accept theory X assumptions, and motivate by recognizing the physical needs of a worker.

Although the construction worker should not be classified as being unskilled, the type of work he performs and the type of environment in which he performs this work often results in it being difficult to address the worker's inner needs. For example, it may be difficult to initiate creativity or satisfy inner personal satisfaction to a laborer whose main task is carrying boards to carpenters. On the other hand, a creative manager may in fact instill such a degree of teamwork among the workers on a construction project, that the workers do indeed obtain personal satisfaction from their work. The techniques used by such a manager include good communication with the workers, instilling pride in the workers, keeping the workers informed as to company objectives, and recognition of good performance. Several of the specific theory Y founded practices used by construction managers for motivating construction workers are discussed in a later section.

Perhaps the more common traditional approach to construction worker motivation is based on theory X. That is, it is held that the only reason the construction worker shows up for work in the morning is to satisfy his physical needs. This is evidenced by the fact that often after accumulating several days pay, the construction worker may be absent from work in order to spend some of his rewards on his physical needs. Of course such a practice is not limited to the construction worker. However, its frequency of occurrence in the construction industry is relatively high.

Assuming theory X assumptions do in fact apply to the construction industry, the motivational techniques used by the construction manager are somewhat constrained by current industry practices. Strong construction labor unions limit the degree of negative motivational methods the construction manager has at his disposal. That is, labor agreements dictate a fixed hourly wage. In addition, the construction manager usually has to justify the firing of a given worker. On the other hand, a construction firm may tend to keep a more productive worker fully employed. That is, when work is slack, the more productive worker may get "the call" from the union hall. However, this is only true to a degree. Seniority rules often play a major factor in assignment of a worker. However, the manager has some freedom in assigning a given worker work tasks. For example, a nonproductive laborer may be assigned to a relatively undesirable task; whereas a productive laborer may be given a more challenging and respected type of work. Again though, this type of theory X motivational technique can only be applied to a degree before it violates accepted industry practices.

In addition to constraining the use of negative motivational methods, current construction industry practices also somewhat constrain the implementation of positive theory X motivational methods. One of the more successful positive motivational methods is the use of piece work. This method is used extensively in the manufacturing industry. The worker is paid as a function of the amount of work he performs. The more production units he completes, the more money he receives in pay. Construction unions have historically opposed the use of piece work. They cite many reasons for their opposition. Included are the variability of the construction product (which results in difficulty in measurement of the production unit), and the protection of the older (and presumably less productive) worker. Union's opposition to piece work has resulted in practically no piece work in the industry. As such, a powerful positive theory X motivational method is not available to the manager.

As in the case of employing negative methods, the construction manager has at his disposal some less direct positive motivational methods. For example, the assigning of overtime work to productive workers in a period of a slack work is a positive theory X method that can be applied by the manager. However, the use of this method may approach a conflict with industry practices.

Undoubtedly the agreement as to the correctness of the two theories, X and Y, will be debated for many years to come. However, the validity of one versus the other is not the real issue to be recognized. What is important is the appropriateness of the motivational techniques that follow the acceptance of the valid theory. Until, and if the validity of one of the theories is accepted, the construction manager will have to continue to attempt to instill construction worker motivation by using both theory X and theory Y methods. In regard to the construction industry, it is likely that both theories in fact apply. It is the degree to which each applies that is at issue.

6.6 Group Behavior

Much of the behavior of the individual employee can only be understood in the context of the group in which he works. Committment to production goals, acceptance of leadership, satisfaction with work, and effectiveness of performance all tend to depend on the relations of a man with his immediate face-to-face co-workers.[12] The importance of considering the effect of group behavior and the environment of the individual worker is especially important in regard to construction productivity and construction personnel management. Very little construction work is done by an individual in isolation. Instead, several laborers including more than one type of craft interact to perform work in the building process. This process of requiring several types of craftsmen working together is often required by labor union rules. For example, many union agreements require the use of a laborer for helping two carpenters. Even if individuals are not mixed together on a given type of work, they still interact with fellow workers during lunch or during nonwork hours. The end result is that as time goes on, groups of workers begin to share common goals and values.

From a social science point of view, a group is more than just a collection of individuals such as construction laborers working together in one location. A group is formed only as a result of interpersonal relations. Sherif and Sherif[13] summarize the process of group formation as resulting from the following four essential characteristics.

(1) A motivational base shared by individuals and conducive to recurrent interaction among them over time.

(2) Formation of an organization (group structure) consisting of differentiated roles and delineated in some degree from that of nonmembers.

---

[12]Bass, B. M., *Organizational Psychology*, Boston, Allyn and Bacon, 1965, p. 190.

[13]Sherif, M., and Sherif, C., *Social Psychology*, New York, Harper and Row, 1969, p. 657.

(3) Formation of a set of norms (i.e., values, rules, and standards of behavior).

(4) More-or-less consistent differential effects on the attitude and behavior of individual members produced by the group properties.

The construction union which includes all construction labor of a given craft is itself a group. It has characteristics that are compatible with the four listed group formation elements. Smaller groups of individuals within a given union and employed at a given project site also share the formation elements.

Groups are often classified as to a given type. One broad classification identifies a group as either a *formal* or an *informal* group. Interactions in formal groups tend to be interpersonal. Examples of formal groups include the business organization, and professional association. While formal groups influence individual workers by their policies, informal groups are often more difficult to control and as such have greater influence on personnel management.

Informal groups result from individuals with common social interests coming together. Informal groups can be further classified as being one of the following three types.

(1) Large groups which arise due to internal politics. These types of groups are often referred to as "gangs" or "crowds."

(2) Groups formed on the basis of common jobs. They often are intimate and work, talk, and even dine together. This type of group is often referred to as a "clique."

(3) Small groups consisting of a few (two or three) close friends. This type of group is often referred to as "subclique."

Each of these three types of informal groups can be observed to be present in the construction industry. One could site many examples of each. For example, union workers gathering for a labor strike or forming a group to protest nonunion work can be classified as a gang or crowd. Such groups in the construction industry normally have an adverse effect on productivity and create personnel management problems.

Cliques are common on a construction project. Often several workers may share a sporting hobby or habit that brings them together in regard to working, talking, and even after hour activities. Such groups can prove beneficial or detrimental to company productivity depending on their goals and values.

Smaller informal groups of two or three workers who reside close to one another typically are friends. They often share common interests and may prefer to work together. Generally this type of small informal group presents few problems in regard to overall personnel management.

As noted, gangs or crowds normally have an adverse affect on productivity and company objectives. As such, when possible, the firm should attempt to prevent these types of informal groups from forming. Communication of goals, and an awareness to the grievances of the workers can go along way to impede the formation of such groups.

On the other hand, the firm can do little to prevent the formation of cliques among its workers. Nothing the firm does can permanently destroy this type of group within the organization. One of the results of the now widely recognized study at the Hawthorne plant at Western Electric[14] was to confirm the existence and importance of such informal groups. In addition to addressing worker productivity as a function of illumination, hours of work, and rest; the Hawthorne studies analyzed the social organization of work groups. The study showed that informal cliques were much a part of the organization. Employees had social needs which they sought to satisfy at work. The employees' efforts to satisfy their social needs resulted in a system of cliques, rivalries, and grapevines, all of which exerted an influence on employee behavior and practice.

Even if a firm can prevent the existence of cliques among its workers, it may not prove advantageous to do this. If the goals of the clique are consistent with that of the firm, the firm will reap the benefits. On the other hand, a clique may prove to be a productivity constraint if its goals or values differ from that of the firm. Adverse clique goals and values can be made compatible with the firm by proper leadership. It is the manager's duty to instill meaningful and explicit group goals. Without such group goals, group members are unlikely to share common work objectives. If the group goals are vague so that workers interpret group goals differently, the possibility for decreasing nonproductive use of time is lessened.

The manager also has the duty to see to it that workers in the work group see the relationship between their personal objectives and the group goals. If this can be done, higher productivity will result. Group values favoring higher productivity are likely to develop when workers understand group goals, see the relationship between their own objectives and that of their group or clique, and find meaning and satisfaction in the work itself.

[14]Committee on Work in Industry, National Research Council, *Fatigue of Workers: Its Relation to Industrial Production*, New York, Reinhold Publishing Company, 1941, pp. 56–57.

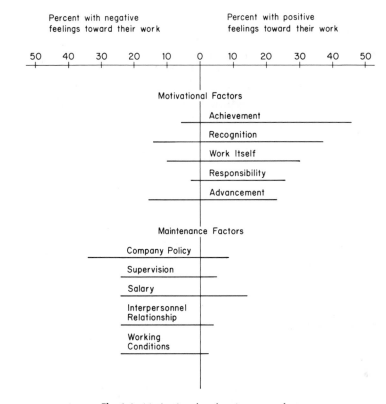

Fig. 6.4. Motivational and maintenance factors.

Herzberg[15] described two independent sets of factors that influence a worker's and a group of workers' satisfaction and performance. His *motivation-maintenance* theory suggests that a worker or group's job satisfaction comes from *motivational factors* while *maintenance factors* result in dissatisfaction. Figure 6.4 illustrates the result of this theory. As is shown in the illustration, Herzberg concluded that one set of factors lead to positive job feelings while yet another set of factors lead to negative job feelings. For example, a worker or group are affected positively when given meaningful responsibilities such as being given the task of "seeing to it that a slab is formed to the proper elevation." On the other hand, if a laborer is asked to work in a sweaty, enclosed environment he will often have a poor morale and as such be less than fully productive. However, if this worker had been asked to

[15]Herzberg, F., *The Motivation to Work*, New York, Wiley, 1959.

work in an ideal environment, this environment in itself would not lead to added productivity. In summary, some factors tend to motivate worker productivity, others merely maintain existing productivity. However, if these maintenance factors are not favorable they will prove to be constraints to productivity. Understanding the effect of these factors will aid the construction manager in motivating individual workers and in making the goals and values of the informal groups within his firm more compatible with those of the firm.

6.7 Management By Objectives

Earlier sections have discussed productivity and personnel management as they relate to the manager, the individual worker, and the group. It is only natural that we expand our scope to a discussion of how we might bring the considerations of each of these individuals or groups of individuals under one roof. In particular, we need a means of integrating the concerned parties into the firm such that overall company goals can be accomplished. The concept by which we might do this is referred to as *management by objectives* (MBO). This concept suggests the need for a hierarchy of compatible objectives within the company organization. In addition, the concept suggests that these objectives identify the economic contribution of each segment of the organization in measurable terms.

The MBO process is merely a systematic formulation of the process of managing subordinates. However, unlike most management approaches, MBO is based upon the assumption that individuals respond better to specific short term goals and objectives than they do to vague long term goals that are incapable of measurement. MBO is particularly useful to the firm that consists of several operating units or departments. The construction firm has such a characteristic. In addition to the several somewhat separate functions that must be carried out by the firm (marketing, planning, procurement, control, accounting, etc.), the firm often is involved with the building of projects at several locations during a given period of time.

The MBO concept focuses on the economic contribution of each of the operating units in the firm. In order to achieve the firm's overall stated objective, the specific objectives of the individual operating units that make up the firm need to be compatible. The degree to which the firm defines operating units is left open. That is, the construction

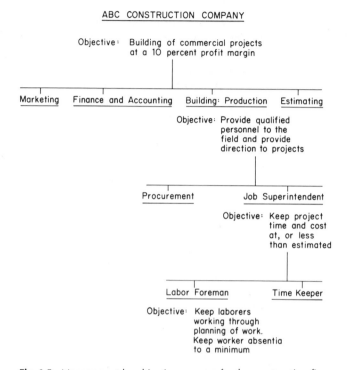

Fig. 6.5. Management by objective program for the construction firm.

firm may define individual projects it builds as its smallest operating unit or it may actually break the project into individual work packages (i.e., excavation work, concrete work, etc.) and identify these as the smallest operating units. Since individual operating units have designated types of work, specific objectives will not be identical, but they do have to be compatible. The MBO approach to obtaining this compatibility is to ascertain that in each of the several areas of work, the objectives at each operating unit level contribute to those at the next higher operating unit level. This process is referred to as the *hierarchy of objectives*.

Let us consider such a hierarchy of objectives for an average construction firm. Fig. 6.5 illustrates a typical hierarchy of objectives for such a firm. It should be noted that as shown in the illustration, the overall company objective predominates. The division and project objectives are made compatible with this objective. Further, note that the objectives at each organizational level are defined in terms of measurable goals. As such, each operating unit can be meaningfully evaluated as to its performance over a specific period of time with the goals specified for that period of time.

In order to have a successful management by objective program, the firm must totally commit itself to it. Organizing, planning, directing, and controlling are influenced by the MBO program. Personal committment to the identified goals of the firm and operating units makes it more likely that these goals will be accomplished. This includes involving nonmanagement personnel as well as management personnel. This type of process not only brings in more opinions and expertise, but it serves as a motivation tool. For example, if the construction firm's project foreman is asked to participate in project planning he might be able to use his experience in developing a more optimal project plan. Equally important is the fact that asking for his advice and participation will tend to satisfy his inner personal needs which will aid in motivating him in carrying out the actual work.

The gathering of interdisciplinary types of skills is also encouraged when determining the company or individual operating unit objectives. Individuals too close to the task often fail to recognize external factors that affect the setting of the objectives for the task. The employee responsible for material procurement and the project estimator may be able to view the firm's planning task more objectively than the firm's project planner.

In summary, the implementation of the MBO concept can have several positive effects in regard to firm objectives and personnel management. The following are examples of these positive effects.

(1) Provide coordination in the company organizational structure.
(2) Fully utilize expertise of all company personnel.
(3) Provide for a means of measuring the performance of the firm, the operating units, and the individual workers.
(4) Encourage worker productivity by addressing his inner job satisfaction.
(5) Encourage a friendly atmosphere among operating units and individual workers.
(6) Provide a basis by which company and operating unit objectives can be modified based upon an evaluation of past performances and stated objectives.

6.8 Modeling Productivity

The U. S. government through its Price Commission has discovered a relationship between industry and company productivity and the industry's or company's ability to measure and model its productivity. Significantly, companies with the largest increases in productivity are those that are best able to document and understand their production.

This point is especially important in regard to construction industry productivity. There is probably no industry that keeps fewer records than the construction industry. Too few construction firms attempt to model or document work production at even the most gross level.

It should be pointed out that one should not entirely fault the construction firm for the industry's lack of a single best means of measuring productivity. Admittedly, it is a difficult task in that many factors affect construction work productivity. Besides many of the engineering and management factors that effect construction productivity, psychologic and sociologic factors relate to the problem. These factors are often difficult to quantify and unify in a model.

Modeling construction method productivity as a function of productivity parameters enables the measuring, predicting, and improving of productivity. Several attempts have been made at applying scientific models that have been used extensively in various manufacturing industries to the modeling of construction method productivity. Included in these models are the following.

(1) Time Study
(2) Work Sampling
(3) Motion Analysis
(4) Balancing Model
(5) Learning Curve
(6) Regression Analysis
(7) Linear Programming
(8) Dynamic Programming
(9) Queueing
(10) Simulation
(11) Network Models
(12) Production Function
(13) Dallavia Model

The list is not intended to be complete. The point to be made here is that several of these models are very limited in scope and often not compatible with the modeling of construction productivity. Of the models listed, time study, work sampling, and motion analysis are most identified with the modeling of the individual worker. In addition, unlike several of the other models listed, these three models are somewhat general in that they can be used to model several types of worker production. As such, these three models will be discussed by means of examples. The interested reader is asked to turn to any of the many scientific management books in print for a discussion of the less general models listed. In addition to the traditional models a model developed by the author will be presented.

6.8.1 Traditional Models

Time Study. The objective of time study is to determine the "standard" time for an operation. By standard time is meant the time required by a qualified worker to perform the operation by a specified method while working at normal tempo. As such, time studies do not attempt to determine the optimal inputs or method for the production of an output; it only evaluates the time associated with a particular method. Of course a "best" method can be selected from those analyzed by time studies, but this approach is an "after the fact" approach. That is, various methods have to be tried and then the best is determined. There is no assurance that this best method is the optimal method.

Time studies of a method of doing an operation are accomplished by means of collecting data for the method while the operation is being performed. A number of representative observations of the times required for performing an operation using a specified method are taken.

A "selected" time to complete the operation is then determined by means of an averaging approach such that

$$\text{selected time} = \frac{\text{(operation time for representative observations)}}{\text{(number of representative observations)}}$$

The question to be asked is what should be the number of representative observations taken. Riggs[16] suggests using a formula based on standard error of the mean for determining the number of observations to be taken. His formula is based on confidence levels and precision levels. There exist quicker methods for determining the number of observations to be taken. The point is, once the number of observations to be taken is determined, the selected time for the operation can be determined.

The next step in determining the standard time for a method of doing an operation by means of time study is to determine the method's "normal time." Determining normal time implies that we may want to bring the work performed to a normal pace. The selected times do not

[16]Riggs, James L., *Economic Decision Models for Engineers and Managers*, New York, McGraw-Hill, 1968

account for items such as worker fatigue or his "tightness" or "looseness." A normal pace is often defined as one that can be maintained by an average worker during a typical working day without undue fatigue.

There are many approaches to setting rate factors for determining normal time. The observer in some consistent manner determines a rating factor for the work being observed. The normal time is then determined as follows.

normal time = (selected time) × (rating factor)

For example, assume that the selected time for doing an operation is determined as 60 minutes and the observer rates the work observed as 110% normal. The normal time for the operation is determined as

normal time = (60 min.) × (1.10) = 66 minutes

The "standard" time is the normal time plus allowances for interruptions. These may be personal allowances, fatigue allowances, or delay allowances. Unions sometimes necessitate personal allowances. This is usually in the form of rest periods which in the United States average about 5% of total work time.[17] Fatigue allowances are generally made due to the fact that worker production often decreases as a worker gets tired. After setting a 5% fatigue allowance, the time associated with a method is extended 5%. Delay allowances are for such things as machine breakdowns, bad weather, defective materials, etc. These are external inescapable interruptions.

A total allowance is determined by summing individual allowance percentages. The standard time for a method of doing an operation is then determined as follows.

standard time = normal time + (normal time) × (total allowance)

For example, considering the previous example where the normal time was 66 minutes, assume that the total allowance is 15%. The standard time for doing the specified method for the operation is as follows.

standard time = 66 minutes + (66 minutes × (.15)) = 76 minutes

Work Sampling. As the name suggests, work sampling involves observing a portion or sample of the work activity. Then, based on the findings in this sample, some statements can be made about the activity. For example, if we were to observe a concrete finisher at 100 random times during the day and found that he was involved in cleaning his tools 20 of the 100 times, we would estimate that the concrete finisher spent 20% of his time directly on cleaning his tools. In regard to planning a construction method, the result of this observation might lead to

[17]"Union Philosophy Surrounds Productivity Measurement Conference," *The Contractor,* November, 1972 p. 22.

the supplying of an additional laborer to the crew to clean the tools and free the finisher for productive work.

' Like time study methods, work sampling is done by direct observations; however, unlike time study the observations are made without a stopwatch. Many times only a glance is needed to determine the activity state, and the majority of studies require only several seconds of observation. Observing an activity even 100 times may not, however, provide the accuracy desired in the estimate. In order to define this estimate, three main issues must be decided.

(1) What level of statistical confidence is required?
(2) How many observations are needed?
(3) When should the observation be made?

The level of confidence required is usually set out by the model user. By means of statistical concepts the number of observations required for a defined percent confidence level can be made in terms of the absolute error. Absolute error is the actual range of observations. For example, let us assume that a contractor estimates that labor spends approximately 10% of its time idle. Assume, further, that he would like to be 95% confident that the findings of his work sampling study will be within the absolute error range of plus or minus 2%; that is, if his study shows that labor spends 10% of its time idle, he is 95% confident that the true percentage lies between 8% and 12%. Using a formulated statistical table, the contractor could then find the required number of observations. For the cited example with a 95% confidence limit, a 2% absolute error, and an estimate of 10% of total work time as idle time, a statistical table indicates that 900 observations are required.

From a procedural standpoint, the number of observations to be taken in a work sampling study are usually divided equally over the study period. Thus, if the 900 observations are to be made over a 10-day period, the observations are usually scheduled at 900/10, or 90 per day. Each day's observations are then assigned a specific time by using a random number table.

The observations are then taken and the state of the activity recorded at each observation. Let us assume that having taken 900 observations, the contractor finds that 11% of the laborer's time is idle time. Thus, he can state with 95% confidence that between 9% and 13% of labor's time is idle time. More detailed work sampling applications could then be performed to determine the breakdown of the idle time.

Motion Analysis Models. Motion analysis and motion analysis models can be traced to the early studies of Frederick Taylor[18] and Frank

---

[18]Taylor, Frederick W., *Scientific Management*, New York, Harper and Row, 1974.

and Lillian Gilbreth.[19] The objective of motion analysis is to determine the best possible way to perform an activity. It is directed toward the development of optimal procedures and working conditions. Several aspects of an activity are investigated in a motion study. The main component of the motion analysis study concerns itself with the set of human movements used in the activity.

By focusing in the set of human movements, motion analysis attempts to

Increase the efficiency of activities

Eliminate as many unnecessary motions as possible

Reduce physical fatigue

Make the activity safer

Improve the layout of the work plan

Improve the materials handling process

Standardize the optimum procedures and working conditions

Several principles of motion study were developed by the Gilbreth's. These principles guide the analyst in improving jobs so that they require less time and effort. A few examples of these principles are as follows.

(1) The two hands should begin as well as complete their motions at the same time.

(2) The two hands should not be idle at the same time except during rest periods.

(3) Hand motions should be confined to the lowest classification with which it is possible to perform the work. The general classification is as follows.

    (a) Finger motions

    (b) Motions involving fingers and wrist

    (c) Motions involving fingers, wrist, and forearm

    (d) Motions involving fingers, wrist, forearm, and upper arm

    (e) Motions involving fingers, wrist, forearm, upper arm, and shoulder

(4) Smooth continuous motions of the hands are preferable to zigzag motions involving sudden and sharp changes in direction.

To enable the charting or modeling of motions, the Gilbreths developed a set of "therbligs." A *therblig* is a basic elementary motion. It can be used to model and describe different methods. Typical therbligs used by the Gilbreths are as follows.

---

[19]Gilbreth, Frank B., *Motion Study, A Method for Increasing the Efficiency of Workmen*, New York, Van Nostrand, 1911.

Therblig	Abbreviation
Search	Sh
Grasp	G
Transport empty	TE
Transport loaded	TL
Hold	H
Position	P
Rest for fatigue	R

Closely related to the concept of using therbligs to model activities is the use of process charts. Process charts are graphic methods of describing a particular job. In motion study, these charts are constructed for the existing process. The motion study analyst examines them and attempts to improve the process. The following symbols are used in process chart modeling.

o	indicates an operation
▼	indicates a storage
→	indicates a transportation
□	indicates an inspection
D	indicates a delay

The process chart can be used for modeling a construction activity. For example, let us consider the construction activity in which a laborer mixes mortar, inspects it, transports it to a bricklayer, and returns. The process chart model for the activity might be as follows.

Symbol	Distance (yards)	Time (seconds)	Activity
o		1120	mixing
□		120	check quality
→	19	300	transport with fork lift
D		120	awaits help from bricklayer
→	19	152	return to mixing site

The process chart can also be used for a more detailed modeling of the activity. That is, it might be used to chart the actual hand movements of the laborer in question.

6.8.2 Method Productivity Delay Model

In this section a model will be discussed that has been developed by the author for modeling construction method productivity. The model is referred to as the Method Productivity Delay Model (MPDM).[20] It can be viewed as an alternative to the more traditional work sampling, time study, and motion analysis models. The objective of the model is to provide the construction firm a practical means of measuring, predicting, and improving productivity.

An overview of the MPDM is shown in Fig. 6.6. The model is broken into four elements. These consist of the collection of data, the processing of data, the structured model, and the implementation element. Each of these elements will now be discussed separately.

Collection of Data. The purpose of the collection element is to collect method productivity data to be used as a basis for modeling the method productivity. It addresses the determination and collection of three types of information.

(1) Identify the "production unit."
(2) Identify the "production cycle."
(3) Collect data concerning the time required for the completion of production cycles and document productivity delays.

The definition of a method's production unit serves as the basis for measuring, predicting, and improving method productivity. The "production unit" is an amount of work descriptive of the production which can easily be visually measured. Typical examples of production units are

(1) arrival of a scraper in a borrow-pit,
(2) releasing of concrete from a crane bucket,
(3) placing of one row of concrete blocks on a wall,
(4) placement of a structural member.

---

[20]Adrian, J. J., *Modeling Construction Productivity*, Thesis presented for partical fulfillment of degree of Doctor of Philosophy in Civil Engineering, University of Illinois, Urbana, Illinois, October, 1974.

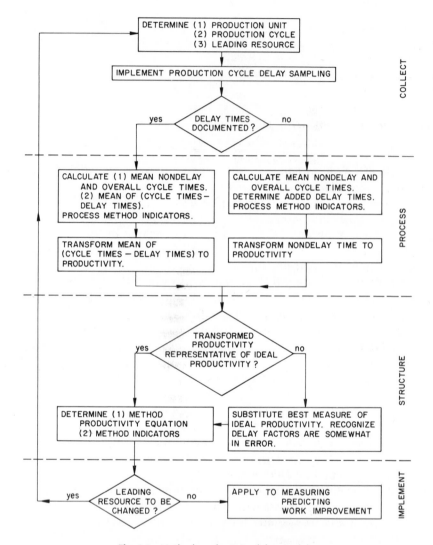

Fig. 6.6. Method productivity delay model.

A "production cycle" is the time between consecutive occurrences of the production unit. The production unit cannot be defined independently of the other elements of the model. The definition of the production unit dictates the detail used to measure method productivity. If the production unit is defined in too broad a context the collected productivity information may be of little aid in productivity measurement, prediction, and improvement. For example, if the production unit is defined as the completion of the placing and finishing of concrete for a wall section of 200 square feet, the collected production cycle times and delay information may be too broad to focus on parameters that affect productivity. On the other hand, too detailed a definition of the production unit may curtail the model user's ability to identify productivity delays or even the completion of a production cycle. For example, if the placing of a single brick is identified as the production unit when four masons are simultaneously placing bricks, the model user will find it difficult to document the successive completion of production cycles, let alone cite productivity delays.

The data collected in documenting the production cycle times and delays serve as the basis for the delay information part of the productivity equation that is part of the MPDM. The documented production cycle times serve as a basis for the first part of the productivity equation.

The following are documented.

(1) Time required to complete production cycle.

(2) Occurrence of productivity delay.

(3) If more than one productivity delay type is found in a given cycle, the total delay of the cycle is allocated by approximate percentage or by documented times.

(4) Any unusual events that characterize a given production cycle.

A data collection form, along with example data is shown in Fig. 6.7. The procedure for collecting the data is referred to as Production Cycle Delay Sampling (PCDS).

Documenting production cycle times is straightforward. The model user merely clocks the time between occurrences of the production unit. If the method is very complex or the production cycle times are very short, such that visual inspection is impossible or inaccurate, a filming procedure such as time lapse can be used to document the method productivity.

Citing and documenting production cycle delays, whether they are single or multiple type delays, requires a degree of skill from the MPDM user. The model user's ability to single out productivity delay types normally increases with his practical experience and decreases as the complexity of the method in question increases. The types of delays identified may vary depending on the construction method. Construction method delays can normally be identified that are observable and independent of one another. The following example of the MPDM will consider five delay types: environment, equipment, labor, material, and

PRODUCTION CYCLE DELAY SAMPLING

Page 1 of 1
Method: Crane Bucket Concrete Pour

Unit: Seconds
Production Unit: Concrete Drop

Production Cycle	Production Cycle Time (sec.)	Environment Delay	Equipment Delay	Labor Delay	Material Delay	Management Delay	Notes	Minus Mean Nondelay Time
1	120			✓				27
2	126		✓					33
3	98						✓	5
4	112		✓					19
5	108							15
6	1122					✓	CRANE MOVE	1029
7	116		✓					23
8	214		✓					121
9	92						✓	1
10	88						✓	5
11	100						✓	7
12	312		✓					219
13	110			✓				17
14	666		90%	10%				573
15	146		25%	75%				53
16	120		✓					27
17	138		✓					45
18	144		20%	80%				51
19	598	✓					CRANE SLIP	505
20	118		✓					25
21	138		✓					45
22	108						✓	15
23	98						✓	5
24	120			✓				27
25	116			✓				23
26	368		✓					275
27	118		✓					25
28	140		✓					47
29	136			✓				43
30	138			✓				45
31	154			✓				61
32	396		✓					303
33	96						✓	3
34	286		✓					193
35	80						✓	13
36	82						✓	11
37	84						✓	9
38	212			✓				119
39	78						✓	15
40								

Fig. 6.7. Production cycle delay sampling.

management. If the user finds it convenient to add or delete from these five types, the MPDM procedure remains unchanged. Examples of the five types of delays follow.

(1) Environment: Change in soil conditions, change in wall section, change in roadway alignment
(2) Equipment: Stationary production equipment in transit, equipment operating at less than capable production rate.
(3) Labor: Workman waiting for another workman, workman loafing, worker fatigue, workman not productive because of lack of knowledge of his work.
(4) Material: Material not available for equipment or labor demand, material defective.
(5) Management: Poor planning of method resource combination and placement, secondary operation interfering with method productivity, poor method layout planning.

Model Processing and Structuring. The processing element of the MPDM provides the connection between the model's collected data, the structured method productivity equation, and the accompanying measure of risk and variability. The processing consists of adding, subtracting, multiplying, and dividing; the procedure possesses the desired model attributes of ease and economy of implementation. The processing data formulated from the collected data shown in Fig. 6.7 is processed by means of the form shown in Fig. 6.8. The form and entries are intended to be self-explanatory.

The first part of the structured MPDM as shown in Fig. 6.9 is a method productivity equation that relates overall or actual method productivity to ideal method productivity as a function of the identified productivity delay types. This method productivity equation is used directly to aid in measuring, predicting and improving method productivity.

"Ideal productivity" is that productivity which occurs when productivity delays are absent. The nondelay production cycles documented in the collection of data (Fig. 6.7) are, in fact, ideal productivity cycles if all delays have been cited. However, if conditions exist which indicate some delays are not being detected, the model user should select other techniques for determining ideal productivity. Even if the nondelay cycles appear adequate as a measure of ideal productivity, it may be beneficial to compare the calculated productivity with a historical record.

The nondelay production cycle time is transformed into production per time period interval for which productivity is to be measured,

MPDM PROCESSING

Method:			Unit: Production Unit:	
Units	Production Total Time	Number of Cycles	Mean Cycle Time	$\Sigma[\mid$(Cycle time) $-$ (non- dealy cycle time)$\mid$]/n
(A) Nondelayed Production Cycles	1112	12	92.6	8.7
(B) Overall Production Cycles	7596	39	194.7	104.5

DELAY INFORMATION

	Environment	Equipment	Labor	Material	Management
(C) Occurrences	1	17	11	0	1
(D) Total Added Time	505	1939	500	0	1029
(E) Probability Of Occurrences*	.026	.436	.287	0	.026
(F) Relative Severity**	2.59	.58	.23	0	5.28
(G) Expected % Delay Time Per Produc- tion Cycle***	6.7	25.4	6.6	0	13.7

*Delay cycles/total number of cycles.
**Mean added cycle time/mean overall cycle time.
***Row E times row F times 100.

Fig. 6.8. MPDM processing.

MPDM STRUCTURE

Crane Bucket Concrete Pour

Production unit: Concrete drop

1. *Productivity equation*

$$\frac{\text{Overall method}}{\text{productivity}} = (\text{Ideal productivity}) (1-\text{Een}-\text{Eeq}-\text{Ela}-\text{Emt}-\text{Emn})$$

18.5 units/hr. = (38.9 units/hr) $(1-.067-.254-.066-.137)$

where   Een = expected environmental delay time as a decimal
           fraction of total production time.
         Eeq = expected equipment delay time
         Ela = expected labor delay time
         Emt = expected material delay time
         Emn = expected management delay time

2. *Method indicators*

(A) Variability of method productivity

Ideal cycle variability = 8.7/92.6 = .09
Overall cycle variability = 104.5/194.7 = .54

(B) Delay information

	Environment	Equipment	Labor	Material	Management
Probability of occurrence	.026	.436	.287	0	.026
Relative severity	2.59	.58	.23	0	5.28
Expected % delay time per production cycle	6.7	25.4	6.6	0	13.7

Fig. 6.9. MPDM structure.

predicted, and work improvement is to be performed. This time period interval will normally be in units per hour or day. The mean nondelay production cycle time for the example is 92.6 sec. The ideal productivity calculated on an hourly basis is

$$\frac{(60 \text{ min/hr}) \times (60 \text{ sec/min})}{92.6 \text{ sec/unit}} = 38.9 \text{ units/hr}$$

If the calculated value is not considered reliable, the value determined in some other manner may be used as the ideal productivity. If the production unit is appropriately defined and the model user is skillful in detecting errors this substitution will seldom be warranted.

The environmental (Een), equipment (Eeq), labor (Ela), material (Emt), and management (Emn) factors in the right-hand side of the productivity equation shown in Fig. 6.9 relate the method's ideal productivity to the method's overall productivity. The factors, which can have values ranging from 0 to 1, are the decimal fraction of total production time caused by each delay type. The factor 1 minus the sum of Een, Eeq, Ela, Emt, and Emn relates the probability of productive work being performed. The left-hand side of the productivity equation in Fig. 6.9 is the "overall method productivity."

Part 2 of the structured model shown in Fig. 6.9 contains "method indicators." The information set out in this segment of the model will be used as indicators to predict and improve method productivity.

Four types of information are set out in the "method indicator" part of the structured MPDM. The first, "variability of method productivity," gives a measure of the variable nature of both the nondelay productivity cycles and the total overall productivity cycles. These are determined as follows.

$$\text{Ideal Cycle Variability} = \frac{\dfrac{\sum \left| \left(\begin{array}{c} \text{Nondelay} \\ \text{cycle time} \end{array} \right) - \left(\begin{array}{c} \text{Mean nondelay} \\ \text{cycle time} \end{array} \right) \right|}{\text{Number of nondelay cycles}}}{\text{Mean nondelay cycle time}}$$

$$\text{Overall Cycle Variability} = \frac{\dfrac{\sum \left| \left(\begin{array}{c} \text{Overall cycle} \\ \text{time} \end{array} \right) - \left(\begin{array}{c} \text{Mean nondelay} \\ \text{cycle time} \end{array} \right) \right|}{\text{Number of total cycles}}}{\text{Mean overall cycle time}}$$

Nondelay cycle times are durations of cycles in which no delays are detected. Overall cycle times are the durations of all cycles without regard for detection of delays. For the data shown in Fig. 6.7 and processed in Fig. 6.8, the "variability of method productivity" is .09 for the ideal cycles and .54 for overall cycles.

The three other indicators in this part of the model relate to selected productivity delays. They are the "probability of occurrence," "relative severity," and the "expected percent of delay time per production cycle." These indicators are used in analysis of potential work improvement.

Model Implementation and Benefits. The MPDM calculated nondelay productivity rate and the overall productivity rate represent measured productivities. Measuring is one of the objectives of the model. The derived productivity equation provides the basis for method productivity prediction. The factors relating method ideal productivity to overall method productivity may be predicted or calculated from past data.

The constant in the method productivity equation, the "ideal productivity," should be fixed. For a given construction method some variation exists in the time of ideal production cycles; however, this variability is small compared to the variability in the cycle times for overall production cycles.

The delay factors can all be considered variables. Although the delay factors (E's) are given values as a result of collection of data from the previous performance(s) of the method in question, they may take on new values for a future occurrence of the construction method.

When a contractor is faced with a construction method for which he has collected MPDM data, he should focus attention on the calculated delay factors. He might determine that one or more of the factors will be lower or higher on the upcoming performance of the method. The previously determined delay factors should therefore be adjusted. This adjustment in delay factors will result in prediction of a new overall method productivity.

The MPDM user cannot assume that actual results will correspond to predicted values. If the method's leading resource is changed in quantity, a new method results and MPDM prediction becomes difficult. If only support resources are changed, prediction is still not precise. For example, three support laborers might be used on a construction method and the MPDM for the method may indicate a 30% labor delay factor. How much of a reduction in the delay factor will occur if an additional laborer is used for the method? The MPDM does not yield a single prediction, however, it does indicate that the method productivity should increase between 0% and 30%. Further consideration of the interdependencies between the method's resource parameters and the other delay factors should provide the MPDM user with a means of estimating the actual reduction in the delay factor and the corresponding increase in method productivity.

Once the construction productivity for the new method is documented, the prediction can be evaluated. This evaluation should serve as a means of better predicting future method productivity.

The contractor should also be concerned about the reliability of his prediction or the variability of productivity. As an aid in judging the variability of the productivity of a method the MPDM user should focus on "Variabilities of method productivity." In particular, the higher the overall cycle variability and the ideal cycle variability, the less dependable the productivity prediction. Ideally, these ratios should be small.

Of the three tasks of measuring, predicting, and improving method productivity, the MPDM is probably the most useful in the work improvement task. Consider the structured MPDM in Fig. 6.9 which was derived from the data collected in Fig. 6.7 and processed in Fig. 6.8. Inspection of the MPDM structure for the method, indicates that the equipment delay and the management delay are critical as they result in large percent production delay times. Attention should possibly be focused on these two types of delays when trying to improve productivity.

6.9 Applications to the Construction Industry

Previous sections in this chapter have addressed personnel management concepts and principles. In reality, there has been a lack of documentation of applications of these concepts and principles to the construction industry. This is not to say that the concepts and principles do not apply. The more plausible explanation is that the construction industry in general has not paid much attention to the problems of productivity and personnel management. In addition, the industry's nonacademic characteristics have resulted in little documentation of those applications of personnel management concepts and principles that have been employed by other types of firms.

Increasing awareness of the higher costs of direct labor are starting to stimulate personnel management programs in the construction industry. As they grow in number, such programs will start to be more frequently documented in industry literature. Within the past few years, a few of these programs have been documented. In particular, Schrader[21] has researched these programs and documented their positive and negative effects. Some of these personnel management programs are summarized in the following paragraphs.

As discussed in previous sections, the individual worker has several needs. Whereas some of these needs are physical in nature (shelter, security, etc.), others tend to be inner personal in nature (i.e., satisfaction with work, pride, etc.). Somewhat consistent with the previously discussed theory Y concept, Schrader places emphasis on a construction worker's inner needs such as his sense of belonging and status. He argues that the strong labor unions have provided the worker with sufficient wages, security, and safety. As such, these physical needs are somewhat secondary merely because they are assumed to be present.

Several documented productivity personnel management programs are centered around this concept of satisfying a worker's inner needs and the assumption that theory Y is valid. For example, one large firm has a program whereby they have a weekly meeting and award performance awards and certificates to workers that show pride in their work by exhibiting good safety practices, good job "housekeeping," and productive work practices. Such a program was reported to increase worker productivity on the order of 20%.

Other documented construction motivation programs are more consistent with theory X concepts. In particular, the worker is rewarded with physical benefits for high productivity. The Fred Weber Contractor Company in St. Louis is well known for this type of program. The firm offers a type of profit sharing program to its workers. Bonuses are paid in the form of a share of profits. Watches and cars are given to productive workers who have been with the firm for a given number of years. This approach of relating to the physical needs of the worker as a motivational tool has resulted in the firm having high productivity and reduced costs. It has been said that other firms in the same geographic area have had difficulty competing against the firm in the competitive bidding environment because of this higher productivity.

Personnel management concepts as they relate to the needs and values of groups of construction workers have also been documented.

[21]Schrader, C. R., "Motivation of Construction Craftsmen", *Journal of the Construction Division*, New York, American Society of Civil Engineers, September, 1972, pp. 257–273.

Several years past, Van Zelst[22] conducted research to measure the effect on construction project productivity when friends worked together. Workers were permitted to work with the people with whom they most liked to work. The result was a 5 % increase in productivity. In addition the men tended to be happy with their work and as a result there was less worker turnover.

As discussed earlier, productivity can usually be increased if workers' goals are made consistent with company goals. As such, it is often beneficial to inform workers as to the company's objectives. A management by objective approach has this advantage. Emery Air Freight Corporation provides daily feedback to its workers on how their work compares with company goals.[23] Such a program has resulted in substantial cost savings. Yet another firm has used a program that might be considered to be a modification of the management by objectives concept. Crews are given the estimated time and cost for individual work packages as estimated by management. The project superintendent then measures the forearm and his crew's performance against this estimate and informs them of the results of the comparison. The result is that individual crews have goals (the work packages are usually small and take only a few days to complete) to work towards. The result of this type of program led to cost savings approaching 50% for select work packages.

Other personnel management programs or program elements that have been implemented by various construction firms include the following.

(1) Orientation program for new workers. This includes discussion of the history of the firm, their goals, safety programs, and benefits to employees.

(2) Guarantee workers a minimum amount of work per year. For example, some, if not all of the workers, are guaranteed 30 hours of work 45 weeks a year.

(3) All company promotions are made from within. These promotions are based on merit rather than only seniority.

(4) Project and company newsletters. These newsletters highlight promotions, good performance, safety awards, and general stories about workers such as hobbies, births, etc.

---

[22]Jones, W. L., *Human Factors as They Affect Method Improvement in Construction*, Stanford University, Department of Civil Engineering, Stanford, September, 1964.

[23]Schrader, C. R., "Boosting Construction Worker Productivity," *Civil Engineering*, October, 1972, p. 62.

(5) Regularly occurring lunch meetings. Awards may be given. A speaker may be invited to address technical or nontechnical subject matters.
(6) Special events such as steak frys, company dinners, or family cookouts.
(7) Sponsorship of company teams and clubs such as a bowling team or wife's social club.
(8) A company channel whereby workers can readily voice their opinions and complaints. Such a channel can be a phone line or a suggestion box.

It should be observed that all of the program elements listed relate to one or more of the personnel management concepts discussed in earlier sections. Innovative management undoubtedly can create other effective motivating practices. The point to be made is that such motivational programs will quickly pay for themselves. The cost of such a program is usually nominal. While the benefits may be somewhat difficult to measure, experience has shown that they normally far outweigh costs.

6.10 Summary

The construction industry has traditionally observed only slight increases in its productivity. While some of the reasons for only limited increases in productivity can be traced to outdated building codes, lack of industrialization techniques, the variable environment in which the construction product is built, and uniqueness of the construction product and industry itself; undoubtedly labors' unwillingness to be fully productive can in many cases be related to less than ideal productivity. However, the individual worker cannot be totally faulted for his less than optimal productivity. By practicing personnel management concepts and practices, management could often better motivate the construction worker.

While not totally a science, personnel management is in fact based on various theories and well-founded principles. While some of these theories conflict as to their assumptions (i.e., theory X versus theory Y), the implementation of any one of them is likely to result in some positive motivational benefits. The area of personnel management does not limit itself to the study of the individual worker. The recognition of a group of workers and their place in the organizational structure plays an important role in motivational theory and productivity. As such, consideration of formal and informal groups, and the concept of management by objectives can be considered part of the personnel management area of study.

There has been a noticeable lack of implementation of the concepts and principles of motivation and personnel management in the construction industry. However, as labor costs continue to substantially increase, the lack of recognition of this subject area will become even more detrimental to the construction firm. A few construction firms have started to recognize the importance of the motivation of its workers and as such have implemented various types of personnel management theory founded programs. These have ranged from profit sharing programs to letting workers choose with whom they want to work. The end result is that the firms that have implemented such motivational programs have usually obtained benefits (e.g., higher productivity, reduced costs, less worker turnover) that exceed the normally nominal costs of implementation of such a program.

Case 6.1. Moto Construction Company:
Motivating Middle Management

The Moto Construction Company is a progressive construction management firm whose management group has always prided itself on the high level of employee relations in the company. The company's philosophy is primarily reflective of the fact that the founder of the firm, who has since passed away, believed that the firm's success had to be based on complete employee committment to its objectives. The company, unlike many construction related firms, had a fringe benefit system, and an employee suggestion system that has provided a generous financial incentive for suggestions that result in improvements in the firm's management. The profit sharing program, by which the company contributes a fixed percentage of its profits to an employee investment and retirement fund has also been credited as being a major factor in promoting a high level of morale in the company.

Typical of the results of Moto's motivation programs is Jack Egan. As overall company project superintendent, individual project superintendent motivation has never been a problem. However, within the past two years, the construction industry has been victim of a slow-down. In response to market conditions and competitive factors in the industry, Moto Company has had to make personnel reductions and merit increases have been largely curtailed. Since company profits were low last year, so was the contribution to the employee profit sharing fund.

The general economic "tightening of the bolt" within the firm has meant that fewer company foreman and superintendents are available to do the same work. Jack Egan was gratified at the response of the foremen and superintendents during the first several months of the economic slowdown. Several of them worked overtime in order to complete required work. Recently, however, Mr. Egan has detected several attitudes that he believes are indicative of a developing prob-lem. On three specific occasions he has heard personnel complaining about the overtime work necessary to complete assigned work. As one of his superintendents stated, "Moto is getting a lot of free labor under the present arrangement, and I don't see any end in sight." Although it is not clear if the two are related, a few superintendents have also left the firm recently in order to accept job offers with other companies.

John Egan has recently brought the occurrence of these events to you, Moto's personnel director. Should you be particularly concerned by the fact that a few of the superintendents left the company and what can you do to improve the motivational climate?

Case 6.2. Makum Construction Company: Leadership and Supervising

Ralph Spears was overall project superintendent of the Makum Construction Company. He had the reputation of being a hard-nosed boss who demanded strict adherence to his instructions, as well as informal control methods. When he was first promoted to project superintendent two years ago, a considerable amount of discord de-veloped in the Makum Company. During the first 9 months of his appointment 5 job foremen under his jurisdiction had quit the firm. However, just about the time that Eugene Hancock, the company's president, was about to remove Spears from his job, the problems sub-sided as the remaining job foremen and those he hired accepted his style of leadership. Although Spears encouraged participation of his foremen during the planning stage of a project, once he made procedure and scheduling decisions, he expected strict compliance.

During his period of superintendent, Ralph Spears reduced overall project costs by 6% while meeting all time schedules for the projects. He had the reputation of running a tight and efficient operation. Largely because of his performance record he was offered an irresistible offer with another firm, and after adequate notice left the Makum Construction Company.

Ralph Spears unexpected departure left a gap in the firm. Eugene Hancock decided to appoint one of the firm's current foremen, Mike Nicek, the new overall project superintendent. Another foreman was hired to fill Mike's previous position. Mike was regarded as a highly competent job foreman, and he saw his new position as an opportunity to gain greater experience along with an increase in pay.

Mike Nicek was a strong believer in management by objectives. He believed in assigning tasks in terms of the objectives and leaving it up to the individual job foreman to formulate the necessary procedures and plans to accomplish the objectives. He was available for advice; however, he avoided becoming involved in every detail.

After his first few months at his new position, things were not going well. Costs were above estimates and three/four projects were behind schedule. In discussing the problem with the job foremen, Eugene Hancock found that the foremen did not believe that Mike Nicek understood the work he was supervising. He was not acting like a supervisor. He refused to specify how goals were to be accomplished and then held the individual foreman responsible when projects costs were high or the project was behind schedule. Therefore, the foremen were frustrated.

What should Eugene Hancock, as president of the Makum Construction Company do, if anything?

Case 6.3. Block Construction Company:
Modeling Productivity

Block Construction Company is a masonry contracting firm. Lately the firm has become concerned about the productivity of placing concrete block in vertical walls. Currently it utilizes a labor crew of four masons and two laborers. The two laborers mix mortar and transport the on-site concrete block to the four masons.

As a means of evaluating and improving productivity for placing concrete block, Block Company has hired you to collect productivity data for the method. The collected data are shown in the data collection form.

Each production cycle shown represents the placing of four concrete blocks. In a normal cycle this represents a single block placed by each mason. Most if not all of the environment delays result from the

PRODUCTION CYCLE DELAY SAMPLING

Page 1 of 1
Method: Placing Concrete Block

Unit: sec
Production Unit: four blocks

Production Cycle	Production Cycle Time (sec.)	Environment Delay	Equipment Delay	Labor Delay	Material Delay	Management Delay	Notes	Minus Mean Nondelay Time
1	68				✓			47
2	32				✓			11
3	16						✓	5
4	24						✓	3
5	20						✓	1
6	24						✓	3
7	28							7
8	120			✓				19
9	24						✓	3
10	28				✓			7
11	20						✓	1
12	16						✓	5
13	16						✓	5
14	32				✓			11
15	28	✓						7
16	264			✓				243
17	32				✓			11
18	32				✓			11
19	32				✓			11
20	24						✓	3
21	36				✓			15
22	40				✓			19
23	32				✓			11
24	764			✓			✓	743
25	20							1
26	40				✓			19
27	24						✓	3
28	20						✓	1
29	32				✓			11
30	32				✓			11
31	40	✓						19
32	248			✓			✓	221
33	20							1
34	36						✓	15
35	20							1
36	36							15
37	24						✓	3
38	80							59
39	44	✓						23
40	420				✓			399

need to change the scaffolding and the placement of block around lintals. Much of the labor delay shown results from the fact that after placing several rows of block, the masons move to the other side of the placed blocks to strike them off. The material delays shown represent the time masons wait for laborers to furnish blocks for placement.

Block Construction Company has decided that a change in the method may be warranted. What change should be made and what is the expected benefits versus cost of such a change?

Chapter 7

Cost Accounting: Planning and Controlling Costs

7.1 Introduction

Normally one thinks of the accounting process as being aimed at the producing of financial statements for the external use by stockholders, government agencies (e.g., Securities Exchange Commission), and other outside parties (e.g., banks, bonding companies, etc.). However, a properly designed accounting system should also prove useful as an internal management tool. In particular, it should provide information for the following two internal purposes.

(1) Information for managers for use in planning and controlling every day routine company operations.
(2) Information for managers for use in making nonroutine decisions such as plant expansion, expansion of product lines.

Although it aids as a means of producing company financial statements, *cost accounting* focuses on the two internal objectives. As such, cost accounting is commonly referred to as *managerial accounting*. By either name one can think of cost accounting as a system of procedures, forms, records, and statements that satisfy the three identified accounting purposes with emphasis on the two internal purposes.

For many years, cost accounting was thought of as a tool for product and inventory pricing and valuation. As such, it served only the planning purpose. However, today cost accounting addresses several other purposes of which control is one of the most important. As such, cost accounting addresses the two widely recognized internal management responsibilities of planning and control. Planning and controlling while being related are quite different functions. Planning can be thought of as management's defining a systematic and formalized plan for directing the future operations toward desired objectives. Cost accounting information is extremely valuable for aiding in management planning decisions.

The program and actions developed in the planning process play a significant role in the control process. No cost, revenue, or process (e.g., man hours expended) can be controlled unless actual results can be compared with some standard that was developed as part of the planning process. On the other hand, the process of control involves more than just comparing actual results with plans. The action taken by management is the critical step in the control process. If management does not take action when the cost accounting system indicates inefficiencies, then costs are not controlled.

Planning and control decisions require a high volume of information that frequently consists of both monetary and nonmonetary data. Nonmonetary data includes hours worked, material used, equipment use, etc. Unlike *financial accounting*, which focuses on the production of financial statements, a properly designed cost accounting system addresses this nonmonetary information in addition to select monetary accounting data. The components of such a system are discussed in the following sections.

7.2 Cost Accounting in the Construction Industry

There is probably no type of firm that needs an effective cost accounting system more than the construction firm. However, it is also true that there is no type of firm that lacks such a system more than the construction firm. It is not unusual to find a construction firm which has very little idea of the amount of gross profit or loss on any given contract until the project has been fully completed. In addition, the firm has only an estimate or faint idea of how a project is progressing as to the project plan. Various reasons can be cited for the failure of firms within the construction industry to implement an effective cost accounting system. Most of these reasons center around the following.

(1) The typical firm is small and often lacks accounting experience.
(2) Wide fluctuations in labor and material costs present recording difficulties.
(3) Worker productivity is often difficult to document and control.
(4) Varying environment and job contingencies result in cost and productivity documentation problems.
(5) Decentralization of the manufacturing process (projects built a distance from a firm's central office) create accounting communication problems.

The reasons cited for difficulties in implementing cost accounting systems in the construction industry do not justify the failure to install such a system. When one considers the need and advantages of an effective cost accounting system to the construction firm, each and every firm can easily justify the time, effort, and cost of installing such a system. Let us consider why it is necessary that the construction firm recognize and implement an effective cost accounting system.

The construction firm's cost accounting system directly affects five different vital aspects of the firm's operations. These are as follows.

(1) Control of project production and costs.
(2) Prediction and control of cash flow.
(3) Enable project estimating and planning.
(4) Provide the means of evaluating personnel.
(5) Enable and facilitate negotiations with bankers and bonding companies.

The control aspect of a cost accounting system was discussed previously. In order to have an effective cost control program, the trend of the cost must be determined as soon as possible and compared against the progress of the plan such that any required corrective action by the manager can be taken. The means by which a firm performs this task can be identified as its cost accounting system. Alternatively, such a system is sometimes referred to as *cost engineering*.

The control aspect cannot be overemphasized in regard to the operation of the construction firm. If one were to investigate the reasons behind many of the reported construction firm failures, lack of control, whether production or cost, would be identified as the underlying cause. Typically, the construction firm operates on a relatively small profit margin. Net profit margins are often 1.5% or less. In a recent survey it was found that only 9 of 61 lines of business studied operated on a smaller profit margin than the construction firm.[1] As such, the construction firm relies on performing a large dollar volume of work at a relatively small profit margin in order to provide adequate profits. This lack of a high profit margin and the need for performing a large dollar volume of work results in substantial financial risk for the firm. Without adequate control, the risk is increased.

The need to have a means of quickly documenting project production and costs are emphasized by the fact that the firm's planned production and costs are often somewhat crude estimates. Unlike several manufacturing industries that perform repetitive types of work tasks,

[1]O'Brian, J. J., and Zilly, R. G., *Contractors Management Handbook*, New York, McGraw-Hill, 1971, p. 19.

the construction firm is often faced with new types of projects and work tasks. As such, the firm cannot be very deterministic in planning its project production and costs. The end result is that actual project production and costs may substantially differ from those planned. Some of the differences may be due to improper control, the rest may be identified with a less than accurate plan. In fact, several construction firms use this type of argument in trying to justify their lack of an effective cost accounting system; that is, they argue that control loses its meaning when confronted with a less than deterministic plan. Undoubtedly a more deterministic plan will facilitate control. However, it does not follow that unplanned production or costs will completely defy control.

The actual carrying out of the construction project control task by means of a cost accounting system is made difficult by several characteristics of the industry. The variable nature of the project (and the type of work, production, and costs), the industry's high dependence on labor, the somewhat variable and unpredictable nature of construction labor productivity, and the relatively variable geographic distances of the manufacturing process (i.e., the construction project) from the firm's central office all create cost accounting implementation difficulties. The end result is that several unique procedures and forms for data documentation are necessary for implementing an effective system for the construction firm. These procedures and forms are discussed in following sections.

The documentation and analysis of project and company costs by way of a cost accounting system provides the construction firm with a means of carrying out the ever so important prediction and control of cash flow. *Cash flow* is the net effect of cash receipts and disbursements for a specified period. In particular, cash flow analysis relates to the determination of available liquid (readily available) assets that are available to the firm at any given time. Because of the nature of the business it performs (i.e., large dollar sized projects), the construction firm does well if it can maintain 5% of its contract amounts outstanding as liquid assets (i.e., cash, readily negotiable securities, etc.). The bonding company may in fact require the firm to maintain this ratio at 10%.[2]

Many a construction firm has failed financially as a result of its inability to predict cash flow requirements. A properly designed cost accounting system can go a long way in remedying a firm's inadequate cash flow analysis.

[2]Wolkstein, H. W., *Accounting Methods and Controls for the Construction Industry*, Englewood Cliffs, Prentice-Hall, 1967, p. 100.

Currently, cost accounting is normally thought of as a control tool. However, one does not have to go back very many years to find that management focused on cost accounting as only a planning tool. In particular, cost accounting was used almost exclusively for product pricing. It is in this context that accounting can be used by the construction firm in carrying out of the project estimating task. Estimating can be viewed as the predicting and planning of the costs of a future project. Even recognizing the somewhat unique nature of each construction project, several types of similar work are common to each and every project. Each building constructed normally has foundation excavation, concrete footings, foundation walls, etc. By gathering, formulating, and analyzing cost data from past and current projects, the construction firm can use this data as the bases for estimating future projects. This is not to imply that unique job site factors should not be recognized for each new project. However, an accurate project estimate can be made by using historic data and adjusting the data for unique job site factors (i.e., expected rainfall, project layout, worker morale, etc.).

A firm's cost accounting system can be effectively integrated with the construction firm's estimating system. The two systems are very compatible and compliment one another. With the increasing availability of data processing devices (i.e., large memory computers, time-sharing computer systems, sophisticated calculators) it is possible to integrate the firm's cost accounting and estimating tasks with other required tasks such as payroll and overall project and method planning. Such an integrated system is shown in Fig. 7.1. Total management systems such as the one illustrated in Fig. 7.1 are finding their way into the larger construction firms. The trend is toward making them feasible for the middle and even the small sized firms. It should be noted that the cost accounting subsystem is the fundamental element to the overall management system shown.

Somewhat related to the control aspect of cost accounting, is the evaluation of company personnel. Without the use of cost accounting it is difficult, if not impossible, to associate production and cost inefficiencies with a given worker, foreman, superintendent, or manager. In addition, it is also difficult to pinpoint and recognize rewardable efforts on the part of company personnel. Cost accounting, by means of formalized data collection procedures and by means of analysis of documented production and cost, focuses on the reasons for good or poor performance. Cost accounting places emphasis on what is commonly referred to as *responsibility accounting*. Responsibility accounting recognizes various responsibility centers within the firm, and holds

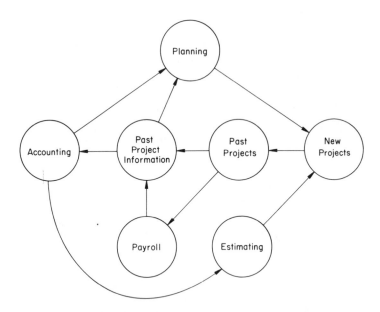

Fig. 7.1. Integrated cost accounting system.

each of these responsibility centers accountable for its actions. This type of accounting system is also referred to as *activity accounting.*

A properly designed responsibility accounting system structures responsibility centers consistent with individual areas of control. If a given manager has the duty of controlling a given segment of production and costs, the accounting system defines him and his segment of responsibility as a responsibility center. All company production and costs are assigned to one of the defined responsibility centers. By focusing on these centers, the firm thereby has a means of pinpointing inefficient and rewardable personnel performance. Such recognition can be in the way of worker reassignment, termination, promotion, or increased wages.

Cost accounting and financial accounting (discussed in following chapters) are not totally independent of one another. For one, the record keeping that is part of a cost accounting system serves as the data bank upon which financial statements are based. Equally important is the fact that the firm's cost accounting system is often evaluated as a means of determining the acceptability and reliability of the produced financial statements.

Of the possible types of legal business structure, only the corporation is committed to the publishing of regular (quarterly or annual) financial statements to its owners. In the case of the corporation, the owners are the stockholders. The various Securities and Exchange Commission (S.E.C.) laws require this reporting to the firm's stockholders. Even when financial statements are not required by stockholders, the construction firm may be forced to prepare various types of financial statements for other purposes. In particular, banks require financial disclosure through financial statements when considering a construction firm loan application. Bonding companies usually require similar types of financial statements from the construction firm.

Many of the financial statements which the construction firm has to submit to outside parties must be *audited* by a Certified Public Accountant (C.P.A.). In particular, the S.E.C. requires audited financial statements. Banks and bonding companies may also require that statements submitted to them be audited. They do this to add strength to the correctness of the statements.

The procedures used by a C.P.A. in auditing a firm are aimed at his expressing an *opinion* on the fairness of the statements in question. Ideally, the C.P.A. will find that the statements "fairly present the financial position" of the firm and thus issue an *unqualified* opinion. However, circumstances may prevent this and lead to a qualified, adverse, or disclaimer of opinion. In determining the fairness of the statements the auditor follows certain auditing standards. Of the ten auditing standards, the standard relating to an evaluation of a firm's internal control, is especially relevant to the auditing of the construction firm and the construction firm's cost accounting system. The auditing standard in question reads as follows.

> There is to be a proper study and evaluation of existing internal control as a basis for reliance thereon and for the determination of the resultant extent of the tests to which auditing procedures are to be restricted.[3]

This evaluation of company internal control presents problems in regard to the auditor and his evaluation of the fairness of financial statements and his writing an opinion on them. In particular, small firms often lack good internal control practices. This is especially true in the case of the small construction firm. An American Institute of Certified Public Accountants guide on the auditing of construction firms cited the following six internal control weaknesses and deficiencies in construction firms.[4]

[3]"Statement of Auditing Standards," *American Institute of Certified Public Accountants,* New York, 1973, p. 13.

[4]"Audits of Construction Contractors," *American Institute of Certified Public Accountants,* New York, 1965, p. 43.

(1) Failure to periodically evaluate contract profitability on a realistic basis.
(2) Inadequate control over estimating and bidding on new contracts.
(3) Inadequate contract cost records.
(4) Weaknesses in billing procedures.
(5) Inadequate control of construction equipment and lack of adequate cost records applicable to the equipment.
(6) Poor control of job site payrolls and other disbursements.

Each of the cited internal control weaknesses relates to the firm's lack of an effective cost accounting system. Better record keeping, accounting procedures, and production and cost control can do much to relieve the rather widely held view by bankers, sureties, and investors of the unacceptable nature of construction firm's financial information.

7.3 Cost Accounting Terminology

Every technical subject matter seems to possess some basic terminology or jargon. Cost accounting has its share of terms or jargons that have to be understood. The reader should be alerted to the fact that the terms are quite numerous. In addition, some difficulty is created by the fact that the meanings of a few of the terms are not universal. Nonetheless, if we are to proceed in following sections with a discussion of cost accounting concepts as they relate to the construction industry, we must first learn the language of the subject matter.

The very term "cost" is subject to many interpretations. One interpretation is that cost is anything one has to give up. This interpretation would include one's time, energy, in addition to dollars, or nonmonetary products exchanged. However, cost as it relates to accounting study is more limited. Cost in an accounting sense is dollars exchanged for goods or services. It is this meaning of cost that will be implied in this chapter. Dollars paid for material, for labor, or for a bond or insurance are examples of cost to the construction firm.

A properly designed cost accounting system assigns the various types of costs that occur to certain defined cost objects. A *cost object* is an activity or part of an organization for which a separate determination of cost is needed. The cost objects are defined in a manner consistent with the decision making needs of management. For example, if the construction firm desires to have each project superintendent responsible for individual job overhead, then a job overhead cost object should be set up for each individual job. Similarly, the segregation of overtime labor hours from normal working hours may be the result of management's desire to analyze overtime policies. It may choose to allocate such overtime labor costs to job overhead rather than to direct cost. Regardless of its decision or policy as to the given cost, the firm's very decision to segregate the cost results in the creation of a cost object. Various construction work items such as concrete slab work, footings, masonry walls, etc., are commonly segregated as to data collection. Each of the work items is thus identified as a cost object. Cost objects can be identified as individuals, work items, or even segments of one's business.

Costs in an accounting sense are often identified as to their behavior as a function of time or as a function of how they relate to the makeup of the product produced or service performed. Terminology such as variable or fixed, unit or total, and product or period are used for such purposes.

Costs that vary directly with changes in activity are called *variable costs*. Examples of variable costs are costs of material and labor used in the production process, and equipment hours expended in the manufacturing process. *Fixed costs* are those that vary with the passage of time despite changes in the level of activity. A secretary's wages, and the salary of an estimator or a superintendent employed the full year regardless of the availability of company jobs can be considered fixed costs. It should be noted that a fixed cost may vary if the level of activity changes substantially. For example, if a construction firm reorganizes such that it reduces its volume by 50%, it may see it necessary to lay off an estimator or two. As such, the fixed cost is no longer "fixed." The end result is that when speaking about a fixed cost, one must recognize the existence of the relevant range of business activity. The *relevant range* is that level of activity for which the firm budgets and expects to operate. As such, the definition of fixed cost is valid only for the firm's relevant range of activity. To illustrate the problem of fixed costs not being fixed over unexpected activity levels, the term *semifixed* is introduced. The concept of variable cost, fixed cost, and semifixed cost are shown graphically in Fig. 7.2.

It should be noted that what is a variable cost to one firm, might in fact be a fixed cost to another firm. For example, one construction firm hires and fires job superintendents as a function of workload, whereas another firm may keep a given number of superintendents on its payroll regardless of level of workload. The advantages and disadvan-

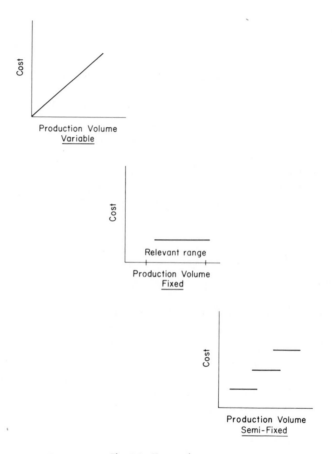

Fig. 7.2. Types of costs.

tages of each of these policies is not at issue here. What is at issue is the fact that the superintendent's costs to the first firm are variable, whereas to the latter firm they are fixed.

Most firms operate by means of absorbing both variable and fixed costs. Many of its production costs (those directly related to making a product) tend to be variable, whereas selling and administrative type costs tend to be fixed. The behavior of all of a cost object's costs (including variable and fixed) taken together are expressed as cost *functions*. A simple cost function is illustrated in Fig. 7.3. Needless to say, not all cost functions are as simple as that shown. The concept of cost functions, variable costs, and fixed costs are used in cost-volume-profit analysis and in variance analysis. These types of cost accounting analyses are discussed in following sections.

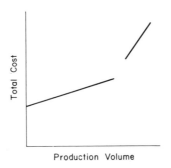

Fig. 7.3. Cost function for an activity.

Costs associated with a product are classified as either being unit or total costs. *Total costs* merely represent the sum of all of the costs associated with the type of production or cost object in question. For example, the sum of the costs of placing 25 cubic yards of slab concrete, 20 cubic yards of wall concrete, and 5 cubic yards of footing concrete might be $1,000. This $1,000 represents the total cost of placing the 50 cubic yards of concrete. *Unit costs* can be thought of as average costs. They merely represent the total cost of the production in question divided by a defined unit of the total production. For example, for the concrete work the common production unit can be identified as a cubic yard of concrete. As such, the unit cost of the concrete is calculated as $1,000 divided by 50 cubic yards resulting in $20 per cubic yard.

Note should be made of the importance of the identification of the base or *common production unit* in the unit cost calculation. Different bases can be defined for a given type of work and each different base will result in a different calculated unit cost. For example, three types of concrete placement were considered in the calculation of the unit cost of placing a cubic yard of concrete. If one would limit the type of production unit to a given type of placement, such as the placing of slab concrete the unit cost of placing a cubic yard of concrete would likely be different. If $250 of the $1,000 total cost is associated with placing the 25 cubic yards of slab concrete, the unit cost per cubic yard of placing slab concrete is calculated as $250 divided by 25 cubic yards or $10 per cubic yard. The consideration of the base in the unit cost calculation is especially relevant when considering the several different possible bases one might identify when singling out the various types of construction work performed. That is, one might single out total concrete or in fact make more detailed bases such as footing concrete, 4 inch slab on grade concrete, 6 inch suspended slab concrete, wall concrete, etc. In addition, the production unit might be cubic yards of concrete, square feet of concrete, or linear feet of concrete.

An important classification in regard to how costs are reported in the financial statements of a firm is the classifying of costs as product or period costs. Costs that are expended in the transformation of materials into a useful product are referred to as *product costs*. These types of costs can be thought of as "attaching" to the product. Carpenter and ironworker wages, concrete and steel costs, and even job superintendent's (assuming he is allocated to the supervision of the production process) wages are product costs. In general, *production* related costs are identified as product costs. Product costs are sometimes referred to as *inventoriable costs*.

Period costs do not directly result from the manufacturing of the product. They are costs that relate to the *selling* of the product and the overall *general administrative costs* of operating the firm. They do not "attach" to the product produced. Secretarial wages, estimator's wages, and office equipment are examples of construction firm period costs. Note that if the secretary or estimator is "assigned" to a given job, these labor costs can be considered as product costs.

Product costs are closely related to the concept of variable costs. While many product costs are in fact variable, not all product costs are variable costs. The wages of a superintendent may be a fixed cost to a construction firm. On the other hand, his time and wages associated with his supervision of a given project may be considered product costs for that project.

It is also true that while most period costs are fixed in nature, there are exceptions. Personnel responsible for finding work may be paid a commission based upon the dollar volume of work contracted. This cost while not attached to the work itself, is in fact a variable cost.

The concept of product and period cost has implications as to the financial statements and tax liabilities of the firm. Whereas product costs are visualized as attached to the product, they are identified as being part of an inventory of products that the firm maintains or holds at the end of a reporting period. As such, these costs are not viewed as expenses to the firm until the inventory is sold. Instead, they are temporarily viewed as assets. On the other hand, period costs do not attach to the manufactured product and as such, are viewed as expenses in the period in which they occur. The difference between the two accounting procedures is very important in regard to construction work because of the rather common long duration of a construction project. That is, the construction project, which can be viewed as inventory or work-in-progress, may be in that status for two or three years. Rather significant differences in financial statements and tax implications result from the alternatives of viewing a cost as a product or period cost. These differences will be highlighted in a later section.

Perhaps the most meaningful classification of cost for use in a cost accounting discussion is the classification of costs as to elements of manufacturinng costs. Three elements of the costs of manufacturing a product are identified. They are as follows.

(1) Direct material costs
(2) Direct labor costs
(3) Overhead costs

Direct material costs are those costs that constitute an appreciable part of the finished product. Concrete, steel, and lumber costs are all direct costs of the construction firm. Certain minor materials such as nails or glue may be identified as *indirect material* (i.e., a project overhead cost) rather than a direct cost. This is only for convenience since it may be difficult to assign a given number of nails or glue to a given project or work item. However, difficulty by itself does not justify identifying a given cost as an indirect cost. If the item is material in amount then it is necessary, regardless of the difficulty, to identify it as direct and relate it to the given work item in question.

Direct labor costs are those costs involved in the transformation of material into a product. Laborer, carpenter, ironworker, and foremen wages are all examples of direct labor costs. *Overtime premiums* are sometimes more appropriately assigned to overhead than to direct labor. This is the case when overtime results because of external conditions. For example, if laborers are pulled off project A in order to finish project B, the later occurrence of overtime on project A (in order to finish the project A on schedule) does not justify penalizing project A with the overtime premium. It is more appropriate to directly charge this time to project B, or to charge the premium to overhead.

Overhead includes all of the costs necessary to the manufacturing operations of the firm that cannot be directly identified with the product. Overhead is also referred to as *factory overhead, manufacturing expense,* or *indirect manufacturing.* The latter term is probably the most descriptive of the actual costs in question.

Overhead is identified as either being variable overhead or fixed overhead. *Variable overhead* includes such items as supplies and indirect labor. An estimator's time is most appropriately identified as indirect labor. In addition, a job superintendent can be appropriately identified as indirect labor (i.e., variable overhead) rather than direct labor. *Fixed overhead* includes such construction costs as insurance for the firm's central office, depreciation of its building, and some office supervisory salaries.

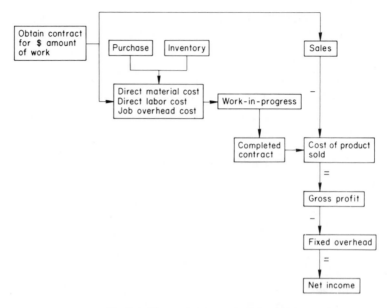

Fig. 7.4. The production and sale cycle.

Two less significant terms are sometimes used in the grouping of direct material, direct labor, and overhead. *Prime costs* consist of the sum of direct material costs and direct labor costs. *Conversion costs* consist of the sum of direct labor costs and overhead costs.

The various manufacturing costs and nonmanufacturing costs that have been discussed can be brought together by means of an illustration that focuses on the flow of the firm's product through its production and selling cycles. Such an illustration is shown in Fig. 7.4. The illustration assumes that the firm is in the business of manufacturing a product. This is of course the case in regard to the construction firm. On the other hand, if a firm does not manufacture a product but merely buys and resells it (i.e., a retail firm) then for all practical purposes, the direct labor aspect of the manufacturing process would be absent in Fig. 7.4.

One other classification of costs should be mentioned before leaving our discussion of terminology. A cost is either a historic cost or a budgeted or predetermined cost. A *historic cost* is one that is determined from the record of an actual cost. Most construction estimating systems are based on historic costs. *Budgeted* or *predetermined costs* are estimates and predictions of what costs should be. These costs are often based on historic costs and an analysis of the work performed.

The result is that a *standard cost* can be determined. This concept is discussed in detail in the following sections.

7.4 Accumulation of Cost—Bookkeeping

Bookkeeping is a necessary ingredient to a construction firm's cost accounting system. Bookkeeping entails the procedures, forms, and distribution channels for the collection and formulation of production cost data. The bookkeeping system is aimed at providing the firm a means of project cost control and a means of determining project costs. In addition, the documentation and classification of costs by means of a bookkeeping procedure are necessary in order to produce reports that are required by the multiplicity of taxes that have been placed on all forms of business.

Bookkeeping is a rather cumbersome process. It requires many hours of clerical work in addition to the time and cooperation of those initiating the production cost reports (i.e., timekeeper, foreman, etc.). As such, bookkeeping is often a significant business cost in itself. However, this cost is necessary in order to prohibit much greater costs due to a lack of control.

The bookkeeping process in the construction industry is made difficult by the fact that project costs are incurred at a distance from the location at which the accounting for them is done (i.e., the home office). Normally, the construction project is not large enough in regard to cost or long enough in regard to duration to justify setting up an entire bookkeeping personnel team at the project location. This is not to say that it has not been done occasionally. On large power plants or similar projects, the construction firm may in fact set up a "home office— branch office" at the project site. However, it is much more common to periodically send the required bookkeeping cost data from the field office to the home office. This distance between the location of the occurrence of costs and the location of formulating them creates several problems in regard to control. In addition to requiring more forms and procedures, the distance creates problems in regard to the time at which the cost data is received, formulated, and analyzed for control purposes. The following discussions of bookkeeping will assume that bookkeeping data is sent from the field to the home office.

In the previous section three elements of manufacturing costs were identified. These were direct material costs, direct labor costs, and overhead costs. Bookkeeping for each of these construction costs and other project related costs will now be discussed.

7.4.1 Material Costs

The bookkeeping for construction materials has to recognize some of the unique characteristics of the industry. Most construction material is delivered directly to the project site. In other types of manufacturing industries, material is first received by a central receiving location and in turn distributed by means of a purchasing department. This latter process facilitates better control of the material costs. Material buying for a construction project is normally planned at the time of estimating a project's cost. This often differs from other manufacturing industries where material buying is planned and carried out throughout the manufacturing process.

Regardless of when construction material is purchased or to where it is initially delivered, the objectives of bookkeeping for material are the following.

(1) Control of purchasing
(2) Control of receiving
(3) Identification of materials to projects and work items
(4) Protection against theft, misplacement, and damage

Construction materials are normally purchased through one of two procedures. For one, the material may be purchased as needed by means of purchase orders. Secondly, the material may be purchased for the entire lump sum contract. Purchasing material as needed (i.e., as indicated by individual purchase orders) has the advantage that a great number of problems associated with the production against theft, misplacement, and damage are eliminated. If the material is to be purchased by purchase orders, the initial request comes from the field. Only authorized personnel should be permitted to initiate a purchase order. More than likely the project superintendent will be responsible for initiating such a request. *Purchase requisition* forms should be used for initiating this type of material request. Such a form is shown in Fig. 7.5. A good system is to have triplicate forms such that a copy of the purchase requisition is kept by the field office and a copy is delivered to both the accounting and engineering or planning departments. This will provide the accounting department a means of controlling purchase requests against invoices and receiving statements. In addition, a

PURCHASE ORDER

TO

ORDER
NUMBER

DATE

JOB

PLEASE DELIVER THE FOLLOWING ORDER TO:

SHIP TO

JOB NO.

F.O.B.

TERMS

SHIP VIA

DELIVERY TO BE MADE ON OR BEFORE   OR RIGHT IS RESERVED TO CANCEL ORDER

In Accepting Verbal Orders, Purchase Order Number Must be Obtained Before Making Delivery.

QUANTITY	DESCRIPTION	PRICE	AMOUNT

INVOICES MUST STATE ORDER NUMBER AND POINT OF DELIVERY.

PRICES ON THIS ORDER NOT SUBJECT TO CHANGE.

PRACTICAL   FORM 113-A   BY _____

FRANK R. WALKER CO., PUBLISHERS, CHICAGO

Fig. 7.5. Purchase requisition form. (Frank R. Walker Company.)

form will alert the engineering or planning department as to the progress of the project and material usage versus the predetermined project plan.

Let us assume that the material requested in the field is not kept in inventory by the form. If such is the case, the home office will send a *purchase order* to the material supplier that is selected. The material supplier will be requested to deliver the material to the job site. The supplier might send the invoice for material ordered to either the home (central office), the field office, or both. Because the field office is removed from the actual purchase or paying of the purchase price, the invoice must eventually be received by the central office. As such, it is preferrable if the invoice is sent directly to it.

The next step in the process is the potential bad link in the control process. Because the material is sent directly to the field, it is the field personnel that are responsible for checking to see that the material delivered corresponds to that requested and eventually paid for by the home office. That is, field personnel are responsible for counting or measuring, inspecting, and signing for each incoming delivery. The key to performing this vital step in the control process is the assignment of the duty to dependable individuals who make themselves available when in fact the material is delivered.

On large projects this usually creates little difficulty. The project is large enough to justify the employment of a warehouseman or receiving clerk who is held responsible for the accountability of incoming materials. On the smaller job, it is common to allocate this responsibility to the timekeeper. On even smaller jobs, the responsibility is sometimes given to the foreman. These latter two practices, especially the latter of the two, are generally less preferrable than that of having a full time receiving clerk. The fact that the timekeeper or foreman is responsible for other tasks often results in his viewing the material receiving responsibility as somewhat secondary. This view can result in a haphazard control procedure. Subcontractors will often arrange with the general contractor to have the general contractor's personnel receive the subcontractor's material. The potential for adequate control is not decreased by this practice.

Whoever is responsible for acknowledging the receipt of materials will normally be requested by the supplier to sign for the material. Since his signature has legal implications (i.e., title passes), the individual signing should first assure himself as to the quantity and quality of the material. If the material is inferior he should not accept it. In addition, his failure to inspect the material in a responsible manner removes his right to later reject the material.

```
┌─────────────────────────────────────────────────────┐
│                    ABC  COMPANY                       │
│                  Receiving  Report                    │
│                                                       │
│                              No.  215                 │
│                              Date 5-21-1974           │
│                                                       │
│      Received from: Steel Supply Co.   Paid           │
│                                                       │
├──────────────┬──────────────────┬───────────────────┤
│   Quantity   │   Description    │   Condition        │
├──────────────┼──────────────────┼───────────────────┤
│              │                  │                    │
│   30 lbs.    │    3 d nails     │    Good            │
│   10 feet    │    #3 rebar      │    Good            │
│              │                  │                    │
│              │                  │                    │
├──────────────┴──────────────────┴───────────────────┤
│      Received by:  J. Cox                             │
│      Inspected by: S. Wilson                          │
│                                                       │
└─────────────────────────────────────────────────────┘
```

Fig. 7.6. Receiving report form.

The field office, by way of the individual responsible for acknowledging receipt of construction materials, should account for all materials received for the project in a weekly production report, or it may be
a separate report such as the one shown in Fig. 7.6. Here again, the form
should be sent to both accounting and the engineering or planning departments. The departments use the report in a continuing evaluation
of the progress of the project.

If it is feasible for the firm to maintain a central supply of materials
that are needed for building its various projects, such a system offers
the firm a means of better control over purchasing and receiving materials. In addition, through centralization and bulk purchasing the firm
may be able to purchase materials more economically.

The bookkeeping and control process differs when a centralized
inventory of materials is kept by the construction firm. Purchase requisitions are still initiated in the field. Such a purchase requisition is

sometimes referred to as a *stores requisition*. If an adequate supply of the material is not on hand, the central office may initiate a purchase order to a supplier. However, not every stores requisition necessarily initiates a purchase order. Control of material ordered, received, and sent to projects is now centralized. This is done by individual material accounts referred to as *stores ledgers*. Each type of material is accounted for in subsidary ledgers referred to as *stores cards* which are in turn summarized in the control stores ledger. Purchases are entered into a company register and when received are entered in the stores card for the material. A stores card for a material is shown in Fig. 7.7. Purchases are listed as to their unit price, and by means of one of several available inventory flow methods, cost levels of inventory are maintained and adjusted for material issues.

The issues of materials as reported by the stores requisition forms are periodically analyzed by the home office as a way of controlling the usage of materials on the various projects. Such an analysis form is shown in Fig. 7.8. This analysis serves as a means of evaluating project progress.

The fourth objective of bookkeeping for material cost, that of protecting against theft, misplacement, or damage may seem removed from the cost accounting process. However, the analysis of purchases, deliveries, and issues can be used to alert the firm to this loss of material. Without an effective cost accounting and bookkeeping system, such losses may never be apparent to the firm and they will continue to be accounted for as ordinary project expenses. Determination of acceptable material wastage factors is part of an effective cost accounting system. In addition, protection of material through the setting out of authorization and security procedures are important elements of the cost accounting and bookkeeping system. If it is worthwhile keeping an inventory of construction materials, it is worthwhile maintaining adequate protection and control over it. Usually, it is financially rewarding to employ an individual on a project site to receive, protect, and to do general housekeeping for project materials. This is especially true when the project is of a size where there is a large buildup of construction materials on the project site.

7.4.2 Labor Costs

Whereas the lack of proper documentation and control of construction materials seldom leads to overall project nonprofitability, such

MATERIAL COST RECORD

NAME OF WORK

ARCHITECTS OR ENGINEERS

LOCATION

OWNER

SHEET NO.

JOB NO

FORM 105

FRANK R. WALKER CO., PUBLISHERS, CHICAGO

Quan-tity	Unit Price	AMOUNT	Quan-tity	Unit Price	AMOUNT	Quan-tity	Unit Price	AMOUNT	Quan-tity	Unit Price	AMOUNT	Quan-tity	Unit Price	AMOUNT	
															1
															2
															3
															4
															5
															6
															7
															8
															9
															10
															11
															12
															13
															14
															15
															16
															17
															18
															19
															20
															21
															22

Fig. 7.7. Material stores card. (Frank R. Walker Company.)

ABC COMPANY
Stores Requisition Analysis   Week ended _____

Date	Req. No.	Material units	Direct Malt. Total $	Job 101	Job 102	Job 103	Indirect Malt. Total $	Maintenance	Job 101	Job 102	Job 103
5-17-74	101	100	125.00		125.00						
5-21-74	108	215	135.00	135.00							
5-22-74	109	106	193.00		193.00						
5-30-74	112	2					35.00	35.00			

Fig. 7.8. Stores requisition analysis form.

practices in regard to labor productivity and costs are one of the prime causes for project and company financial loss. Labor is the most variable of all construction costs.

Construction project labor bookkeeping is commonly referred to as timekeeping. The actual timekeeping process has two objectives. For one, it determines the total amount of time for which each worker is to be paid. As such, the process is part of the firm's payroll task. Of more importance in regard to control and cost accounting is timekeeping's contribution to allocation of labor hours and costs to the various project work items.

The actual timekeeping on a construction project is normally done by project foremen or a timekeeper. The employment of a timekeeper is usually not justified on small construction projects. Instead, foremen are given the responsibility of daily documentation of worker hours both as to their amount of hours and the allocation of the hours to the performed work items. He does this by means of recording the hours in a small book kept in his pocket or by filling out a time card at the end of the day. Because such time cards are stored at the field office there is little chance that they will be lost and as such, this procedure is preferred. Such a form is shown in Fig. 7.9.

If a project is of a size that can justify the employment of a timekeeper (Note: the timekeeper can also be responsible for receiving and protection of project materials), better potential for control results than if foremen are assigned the timekeeping responsibility. The timekeeper generally has more time and is more committed to the timekeeping task than are foremen. In addition, there is likely less potential for collusion between the timekeeper and workers than there is between a foreman and his workers. That is, a foreman often is involved in working with his workers. His closeness to his workers encourages such a practice as the foreman's reporting a worker's hours even though the worker is absent for the time period.

When a project is spread out over a relatively large area, the timekeeper may have difficulty documenting late starting or early quitting of individual workers. In addition, there may be so many workers on the project site that he may in fact fail to observe and document the absence of a given worker. Such a failure will lead to documenting and payment of wages for which no work is performed. There are several well-known procedures for documenting the starting and finishing time of a worker. Probably the most frequently used timekeeping device used in the manufacturing system is a time clock. Workers insert a card into a punch type device which records the time of the day on the card. Time clocks have not proved popular in the construction industry. The mobility of the construction project, workers' general dislike of

WORK ITEM		WED	THR	FRI	SAT	MON	TUE	TOTAL
	ST							
	ST							
	ST							
	ST							
	ST							
	ST							
	ST							
TOTAL								

NAME _____

CRAFT _____ WEEK ENDING _____

Fig. 7.9. Time card form.

them, and the difficulty associated with monitoring such a system are some of the reasons for the nonpopularity of such a device in the construction industry.

An alternative to the use of a time clock is the use of a badge procedure. Small metal badges with numbers on them are kept at a central location which is maintained by the project timekeeper. Upon arriving for work, a worker picks up his badge with his assigned number and pins it on his work uniform. At the end of the day he returns the badge. Such a procedure ensures documentation of a worker's presence, his starting time, and his quitting time. In addition, it brings attention to long absences of a given worker. The main difficulty of the badging system is that workers have to report to a central location to pick up and return their badges. Such a procedure may prove time consuming when workers are spread out over a project.

An alternative to the badging system is to have workers continuously wear a badge number. This badge is not turned in, but is kept by the worker. The timekeeper in making his rounds documents the presence of workers by noting their number. Such a procedure is especially advantageous when many workers are employed and the timekeeper does not know each one by face. This procedure while proving useful to the documenting of the presence of a worker, does not aid in noting whether a worker starts or quits on time.

Regardless of whether a foreman or a timekeeper is responsible for documenting labor time, occasionally an individual from the home office should visit the construction project to check the foreman's or timekeeper's report as to who is working. This provides a means of control in regard to potential collusion between a worker and the foreman or timekeeper.

Regardless of whether the foreman or timekeeper makes out daily time cards they have to be sent to the home office. Preferably, the time cards should be sent in daily. At the minimum, they should be sent in weekly. These *weekly reports* lack the control potential that *daily reports* offer. The quicker labor inefficiencies or overruns are recognized, the better the chance for corrective management. In addition, weekly reports encourage fraudulent reporting procedures. A worker might be laid off on Tuesday and carried on the payroll through Friday due to fraudulent timekeeping.

The daily or weekly labor cost reports that are turned in by the foreman or timekeeper should indicate both total worker hours and also the allocation of the hours to project work items. However, the project foreman cannot be expected to document a very detailed analysis of his workers' time. That is, it is awkward to require him to account for coffee breaks, inefficient production, etc. His effectiveness as a foreman might be weakened if he is asked to be a watchdog of his workers. This is yet another reason for justifying the employment of a timekeeper on a project.

The daily or weekly cost reports that are sent to the home office are used by the accounting, payroll, and engineering or planning departments. The payroll department uses the reports to initiate worker paychecks. The individual in charge of this payroll function is referred to as the *paymaster*. The accounting, and engineering or planning departments record the labor costs and analyze them as to the individual project work items. The costs are often summarized by a form such as the one shown in Fig. 7.10. This analysis, an important part of the cost accounting system, serves to bring attention to cost overruns, work improvement, and potentially costly delays. This can be done by comparing labor hours expended per unit of work item production performed with planned labor hours per unit of work item. Productivity trends can be singled out and analyzed. More and more firms are starting to use documented work item labor costs as a means of estimating future projects. Several of these firms are transforming the work item labor costs into man-hours for their future estimating. These man-hour records are less sensitive to changes in labor notes in regard to future estimates.

In addition to the timekeeping aspect of accounting for labor, other labor bookkeeping procedures include forms and authorization procedures for hiring and firing employees, handling of payroll fringe benefits and payroll deductions. These procedures have a less significant role in the control process and vary substantially from firm to firm. As is true of any reporting process, the benefits of the documenting procedure should outweigh the costs of implementation in order to justify the procedure.

7.4.3 Overhead Costs

The construction firm has to recognize two types of overhead costs in its bookkeeping process. For one, there is always some type of overhead costs that are directly related to a project. Equipment costs, supervision costs, and testing costs are examples of these types of costs. These costs are referred to as *job overhead* or *direct overhead*. In addition to direct overhead, indirect overhead costs must be recognized and

LABOR DISTRIBUTION REPORT

NOTE:—This report must be made out and sent in with Pay-roll each Period. Total on Distribution must balance with Pay-roll Total.

REPORT NO. _____

SHEET NO. _____

JOB NO. _____

NAME OF WORK		LOCATION					PAY-ROLL ENDING				
CLASS OF WORK	OCCUPATION						Total Hours	Hourly Rate	AMOUNTS	TOTAL COST THIS WEEK	TOTAL COST TO DATE

Fig. 7.10. Time card analysis form. (Frank R. Walker Company.)

allocated to individual projects. Such costs as secretarial wages in the home office, depreciation of the home office building, and management's automobile expenses are referred to as *indirect overhead*. Indirect overhead is also referred to as *office overhead* or *general overhead*. Each and every overhead cost, regardless of whether it is direct or indirect, must be allocated to the projects the firm builds in order that the cost can be recovered.

The identification as to what is overhead or how the identified overhead is allocated to various projects varies significantly from firm to firm. For example, some firms handle equipment costs as direct costs, others view them and account for them as overhead costs. Similarly, some firms may allocate office overhead to projects as a function of the expected duration of the projects, whereas others will allocate it to projects as a function of the total direct cost of the projects.

Bookkeeping for overhead focuses on control. Predetermined overhead application rates are determined and are multiplied by the relevant job cost factors (e.g., total direct cost) to yield total overhead cost to be included in the estimate for a project. Then as overhead costs are incurred, they are charged to the various projects. The control of these costs is accomplished by comparing the estimated overhead to that incurred. In addition, the documentation of the actual overhead costs aids in the determination of future overhead application rates.

It is often appropriate to allocate the various types of overhead to projects on different bases and to select the different bases according to the particular needs of the firm. Since these bases differ and since the types of costs differ, let us now discuss separately direct project overhead and indirect project overhead. Direct or job overhead includes the cost of the following.

(1) Equipment
(2) Job superintendent
(3) Small tools
(4) Field office
(5) Field office supplies
(6) Job insurance
(7) Bonds

The list of such costs could be lengthened depending on the type and size of the project and construction firm.

Equipment bookkeeping is especially important when one considers the substantial dollar amount of equipment used on the construction project. Some firms use special forms such as the one shown in Fig. 7.11 to achieve physical control on their equipment. Equipment bookkeeping should have two objectives.

ABC COMPANY Equipment Usage		
Equipment No. 112		Type Scraper 6 yd.
Job Distribution		*Hours Worked*
Bulk Excavation	Job 101	3
Cut and Fill	Job 102	4
Total hrs. worked		7
Repair time		0
Idle time		1
		Operator James J. Brown

Fig. 7.11. Equipment usage form.

(1) Control of the use of the equipment such that its location can be determined and adequate maintenance applied.

(2) Determination of the hourly cost of the equipment such that the cost can be allocated to projects.

The need for control of the usage of equipment is self-explanatory. Unless the location of equipment is known, project planning, equipment maintenance, and project cost determination will all be done in a haphazard manner. In addition, documenting of equipment usage (i.e., hours of performance, productivity) will aid in future decision making regarding equipment selection.

Equipment costs are best allocated to a project on the basis of expected hours of usage. As such, hourly usage costs must be determined. If equipment is rented, the determination of this hourly cost is straightforward. On the other hand, if company equipment is used, the calculation of the predetermined hourly cost is more complex. In addition to the recognition of the purchase cost and the depreciation cost of the equipment, down-time including idle equipment time and equipment maintenance time have to be recognized in the rate determination. As such, equipment repair and maintenance costs should be kept and analyzed. This can be done by keeping separate cost ledgers for each piece of major equipment. Such a ledger is shown in Fig. 7.12. The ledger provides for documenting repairs and maintenance performed on the equipment. As to the allocation of these costs to a project, major extraordinary repairs should usually be added to the cost of the equipment and depreciated (allocated) over several projects, rather than have

EQUIPMENT AND DEPRECIATION RECORD

SHEET NO.

KIND OF EQUIPMENT

DESCRIPTION

PURCHASED FROM		SERIAL NUMBER

DATE ACQUIRED	HOW ACQUIRED						APPRAISED VALUE

FORM 137

		ESTIMATED LIFE YEARS	DEPRECIATION YEARLY RATE		DATE APPRAISED

FRANK R. WALKER CO., PUBLISHERS, CHICAGO

DATE			DESCRIPTION	Folio	ORIGINAL COST AND CAPITAL REPAIRS DR.	DEPRECIATION PER YEAR MEMO.	DEPRECIATION TOTAL TO DATE CR.	PRESENT BOOK VALUE MEMO.	OPERATING REPAIRS DR.	RENTALS CHARGED OR RECEIVED CR.	
Mo.	Day	Year									
1			MACHINE COST								1
2			ADDITIONAL EQUIPMENT COST								2
3			FREIGHT, TRUCKING, ETC.								3
4			OTHER CHARGES								4
5											5
6			TOTAL ORIGINAL COST								6
7											7
8											8
9											9
10											10
11											11
12											12
13											13
14											14
15											15
16											16
17											17
18											18
19											19
20											20
21											21
22											22

Fig. 7.12. Equipment ledger form. (Frank R. Walker Company.)

the project on which the cost took place absorb the entire cost. Otherwise, there would be a distortion of project costs in that a single project is burdened with the entire repair cost whereas the repair will also benefit future projects. The overriding objective in any allocation of overhead should be on the basis of benefits and costs assignable to individual projects.

Equipment timekeeping can normally be done in a manner very similar to that for labor timekeeping. A timekeeper can allocate equipment time to the various work items in the same manner he allocates labor time.

Other direct overhead costs are usually best allocated on the basis of project total direct cost. For example, a firm may determine a rate of 10% of total direct cost as a job overhead rate (excluding equipment). Thus, if the total material and labor direct cost sum to $500,000, the job overhead is calculated as $50,000. In most cases such an allocation of job overhead will not heavily overburden any one construction project. However, this is not without exception. For example, if a project has very expensive material units such as steam turbines or generators, the large direct material cost will result in a large total direct cost. However, the project overhead is likely to be more of a function of the labor time and cost than it is the material cost. As such, the project in question will likely be overburdened with overhead costs. The end result is that careful analysis must be done if job overhead costs are to be accurately matched against project benefits. In truth, it is not likely that the individual construction firm can develop cost figures to the point which a totally accurate allocation can be obtained. The varying nature of the construction project and its cost ingredients make the analysis of individual project overhead bases very subjective. The end result is that allocation on the basis of direct cost will usually prove adequate.

Indirect overhead or general overhead costs are generally fixed costs. Costs such as clerical salaries, home office expenses, and salaries of management are generally not dependent on the amount of project work being performed. The costs are more a function of duration than they are a function of project direct costs. As such, a duration basis for allocation of general overhead to projects is most appropriate. For example, if a company's total expected annual general overhead is $50,000 and total yearly "weekly" project duration is 500 weeks (e.g., 10 projects each of 50 week duration) than a single 50 week project should be allocated $100 per week or $5,000 total.

The determination of direct or indirect overhead rates and expected project overhead are only the first step in the control process. The process is only complete upon comparing actual overhead costs to those budgeted, and taking corrective management action when appropriate. Such corrective actions may be a cost reduction program (layoffs, belt tightening), or may be in the form of better control through better efficiency in the form of more productive use of overhead equipment and material and more productivity from management personnel.

7.5 Document Flowcharting

One inherent danger with the use of forms for the bookkeeping function is the overuse of such forms. Each form used results in the requirement of labor hours in filling out, interpreting, and filing the form. A form should not be used unless it proves to be a vital link in the success of the information system. Redundancy should be eliminated wherever and whenever possible.

The preparation of *document flowcharts* provide the firm an useful means of analyzing a set of forms used. The document flowchart illustrates the flow of documents relating to a particular transaction. For example the flow of a payroll or material transaction through various individuals or divisions of the firm can be illustrated and analyzed by means of a document flowchart.

While there has been no universal standardization of document flowcharting symbols, the set of symbols illustrated in Fig. 7.13 have fairly widespread usage in document flowcharting. The first step in the construction of a document flowchart is to draw columns by means of vertical lines on a blank sheet of paper. One column is drawn for each individual, or company division involved in the flow of the document in question. The name of the individual or division is identified at the top of column. The origination of each document is shown on the chart as to the individual or division. The name of each document is inscribed within the symbol used for the document.

As a means of presenting an example of a document flowchart let us consider the paryoll system shown in Fig. 7.14. The figure illustrates a document flowchart for a payroll system. The number and type of documents and individuals and divisions is not meant to be representative of that required for each and every construction firm. The size, type of work performed, and personnel of the firm dictate the actual payroll bookkeeping system most appropriate for a given firm.

Independent of the characteristics of the given payroll bookkeeping system, the procedure of document flowcharting remains unchanged.

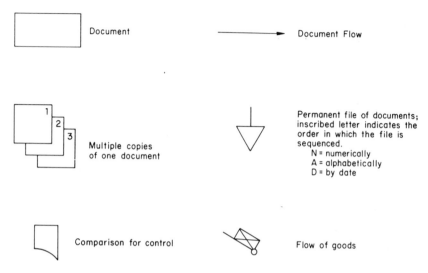

Fig. 7.13. Document flowcharting symbols.

As can be observed in Fig. 7.14, the initial document is the timekeeping card initiated by the foreman. This form is filled out in duplicate. One copy is sent to payroll where it serves as the basic document for preparing the payroll register. Duplicate copies of the payroll register are made, one copy being sent to accounts payable, whereas the other copy serves as a means of a check in that the payroll total is to be compared to labor cost summarized on the job ledger. In addition to the time cards that are input to the payroll division, the payroll division receives a document, prepared by the personnel department, that indicates payroll calculation changes. For example, a given worker may have had a change in the number of his dependents which would result in a different payroll calculation as to withholding tax.

The second copy of the time card is shown in Fig. 7.14 as being input to the cost distribution division. The purpose of this cost distribution is to allocate actual worker hours to given work items and jobs. Naturally the format of the time card must be such that the worker hours are distributed on the form in an order that enables the cost distributions. Duplicate copies of the cost distribution form serve as input to the job ledger and to estimating cost data files. These data files will later be used to aid in the estimating of future projects. The estimate for the ongoing projects is also compared to the job ledgers as a means of control on ongoing projects.

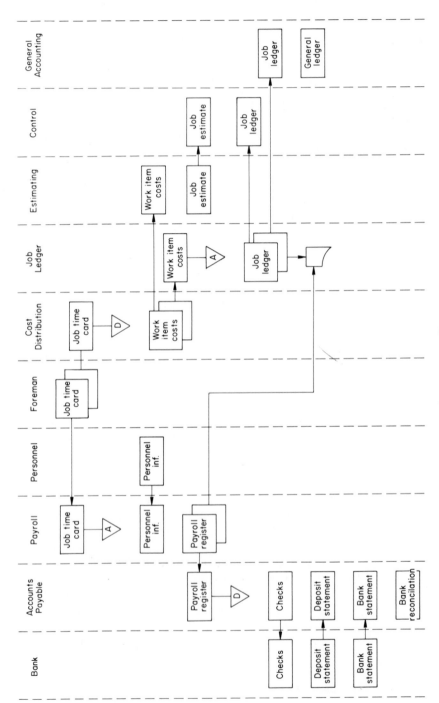

Fig. 7.14. Payroll system.

As indicated earlier, the job ledger labor costs are compared to the payroll register as a double check. Naturally both should total to be equal. If they don't, the difference should be traced and corrected. The payroll system shown in Fig. 7.14 concludes with the writing of checks and the receipt of a bank statement and the summarizing of the job ledgers in the general account ledgers.

The document flowchart shown in Fig. 7.14 serves several purposes. For one it indicates responsibility of individuals and divisions. In addition, it serves as a means of evaluating the overall bookkeeping system. It serves as a means of eliminating redundant forms and information while facilitating the development of a system that recognizes the overall system input of each of the individuals or divisions. Finally the document flowchart provides a means of tracing accounting errors should such errors develop.

A document flowchart for the requisition and purchasing of material is shown in Fig. 7.15. Once again the system shown is not meant to be representative of the most appropriate material bookkeeping system for each and every firm. For example, the system shown indicates all material is requisitioned by means of material purchases from a vendor. In reality, several construction firms have found it profitable to maintain their own inventory of some materials in which case the job material would be requisitioned from the inventory.

The foreman initiates the material system shown in Fig. 7.15. The material requisition serves as input to the purchasing division which in turn orders the material from a vendor. The purchasing division checks the invoice sent from the vendor by comparing it to the material received (as indicated by the foreman who receives the material). The invoice is then sent to accounts payable and in addition the form indicating the amount of material received is sent to accounting where it is summarized on the job ledger. In addition the material is summarized as to work items such that the amount used can be controlled by comparing it to the amount estimated. Like a payroll system, the material system should recognize control as well as historical record accounting.

Document flowcharts can also be prepared for equipment documents or any forms that are part of the firm's overhead application process. If nothing else such flowcharts force the firm to look at the bookkeeping system as a function of individual forms and individuals and divisions. Viewing the system as a function of the components in itself will likely result in a more efficient bookkeeping system.

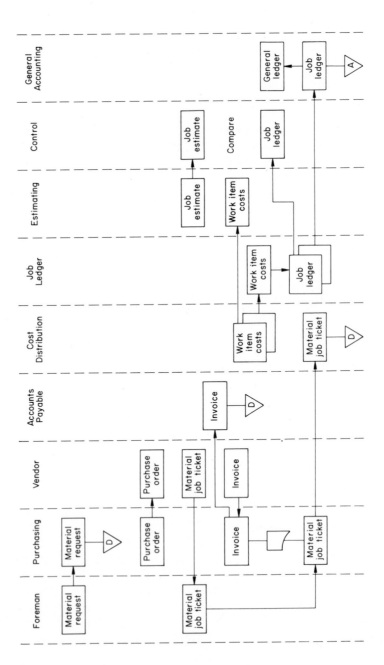

Fig. 7.15. Material system.

7.6 Job Order Costing

The construction industry differs from most other manufacturing industries in that the cost of its product usually has to be estimated before the product is contracted. Manufacturing industries such as the automobile industry measure their direct costs and distribute overhead to their manufactured automobiles. This measured cost is then used as a basis of fixing the selling price. The unit direct costs and overhead costs are relatively constant because of the repetitive characteristics of their manufacturing process. Construction projects do not share this cost characteristic. Even if two projects are similar in their appearance, the different environments in which they are built result in the builder having to predict the costs as a basis of his contract price. This is especially the case in regard to a competitive bid lump sum contract.

The cost plus fixed fee or cost plus percentage contracts do provide the builder an opportunity to determine costs before billing the project owner for the work performed. As such, there is less financial risk for the builder in that he gets paid as a function of his actual costs. He gets reimbursed for his costs plus a negotiable profit.

In order to be able to determine his product costs in order that he can properly determine the "cost" portion of its cost plus contract, the construction firm needs a means of formulating job costs. In the competitive lump sum bid contract process, the need to formulate job costs exists in order that the firm can better estimate costs of a project.

The formulating of job costs relates to the bookkeeping task. The bookkeeping task provides the necessary cost data for the product costing task. The product in the case of the construction industry is the construction project. As such, costs are identified as to a project. In accounting terminology, the construction project becomes a *cost object* or *cost center*.

There are two accounting extremes to product costing. One of these, referred to as *job order* (or *job cost*) *accounting*, is used by firms that manufacture products that can readily be identified as individual units and each of which receives varying amounts of attention and work. Industries that commonly use job order accounting or costing are construction, aircraft, and machinery. *Process accounting* is used for product costing when the firm produces similar units of product using mass production techniques. Industries that use process accounting or costing include textiles, oil, food, and cement.

The main difference between job order costing and process costing is one of the scale of an average. Both costing procedures are merely averaging of costs. However, process costing deals with broad averages and masses of like units whereas job order costing attempts to apply costs to specific jobs. Because of the necessity of many similar units, process costing is not relevant to the product costing of the construction industry's product. As such, only the mechanics of job order accounting or costing are discussed.

The construction industry firm usually builds several projects simultaneously. During construction, each project is considered to be part of the firm's *work-in-progress*. The basic document that is used to accumulate costs for each project that is part of the firm's work-in-progress is called the *job order* or *job cost sheet*. Such a document is shown in Fig. 7.16. The file (referred to as subsidiary ledgers) of job cost sheets for uncompleted projects makes up the firm's work-in-progress and is summed and controlled by a work-in-progress control ledger account.

If material is purchased by means of field purchase requests, the purchase requests discussed in the previous section are used to charge job cost sheets for direct material used. The previously discussed work tickets or time cards that are prepared by a project timekeeper or foreman are used to charge jobs for direct labor used. This process of charging direct material and direct labor to jobs is shown in Fig. 7.17.

Overhead costs are applied to a project's job-cost sheet as a function of a predetermined base or bases. For example, job overhead (direct overhead) might be applied to a project on a basis of 10% of the direct labor cost expended. Similarly, general overhead (indirect overhead) might be applied at a rate of $1,000 per month of project duration. This allocation process is shown in Fig. 7.17.

Actual job overhead costs are summarized in a job overhead control account. If the predetermined overhead base cost per unit (e.g., percent of direct labor cost) is accurately determined and actual job overhead costs are controlled, the applied job overhead will equal the actual job overhead costs. Control of the job overhead costs during construction is facilitated by comparing the actual costs to those applied for a given time period. For example, assuming direct labor costs of $10,000 and a job overhead rate of 10% of project direct labor costs, $1,000 of job overhead would be applied to a job. However, if actual job overhead costs at the point of time in question is $2,000, management should probably investigate the reason for this cost overrun and take any required corrective action.

JOB COST RECORD

NAME OF WORK

ARCHITECTS
OR ENGINEERS

FORM 116

LOCATION

OWNER

SHEET NO.

JOB NO.

FRANK R. WALKER CO., PUBLISHERS, CHICAGO

	Labor	Material	Labor	Material	Labor	Material	Labor	Material	Labor	Material	
1											1
2											2
3											3
4											4
5											5
6											6
7											7
8											8
9											9
10											10
11											11
12											12
13											13
14											14
15											15
16											16
17											17
18											18
19											19

Fig. 7.16. Job cost sheet. (Frank R. Walker Company.)

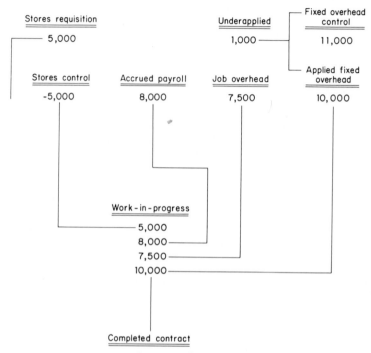

Fig. 7.17. Job cost system.

General overhead costs can be handled in a manner similar to job overhead costs. However, it is usually more difficult to allocate actual general overhead costs to a project. As such, the accuracy of the basis by which these costs are to be applied to the job cost sheets becomes very important. Because actual costs are difficult to compare to the applied costs, control of general costs becomes more difficult. If the allocation base unit is inaccurate, jobs may be underapplied or over-applied. For example, a firm's total annual general overhead cost is expected to be $1,000,000. Expecting 1,000 months duration of work throughout the year, the firm would apply general overhead on the basis of $1,000 for each month of project duration. However, if the firm underestimates its annual general overhead or overestimates its volume of work, too little general overhead will be applied to each and every project. The end result is that the firm will be making less than planned profits on their projects. In fact, if the general overhead is grossly under-stated, the firm may actually lose money on their projects.

Overhead is *underapplied* when the applied amount is less than the actual overhead costs. It is *overapplied* when the applied amounts exceed the actual overhead costs. Proper control should aid in keeping underapplied overhead to a minimum. However, even with adequate control, there is likely to be weekly or monthly differences in the amount of actual overhead costs and those applied. This is due to variations in the nature of such costs. For example, the purchase of small tools (a job overhead cost) may occur at the beginning of a project whereas the cost of this overhead is distributed more evenly over the duration of the project.

There are several accounting alternatives for treating differences between actual overhead costs and those applied. For one, the difference can simply be ignored in recognition of the fact that it is likely to dissappear in the next accounting period for the project in question. On the other hand, if a project is complete, it is best to charge (or deduct) the difference in the actual overhead costs and the applied amount to the job cost sheet.

Projects which are completed are transferred out of the work-in-progress accounts. This is done by eliminating (crediting the account) them from the work-in-progress account and placing (debiting an account) them in a completed contract account. This completed contract account is referred to as a *finish goods account* is many manufacturing industries. The entire job costing procedure is summarized in Fig. 7.17.

7.7 Standard Costs

The construction industry is noticeably absent of work and cost standards. Such standards are a necessary part of a budgeting and control system. Much of the construction industry's inability to substantially increase its productivity can be traced to its lack of determining method work and cost standards. There is a direct correlation between an industry's ability to increase its productivity and its ability to set work and cost standards. The better the industry's potential for setting such standards, the larger is the potential increase in productivity.[5]

No doubt that the uniqueness of each construction project and the variable environment surrounding each project has complicated the task of setting standards. However, lack of usage of cost accounting

[5]Grayson, Jackson, "Man with a Plan," *Constructor*, February, 1973, pp. 37–41.

concepts in the industry can also be cited as a significant reason for the failure to determine and implement meaningful standards.

The concept of standard work and cost can be integrated into the firm's normal costing procedure. For example, the concept of standards is compatible with a job cost accounting system. Standards outline how a given work package (e.g., a construction method) should be accomplished and how much it should cost. As work is performed, actual costs and production are compared with the standard production and costs to reveal variances.

Standard costs can be considered as target costs. They are carefully predetermined costs and should be attainable. They should not be set as ideal standards that require "perfection" on the part of management or the individual worker. However, standards should be set such that the achievement of standard performance is a satisfying accomplishment.

As to direct costs, two different types of standards should be determined. Each construction method should have a standard for direct material and a standard for direct labor. Let us first consider the determination of standards and the analysis of variances for direct material.

A standard amount of material for a given construction method and a standard unit price for the material are first determined. This determination of the amount of material required is probably best determined by personnel such as a foreman. In more sophisticated firms, a method's department may analyze method material requirements and set the standards. The unit price standard for material is likely best determined by cost oriented personnel. Typically, accounting personnel or estimating personnel are best qualified to determine the standard unit price purchase cost for material.

The amount of material actually used and the cost of the material used are compared to the predetermined standards. For example, let us assume we are considering pouring concrete for a 5-¾ inch on-grade slab. The slab is 100 feet square. Let us assume that the standard amount of concrete for this slab is 185 cubic yards. This amount is based on the actual volume and a small wastage percentage based on the actual volume. The estimating department sets $20 as the standard for the cost of a cubic yard of concrete delivered to the site. The comparison and analysis of any variances between actual material and costs and the standards is carried out by means of the *columnar format* shown in Fig. 7.18. The analysis shown in Fig. 7.18 assumes that 192 cubic yards of concrete was used for the slab and the unit price of the concrete was $19.50 per cubic yard.

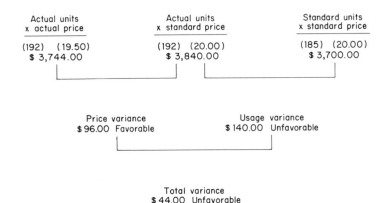

Fig. 7.18. Material cost variance.

The analysis is carried out by focusing on two variances. One is the purchase-price variance and the other is the usage variance. The *purchase-price variance* is calculated by determining the difference between the product of the actual amount of material used and the unit purchase price and the product of the actual amount of material used and the standard unit price. In the example shown this difference is $96. If the amount of material used times the unit purchase price is more than the amount of material used times the standard unit price, the variance determined is considered unfavorable. That is, this is an indication that the material was purchased at an unfavorable price. Responsibility for this type of variance should likely focus on the purchasing or procurement department. This same department should be favorably recognized when the variance is favorable. This occurs when the purchase price is less than the predetermined standard unit price. In the example, there is a *favorable* purchase-price variance of $96.

The second variance determined in the analysis is the *usage variance*. It is calculated by taking the difference between the product of the actual amount of material used and the standard unit price, and the product of the predetermined standard amount of material for the work and the standard unit price. In the example in Fig. 7.18 this difference is $140. If the amount of material used times the standard price is more than the standard amount of material times the standard unit price, the usage variance is unfavorable. Such an unfavorable variance can usually be traced to excessive material wastage, and poor handling and placing procedures. On the other hand, a favorable usage variance exists when the amount of material used times the standard unit price is less than the standard amount of material times the standard unit price. In the example shown, there is an *unfavorable* variance of $140. The responsibility for favorable or unfavorable usage variances should be aimed at the foreman or job superintendent.

The *total material variance* can be determined by summing the purchase-price variance and the usage variance. In the example considered there is a $96 favorable purchase-price variance and a $140 unfavorable usage variance resulting in a $44 unfavorable total variance. It should be noted that merely focusing on the difference between total actual cost and a total standard cost (i.e., the total variance) can be misleading in regard to method efficiency. In the example, the favorable efforts of the purchasing personnel are hidden due to the inefficient usage of material at the job site. Similarly, much of the inefficiency of the usage of material is hidden due to the balancing effect of the favorable purchase price of the material to that determined by predetermined standards. Adequate control can only be determined by focusing on the purchase-price and usage variances.

The determination and analysis of direct labor standards is performed in a manner similar to that for direct material standards. Similar to the material purchase-price and usage variances, a labor rate variance and a labor efficiency variance are determined.

Construction labor *rate standards* are usually set by labor union agreements. As such, they are somewhat outside of the control of management. However, while the rate standard might be set, actual dollars of wages spent may exceed the standard. Overtime pay would be the primary cause for such a difference. In addition, an unplanned change in rates during a project will cause a difference in the predetermined standard and the amount actually paid to workers. This can happen if a union agreement expires during a project and a higher wage is negotiated.

Labor efficiency standards are controllable. However, they are difficult to set. Disputes over labor efficiency standards are much more likely to arise than are disputes over material usage standards. Determining appropriate fatigue, and rest time for workers has to be considered. Union work rules have to be considered also. Time and motion studies are the most widely used method of setting labor efficiency standards. These are usually carried out by personnel acting in a staff position such as an engineer.

The construction industry has not always been receptive to the use of time and motion studies. Management has sometimes failed to apply such techniques in fear of nonacceptance by the labor unions. In addition, construction managers have argued that it is difficult to set labor efficiency standards for workers who are performing varying types of work in varying types of environment. There is no question that difficulty arises. However, this does not indicate that adequately trained personnel cannot determine such standards. Latest practices of several of the more informed construction firms indicate that it is possible to set a meaningful labor efficiency standard. Without such standards, the industry has little means of budgeting and controlling total direct labor costs. Once the labor efficiency standard is determined, project foremen should be held responsible for an efficiency related variance. Time cards and time card summaries that were discussed in the previous section on bookkeeping provide the means of comparing actual labor rates and efficiency with the predetermined standards.

The analysis of direct labor variances is performed by means of a *columnar format* similar to the one used for analysis of direct material variances. The total direct labor variance is separated into two variances: the rate variance and the efficiency variance.

The *rate variance* for a given work package (i.e., a construction method) is the difference between the product of the actual labor hours used to perform the work and the actual price paid for each hour (i.e., the actual rate), and the product of the actual labor hours used to perform the work and the predetermined standard rate. If the actual hours times the actual rate exceeds the actual hours times the standard rate, the variance is unfavorable. Similarly, if the actual hours times the actual rate is less than the actual hours times the standard rate, the variance is favorable.

Let us assume that 70 actual carpenter hours are used to form 3,000 square feet of vertical walls. In addition, the predetermined labor efficiency standard is set as 2.5 carpenter hours per 100 square feet. At the beginning of the project a rate standard of $8.00 per hour was used in setting the budget. However, because the union work agreement terminated during the work and a higher rate was negotiated, the average actual rate used for paying labor for the method in question is $9.50.

Given the above information as to the forming of vertical walls, the rate variance is calculated as shown in Fig. 7.19. There is an unfavorable rate variance of $105.

The *labor efficiency variance* is calculated as the difference between the product of the actual labor used to perform the work in question and the standard predetermined wage rate, and the product of the standard hours for the work in question and the standard predetermined wage rate. A higher actual hour times standard rate than standard hours times standard rate indicates an unfavorable variance. A

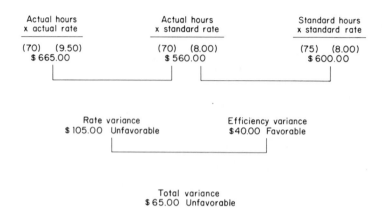

Fig. 7.19. Labor cost variance.

higher standard hours times standard rate than actual hours times
standard rate indicates a favorable variance. As shown in Fig. 7.19,
there is a $40 favorable labor efficiency variance for the form work
method previously described. This is based on the fact that for 3,000
square feet of formwork the standard number of hours is calculated as
2.5 times 30 or 75 hours.

The total *direct labor variance* is the sum of the rate and labor
efficiency variances. For the example considered, there is $105 un-
favorable rate variance and a favorable $40 labor efficiency variance. As
such, there is a $65 unfavorable variance. As is true of the analysis of the
direct material variance, it is necessary to focus on each of the two
ingredients of the total variance in order to assure adequate control.

The determination of standards and the analysis of variances for
overhead recognizes the different nature of job overhead and general
overhead. For the most part, job overhead is variable in that its amount
is dependent on the volume of work the construction firm performs. On
the other hand, construction general overhead tends to be fixed in that
costs such as salaries of secretaries and maintenance of the central
office is more a function of time than of the volume of construction
projects performed.

The previous section on job order accounting discussed the use of
an overhead control account for the comparing of overhead costs to the
amount of overhead applied. When making use of standard costs, this
control account should be replaced with two new accounts, one for
variable overhead (i.e., job overhead) and one for fixed overhead (i.e.,
general overhead).

The determination and analysis of variances for variable overhead is similar to that discussed for direct material and direct labor. As discussed in an earlier section in this chapter, construction job overhead is applied to a project as a function of a basis such as total direct cost, direct labor hours, or direct material cost. Let us assume that a construction firm applies its job overhead to projects as a function of the total direct labor hours estimated for a project. In particular, let us assume that it applies job overhead at a rate of $4 per direct labor hour. The $4 is in effect a *standard variable overhead rate*. The determination of this rate is the responsibility of the cost accounting and engineering personnel.

In addition to setting a standard variable overhead rate, a standard number of direct hours for performing the method in question must be determined. Because of the definition of the allocation basis, this determination is the same as the determination of the labor efficiency standard previously discussed.

Unlike the direct material and labor variances, job overhead variances relate more to the sum of several ongoing activities. For example, actual monthly job overhead costs might be compared to a predetermined, standard monthly overhead cost. If three methods are being performed during the month the sum of the direct labor hours incurred on each of the projects is summed and used as a basis for comparing the actual job overhead costs to the standard.

The *total variable overhead* variance is made up of a spending variance and an efficiency variance. The *spending variance* is merely the difference in the actual variable overhead (i.e., job overhead) incurred during the period in question and the product of the actual direct units of the basis (e.g., actual direct labor hours) and the standard variable overhead rate. Let us assume that the previously discussed firm (i.e., the firm that applied job overhead at a rate of $4 per direct labor hour) incurs $8,200 job overhead during a month in which 2,000 direct labor hours of work is performed. As shown in Fig. 7.20, the spending variance is calculated at $200. This variance is *unfavorable* in that the actual job overhead incurred is greater than the actual direct labor hours incurred times the standard application rate.

The variable overhead *efficiency variance* is calculated as the difference between the product of the actual direct units of the basis (e.g., actual direct labor hours) and the standard variable overhead rate, and the product of the standard (budgeted) units of the basis and the standard variable overhead rate. For the previously discussed example, let us assume that the firm set a standard of 1,950 direct labor hours. An efficiency variance of $200 is calculated as shown in Fig. 7.20. This

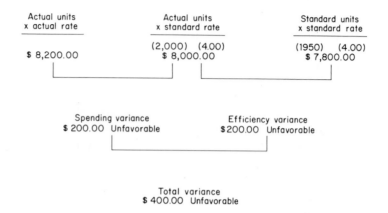

Fig. 7.20. Job overhead variance.

efficiency variance is *unfavorable* in that the actual direct hours incurred times the standard rate exceeds the standard direct hours times the standard rate.

The total variable overhead variance is the sum of the spending and efficiency variances. For the example considered, both the spending and efficiency variances were unfavorable. As such, a $400 unfavorable total variable overhead variance is determined. Part of this variance is related to the fact that more direct hours than budgeted were incurred to perform the work in question. The rest of the variance (one-half of it) can be traced to higher than expected job overhead costs per direct labor hour incurred. This portion of the variance is referred to as the spending variance. Job overhead control should focus on this variance. The efficiency variance results because of the lack of labor production control.

Fixed overhead costs by definition are not variable. As such, no variation occurs in them as a function of time. Since actual and budgeted or standard units of the basis (e.g., direct labor hours incurred or total direct costs incurred) during the time period may differ, the effective unit of cost applied to the basis unit of production may vary.

The total fixed overhead variance consists of a budget variance and a volume variance. The *budget variance* is the difference between the actual fixed overhead costs incurred in a given period of time (e.g., a month) and the budgeted amount of overhead for the time period. For example, let us assume a firm expects to incur an annual general overhead cost of $600,000. As such, they budget $50,000 of fixed overhead to each month. However, if they incur $62,000 of fixed overhead during a given month, a unfavorable $12,000 budget variance occurs.

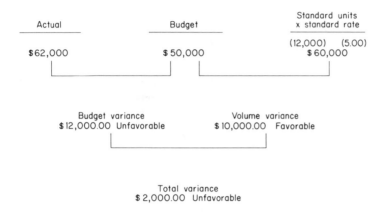

Fig. 7.21. Fixed overhead variance.

As discussed earlier, construction fixed overhead is appropriately allocated on a duration basis. However, within a given month several projects may be ongoing. The monthly overhead budget ($50,000 in the example considered) may be distributed to individual ongoing projects as a function of their total duration or as a function of the amount of work performed on each project during the month. For example, a rate of $5 per direct labor hour might be used. Assume the firm is expecting total labor hours during the year to be 120,000 which is equivalent to 10,000 per month.

A *volume variance* is calculated as the difference in the monthly budgeted overhead and the product of an actual unit of the basis (e.g., 12,000 estimated direct labor hours for the month in question) and the standard rate. As is shown in Fig. 7.21, the volume variance is calculated as the difference between $50,000 and 12,000 hours time $5 per hour. Since the budget amount is less than the budgeted hours times the standard rate (i.e., the amount applied to jobs), a *favorable* volume variance occurs. It is $10,000 in amount.

Summing the $12,000 unfavorable budget variance and the $10,000 favorable volume variance, a total unfavorable fixed variance of $2,000 is calculated. However, unlike the total variable overhead variance, not all of the fixed overhead variance is controllable (i.e., the volume variance). This variance occurs because of seasonal variations in production. The variance is only relevant to product costing. In particular, a volume variance indicates that fixed overhead costs are not properly matched to a unit of production.

Regardless of whether it is a material, labor, job overhead or a general overhead standard, the determination of the standard and the analysis of any variations provide the firm with both a means of budgeting (i.e., project costing) and controlling the budgeted costs. Actual costs are compared to standards. The investigation of the differences provides the indication for corrective management procedures, change of plans or objectives, or even a change in the standard.

7.8 Absorption Versus Direct Costing

Previous sections have addressed the allocation of overhead costs to individual projects. It was suggested that job overhead costs (e.g., variable costs) be allocated to the cost of individual projects as a function of such measures as total direct costs, direct labor costs, or direct labor hours. On the other hand, it was suggested that a construction firm's general overhead (e.g., fixed costs) be allocated to individual projects such that the sum of the costs of the individual projects includes the sum of all the firm's overhead costs.

In cost accounting terminology, the described methods for handling overhead (i.e., allocate all of the overhead to individual projects) is referred to as *absorption costing*. All costs as such become "inventory costs" while the project is in the work-in-progress stage. Thus, if a project takes more than one year's duration, the job overhead and general overhead costs would in affect be carried as inventory from year to year. Thus, the overhead costs would be a company asset until the project was completed and turned over to the owner. The overhead costs would not be recognized as an expense until this time.

An alternative to the traditional absorption costing procedure is *direct costing* (also referred to as *contribution costing*). Direct costing emphasizes the fact that fixed overhead is of a different nature than direct costs or variable overhead. Fixed costs are costs that occur and must be recognized during a given period. As such, direct costing treats these fixed overhead costs as *period costs*. They are not considered to attach to the product (i.e., the construction project). Therefore, they are not considered to be part of a work-in-progress when a project has a duration in excess of the accounting period in question. Instead, the fixed overhead costs are expensed in the period in which they occur.

Much of the argument for direct costing is centered around the different decisions that relate to creating and controlling variable overhead costs versus fixed overhead costs. Fixed costs generally originate in the firm's decisions as to the size of their company and planned growth. As such, these are *committed costs*.[6] On the other hand, variable costs originate because of the daily operation of the firm. Responsibility for these costs are centered on manufacturing personnel. In the construction industry, the personnel responsible for these variable overhead costs would likely be job foremen and superintendents. On the other hand, upper management is generally responsible for the committed costs. Direct costing emphasizes these different levels of responsibility by separately recognizing the two types of costs.

From an accounting point of view, the important difference between absorption costing and direct costing is the different income effects of the two costing methods. This difference is highlighted in Fig. 7.22. As shown, reported net income is lower when using direct costing. Absorption costing yields a higher net income because of the fact that fixed overhead costs are made part of inventory instead of being expensed as they are in direct costing. Note should be made that over several accounting periods, the difference between the reported incomes using the two costing procedures will tend to be eliminated. This is especially the case when volume tends to be relatively constant. However, during periods of wide variation in sales or work performed (e.g., construction project work completed), the reported income using the two procedures will vary substantially.

The important different financial accounting affect of the two costing procedures is witnessed by some of the recent experiences of the industrialized building industry. Industrialized building firms produce and sell their product in a manner similar to the automobile industry. The industrialized building firm produces a product which it in turn may store in its inventory, expecting to sell the product at a later date. For the industrialized building firm, the product may be home modulars or entire prefabricated homes, buildings, or parts of buildings. The typical modular home builder has traditionally built such modulars before orders are received for them. As such, in periods of slack in sales, the firm carries the modulars as an inventory item.

The industrialized building firm has generally used absorption costing for allocating their fixed overhead. Because of the manufacturing process involved, the fixed overhead costs have often proved to be substantial. The end result is that by not expensing these fixed costs in

[6]Boer, G. B., *Direct Cost and Contribution Accounting*, New York, Wiley, 1974, p. 14.

Absorption Costing

Modulars sold 1,000 at $1,000.00		$1,000,000
Cost of units sold Variable:		
1,100 units at $600.00	$660,000	
Fixed manuf. 200.00	220,000	
Less ending inventory 100 units	80,000	
		800,000
Gross Margin		$ 200,000
Less selling and administrative (including variable and fixed)		90,000
Net Income		$ 110,000

Direct Costing

Modulars sold 1,000 at $1,000.00		$1,000,000
Variable manuf. costs	$660,000	
Less ending inventory 100 units at 600	60,000	
Variable manf. costs for units sold	$600,000	
Add variable selling and administrative	40,000	
		$ 640,000
Contribution Margin		$ 360,000
Less fixed costs:		
Fixed manf.	220,000	
Fixed selling and manuf.	50,000	
		270,000
Net Income		$ 90,000

Fig. 7.22. Comparison of absorption and direct costing.

favor of making them part of inventory (an asset), the firm in affect over-states their income. At the same time, they create a higher cost inventory.

Recently, several industrialized building firms have gone from one period of reported high income to the next period of financial ruin. Much to the dismay of investors in the firm, what appeared to be a stable financial firm suddenly collapses. Much of the reason for this suddenness in the change in the financial state of the firm is related to their costing procedure. Because of the choice of absorption costing, income tends to be high as long as the firm continues to manufacture inventory items (e.g., modules). However, sooner or later the costs of manufacturing the inventory have to be recognized. If sales turn downward, the financial effects are significantly negative. Much of the firm's assets are in the form of inventory and the firm faces a severe cash flow problem. Short term debt comes due and the lack of cash either results in bankruptcy or a selling off of the inventory at a reduced price.

The use of direct costing cannot aid in abating sales slowdowns. However, the described suddeness of change from stable or increasing growth to financial ruin would not be as likely to occur if direct costing was used. The large fixed overhead costs of the industrialized building firm would be reported as period costs. In addition, part of the inventory would be reported as period costs. In addition, inventory would only include the sum of the direct costs and variable overhead.

Several construction firms handle fixed overhead (i.e., general overhead) in a manner that approaches direct costing. For example, some construction firms do not allocate their general overhead to the cost of individual projects. Instead they merely use a larger profit margin for their projects to "cover" such overhead costs that are recognized as period costs. The costs are not recognized as part of project work-in-progress. This procedure has the advantage of recognizing and only holding project personnel responsible for those costs that are within their control. On the other hand, there is the disadvantage that there is no assurance that profit margins are set such that all company general overhead will be recovered in that no basis is used for allocating the general overhead costs to individual projects.

7.9 Budgeting and Cash Flow

Previous sections in this chapter have addressed cost accounting from a control point of view. Undoubtedly, one of the strongest arguments that can be made for implementing a cost accounting system is that such a system is a necessary part of any program to control productivity and costs. However, in addition to being a basis for the control task, a cost accounting system plays an important role in the planning function of management. In particular, a properly designed system is instrumental in the determination of budgets and analysis of a firm's cash flow.

A *budget* is a financial quantitative expression of a plan of action for carrying out the firm's objectives. It summarizes the expected impact of all operating and financial decisions on the firm's financial position (i.e., balance sheet), income, and cash flow. In addition to serving as a plan, a budget aids in the coordination and implementation of the plan.

Budgets are generally included in the management process of large firms more than they are in small firms. Small firms such as many small construction firms often lack a cost accounting system and formalized techniques that are necessary parts of budget preparation. The end result is that the small firm often fails financially due to an improper budget or even a lack of budget. For example, several small construction firms have been reported to fail due to the problems that arise when they try to rapidly grow in size. Failure to set out a budget that indicates needed cash flow, collection periods, and sales potential is a major cause for failure when attempting to expand one's business.

Several construction firms have stated that the uncertainties peculiar to their business makes budgets impractical for them and their industry. The is no question that there are some unique uncertainties in the construction industry. However, budgets are not intended to eliminate all uncertainties. Regardless of the type of industry, management will still have to recognize uncertainties even with the best of formalized budgets. The fact that several construction firms have been successful in setting budgets and implementing them is proof of the fact that a budget program will be helpful to some degree to every type and size of firm including the small construction firm.

Several specific advantages of budgets can be cited. These are as follows.[7]

(1) They compel management planning.
(2) They provide expectations that are the best framework for judging subsequent performance.
(3) They promote communication and coordination among the various segments of the organization.

[7]Horngren, C. T., *Cost Accounting: A Managerial Emphasis*, Englewood Cliffs, Prentice-Hall, 1972, pp. 123–124.

Any one of these advantages by itself justifies the preparation of a budget.

Budgets can be of different types and cover different spans of time. From an accounting point of view, a budget may be prepared on a cash or accrual basis. In addition, the construction firm may formulate a budget for a single project or a budget to cover the span of time for several projects, or a month, year, or even ten year period. Whereas a yearly budget may guide the actions of production personnel, a ten year budget might be used by upper management for mapping out growth and capital expenditures. As such, different purposes are satisfied by different budgets.

A somewhat all encompassing type of budget is referred to as a *master budget*. The purpose of the master budget is to integrate the firm's operating and financial budgets. The *operating budget* consists of expectations for sales, cost of materials, labor, and variable and fixed overhead for a period of time such as a year. The *financial budget* consists of expectations for receipts, disbursements, income statement, balance sheet, and flow of cash (often expressed by means of a budgeted statement of the sources and applications of funds). The preparation and format of the income statement, balance sheet, and sources and application of funds statements are discussed in Chapter 9. As such, only the operating budgets and cash receipts and disbursements budgets are discussed here. The preparation of budgeted financial statements is straightforward once these segments of the master budget are set out.

The basic steps in preparing a budget will now be illustrated by means of an example. The budget shown is for a one year span of time. However, the various steps and schedules that make up the operating segment of the master budget are shown only for a quarter of the year. The following schedules that make up the master budget are illustrated.

(1) Contracted work budget
(2) Direct materials budget
(3) Direct labor budget
(4) Job overhead budget
(5) General overhead budget
(6) Budgeted statement of cash receipts and disbursements

Each of the first five budgets listed are support schedules for the statement of cash receipts and disbursements. For example, the contracted work budget shown in Fig. 7.23 provides a means of determining cash intake. This is done by estimating the amount of work to be performed from past contracts and new contracts during the period in

ABC COMPANY
Contracted Work Budget
for the Second Quarter of the 197A Fiscal Year

	Previously contracted work performed this period	New contracts signed this period	Work performed that is contracted this period	Total work this period
Project A	$ 25,000			$ 25,000
Project B		$525,000	$112,000	$112,000
Project C	$135,000			$135,000
Project D		$215,000		0
Project E		$110,000	$110,000	$110,000
				$382,000

Fig. 7.23. Contracted work budget.

question. In the example, this is done quarterly and the contracted work budget shown is for the second quarter.

The construction firm will not receive cash payment during a given time period for all the work performed during that time period. For one, there may be a time lag between the time the work is completed and the time the firm bills the owner for the work. In addition, the owner may be slow paying for the work or he may in fact retain part of the payment until the entire project is judged to be substantially complete. As such, the dollar value shown for the work performed in the statement of cash receipts and disbursements shown in Fig. 7.28 must be adjusted in order to determine the cash received. Although a separate schedule to determine the amount of cash not received for work performed is not shown, a dollar value is shown in the illustration.

The direct material and direct labor budgets for the example in question are shown in Fig. 7.24 and 7.25, respectively. These budgets are determined on the basis of the estimated work completed during the time period as indicated in the contract work budget. It may be appropriate to prepare support schedules of the various types of material used and labor crafts employed. Both the direct material and labor costs are integrated into the disbursements segment of the statement of cash receipts and disbursements.

The job overhead and general overhead budgets are shown in Figs. 7.26 and 7.27, respectively. In order to determine rates for applying the overhead costs to individual jobs, job overhead costs are estimated for a given volume of work (i.e., total cost of work performed of $100,000), and annual general overhead costs are estimated. A job overhead rate of 17% of total cost of work performed is found by dividing the sum of the estimated job overhead costs by the basis of $100,000. Similarly, a monthly general overhead amount of cost to be allocated is determined by dividing the estimated annual costs by 12 months. Using the two bases described, job overhead and general overhead are integrated into the disbursement segment of the statement of cash receipts and disbursements.

The purpose of the statement of cash receipts and disbursements shown in Fig. 7.28 is to aid the firm in its cash flow analysis. In particular, it aids in avoiding unnecessary idle cash and even more importantly focuses on potential cash deficiencies. The importance of mapping the firm's cash flow cannot be overemphasized. It is of such importance that the larger manufacturing firms prepare a similar statement for a span of time of only a week.

ABC COMPANY
Direct Material Budget
For the Second Quarter of the 197A Fiscal Year

	Accrued material cost to be paid this period	Material purchased this period	Material purchased and paid for this period	Total cash paid
Project A	$2,000	$ 8,250	$ 7,150	$ 9,150
Project B	0	$44,000	$44,000	$44,000
Project C	0	$12,000	$ 6,500	$ 6,500
Project D	0	$ 4,000	0	0
Project E	0	$ 4,000	$ 2,000	$ 2,000
				$61,650

Fig. 7.24. Direct material budget.

ABC COMPANY
Direct Labor Budget
for the Second Quarter of 197A Fiscal Year

	Accrued payroll paid this period	Labor cost this period	Labor hours this period to be paid this period	Total cash paid
Project A	$ 9,250	$ 9,250	$ 8,500	$ 17,750
Project B	0	$43,000	$17,000	$ 17,000
Project C	$15,000	$29,750	$26,750	$ 41,750
Project D	0	0	0	
Project E	0	$52,000	$52,000	$ 52,000
				$128,500

Fig. 7.25. Direct labor budget.

ABC COMPANY
Job Overhead Budget
For the Fiscal Year Ending December 31, 197A

For Activity Level of Total Cost of
Work Performed of $100,000

	$ Amount
Supplies	$ 500
Supervision	8,000
Payroll fringe benefits	2,000
Equipment	6,000
Maintenance	500
	$17,000

Job overhead rate (percent
of total work performed)
($17,000/$100,000)   17%

Fig. 7.26. Job overhead budget.

ABC COMPANY
General Overhead Budget
For the Fiscal Year Ending December 31, 197A

	$ Annual Amount
Salaries	$110,000
Depreciation	25,000
Property taxes	12,500
Property insurance	5,500
Interest on mortgage	2,000
Utilities	12,000
Maintenance	85,000
	$252,000
Monthly Overhead Rate: ($252,000/12)	$ 21,000

Fig. 7.27. General overhead budget.

The previously presented budgets (e.g., direct material costs) make up a substantial portion of the statement of cash receipts and disbursements. However, recognition of beginning cash balance, minimum desired cash balance, and financing effects (i.e., amount borrowed, repayed, and interest) must also be recognized in the determination of the ending cash balance. This is illustrated in the example shown in Fig. 7.28. The wide variations in the ending cash balance for the example shown are common in the construction industry. The variable environment, the unique nature of the product, and the duration and method of payment from the project owner are all factors leading to nonuniform cash receipts and disbursements. This being the case, the statement of cash receipts and disbursements takes on added significance.

The budget illustrated can be considered *static*. That is, the operating segment of the budget is based upon the performance of a given number of projects and a given amount of work. The static budget loses some of its usefulness if the actual level of activity varies from the budgeted amount. As such, a *flexible budget* may prove beneficial when the level of activity is somewhat nondeterminable. A flexible budget is prepared for a range of possible activity (e.g., amount of construction work performed). As such, the budget is dynamic because it adapts to changes in volume of activity. For the example master budget discussed, a flexible budget for each quarter for work performed levels ranging from $150,000 to $400,000 might be budgeted. This flexible budget can then be analyzed to determine the possible impact on the firm's cash flow.

ABC COMPANY
Budgeted Statement of Cash Receipts and Disbursements
For the Fiscal Year Ending December 31, 197A

	Quarters				For Year
	1	2	3	4	
Cash balance, beginning	$ 5,000	$ 5,560	$ 28,670	$ 4,020	
Work performed	242,000	382,000	248,000	142,000	$1,014,000
(a) Total available for expenses	$247,000	$387,560	$276,670	$146,020	
Less amount of cash retained by owner	10,000	25,000	43,150	8,450	
(a) Total available for expenses	$237,000	$362,560	$233,520	$137,570	
Less disbursements:					
Materials	$ 51,500	$ 61,650	$56,500	$ 20,540	$ 190,190
Labor	81,400	128,500	62,840	31,000	303,740
Job overhead	41,140	64,940	42,160	24,140	172,380
Applied fixed overhead	63,000	63,000	63,000	63,000	252,000
(b) Total disbursements	$237,040	$318,090	$224,500	$138,680	$ 918,310
Minimum cash balance desired	5,000	5,000	5,000	5,000	
Total cash needed	$242,040	$323,090	$229,500	$143,680	
Excess of total cash available over total cash needed before financing (deficiency)	($ 5,040)	$ 39,470	$ 4,020	($ 6,110)	
Financing:					
Borrowing (beginning)	$ 11,200	$ 0	$ 0	$ 15,000	$ 26,200
Repayments	0	(10,000)	0	0	(10,000)
Interest	(600)	(800)	0	(1,100)	(2,500)
(c) Financing effect	$ 10,600	($ 10,800)	$ 0	($ 13,900)	$ 13,700
Cash balance	$ 5,560	$ 28,670	$ 4,020	$ 7,790	$ 13,700

Fig. 7.28. Statement of cash receipts and disbursements.

7.10 Summary

Cost accounting's main purpose is to help management make decisions. Modern cost accounting systems emphasize the gathering and reporting of information for many types of decisions. Whereas some of these decisions are of a planning nature, cost accounting's real impact is in the area of control. Unless management's plan can be controlled, the plan is of little value.

Cost accounting systems are noticeably absent in the construction industry. Many of the financial failures that occur in the industry are directly related to this absence. In the past, the typical construction firm has ignored implementation of a cost accounting system for several reasons. The difficulty of setting up such a system in the somewhat unique construction industry is likely one of the foremost reasons. Whatever reasons have been given for lack of usage in the past, the reasons have limited merit in today's increasing competitive and sophisticated construction industry. The financially successful firm of the future will find it a must to implement an effective cost accounting system.

The required ingredients of an effective cost accounting system varies somewhat from one industry to the next. For example, whereas job order accounting is appropriate for the construction industry, process accounting is appropriate for the textile industry. Disregarding the type of industry, several cost accounting procedures are a necessary ingredient to any effective system. For example, proper bookkeeping, overhead allocation, and budgeting procedures are common to each and every effective cost accounting system.

Case 7.1. Flow Construction Company: Document Flowcharting

Flow Construction Company has become increasingly concerned with its payroll system. While the system worked well when the firm was small, Flow's increasing volume of work has created several problems. These problems include several instances of underpayment and overpayment of labor, loss of documents for tax purposes, lack of control of labor costs, and little or no correlation between future estimates and the cost of previous projects.

Flow Company typically has three ongoing projects, each being about a $300,000 commercial project. Each project typically has three or four foremen responsible for various segments of the job. These foremen have the responsibility of accounting for the labor time of their subordinates. Typically the foreman fill out a time sheet at the end of the week which summarizes the total hours worked by each of his crew members during the week.

The time sheet is turned into the company's bookkeeper at the end of the week. The bookkeeper uses the time cards to update the labor costs on the job ledgers.

The time cards are then brought to a local bank. For a fee the bank processes the time cards and prepares labor checks for Flow's labor. Flow provides the bank with any changes in personnel information that affects the calculation of the pay checks. The bank provides a monthly bank statement to the firm.

Every three months the bank provides Flow Company with a summary of labor costs. This summary is by crafts (e.g., the total ironworker, carpenter, laborer, etc., costs are summed for the three months and reported separately). Because of the incompatibility of the form of this report with the job ledgers (i.e., all labor costs are summarized together on the job ledgers), presently Flow Company has done little with the three month labor statement.

Completed job ledgers currently are used to aid the firm in estimating future projects. That is, the firm has attempted to correlate the cost of jobs and the overall make up of jobs as an aid in estimating. More often than not, the firm reverts to experience when estimating the cost of a project.

Flow Company has asked you to prepare a document flowchart for their current payroll system. On the basis of this flowchart and recognizing the fact that Flow Company currently has an annual volume of about seven million dollars of work, by means of a document flowchart devise a more efficient payroll system for Flow Company.

Case 7.2. Vary Construction Company:
Variances and Estimating

Vary Construction Company is attempting to implement the use of past project data and variances to improve the accuracy of its estimating system. The firm typically analyzes monthly data to aid it in the estimating of projects to be bid in the following month.

It currently is the end of April and Vary Company has asked you to aid it the determination of various costs to be applied to projects to be bid and performed in the month of May.

On January 1, the beginning of its fiscal year, Vary Company estimated its total annual company overhead (which is considered fixed) to be $240,000. While budgeting it equally over each of the twelve months, it applies it to specific jobs on a bases of $.40 per direct labor hour. This application rate has been determined from an estimate of total direct labor hours for the upcoming year. While variations in direct labor hours have occurred in the months of January, February, March, and April, the firm believes its estimate for the year to be accurate. The actual fixed overhead expenditures by month have been as follows.

Month	Overhead Costs
January	$25,000
February	$25,000
March	$25,000
April	$25,000

On the basis of the first four month costs, it is expected that the monthly fixed overhead cost will remain at $25,000. The estimate of direct labor hours for May is 50,000 hours.

The firm has applied job overhead costs on the basis of $.40 per estimated direct labor hour. April has been the first month that Vary Company has gathered data as to estimated direct labor hours and actual direct labor hours. For the month of April, 40,000 hours were estimated; however 45,000 hours actually took place. The firm actually spent $18,400 on job overhead costs in the month of April.

The 40,000 estimated direct labor hours for April consisted of 30,000 laborer hours and 10,000 carpenter hours. The estimated wage rate for April for the two crafts were $8.00 and $10.00, respectively. Payroll records indicate that a total of $300,000 was paid to laborers and $98,000 to carpenters during the month of April. This was on the basis of 31,000 actual laborer hours and 9900 carpenter hours. It is known that the laborers worked overtime several days in order to keep projects on schedule.

The two main materials that the firm uses are lumber and concrete. During April, drawings indicated lumber use of 8:000 board feet of lumber and 1450 cubic yards of concrete. Actual estimated prices are $2.50 per board foot of lumber, and $34.00 per cubic yard of concrete. Actual price paid averaged $2.25 and $35.25, respectively. Total material costs for April were $21,000 and $6,900 for lumber and concrete, respectively.

The firm expects to bid and perform a single project during the month of May. On the basis of calculations (made before consideration of April's data) estimated carpenter hours and labor hours are 20,000 and 30,000 respectively. The project drawings indicate 7000 board feet of lumber and 1200 cubic yards of concrete. The project will start the first day of the month and is estimated to be completed on the last day of the month.

Using the aid of variance analysis you are to aid Vary Company in determining its bid price for the May project. The firm desires to include a four percent profit margin on total direct cost.

Case 7.3. Over Construction Company:
Overhead Application

Steve Undecid, the chief estimator of Over Construction Company, has accepted your suggestion that job overhead and company overhead be applied on the basis of job direct labor hours. However he has now confronted you with another problem of major importance to the application of overhead.

In determining the appropriate overhead application rates, Steve Undecid recognizes that three different levels of the base (i.e., direct labor hours) can be chosen. These levels are as follows.

Maximum annual capacity: the annual number of direct labor hours should the firm perform work to their physical potential.

Expected annual activity: the annual number of direct labor hours the firm can expect to perform based on last year's performance.

Average annual activity: the annual number of direct labor hours the firm can expect to perform based on an average of the last five years' performance.

The three relevant annual direct labor hours are 220,000, 180,000, and 150,000, respectively.

It is currently January 1, 1975 and Steve Undecid has asked you for your advice in deciding which level of the base to use to determine the overhead application rates. In considering the alternative you should consider the effects on variances, bid amounts, and total application of overhead.

Chapter 8

Capital Budgeting: Planning Long Term Expenditures

8.1 Introduction

Making decisions as to the acquisition of long lived or fixed assets is one of the most important management functions of any firm. These are assets which the firm uses for its means of production. Their expected life is typically greater than a year. Decision making as it relates to these types of assets is commonly referred to as *capital expenditure analysis* or *capital budgeting*.

The greater a given firm's dependence on capital assets (i.e., fixed assets), the greater the importance of capital budgeting to the firm. As to the construction industry, a given firm's dependence on capital assets varies considerably depending on the type of work performed. Whereas the building construction firm may have little need for capital assets, the heavy and highway construction firm typically has a large investment in capital assets. It has been estimated that of every dollar of annual work volume the heavy and highway firm performs, it maintains a forty-two cent investment in equipment (i.e., a capital asset).[1]

Capital budgeting recognizes the time value of money. Owing to the fact that an interest charge is associated with lending and borrowing money, the value of money is dependent on time. The valuation of cash inflows and outflows is made more complex by economic factors such as inflation which affects the true worth of money at a given point in time.

Capital budgeting focuses on the optimal selection of alternative economic proposals. It recognizes cash inflows, outlays, and opportunity costs. As to the construction firm, capital budgeting may be used for selection of projects for which the firm is to bid, analysis of company growth alternatives, and decisions as to financial structure. However its

[1]How To Buy, Rent or Lease: The Tools of Construction, "Engineering News Record," January 12, 1975, p. 41.

295

most practical and widely used application is in the area of equipment analysis and selection. In addition to providing a tool for choosing between alternative types of equipment to be purchased, capital budgeting can aid in the decision to buy, rent, or lease equipment.

The result of a capital budgeting decision is not limited to its effect on capital inflows and outflows. Such decisions affect the financial structure of the firm and as a result may affect the firm's ability to borrow money or the bonding capacity of the firm. Additionally, while the time value of money plays a predominant role in a capital budgeting decision, other economic factors may also be relevant to the optimal decision. For example, effects of depreciation, investment tax credit, and capital gain tax advantages may have an important impact on the optimal choice of alternatives. More often than not these additional factors can be recognized in a capital budgeting analysis.

This chapter focuses on specific techniques that can be used for capital budgeting. Due to their failure to recognize the time value of money, several of the techniques are only approximate as to the solution determined. These techniques are introduced first. The more accurate techniques that include recognition of the time value of money are then presented. Unique construction related factors as they relate to capital budgeting are discussed by means of their inclusion in the examples of the specific capital budgeting techniques.

8.2 Average Investment Method

The average investment method sometimes referred to as the *average rate of return method*, is an easy and quick means of passing judgment on a potential capital asset investment. A serious weakness of the method is that it makes no distinction between revenues and expenses that occur at an early date versus those that occur at a later date. Should the time interval be long, or the interest rate relevant to the analysis be relatively large, the application of the average investment method may in fact result in a serious error in selection of alternatives. On the other hand, more often than not, the relative benefits or disadvantages of two or more alternatives may be great enough that the application of the method indeed focuses on the more optimal solution.

The average investment method merely relates the average earnings or dollar benefits of an asset or alternative to the average investment over its lifetime. Stated as a formula this as follows.

$$\text{Average rate of return} = \frac{\text{average earnings}}{\text{average investment}}$$

Once the average rate of return is calculated for an asset or alternative it can be compared to a desired rate of return of alternatives to aid in the evaluation of the alternative being considered.

For example let us assume that the estimated benefits (e.g., extra dollar work performed or cost savings due to higher productivity) of purchasing a $200,000 piece of construction equipment is $150,000. The estimated average annual benefit is determined by dividing the total expected benefits by the expected life, say ten years. Thus the average earnings are as follows.

$$\text{Average earnings} = \frac{\$150,000}{10} = \$15,000$$

The average investment is calculated as one-half of the original investment. This in effect results in valuing the average investment equal to the average carrying value of the asset as determined by straight-line depreciation, assuming the asset has no salvage value. For the example noted, the average investment of the equipment is calculated as follows.

$$\text{Average investment} = \frac{\$200,000}{2} = \$100,000$$

Finally the average rate of return is calculated as the average earnings divided by the average investment. The result is as follows.

$$\text{Average rate of return} = \frac{\$15,000}{\$100,000} = 15\%$$

Thus the application of the average investment method indicates a 15% rate of return on the construction firm's $200,000 investment in the equipment. This 15% could then be compared to a stated desired rate of return such as one the firm may obtain by other investment alternatives. For example, it may prove advantageous to subout work that would be performed by means of purchasing the equipment. Such an option would likely prove advantageous should the construction firm be able to invest the $200,000 at a return approaching or in excess of 15%.

The average rate of return could also be calculated for purchases of alternative equipment and then be compared to the 15% return calculated for the $200,000 piece of equipment. For example, the average rate of return for a $60,000 piece of equipment with a twelve year life with expected total benefits of $108,000 would be as follows.

$$\text{Average rate of return} = \frac{\$108,000/12}{\$60,000/2} = \frac{\$9,000}{\$30,000} = 30\%$$

Does it follow, that due to the calculated higher rate of return (i.e., 30% versus 15%), that the $60,000 piece of equipment is the better capital budgeting alternative? On the basis of the application of the average investment method, such a conclusion does indeed follow. However the possible errors in such a conclusion should be apparent. For one, as noted earlier, the dollar benefits are not identified as to when they occur. It may be that the entire $150,000 of benefits of the more expensive equipment are obtained in the earlier years of its life whereas the bulk of the dollar benefits obtained from the cheaper equipment are obtained in the last few years of the equipment's life. Owing to the time value of money, surely the money received in early years should be valued higher than an equal amount of money received in later years.

Note also that the two pieces of equipment are expected to have different useful lives. The fact of the matter is that more likely than not the equipment will have to be replaced after the exhaustion of its life. The average investment method has ignored the fact that the outlay of money for replacement will occur two years earlier for the one piece of equipment versus the alternative piece of equipment.

Other important factors not included in the average investment method comparison include the nonrecognition of depreciation expense, investment tax credit, and accelerated depreciation methods for calculation of tax liability. Each of these factors may have an important impact on the optimal economic alternative.

As is true of all the capital budgeting techniques discussed in this chapter, the method fails to recognize noneconomic factors such as quality, preference for a certain manufacturer, serviceability, etc. These factors may be important in addition to the common economic considerations. This is especially the case when the economic merits of alternatives are fairly equal.

However even if the noneconomic factors are completely discounted in the capital budgeting analysis, it should be apparent that one should be careful in putting too much weight on results obtained by the use of the average investment method. At best, the method should be used as a screening procedure to eliminate unprofitable alternatives.

8.3 Payback Method

Like the average investment method, the payback method ignores the time value of money and as such only serves as an approximate method for comparing capital budgeting alternatives. On the other hand, the payback method, as is true of the average investment method, is easy to apply and can in fact be used to eliminate unprofitable alternatives from consideration early in deliberations.

The payback method is a procedure for determining the *payback period*, which is the amount of time required for an asset or alternative to earn enough to return the original outlay. It is calculated as follows.

$$\text{Payback period} = \frac{\text{investment}}{\text{annual net cash flow}}$$

The investment part of the equation merely represents the initial cash expenditure for the alternative. For example, a construction firm may be considering the purchase of a $200,000 piece of equipment. In this case the investment is $200,000.

The annual cash flow is considered as annual cash inflows minus annual cash outflows. Typically it is expected revenues minus expenses plus depreciation (i.e., depreciation is an expense but not a cash expense and as such should be added back to negate its subtraction as an expense). As to construction equipment, the benefits consist of cost savings or added work revenue minus expenses of operating the equipment. The depreciation expense is an operating expense but not a cash expense.

Let us assume that the annual dollar inflows (i.e., cost savings, etc.) minus annual operating expenses from the $200,000 piece of equipment are estimated at $15,000. Additionally the equipment has a ten year life and is being depreciated using a straight line method. Thus the resulting depreciation expense to be included in the annual net cash flow is $20,000. Thus the total annual net cash flow is calculated as follows.

Annual net cash flow = $15,000 + $20,000 = $35,000

The payback period for the $200,000 piece of equipment is calculated as follows.

$$\text{Payback period} = \frac{\$200,000}{\$35,000} = 5.7 \text{ years}$$

This 5.7 year payback period would likely be rounded to six years. Should the firm desire a payback period less than five or six years, the equipment should be ruled to be nonfeasible. On the other hand, should the firm desire a payback period of about ten years, the equipment selection deserves further attention.

The payback method can also be used to compare alternative equipment purchases or alternatives. Thus if one piece of equipment has a payback period of six years versus another piece of equipment that has a payback period of eight years, one can conclude from the use of the payback method, that the equipment with the payback period of six years is more optimal.

An equipment decision based only on the payback method may prove troublesome. The payback method is weak in that it doesn't consider the life of the alternatives. This failure to recognize the lives of the alternatives results in a failure to recognize the overall profitability of alternatives. For example, a piece of equipment with a payback period of six years may have a life of ten years, whereas a piece of equipment with a payback period of eight years may have a life of twenty years. Even though its payback period is less favorable than the alternative piece of equipment, the twenty year life of the asset with an eight year payback period may result in it being the more profitable and optimal piece of construction equipment.

Yet another weakness in the comparison of payback periods of alternatives, is the failure to recognize the timing of the cash flows. This failure to recognize the time value of money can result in serious distortion of the relative economic merits of alternatives. The user of the payback method or the average investment method should be aware of these possible distortions when using these techniques for capital budgeting. The following sections of this chapter address the time value of money and the more rigorous and accurate capital budgeting solution techniques.

8.4 Time Value of Money

Many decisions concerning capital assets affect cash inflows and outflows over a long period of time. It is not unusual for a construction firm to expect a major piece of equipment to last ten or even twenty years. These expectations are confirmed by the fact that the Internal Revenue Service requires that equipment assets be depreciated over no less than 8 years.[2] The long expected life coupled with the fact that at interest rates in existence during the last five years the value of money may double in as short a period of time as ten years, results in the time value of money being of major importance to a capital budgeting analysis.

Associated with time and money is the *interest rate* which the borrower must pay for using money, or the interest rate at which an inves-

---

[2]1974 U. S. Master Tax Guide, "Commerce Clearing House," November 1973, p. 420.

tor may invest money. *Interest* is a rent charged for using money for a period of time. A borrower pays a lender interest for using the lender's money. The interest rate charged by the lender is the ratio of rental charged to the amount of money lent or borrowed for a given time period. When determining the interest rate to be charged, the lender considers the risk of loss of his money, his opportunity costs for the money, and such things as administrative expenses of drawing up and closing the loan. When determining what interest rate he is willing to pay for using money, the borrower compares his expected rate of return from the investment of the money and the interest rate associated with borrowing the money.

The interest rate as it pertains to the availability of money from banks, or savings and loan companies, is related to the state of the national economy. Through monetary policies aimed at controlling the amount of money in circulation and the issuance of debt, the federal government can somewhat dictate interest rates. In practice, the modeling of interest rates as a function of distinct factors is indeed complex.

When making an economic analysis of several possible alternatives involving revenues and costs, not only must the construction firm consider the interest rate it must pay for borrowing money, but also the interest rate associated with investing its income. In reality, the interest rate it is charged versus the interest rate at which it can invest may be quite different, the borrowing interest rate usually being higher.

The interest rate not only applies to the incomes and costs associated with the proposal the firm is considering, but also to the opportunity incomes or costs as they pertain to the proposal in question. For example, even though a firm may have enough of its own money available to finance a project without borrowing, the fact that it may safely invest this money for 6% a year (if the money is not used to finance the project) should be charged against the cost of doing the project.

Similarly, when choosing between alternatives of buying a piece of equipment versus renting it, the opportunity interest income that can be obtained should the equipment be rented, should be recognized in the analysis. Failure to recognize opportunity income, can result in a less than optimal decision.

8.4.1 Interest Formulas

Owing to the existence of an interest rate associated with investing or borrowing money, the value of money to an individual is dependent

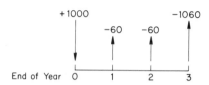

Fig. 8.1. Simple interest.

upon time, i.e., the value of a proposed future sum of money must be discounted to determine its present value. When purchasing equipment with borrowed money, both the interest rate paid for the money, and the time associated with paying it back must be considered to determine the equipment's "true" cost.

In this section, several formulas will be given for determining the value of money at different points in time, given an existing interest rate. These formulas are often referred to as interest formulas. In presenting these interest formulas the following symbols will be used.

i, interest rate per defined time period

n, number of time periods

P, present sum of money

S, future sum of money

R, one of a uniform series of end of period payments

When the interest paid by the borrower to a lender is proportional to the length of time the money is borrowed, it is referred to as a simple interest. The interest paid per period is equal to the amount of money borrowed, multiplied by the interest rate per time period. The total amount of interest paid by the borrower to the lender is equal to the amount paid per period, multiplied by the number of time periods for which the money is borrowed. Having borrowed an amount of money (P) from a lender, the borrower pays back the lender a total sum of money (S) as follows.

$$S = P + Pin = P(1 + in)$$

For example, if a person borrows $1000 from a lender for a 3 year period, at an interest rate of 6%, he then pays $60 interest at the end of each of the 3 years, in addition to the $1000 at the end of the last year. These payments are shown on a time scale in Fig. 8.1. In the figure, a negative payment refers to money the borrower pays the lender.

Very few loans drawn up between two parties are written so that simple interest applies to the loaned money. The more common type of loan drawn up uses compound interest. Suppose you lend the bank $1000. In this case, the bank is the borrower and you are the lender. The

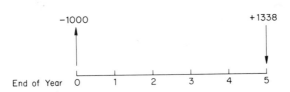

Fig. 8.2. Single payment compound amount.

loan is such that the bank agrees to pay 6% yearly compounded interest for the use of your money. At the end of the first year they credit to your account $60.00 (6% of $1000.00). Assuming you withdraw no money from your account, at the end of the second year the bank credits your account $63.60 (6% of 1060.00). At the end of the third year they credit your account $67.42 (6% of $1123.60). The bank is paying you interest on your balance in your account every time period. If after n pay periods, you decide to make a withdrawal of your initial loan and all your accumulated interest, you would receive a sum of money given by the following formula.

$$S = P(1 + i)^n$$

For example, if you withdrew your accumulated sum of money after a 5 year period, you would receive $1338.00 ($1000 $(1 + 0.06)^5$). The payments are shown in Fig. 8.2, the positive payment representing the money you receive, the negative payment the money you gave the bank.

It should be obvious that there is a great difference between simple and compound interest. For this reason, it is very important for the borrower and the lender to fully understand the type of interest, the relevant time periods, and the interest rate per time period written into a particular loan. Many people, including contractors, have taken out a loan expecting to make certain interest payments, only to discover later they have committed themselves to a larger sum of money. Historically, lenders have been misleading in stating the "real" interest rate associated with a loan to a borrower. For example, a lender may state an interest rate of 1% monthly, leading some individuals to believe that if they obtain a $1000 loan, they will only have to pay an interest charge of $10 a year. Of course, this is not correct. A 1% monthly interest rate is not equal to a 1% annual interest rate. The government has recently taken steps to alleviate this problem by requiring a lender to state the "true" annual interest rate charged on a loan, rather than a weekly, monthly, or quarterly interest rate. The lender is also required to state whether the interest charged is to be simple or compound. Even with these preventive actions by the government, it cannot be overem-

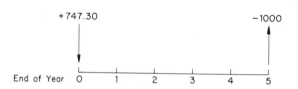

Fig. 8.3. Single payment present worth.

phasized that the borrower should be aware of all liabilities associated with borrowing money.

Regarding the time value of money, an individual may be interested in knowing the worth of some future sum of money to him at the present time. For example, let us imagine an individual is promised $1000 five years from the present. The individual realizes that if he presently had the $1000, he could invest it at the present interest rate and accumulate a sum greater than $1000 by the end of 5 years (at which time he would receive the promised $1000). As a result of this opportunity to presently invest the money at some positive interest rate, the future sum of $1000 is worth less than $1000 to him at the present.

The present value of a future monetary sum is often referred to as the present worth of the sum of money. To determine a future sum's present worth, we need to know how far into the future the sum is to be paid or received, and also the interest rate at which the money could be invested, or in the case of borrowing money, the interest rate associated with borrowing the money. The present worth (P) of a future sum of money (S) may be found by using the following formula.

$$P = S(1 + i)^{-n}$$

The term $(1 + i)^{-n}$ is known as the single payment present worth formula or factor. It assumes a constant i over the relevant time period n. It may be observed that the single payment present worth factor is merely the inverse of the single payment compound amount factor, i.e., finding the future worth of a present sum of money is the reverse of finding the present value of a future sum.

Returning to the problem of finding the present worth of $1000 to be received by an individual 5 years from the present, let us assume the individual could invest the money at an interest rate of 6%. The present worth of the money is equal to $747.30 ($1000$(1 + 0.06)^{-5}$). Figure 8.3 shows the finding of the present worth on a time scale.

By using the single payment compound amount factor and the single payment present worth factor, the true "value of a sum of money

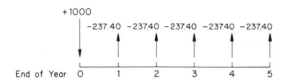

Fig. 8.4. Uniform series—capital recovery.

may be found at any desired point in time. However, to facilitate the actual calculation procedure, which may involve shifting money on a time scale when there are several payments, several other interest formulas or factors have been derived. One of these factors is the capital recovery interest factor. This is useful in determining the equal payments required in a loan in which the borrower is to only pay interest on the unpaid balance. For example, suppose an individual is to repay a $1000 loan in 5 equal end-of-the-year payments, paying a 6% interest rate on the unpaid balance. The equal payments he is to make (R) may be obtained from the following formula.

$$R = P(i(1 + i)^n/((1 + i)^n - 1))$$

The term in brackets is known as the capital recovery factor. Note that the factor is merely the result of summing several single payment compound amount factors. In the above example, the interest factor is found to be 0.2374. The equal payments to be made (R) are found to equal $1000 \times (0.2374)$ or $237.40. The payments involved are shown on a time scale in Fig. 8.4.

Observe that in using the capital recovery factor, we are actually finding a uniform series of payments which are equivalent to a present monetary sum. We may well be interested in reversing the problem, i.e., we may want to know the present value of a uniform series of payments. This may be found by using the following formula.

$$P = R ((1 + i)^n - 1)/(i(1 + i)^n))$$

Note that the term in the brackets, referred to as the uniform series present worth factor, is merely the inverse of the capital recovery factor. The reason should be obvious.

The uniform series present worth factor is useful in determining the present worth of a uniform series of payments. For example, let us suppose an individual is promised $1000 at the end of every year for 5 years. Since he knows he can invest available money at a 6% interest rate, he knows this promised sum of $5000 (5 × $1000) is, in fact, worth less than $5000 at the present time. The uniform series present worth factor for $i = 0.06$, $n = 5$, is found to be equal to 4.2124. Thus, the

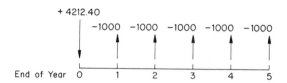

Fig. 8.5. Uniform series present worth.

present worth of the payments is equal to $4212.40 ($1000 × 4.2124).
These payments are shown on a time scale in Fig. 8.5.

Two other interest formulas or factors are of immediate interest
here. These interest factors define the relationships which exist between a future sum of money (S), and a set of uniform series of payments (R). These relationships may be derived from the single payment
compound amount interest factors. One of these interest factors, the
uniform series compound amount factor, determines what equal value
end-of-period payments, invested at an interest rate i and earning interest immediately upon investment, will sum to after n payment
periods. The amount accumulated, which consists of the sum of the
uniform payments and the earned interest, may be determined from the
following formula.

$S = R \left(((1 + i)^n - 1)/i \right)$

The term in the brackets is referred to as the uniform series compound
amount factor. Suppose an individual invests $1000 at the end of every
year into a savings account, which pays 6% compounded interest. The
money starts drawing interest as soon as it is invested. To determine
the amount of money accumulated after 5 years, we calculate the uniform series compound amount factor for $i = 0.06$, $n=5$, and obtain a
value of 5.637. Thus, the sum of money accumulated is found to be the
product of $1000 times 5.637, or $5637.00. This is shown on the time
scale in Fig. 8.6.

The inverse of the uniform series compound amount factor is the
sinking fund factor. The sinking fund factor determines which uniform
series of payments must be made at a given interest rate, to accumulate
a stipulated future sum (S) after a given number of payment periods.
For example, assume an individual desires to invest a uniform series of
payments (each to be made at the end of the year at an interest rate of
6%), so that he has $1000 in savings at the end of 5 years. This uniform
series of payments may be derived from the following formula.

$R = S \left(i/((1 + i)^n - 1) \right)$

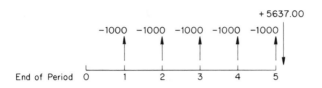

Fig. 8.6. Uniform series compound amount.

Fig. 8.7 Uniform series—sinking fund.

The term in the brackets is referred to as the sinking fund factor. For the above example, the sinking fund factor equals 0.1774. Thus, the uniform end-of-the-year payments which the individual must invest in order to accumulate $1000 after a 5 year period is equal to $1000 multiplied by 0.1774 ($177.40). These payments are shown on a time scale in Fig. 8.7.

It should be observed that the value of any interest factor described, whether single payment compound amount, capital recovery, sinking fund, etc., depends only on the relevant interest rate, i, and the number of payments, n. From this point on, the entire formula will not be written out for a given interest factor. Rather, a shortened notation will be substituted. Single payment compound amount will be abbreviated as (SPCA, i = x, n = y), single payment present worth as (SPPW, i = x, n = y), uniform series present worth as (USPW, i = x, n = y), capital recovery as (CR, i = x, n = y), sinking fund as (SF, i = x, n = y), and uniform series compound amount as (USCA, i = x, n = y). The values of x and y correspond to the given interest rate and the number of payment periods.

The values of the various interest factors as a function of the interest rate, i, and the number of payment periods, n, are available in interest tables. The use of such interest tables eliminates the need to mathematically solve the interest formula. A complete set of interest tables is presented in Appendix A.

8.4.2 Annuities

Closely related to the concept of the time value of money and in-terest formulas is the term *annuity*. The term annuity implies a series of equal periodic payments. The amount of an annuity is the sum of the periodic payments or rents plus the sum of the compound interest on each of them. In this sense an annuity is similar to the concept of the uniform series compound amount.

Two types of annuities are in common use. One is referred to as an *ordinary annuity*, whereas the other is referred to as an *annuity due*. The two types of annuities differ in regard to when the last payment is made. The ordinary annuity is illustrated in Fig. 8.8. It can be observed that the number of payments is one more than the number of interest periods. It is assumed that the first payment is made at the beginning of the time period being considered and the last payment is made at the time at which the sum of payments and interests are calculated.

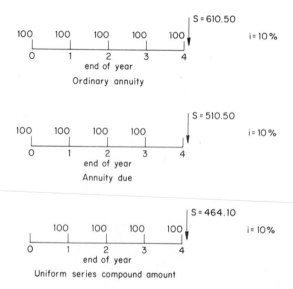

Fig. 8.8. Annuities and compound interest.

The annuity due is also illustrated in Fig. 8.8. The annuity due has an equal number of payments and interest periods. As can be observed in the figure, the last payment is made or received one period prior to the point in time at which the sum of the payments and interests are calculated.

It should be noted that while the ordinary annuity and annuity due are similar to the uniform series compound amount interest factor, differences do in fact exist. As illustrated in Fig. 8.8, the uniform series compound amount factor assumes that the first payment is made after the first time period. The result is that if one were to calculate the value of the payments at any point in time for the ordinary annuity, annuity due, and uniform series compound amount interest factor, three different values would result. This is done for the end of period four in Fig. 8.8.

It is also possible, using the time value of money interest formulas, to calculate the present value of annuities. As one would expect, the present value of an ordinary annuity and annuity due also differ even when they have similar interest rates and time periods.

In reality annuities are merely an application of the interest factors discussed. The commonness of the payment time periods for which the ordinary annuity and annuity due represent has resulted in singling out these payment methods with identifying names. The annuity terms are widely used when discussing capital budgeting alternatives.

8.5 Discounted Cash Flow Analysis

The most general capital budgeting technique in regard to the number and type of problems for which it can be applied is the *discounted cash flow method*. This method is alternatively referred to as the *rate-of-return* method. Using this method, a capital expenditure is viewed as the acquisition of a series of future net cash flows consisting of two elements: the return of the original outlay and the net income or cost savings from the capital expenditure. Should the present value of the net cash inflows discounted at a desired rate of return be in excess of the initial capital expenditure required, then the investment is warranted. Alternately two proposals may be compared on the basis of their respective differences in discounted net cash inflows versus required initial investment.

Let us consider the previously discussed example, whereby a construction firm is considering the purchase of a $200,000 piece of equipment. The estimated annual cash flow due to savings resulting from cost reductions is $15,000, and the increased cash flow due to the depreciation expense is $20,000. Thus the total annual cash inflow is $35,000. In order to determine the feasibility of the capital expenditure using the discounted cash flow method, the future incomes or cash flows are discounted back to the present time and compared to the initial capital expenditure of $200,000. The future cash flows are discounted by means of calculating their present worths at a specified interest rate. The interest rate to be used in the calculation is the interest rate for which the firm could invest the initial capital expenditure had it not purchased the equipment. Alternatively, it is the interest rate at which the firm borrows the money to purchase the equipment. Let us assume that the latter is true in the example, and the effective interest rate (i.e., including closing costs, etc.) for borrowing the money is 15%. The net cash inflow discounted at 15% is calculated in Table 8.1.

The sum of the discounted net cash inflows is $175,595. Because this sum is less than the initial capital expenditure of $200,000 the purchase of the equipment is ruled unfeasible. If the discounted sum more closely approaches the initial cost, the purchase should likely be more closely analyzed. On the other hand, should the discounted sum of cash inflows exceed the initial $200,000 cost, the purchase is economically warranted.

The discounted cash flow method also proves useful when evaluating alternative purchases. For example, let us assume that as an alternative to the $200,000 piece of equipment, the firm has an option of

Table 8.1

Year	Net cash flow	Present value of 1 at 15%	Present value of net cash flow
1	$35,000	.869	$30,415
2	$35,000	.756	$26,460
3	$35,000	.657	$22,995
4	$35,000	.572	$20,020
5	$35,000	.497	$17,395
6	$35,000	.432	$15,120
7	$35,000	.376	$13,160
8	$35,000	.327	$11,445
9	$35,000	.284	$ 9,940
10	$35,000	.247	$ 8,645
			$175,595

Table 8.2

Year	Net cash flow	Present value of 1 at 15%	Present value of net cash flow
1	$14,000	.869	$12,166
2	$14,000	.756	$10,584
3	$14,000	.657	$ 9,198
4	$14,000	.572	$ 8,008
5	$14,000	.497	$ 6,958
6	$14,000	.432	$ 6,048
7	$14,000	.376	$ 5,264
8	$14,000	.327	$ 4,578
9	$14,000	.284	$ 3,976
10	$14,000	.247	$ 3,458
11	$14,000	.215	$ 3,010
12	$14,000	.187	$ 2,618
			$75,866

purchasing a previously described piece of equipment for $60,000. This equipment has an expected life of twelve years and a net annual cash inflow of $9,000 plus $5,000 of depreciation for a total of $14,000.

The present value of the discounted $14,000 inflows are calculated in the same manner as for the $200,000 piece of equipment. The relevant interest rate is again assumed to be 15%. The calculation of the discounted sum is shown in Table 8.2.

For this alternative the discounted sum of the inflows exceeds the initial cost of $60,000. This in effect means that there is a positive economical return associated with the purchase of the equipment. On the basis of the discounted cash flow analysis, clearly the better choice of the two purchases is the $60,000 piece of equipment.

While the discounted cash flow method has recognized the lives of the two alternative pieces of equipment in the calculation of discounted inflows, it has failed to recognize the fact that more than likely the piece of equipment will be replaced with another piece of equipment after its life. This large replacement cost is important in the analysis in that the equipment replacement will take place at a different point in time depending on which alternative is selected. Even recognizing this inadequacy of the method, the reliability and completeness of the discounted cash flow method far exceeds that of the average investment method or the payback method. It is interesting to compare the results that are obtained from the use of the alternative decision analysis techniques as to the equipment selection. The comparison is as follows:

Equipment (initial cost)	Average investment (rate of return)	Payback period (years)	Discounted cash flow	
			Initial cost	Discounted inflows
$200,000	15%	5.7	$200,000	$175,595
$ 60,000	30%	4.3	$ 60,000	$ 75,866

While it is true that each analysis technique indicates that the $60,000 piece of equipment is the better alternative, the relative merit of the $60,000 piece of equipment differs depending on the technique used. For example, using the payback method, the merit of the two pieces of equipment may be ruled about equal in that their payback periods are approximately equal (i.e., 5.7 and 4.3). On the other hand, using the average investment method or the discounted cash flow method, the relative strong preference for the $60,000 piece of equipment is apparent.

It should also be noted that the average investment method indicates a 15% rate of return for the $200,000 piece of equipment. However recognizing the interest rate associated with money and the fact that the cash inflows occur in the future, the discounted cash flow method indicates that the rate of return is actually less than this rate. This is evidenced by the fact that the sum of the discounted net inflows at 15% is less than the required initial expenditure.

Finally it should be observed that the payback period in itself means little. The calculated payback periods of 5.7 and 4.3 have little relationship to whether each of the alternatives has a positive rate of return. Thus we have the argument for the use of the discounted cash flow method.

The use of the discounted cash flow or rate of return method is not limited to determining if the discounted net cash inflows exceed the initial expenditure for an investment alternative. The method can be used to determine the actual rate of return associated with an investment such as the investment in a capital asset. For example, let us assume that the construction firm contemplating the purchase of the previously described $60,000 piece of construction equipment would like to know the true rate of return associated with the $60,000 expenditure.

Because the total net cash inflows sum to $168,000 whereas the initial expenditure is only $60,000, it follows that the rate of return is greater than zero. It can also be concluded from the calculations in

Table 8.2 that the rate of return on the initial expenditure is in excess of 15%. This conclusion follows from the fact that the sum of the net cash inflows, discounted at an assumed interest rate of 15%, exceeded the initial expenditure of $60,000. In effect, this means that had the construction firm invested the $60,000 at a compounded 15% annual interest rate, it would have received less cash inflows than those that it received from investment in the equipment. Thus the return associated with the $60,000 equipment investment must be greater than 15%.

Having decided that the actual rate of return is in excess of 15%, the next step in determining the actual rate of return centers around the use of trial and error. The complex mathematic nature of interest formulas (i.e., they are not linear) results in the necessity for use of the trial and error method. Using such a method, a rate of return is selected on the bases of eliminating unfeasible values (i.e., in this case all values less than or equal to 15% have been determined unfeasible), and an analysis of previously calculated discounted net cash inflows versus initial expenditures. For example, from Table 8.2 it was determined that the sum of the discounted net cash inflows equals $75,866. This sum, discounted at 15%, is quite a bit in excess of the $60,000. On this basis it follows that the next trial and error iteration should be quite a bit in excess of 15%. Perhaps 25% would be a good estimate. On this basis, the sum of the discounted net cash inflows is calculated in Table 8.3.

From the calculation in Table 8.3 it is determined that the sum of the net cash inflows discounted at 25% is less than $60,000. This in effect means that had the firm invested $52,152 in the equipment and

Table 8.3

Year	Net cash flow	Present value of 1 at 25%	Present value of net cash flow
1	$14,000	.800	$11,200
2	$14,000	.640	$ 8,960
3	$14,000	.512	$ 7,168
4	$14,000	.4096	$ 5,734
5	$14,000	.3277	$ 4,588
6	$14,000	.2621	$ 3,669
7	$14,000	.2097	$ 2,936
8	$14,000	.1678	$ 2,349
9	$14,000	.1342	$ 1,879
10	$14,000	.1074	$ 1,504
11	$14,000	.0859	$ 1,203
12	$14,000	.0687	$ 962
			$52,152

Table 8.4

Year	Net cash flow	Present value of 1 at 20%	Present value of net cash flow
1	$14,000	.833	$11,662
2	$14,000	.694	$ 9,716
3	$14,000	.579	$ 8,106
4	$14,000	.482	$ 6,748
5	$14,000	.402	$ 5,628
6	$14,000	.335	$ 4,690
7	$14,000	.279	$ 3,906
8	$14,000	.233	$ 3,262
9	$14,000	.194	$ 2,716
10	$14,000	.162	$ 2,268
11	$14,000	.135	$ 1,890
12	$14,000	.112	$ 1,568
			$62,160

received the annual cash inflows of $14,000 for twelve years, the effective rate of return on the investment would be 25%. However because the firm had to invest more than $52,152 (i.e., the equipment purchased required an expenditure of $60,000), it's actual rate of return is less than the 25%.

We have now bounded the solution. The actual rate of return is between 15 and 25%. If it is desirable to further focus in on the actual rate of return, the next iteration would be carried out at a rate somewhere between 15 and 25%. The next trial might be made at 20%. This is done in Table 8.4.

While the sum of the net cash inflows discounted at 20% does not exactly equal $60,000 it is in fact relatively close. Any further centering in on the actual rate of return may not be beneficial in that there is a degree of uncertainty associated with the expected annual net cash inflows. More likely than not the rate is close to 21%.

The trial and error method has resulted in the determination of approximately a 21% rate of return for the equipment expenditure. Having calculated this rate of return, it can be compared to the expected rate of return for alternative investments to determine if the equipment purchase is warranted.

It should be noted that while the actual rate of return was determined using a trial and error method, in reality the rate of return could have been determined in a more straightforward procedure. In particular, because each of the expected annual cash inflows was equal in amount, the rate of return could have been solved from the following equation.

$60,000 =

($14,000) × (uniform series present worth factor)(for n = 12, i = ?)

Using interest formula tables, the value of i (i.e., the interest rate) could be found that results in the equation being valid. This interest rate would in effect be the rate of return.

This direct application of finding the rate of return can only be used should the expected inflows be equal in amount. More often than not they may vary (i.e., both expected revenues and expenses may vary from year to year) and when this is the case the trial and error method must be used. Because of this likelihood, the calculations in Tables 8.1–8.4 are carried out in a manner that is general (i.e., the inflows may be equal or unequal).

8.6 Annual Cost Method

Evaluation and analysis of proposed construction equipment expenditures should not limit themself to an evaluation of initial cost. Because of the expected long life of most equipment purchased it is necessary to recognize annual costs associated with operating equipment throughout its life.

As to construction equipment, annual costs include normal maintenance and equipment repairs. Depreciation costs can be ignored in that they are noncash costs. In fact a rigorous analysis may actually recognize cost savings associated with the income tax depreciation deduction.

Using the annual cost method, an annual cost for the investment or purchase being considered is determined; that is, all costs associated with the equipment being considered are expressed as an annual cost. Both normally occurring annual costs such as maintenance and repair costs and lump sum costs such as the initial capital expenditure are expressed as an annual cost.

Regularly occurring maintenance and repair costs can typically be expressed as annual costs. As such they normally present no difficulty as to being handled as annual costs in the annual cost method. On the other hand, should the actual expected repair and maintenance costs be nonuniform as to their amount from year to year, it is necessary to transform them to equal amounts using time value of money interest formulas.

As noted earlier, all costs are expressed as annual costs when using the annual cost method. As such it is necessary to transform an initial equipment expenditure into equal annual costs over the life of the equipment. This is accomplished through the use of the capital recovery interest factor. In addition to distributing the initial purchase expenditure over the life of the asset, an interest cost is recognized and accounted for in the calculation of the annual cost. The requirement for recognition of an interest cost acknowledges the fact that the firm purchasing a piece of equipment will likely have to obtain a loan for which there will be an interest expense. Even should the firm have the required purchase price available, the fact that it could invest this amount of money at a given interest rate results in the need to acknowledge an interest cost in the annual cost method. While such a potential investment interest rate will likely be less than the rate associated with a loan, it still should be recognized in the calculation of the annual cost.

The calculated annual cost serves as an indicator. By itself the value of the indicator (i.e., the annual cost) serves little purpose. However the indicator compared with a similarly calculated indicator for another investment alternative provides a means of determining the more economic alternative.

Let us assume that a construction firm is faced with purchasing one of two alternative pieces of equipment from different manufacturers. Other than the initial costs and the expected annual maintenance and repair costs, the two pieces of equipment are similar, that is, they have equal lives, are equally dependable, and can perform an equal amount of work in a given period of time.

The initial cost of one piece of equipment, equipment A, is $165,000 whereas the initial cost of the other piece of equipment, equipment B, is $180,000. Both pieces of equipment have an expected life of ten years with little or no salvage value expected at that time. Based on information collected by the construction firm, information it has obtained from its competitors, and information obtained from the two equipment manufacturers, the firm estimates the annual maintenance and repair cost to be $14,000 and $12,000 for equipment A and B, respectively.

The firm plans on financing the initial purchase through an agreement with the equipment manufacturer. The loan will be for ten years and at an annual interest rate of 10%. Note that each of the manufacturers might have offered a different interest rate or period in which the loan was to be repaid. This would cause no problem in the annual cost analysis. Each alternative would recognize its own interest rate. Assuming a 10% interest rate for the two alternatives, the calculated annual cost for each alternative is calculated as follows.

Equipment A

Annual cost = $165,000 (capital recovery factor) + $14,000
                        (n = 10 i = 10)
$40,853 = $165,000   (.16275)   + $14,000

Equipment B

Annual cost = $180,000 (capital recovery factor) + $12,000
                        (n = 10 i = 10)
$41,295 = $180,000   (.16275)   + $12,000

Based on the calculation of annual costs, it is apparent that the more economic piece of equipment is equipment A. Thus the lower initial cost of equipment A should be given more weight than the lower annual maintenance and repair cost of equipment B. This conclusion cannot be reached unless the annual cost calculation is made. That is, it may be misleading to merely sum the total costs and divide by the life of the asset. The time value of money has to be recognized in the calculation.

The example considered assumed that the two alternative pieces of equipment had equal lives. The annual cost method can be used to compare alternatives that have unequal lives. However it should be recognized that the analysis is somewhat incomplete unless recognition is made of the unequal time periods. That is, should one piece of equipment have a life of five years and another have a life of ten years, the annual cost calculations should recognize that the five year life equipment will have to be replaced after five years. More likely than not, the replacement cost will be greater than the initial cost.

The above example of comparing equipment A and B assumed that the two types of equipment have no salvage value after their expected life. In many cases the equipment has a salvage value in that it has a trade-in value. Recognition of salvage values in the annual cost calculation requires an extension of the calculations. Let us assume that in the previous example, equipment A has an expected salvage value of $10,000 and equipment B has an expected salvage value of $30,000. The general formula for computing the annual cost of an asset that has an expected salvage value after its useful life is as follows.

Annual cost = (Initial cost−Salvage value) (Capital recovery factor)
                 + Yearly cost + (Salvage value) (Interest rate)
For equipment A and equipment B the calculation is as follows.

Equipment A

Annual cost =($165,000 − 10,000)(.16275) + 14,000 + (10,000)(.10)
  $40,226 =$25,266 + 14,000 + 1,000

Equipment B

Annual cost =($180,000 − 30,000)(.16275) + 12,000 + (30,000)(.10)
  $39,412 =$24,412 + 12,000 + 3,000

Whereas equipment A was more economic when the salvage value
was absent, the calculations above indicate that the introduction of
salvage values has resulted in equipment B being the more economic
equipment. Thus should salvage values be expected, it is necessary to
recognize them in the annual cost calculations.

The annual cost method focuses on selecting the best alternative
based on minimizing of costs. It should be noted that other considerations may also be important in the analysis of alternatives. Equipment
productivity, dependability, and flexibility are among these other alternatives. The relative importance of these types of considerations
increases as the difference between the calculated annual cost of alternatives decreases.

8.7 Present Worth Method

Similar to the annual cost method, the use of the present worth
method results in an indicator that can be computed for evaluating the
economic benefits of alternatives. This is done by calculating the dollar
present worth of alternatives.

The present worth of an investment alternative is the sum of the
initial cost or benefit and the future costs or benefits discounted back to
the present time. Whereas some problems may concern themselves
with a comparison of costs, others may address a comparison of benefits such as revenues.

In the case of the decision to purchase a piece of construction
equipment both initial costs and future yearly maintenance and repair
costs must be recognized. The initial purchase cost is a present cost and

as such needs no transformation as to a present worth calculation. Yearly maintenance and repair costs are future costs. Consistent with time value of money principles, the further into the future an expenditure takes place, the less expensive (in terms of present dollars) the expenditure. Thus the yearly maintenance and repair costs have to be discounted in order to express them as present costs.

Several different bases for determining the interest rate for discounting the future costs can be used. For example, a case can be made for using the average borrowing rate at which the firm obtains its financing, yet another case can be made for tying the rate used to the average prime rate expected over the years of life of the asset. Perhaps the strongest argument can be made for using the interest rate for which the firm could invest money equal in value to the costs of the yearly maintenance and repair costs if the equipment was not purchased. In effect this is the opportunity interest rate.

For purposes of demonstrating the use of the present worth method, let us consider the same example considered in the previous section. In particular, let us assume a construction firm is considering the purchase of a piece of construction equipment and is trying to evaluate the economic merits of equipment A and equipment B. Equipment A has an initial cost of $165,000 and an expected annual maintenance and repair cost of $14,000. Equipment B has an initial cost of $180,000 and an expected annual maintenance and repair cost of $12,000. Both pieces of equipment have an expected useful life of ten years with no expected salvage value at that time.

Equipment A

Present worth of costs = $165,000 + $14,000   (Uniform series present)
                                                (worth factor)
                                                (n = 10 i = 10)

$251,016 = $165,000 + $14,000 (6.144)

Equipment B

Present worth of costs = $180,000 + $12,000   (Uniform series present)
                                                (worth factor)
                                                (n = 10 i = 10)

$253,728 = $180,000 + $12,000 (6.144)

Because of the smaller value of the present worth of the cost of equipment A versus equipment B, it is judged the more economic purchase. The same result is obtained as was when the annual cost method was used (i.e., assuming the salvage values were ignored). This is not unexpected in that the present worth method merely moves various amounts of money to a specific point in time. The same was true of the annual cost method. Because the amounts of money are the same, the indicators derived using the two analysis methods should point to the same alternative as being the more economical.

The example discussed has used the present worth method to determine the least expensive piece of equipment. If the amounts of money being considered in a problem are incomes, the present worth method can still be used. However in this case the alternative with the larger present worth should be chosen as the best alternative.

Both equipment A and equipment B had expected lives of ten years in the example discussed. A present worth comparison becomes somewhat meaningless unless the alternatives are considered for an equal time period. For example, if equipment B has a life of five years, then clearly its total present worth cost would be less than that of the ten year life equipment A. However this means little in that equipment B will have to be replaced after the five years. As such the calculated present worth costs would have little meaning unless the costs of replacing and maintaining another five year piece of equipment were introduced into the calculations.

The present worth method can be used as a substitute for the annual cost method and vice versa. However, the necessity of comparing equal lifes is more vital to a present worth calculation. As such, the annual cost method is often preferred.

8.8 Tax Considerations

The preceding sections of this chapter have focused on selection of a capital asset based on the minimizing of the effective (i.e., time value of money considerations) purchase cost and maintenance and repair costs or the maximizing of revenues or cost savings. While the analysis is useful as to the selection and purchase of equipment, it remains somewhat incomplete.

Naturally the selection of construction equipment may and should include recognition of nonmonetary considerations. Considerations such as equipment productivity, reliability, and flexibility as to the types of work it can perform are important to the analysis. The willingness of the manufacturer to service the equipment and the compatibility of the equipment with the firm's existing fleet of equipment are additional important considerations.

In addition to these somewhat nonmonetary factors are certain tax related considerations that can play heavily in the merit of a given investment alternative. Included in these tax related considerations are depreciation, utilization of available investment tax credits, and potential savings through recognition of capital gains. Recognition of the impact of these economic related factors is especially important in the decision to buy, rent, or lease a specific type of equipment. This is true because while the advantages affect an alternative such as when buying the equipment, the advantages may be absent as to the other alternatives. Failure to recognize this can completely distort a meaningful analysis.

8.8.1 Depreciation

Accounting methods for depreciating an asset such as construction equipment are presented in Chapter 9. Assuming the method used is acceptable to the Internal Revenue (i.e., a taxpayer is not free to depreciate an asset in any manner he chooses), the calculated depreciation expense is a deductible expense to the firm in determining its income tax liability. Considering the fact that a firm may have an effective tax rate approaching 50%, each dollar of depreciation expense can in effect provide the firm with a fifty cent increase in its cash flow.

In the discussion of the discounted cash flow method in a previous section, the increase in cash inflows due to the depreciation expense were recognized. In effect this recognition affected the comparison of alternative purchases in that the annual depreciation expense differed for the alternative purchases.

The recognition of the depreciation expense in a time value of money analysis becomes even more important should one alternative be to buy and yet another alternative be to rent or lease. When one rents or leases a business asset, the annual or monthly cost paid is fully deductible for calculation of tax liability. Typically the expense, and therefore the tax deduction is linear with time. For example, a lease agreement with an equipment manufacturer may call for equal end of year payments of $15,000 for ten years. Thus the annual yearly tax deduction would be $15,000.

Let us assume that rather than lease the construction equipment, the construction firm purchases it and agrees to pay for it in ten annual installments of $15,000. While the firm's annual ownership cost is $15,000, it may in fact be able to deduct a larger amount as to its tax liability.

For one, there may be little relationship between the actual expected life of the equipment and the number of years over which the financing takes place. Secondly the government in attempting to alleviate many disputes between asset owners and the internal revenue has provided asset life guidelines that are typically advantageous to the tax entity. In order to increase its deductions in early years (i.e., consistent with time value of money benefits), the firm would like to depreciate its assets over a short period of time. The *Class ADR system*[3] recently adopted by the government has resulted in allowing the tax entity to utilize short lifes in the depreciation calculation. For construction equipment the allowable lifes ranges from eight to ten years. Typically the actual life of a piece of equipment may exceed this.

The benefit of being able to recognize depreciation faster than actual payments relates to the concept of being able to recognize dollar deductions sooner and as such obtain the increased cash flow sooner. For example, let us assume that the piece of construction equipment that is to be financed by means of ten annual $15,000 payments is considered to have a life of eight years for tax purposes. Assuming the total $150,000 is the cost of the asset (i.e., in reality some of the cost is an interest cost and this type of cost can only be deducted in the year paid) the annual depreciation cost using a straight-line depreciation method is $150,000/8 or $18,750. This deduction can be taken in each of the first eight years.

While it is true that the total deduction is the same as if the asset is leased versus purchased, the timing of the deductions affects the economic worth of the alternatives. This is evident by a calculation of their present worths. Let us assume that the relevant interest rate is ten percent. The discounted present worth of depreciation savings are calculated in Fig. 8.9. As can be observed from the calculation, the purchasing of the equipment results in a larger present worth deduction. The importance of such a consideration in an analysis method such as the discounted cash flow method increases as the cost and depreciation or financing cost increases.

[3]Sommerfield, R. M., Anderson, H. M., and Brock, H. R., *An Introduction to Taxation*, Harcourt Brace Jovanovich, Inc., 1972, pp. 314, 315.

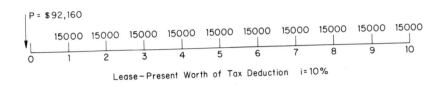

Lease–Present Worth of Tax Deduction   i = 10%

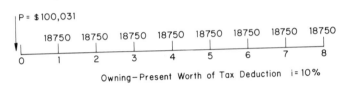

Owning–Present Worth of Tax Deduction   i = 10%

Fig. 8.9. Present worths of tax deductions.

In addition to the benefit of being able to utilize a shorter life for a purchased asset, the availability of *accelerated tax deduction methods* can further add to the time value of money benefits. While it is left to the next chapter to discuss these accelerated depreciation rates, suffice it to say that the tax entity can accelerate the depreciation deduction. The advantage of being able to deduct a greater portion of the total allowable deduction sooner should be evident. There are constraints on how much the deduction can be accelerated. However, the constraints are quite liberal, and the tax entity can often use a method that has the effect of doubling an otherwise linear deduction rate for early year calculations.

As to speeding up the depreciation of an asset to improve the economic merit of purchasing the asset, yet another "tax loophole" or incentive is available to the construction firm. *Additional first year* depreciation is available on qualified assets. Qualified assets include tangible assets that are purchased after 1957 and have an estimated useful life of at least six years. Construction equipment typically satisfies this criteria.

An allowance equal to 20% of the cost of qualified assets may be deducted in addition to depreciation under the normal methods. The additional deduction is limited to $10,000 per year per tax entity.

The intent of allowing the tax entity the additional first year deduction is aimed at aiding the small firm in its early life. More often than not the first year is a crucial year in regard to the firm's cash flow. It should be noted, that in total, the allowable depreciation deduction for an asset remains unchanged. However the speeding up of the depreciation, done by granting the additional first-year deduction, gives the firm time value of money benefits.

From the discussion of depreciation benefits, one might conclude that it is always better to purchase an asset rather than rent or lease it. Naturally this is not true. A firm normally doesn't purchase an asset for its tax benefits. Instead it is purchased because it is needed to carry out the business of the firm. Should a firm only need a specific type of equipment for a year, there obviously is no advantage of having a purchased piece of equipment stand idle for nine more years merely because of the available tax deduction. Thus the utilization of the equipment should be foremost in the analysis of the equipment. Assuming two alternatives have similar utilization, the time value of money and depreciation considerations are necessary to a meaningful analysis.

Purchasing or leasing a given piece of equipment represent the extremes of the options available to the construction firm. In between these extremes are various types of *lease purchase agreements*. The essence of these agreements are aimed at lease payments that can be applied to the purchase cost should the firm decide to purchase the asset. Because of the advantage of not having to recognize on the firm's balance sheet future lease payments as liabilities versus the recognition of indebtedness of purchased assets, firms have been known to try and make a purchase appear as a lease through a lease purchase agreement. This advantage of leasing equipment will likely diminish as the accounting rules change to require full disclosure of lease commitments.

8.8.2 Investment Tax Credit

The advantages of purchasing equipment are not limited to utilization of depreciation deductions. From time to time governments have attempted to stimulate economic growth by granting an incentive to firms to purchase capital assets. The presence of this incentive and the degree of the incentive have varied over time. It's presence is referred to as an *investment tax credit*. When such a credit is in existence or expected to come into existence, it should be recognized in the capital budgeting analysis.

In its present form, the investment tax credit is seven percent of "qualified" investment. Qualified investment basically means that the asset is to be used in the firm's production process. Construction equipment meets this requirement. The principle types of assets excluded from being qualified are land and buildings.

The investment tax credit differs from a depreciation expense in that the credit is subtracted from the tax entity's tax liability rather than used to determine the tax liability. Whereas a dollar depreciation deduction may result is something less than a fifty cent lessening of the tax liability, a dollar investment tax credit results in a lessening of a dollar tax liability. Additionally, the use of the credit has no subsequent effect on the depreciation deduction.

As the investment tax credit now stands, the tax entity is entitled to a tax credit of 7% of the cost of the asset purchased in a given year. The expected life of the asset has to exceed seven years in order to obtain a fully 100% usage of the tax credit. The percentage decreases as the life decreases. For example should the firm obtain a $50,000 piece of equipment with an expected life of ten years, it is entitled to a full 7% tax credit or $3,500. On the other hand, should the expected life be only three years, the firm is entitled to one third of this or $1,167. Recapture rules exist to handle the case where equipment has been estimated to have a life of seven or more years only to be replaced after less than seven years.

Presently the maximum investment tax credit a firm can recognize in a given year is $25,000. However there is a carryover privilege should the calculated amount a firm is eligible for exceed this amount. There are many other exceptions and additions to investment tax credit application that cannot be covered in detail here. Needless to say a good tax accountant can quickly earn his keep in advising the construction firm of these guidelines.

The existence of the investment tax credit brings attention to the firm's need for proper tax planning when purchasing equipment. Equally important as the recognition of the tax credit, is the recognition of the information to the complete analysis of a capital budgeting analysis. Failure to recognize the credit when in fact it is available can lead to the leasing of equipment when in fact a more thorough analysis would prove purchasing to be more economical.

8.8.3 Capital Gain Considerations

For many years there has been tax preference given to capital gains. While even the definition of "capital gain" is very complex, essentially a capital gain is a financial gain from the sale of a qualified asset that has been held by the owner for a specified period of time. If such a gain qualifies, it is taxed at only one-half the rate that would apply to the gain had it not been a capital gain.

The existence of this favorable capital gain treatment should not be ignored in the capital budgeting analysis. The tax liability savings can often prove to be substantial.

The gain a construction firm would have from the sale of a piece of equipment would be the difference between the amount it realized in the sale and the tax base. Essentially the tax base is the initial purchase cost minus the depreciation taken on the equipment. Because of the relatively high resale value of construction equipment, the "gain" to be reported may have a significant impact on the economic analysis of alternative pieces of equipment or alternative means of obtaining the equipment. If equipment is kept up, held for a mandatory period, and well placed as to selling it, the construction firm may be able to generate income that is taxed at a rate considerably less than the rate that applies to their "operating income."

In reality capital gain treatment is very complex. Whereas certain types of assets qualify for capital gain treatment, others do not. Additionally, should the firm utilize accelerated depreciation rates in depreciating its eligible equipment, certain rules must be followed as to recapturing the accelerated portion in the capital gain calculations. Perhaps no portion of the tax law is as complex as capital gain taxation. As is true of many areas of taxation, the benefits of seeking a competent tax accountant typically more than warrants the expense. This seeking of advice can go a long ways in limiting tax liability. Additionally, the information is necessary to a complete and meaningful capital budgeting analysis. Failure to recognize the amount of gain eligible for capital gain treatment can be as important as the failure to recognize a replacement cost in the analysis of the economic merit of purchasing a piece of equipment.

8.9 Summary

The importance of capital budgeting to the individual firm is dependent on the type of work the firm performs. Whereas the building construction firm is more dependent on utilization of labor in performing its work, the heavy and highway firm's very existence is dependent on a large dollar volume of equipment. This high dependence emphasizes the need to fully analyze initial and future costs when purchasing, renting, or leasing equipment.

The average investment method and payback method are capital budgeting tools aimed at the selection of the most economical investment alternative (i.e., piece of construction equipment). Both methods ignore the time value of money and as a result are only approximate in their analysis of alternatives. The main use of the methods is for screening the feasibility of investment alternatives.

The life of many types of construction equipment exceeds eight or ten years. This relatively long life necessitates the need to recognize the time value of money in an economic analysis of alternative types of equipment. The discounted cash flow method, the annual cost method, and the present worth method all recognize the time value of money in their economic analysis of long term assets.

In selecting a given type of equipment nonmonetary as well as monetary considerations must be recognized. Expected equipment productivity, reliability, and flexibility should be considered along with purchase cost and expected maintenance and repair costs. Additionally, tax considerations such as depreciation deductions, investment tax credits, and capital gain savings can effect the selection of the best equipment and as such should be included in the capital budgeting analysis.

Case 8.1. Neway Construction Company: Rate of Return

Neway Construction Company specializes in the placement of concrete for five to ten story buildings. For several years the firm's method of placing the concrete has centered around the use of a crane and several Georgia buggies which receive the concrete from a bucket attached to the crane and are moved horizontally by labor.

This method of placing concrete has worked well for the firm over a number of years. However their company owned crane is closely approaching the point in time at which it will have to be replaced. Additionally, the increasing cost of labor (i.e., much labor is used in their current method) has resulted in their concrete placement costs becoming high to the point where the firm is having a difficult time remaining competitive.

The result is that the firm has started to investigate the possibility of purchasing equipment for the vertical pumping of the concrete. While such equipment is expensive, it typically results in a reduction of required labor time.

The annual labor cost savings from the use of pumping equipment versus a crane are estimated at 12%. Since the labor cost associated with this activity annually approached one million dollars, this is a potential of $120,000 savings.

Whereas another similar crane is estimated to cost $80,000, the cost of the pumping equipment is $180,000. Additionally the estimated annual maintenance cost will likely increase by $6,000 (i.e., currently it is $5,000 when a crane is used). Both the crane and pumping equipment have estimated lives of ten years with little to no salvage value expected at that time. Both types of equipment can be financed through a 10% loan. The equipment is to be depreciated linearly.

In evaluating the feasibility of purchasing the pumping equipment the firm would like to obtain or exceed their current 5% rate of return on concrete work. Independent of their ability to cut labor costs, fixed overhead costs other than equipment costs are estimated to remain the same. Should the firm purchase the pumping equipment or purchase another crane?

Case 8.2. Joice Construction Company:
Initial and Future Costs

Joice Construction Company is currently trying to decide between the purchase of two alternative pieces of construction equipment. The company is a general contracting firm and is in need of excavation equipment.

The company's main need is for an excavator in that such a piece of equipment will be used almost every day. Additionally the firm has less frequent need for a trenching machine. Its usage is estimated at three days a month for the foreseeable future.

The firm has found two manufacturers that can satisfy the needs of the firm. Exco Company manufactures an excavator that it will sell to Joice Company for $80,000. The equipment has an expected life of eight years and can be financed through ten annual end of year payments of $12,000 each. The expected annual maintenance and repair cost is expected to be $2,000 for the first year and increase linearly to $8,000 for year eight. At the end of year eight it is estimated that the equipment can be traded in for $10,000.

Multo Company manufactures an excavator that through means of an included attachment can be converted into a trenching machine. The purchase cost of this machine is $110,000 and the equipment has an expected life of ten years. The equipment can be purchased through annual installments of $14,000, $11,000 of which is principle and $3,000 of which is interest. At the end of its expected ten year life the equipment is estimated to have a $10,000 trade-in value. The annual maintenance and repair cost are estimated to be approximately one-tenth of the undepreciated portion of the equipment.

Should Joice Company decide to purchase the excavator from the Exco Company, they will have to rent a trenching machine when it is needed. Current rental costs are $100 per day and are expected to increase five percent each year. The owner of the leased equipment is responsible for any required maintenance and repair costs.

The Joice Company plans to depreciate purchased equipment using a straight-line method (i.e., linearly over its life). It's cash position is such that they choose not to take any additional first year depreciation. The investment tax credit is nonexistent during the year in which the equipment is to be purchased. The firm's tax rate is approximately 40%.

From which manufacturer should the Joice Company purchase its equipment?

Case 8.3. Ndcash Construction Company:
Depreciation Benefits

Ndcash Construction Company has been doing business for one year. Like many new firms, cash flow problems have and continue to confront the firm. As such much of their current efforts are centered on the improving of their cash flow.

In order to continue its operations the company will have to gain access to the use of a crane. It expects almost continuous use of the equipment throughout the life of its business which hopefully will be greater than a year.

The firm has an option of leasing the equipment or purchasing it by means of a finance loan with the equipment manufacturer. The annual cost for leasing the equipment is $12,000. Should the firm purchase the equipment, the total price would be $180,000 payable over twelve years. In addition to the yearly principle of $15,000, a yearly interest cost of $1,500 is to be paid to the manufacturer thus resulting in a total annual cost of $16,500.

The firm has sought advice from its accountant and determined that if purchased, the equipment can be depreciated in as few as nine years.

However in order to be eligible for additional first year depreciation, the equipment will have to be depreciated using a straight-line method (i.e., linearly). The equipment is eligible for the investment tax credit which at this time is 7%. The firm expects to have a taxable income that will result in a tax rate of 40%.

Assuming that improvement of their cash flow is foremost in their decision to lease or purchase the needed equipment, what action should Ndcash Company take?

Chapter 9

Financial Accounting: Holding the Firm Accountable

9.1 Introduction

The main objective of financial accounting is to provide relevant and understandable data concerning the financial affairs of a company to external parties. These external parties may be potential investors, creditors, taxation bodies, and labor management agencies. In addition to the objective of providing data to external parties, financial accounting also serves the needs of the management of the individual firm. In particular, financial accounting like cost accounting, can provide formulated and relevant data for the decision making needs of management. This latter benefit of financial accounting will be emphasized in this chapter.

Financial accounting theories and practices are numerous. It is difficult to give a comprehensive treatment of all of the theories and practices in a single book, let alone a single chapter. The difficulty of discussing relevant financial accounting theories and practices is increased due to the fact that different practices apply to different types of firms. For example, different reporting requirements apply to proprietorships and some corporations. Certain types of corporations are required by the Securities Exchange Commission (S.E.C.) to publish annual financial statements that conform to a defined format. Such statements may be required to bear the signature of a Certified Public Accountant (C.P.A.). These *audited* statements have to be consistent with announcements and publications of proper accounting procedures and reporting issued by the American Institute of Certified Public Accountants (A.I.C.P.A.). In contrast to the corporation in need of audited financial statements, is the small proprietorship operated by a single individual or a small group of individuals. Other than requiring financial statements for satisfying the needs of a potential lender of money (i.e., a banker) or a bonding company, a small construction firm may implement any style or detailedness of financial accounting. This freedom in financial reporting does not imply that the small firm should ignore proper and detailed financial accounting. In fact, this freedom is undoubtedly the reason for the lack of adequate financial accounting on the behalf of the typical construction firm. Since such accounting aids in the management decision making process and in the ability of the firm to obtain needed capital from creditors and investors, the lack of adequate accounting relates to the high rate of bankruptcy in the construction industry.

Financial accounting practices also vary somewhat as a function of the nature of the work a firm performs. For example, different revenue recognition practices are followed by the automobile industry, the mining industry, and the construction industry. The construction industry is especially unique in regard to financial accounting. The nature of the work performed, the relatively long duration of the typical construction project, and the type of legal structure of the typical construction firm all lead to somewhat unique financial accounting practices. The uniqueness of the construction industry and the importance of financial accounting practices for the industry have led to special construction accounting announcements by the A.I.C.P.A.

The importance of proper financial accounting practices has been increasingly recognized by the construction industry. Several firms, even those small in size, have seen it necessary to employ a full time accountant to handle the firm's financial and cost accounting tasks. Such an employee has usually rewarded the firm with better control of its operations; a better image of the firm in respect to bankers, investors and bonding companies; and substantial tax savings.

The following sections of this chapter will focus on financial accounting with an emphasis on its application to the construction firm. After a brief discussion of basic financial accounting theories, principles, and procedures, items relevant to a firm's producing of an income statement, statements of financial position, and statement of changes in financial position will be discussed, respectively. The discussion of taxes as they relate to accounting is discussed in this and previous chapters.

9.2 The Accounting Cycle

The entire accounting process is aimed at summarizing and classifying financial data. The financial data is classified into common

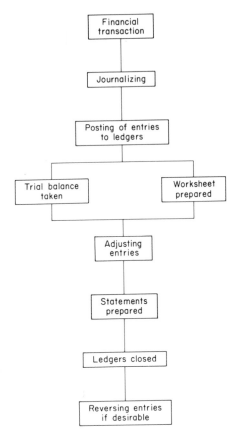

Fig. 9.1. The accounting cycle.

elements such as cash, receivables, sales, expenses, etc. Whereas some of these elements (referred to as accounts) relate to a company's income statement, others relate to its statement of financial position (i.e., its balance sheet).

The process by which financial transactions of the firm are summarized and classified into individual accounts is part of the *accounting cycle*. The cycle is summarized in Fig. 9.1. This cycle begins with the occurrence of a *financial transaction*. Financial transactions are of two types. For one, external transactions result from financial dealings with outsiders. Examples of such transactions include a construction firm's receiving of cash from a project owner, its purchase of concrete from a supplier, and its payment of wages to construction workers. A second type of transaction recognized in the accounting cycle is the internal transaction. Examples of such transactions include a construction firm's depreciating its equipment and the firm's use of lumber from its warehouses.

It is sometimes difficult to recognize the occurrence of a financial transaction. This is especially the case in regard to internal transactions. Several *generally accepted accounting principles* (G.A.A.P.) aid in the recognition of transactions. In particular, seven different G.A.A.P. directly or indirectly relate to the recognition of financial transactions. These are as follows.

(1) The revenue principle
(2) The matching principle
(3) The objectivity principle
(4) The full disclosure principle
(5) The cost principle
(6) The consistency principle
(7) The exception principle

These well-founded accounting principles are not limited in scope to the question of financial transaction recognition. Their relation to other financial procedures will be discussed intermittently throughout the chapter.

The *revenue principle* in effect defines revenue and indicates the point of time at which it should be recognized. Revenue recognition should include all changes in the net assets of the firm other than those arising from capital exchanges. An asset can be thought of as something that adds value to the company. A capital exchange involves an asset which can be used by a firm for a relatively long period of time in producing a product or service. As such, a construction firm purchasing or selling a major piece of equipment (e.g., a scraper) is a transaction but not a revenue transaction. This transaction involves a capital asset. On the other hand, the revenue received from building a project and interest income are considered as revenue transactions. The purchase of small hand tools is properly recognized as a revenue transaction (actually a contrarevenue transaction in that it is an expense) in that the tools will likely have a short life in regard to the firm's production process. As we will see later, revenue transactions mainly affect a firm's income statement, whereas capital transactions mainly affect the firm's statement of financial position.

In general, the revenue principle states that revenue transactions (for that matter any transaction) should be recognized when an exchange has taken place. As such, the primary test of recognition is the point of sale or the time at which the actual services are performed. Taken on face value, the revenue principle in effect states that a construction firm should only recognize income from a project when the project is turned over (i.e., ruled substantially completed) to the owner. As we will discuss in a following section, this is not always true in practice. There are noticeable exceptions taken to the revenue principle. For one, a firm may adopt a cash accounting system, or an accrual accounting system. The point of time at which revenue and expenses are recognized is dependent on the selection of these two different systems. In addition, there are modifications of the revenue principle that have been adopted to conform to the unique characteristics of certain industries. The construction industry is one of these industries.

The *matching principle* relates to financial transaction recognition in that it requires incurred costs related to revenue in a given period to be matched to that revenue in the period. For example, if a construction firm performs work and receives revenue for the work performed, then the cost incurred to perform the work should be matched to the recognized revenue. This is true even if the expenses are paid for in a later period. If the revenue is recognized in 1975, the expenses should be recognized in 1975, even if they are not paid for until 1976. As is true of the revenue principle, in practice there are exceptions to the matching principle. Such an exception occurs when the cash method of accounting is used.

The *objectivity principle* states that to the fullest extent possible, transaction recognition should be based on objective data and determinations. Subjective estimates should be avoided. The percentage completed method of recognizing revenue (discussed in a later section) used by many construction firms is in conflict with the objectivity principle in that it requires estimates. However, situations result in inadequate disclosure (yet another accounting principle). As such, the violation of the objectivity principle is justified.

The *full disclosure principle* requires that financial statements report all significant information relating to the financial affairs of the firm. As such, any financial transaction that would affect the actions of a potential investor or creditor should be disclosed. Perhaps more important in its relation to transaction recognition is the principle's affect on reporting potential transactions. In particular, full disclosure requires that conditions that may affect future financial transactions be disclosed. For example, a potential loss on a construction project may need disclosure even though the actual loss has not yet occurred. Such information usually has to be evaluated by an accountant in order to determine if disclosure is in order.

The *cost principle* while not directly related to the recognition of a transaction, does relate to the financial value associated with a transaction. The cost principle holds that cost is the appropriate basis for transaction recognition. As such, when the construction firm purchases a piece of equipment, the cost incurred for purchasing the equipment should be the value assigned to the equipment. The firm might believe they got a "buy" in that the equipment is worth more than the cost. However, cost remains the appropriate amount recognized in the transaction. When cash is not a part of a financial transaction, the basis for the amount of transaction recognition is the cash equivalent of the asset received or exchanged, whichever is more clearly evident. For example, the construction firm may exchange a piece of its equipment for that of another firm. The new piece of equipment should be valued at the dollar cost for purchasing a similar piece of equipment. If such a cost can not be determined, then the dollar cost for purchasing a piece of equipment similar to that given up should be used for valuing the new asset. In general, *replacement cost* should be used as the cost basis rather than realization cost (i.e., the amount for which the equipment given up can be sold).

The *consistency principle* requires that the firm be consistent in its application of accounting principles and procedures (several alternative accounting procedures exist for a single transaction) from one period to the next. As to transaction recognition, the principle requires that a given type of transaction be recognized and handled in a similar manner in different accounting periods. Thus, if the purchase of small tools is recognized as an expense transaction in one period, a similar purchase should not be viewed as a capital transaction in yet another period. A.I.C.P.A. announcements have required that disclosure be made on audited statements of the lack of consistency in a firm's accounting procedures. In fact, if a material change occurs in the financial transactions due to the inconsistency, the accountant is required to qualify his statements as to the fairness of the financial statements of the firm.[1]

The *exception principle* recognizes that one or more of the previously listed accounting principles may be inoperative or impractical in certain infrequent situations. As such, the exception principle cites three concepts that conflict with the previously listed principles, but are in fact widely recognized and used in practice. One of these exceptions is the *materiality concept*. This concept recognizes that it may not always be practical to recognize every minute transaction. For example, theoretically, every time a construction superintendent requisi-

---

[1]Committee on Auditing Procedure, AICPA, *Statements on Auditing Procedure No. 33*, New York, 1963, p. 42.

tions drinking cups from the company's central office for use on the project site the cups should be treated as a job expense (assuming they are viewed as an asset by the central warehouse). However, the cost of the cups requisitioned is likely to be immaterial in regard to the impact on the total job expense or company financial statements. As such, because of the immaterial nature of the transaction it is not necessary to recognize the transaction. However, this does not imply that the actual purchasing of the cups by the central office should not be recognized. The total cost of the cups is material and as such has to be incorporated into the financial statements. This is generally done by recognizing a periodic expense transaction or expensing the cups as purchased.

The *conservatism concept* is another example of the exception principle. This concept holds that when there are several *reasonable* possibilities in regard to an event or recognizing a transaction, the least favorable alternative should be recognized. For example, in estimating its uncollectable receivables, the firm should recognize in its accounts the largest amount that can be reasonably expected. The application of the conservatism concept has often been attacked by nonaccountants and accountants alike.

The final exception principle concept is that of *industry peculiarities*. In certain situations the uniqueness of a given industry in itself justifies exceptions in the application of generally accepted accounting principles. The use of the percentage completion method for recognizing revenue in the construction industry is such an exception. This and other exceptions as to accounting principles and practices in the construction industry are discussed in following sections.

The financial transaction is normally accompanied by the receiving or sending of a document. Payroll cards, material invoices, and billings to owners are typical documents that are evidence of a transaction. These documents were discussed in an earlier chapter on cost accounting.

Once a transaction occurs it is entered into a *journal*. A journal is merely a notebook of documented financial transactions. Normally, a firm has a general journal and several special journals. Special journals are used to record similar and repetitive types of transactions. For example, a construction firm may have a *special project journal* for each and every project. Individual project transactions are documented in individual project journals. In addition, the construction firm may find it useful to keep special journals for cash receipts and cash disbursements.

All of the transactions that are entered in special journals are eventually summarized. Less repetitive transactions (those not entered into

September, 1974	General Journal		
Date	Accounts	Debit	Credit
9/8	Work in Progress—Job 101	375.00	
	Cash		375.00
9/10	Equipment—Truck	2,825.00	
	Accounts Payable		2,825.00
9/13	Cash	385.00	
	Note Payable		385.00
9/23	Work in Progress—Job 101	1,261.50	
	Accounts Payable		1,261.50
9/30	Depreciation Expense	843.00	
	Accumulated Depreciation—Trucks		843.00
9/30	Accounts Receivable	826.00	
	Billings on Project 101		826.00
9/30	Accounts Payable	362.00	
	Cash		326.00

Fig. 9.2. General journal.

Project Journal   *Job 101*

Date	Supervision	Labor	Small tools	Material	Billings	Advances
9/21/74	250.00	125.00				
9/23/74			236.50	1,025.99		
9/30/74				826.00		
10/ 4/74					2,540.00	
10/ 4/74		1,425.00		812.50		
10/ 6/74	350.00					125.00
10/12/74		2,150.35		4,132.64	4,125.00	
10/21/74				235.26		

Fig. 9.3. Project journal

any special journal used by the firm) are entered in the general journal. It is this general journal which provides control and the means of producing financial statements for the firm. A typical page from a general journal and a project journal used by a construction firm are illustrated in Figs. 9.2 and 9.3.

The mechanics of making individual financial transactions in any journal are centered around the concept of debits and credits. Assuming a double entry system is used for each transaction, equal debits and credits are entered into the journal. A debit can be thought of as a journal entry that increases a firm's assets or expenses, or decreases its liabilities, owner's equity, or sales. On the other hand, a credit journal entry decreases a firm's assets or expenses or increases its liabilities, owners's equity, or sales. Each transaction affects two or more accounting elements or accounts. For example, a transaction may involve debiting two asset accounts and crediting a liability account. Similarly, it may involve debiting a single expense account and crediting an asset account. The important point to remember is that the sum of the debit entries and credit entries for each transaction must equal one another.

The format used for entering a transaction is as follows.

Equipment	2,500.00	
Cash		2,500.00

The debit entry (i.e., equipment) is listed first. After all of the debit entries are listed, the credit entry (i.e., cash) or entries are listed. Typically, these credit entries are indented as shown such that they can be easily differentiated from the debit entries. Typical journal entries are illustrated in sections that follow.

The recorded journal transactions are transferred to summarizing sheets which group transactions of a specific type. This procedure is referred to as posting and summarizing sheets are referred to as ledgers. As was the case in regard to journals, the firm may keep a set of general ledgers and a set of special ledgers referred to as subsidiary ledgers. The general ledger provides information for the basic financial statements. For example, all cash transactions entered into the firm's journals are summarized in the cash ledger at a given point in time such that the cash account can appropriately be reported in the financial statements. Similarly, an equipment ledger is used to summarize the value at which the firm's equipment is to be reported in the financial statements.

Subsidiary ledgers are used to supply details in various selected accounts. For example, rather than keep an account receivable (i.e., an asset account) ledger for each and every individual firm who owes the

General ledger accounts receivable*			
	Debit	Credit	Balance
May 31, 74	3,520		
		2,120	1,400 Dr

*Note: Amounts Posted at End of Month

Debits
&
Credits
Summed
&
Trans
ferred

Accounts receivable ledger**			
R. J. Jones Co.			
Date	Type	Debit	Credit
5/ 3/74	S	825	
5/18/74	CR		1,450
5/21/74	S	936	
L. Roecker Co.			
Date	Type	Debit	Credit
5/ 8/74	S	1,759	
5/21/74	CR		670

**Note: Amounts Posted Daily.

Fig. 9.4. Posting and subsidiary ledgers.

firm in question money, subsidiary ledgers may be used for each, and the ledgers controlled by the general accounts receivable ledger. The concept of posting, ledgers, and subsidiary ledgers for a typical construction firm is summarized in Fig. 9.4.

Intermittently (i.e., especially when financial statements are to be prepared) the accuracy of the journalizing and posting procedures should be checked. This is done by means of performing a trial balance. A trial balance is merely a listing of all accounts in the ledgers and their balances, showing the total of accounts with debit balances, and the total of accounts with credit balances. The sum of the debits should equal the sum of the credits. If not, the error should be found by tracing backwards in the journalizing and posting process. A trial balance is often made using a segment of a document referred to as a *worksheet*. Such a worksheet and trial balance are illustrated in Fig. 9.5.

The worksheet provides the means of transforming ledger data to the trial balance. The worksheet also incorporates adjustments that are necessary because of changes in expense, revenue, assets, and liability accounts. Adjusting entries are discussed in a following section. The typical worksheet also segregates income statement data and balance sheet (more appropriately referred to as a statement of financial position) data in order to facilitate the preparation of the two statements. A typical worksheet format is shown in Fig. 9.5.

Once required adjusting entries are made and the worksheet is prepaid, financial statements can be prepared. Historically, these statements consisted of the *income statement* (less appropriately referred to as a profit and loss statement) and a *statement of financial position* (less appropriately referred to as a balance sheet). In addition, an

Account	Trial Balance Dr.	Cr.	Adjusting Entries Dr.	Cr.	Income Summary Dr.	Cr.	Balance Sheet Dr.	Cr.
	ABC CONSTRUCTION COMPANY Worksheet Fourth Quarter 1975							
Cash	51,200						51,200	
Accounts Receivable	5,000						5,000	
Raw Material	9,500			500			9,000	
Equipment	93,300						93,300	
Acc Depr—Equipment		300		1,000				1,300
Plant	51,000						51,000	
Acc Depr—Plant		5,000						5,000
Accounts Payable		21,000		4,100				25,100
Notes Payable		32,000						32,000
Capital Stock		58,500						58,500
Retained Earnings		87,200	5,600					81,600
Billings		110,000				110,000		
General Overhead	21,000				21,000			
Project Expenses	83,000				83,000			
Net Income					6,000			6,000
	314,000	314,000	5,600	5,600	110,000	110,000	209,500	209,500

Fig. 9.5. Typical worksheet.

A.I.C.P.A. pronouncement[2] has made it mandatory for corporations (those that qualify under S.E.C. definition) to also publish a statement referred to as the *statement of changes in financial position.* Previously this statement was referred to as the "funds statement." It is felt that the statement of changes in financial position provides information that is necessary to the investor or creditor and is not clearly apparent in the income or financial position statement.

The statement of financial position reports on the assets, liabilities, and owner's equity accounts at a given point in time. On the other hand, the income statement and statement of changes in financial position relate to a *period* of time. The income statement reports on the revenues and expenses for a period of time, and the change in financial

[2]AICPA, *Opinions of the Accounting Principles Board, No. 19,* New York, March, 1971, p. 373.

ABC Company
Income Statement
For the Year Ended December 31, 1975

Revenue:		
Gross Sales		$150,000
Less: Discounts	$ 5,000	5,000
Net Sales		145,000
Cost and Expenses:		
Merchandise Inventory Jan. 1	45,000	
Purchase	25,000	
Total Goods Available	70,000	
Less: Merchandise Dec. 31	15,000	
Cost of Goods Sold		55,000
Gross Margin on Sales		90,000
Operating Expenses:		
Selling Expenses		
Advertising	20,000	
Salaries	20,000	40,000
General and Administrative:		
Office Expenses	2,000	
Office Payroll	12,000	14,000
Income from Operations		36,000
Deduct: Other Expenses		
Interest on Notes	12,000	
Add: Other Income		
Interest Income	14,000	2,000
Net Income before Taxes		$ 38,000
Less: Provision of Taxes		12,000
Net Income for the Year		$26,000

Fig. 9.6. Income statement.

position statement relates to changes in working capital, asset, liability, and owner's equity accounts over a given period of time. Typical formats for the three discussed statements are illustrated in Figs. 9.6–9.8. It should be noted that various statement formats are found in practice. For example, rather than report operating revenue separately from nonoperating revenue as is done in Fig. 9.6 (this is referred to as a *multiple step* income statement), all revenue may be reported first followed by a listing of all expenses (this is referred to a *single step* income statement). The form of the balance sheet also varies. In addition to various formats, the actual names of the owner's equity accounts will vary depending on whether a firm is a proprietorship, partnership, or corporation. As will be discussed later, the statement of changes in

ABC Company
Statement of Financial Position
December 31, 1975

ASSETS		LIABILITIES	
Current Assets:		Current Liabilities:	
Cash	$ 10,500	Accounts Payable	$ 4,500
Marketable Securities at Cost	5,500	Accurred Income Taxes	2,000
Receivables	8,000	Total Current Liabilities	6,500
Other Current Assets	2,000		
Total Current Assets	26,000		
Investments:		Long Term Liabilities:	
Equity in Trucko Constr. Co.	54,500	Deferred Federal Taxes	8,400
Warehouse Building—Canton, IL	43,500	Other	2,600
Total Investments	98,000	Total Long Term Liab.	11,000
Property and Equipment:		STOCKHOLDERS EQUITY	
Office Building	124,000	Contributed Capital:	
Less Acc Depr	24,000		
Net	100,000	Preferred Stock $50 par	55,000
Equipment	125,000	Contribution in Excess of	
Less Acc Depr	43,000	par-preferred stock	27,000
Net	82,000	Common Stock $10 par	90,000
Total Plant and Equipment	182,000	Contribution in Excess of	
		par-common stock	21,000
		Total Contributed Capital	193,000
Deferred Charges:		Retained Earnings:	
Organization Cost	16,400	Reserve for Sinking Fund	21,000
Unamortized Debt Expense	8,600	Unappropriated	99,500
Total Deferred Charges	25,000	Total Retained Earnings	120,500
Total	$331,000	Total	$331,000

Fig. 9.7. Statement of financial position.

financial position can be prepared on a cash basis or a working capital basis. The result is a difference in statement format. It should also be noted that some firms may prepare an additional financial statement referred to as a *retained earnings statement*. However, more often than not this statement is contained within the income and financial position statements. The content and construction industry peculiarities as related to financial statements are discussed and illustrated in following sections.

Upon preparing financial statements, ledgers are *closed*. This is done by eliminating income related accounts (referred to as nominal accounts). In particular, any net income or loss is closed to the real account referred to as the retained earnings account. The revenue and expense accounts are as such cleared and readied for the documenting of transactions in the next accounting period. Infrequently, *reversing* entries are made as a matter of providng a means of conveniently handling the next period data. The infrequency of their use does not justify their discussion here. The closing of ledger accounts signals the end of the accounting cycle for a given time period. New financial transac-

ABC Company
Statement of Changes in Financial Position—Working Capital Basis
For the Year Ended December 31, 1975

Working Capital Generated:
  From Operations:
    Net Income before Extraordinary Items $ 33,000
    Add: Depreciation   2,000
    Total Working Capital Generated from Operations $ 35,000
  Extraordinary Items Generating Capital
    Permanent Investment Sold   48,000
      Total Working Capital Generated   83,000
Working Capital Applied:
  Land Purchased   53,000
    Total Working Capital Applied   53,000
      Net Increase in Working Capital $ 30,000

Financial and Investing Not Affecting Working Capital:
  Bonds Acquired by Issuing Common Stock $125,000

Changes in Working Capital Accounts

| | Balance Dec 31 | | Working Capital |
	1974	1975	Increase (Decrease)
Current Assets:			
Cash	25,000	35,000	$10,000
Accounts Receivable	27,000	24,000	(3,000)
Total Current Assets	52,000	59,000	
Current Liabilities			
Accounts Payable	37,000	14,000	23,000
Total Current Liabilities	37,000	14,000	
Working Capital	$15,000	$45,000	$30,000

Fig. 9.8. Statement of changes in financial position.

tions that occur in the following time period initiate the starting of a new cycle.

9.3 Typical Transactions

The typical construction firm engages in many types of financial transactions. Although the type and size of the construction firm plays an important role in characterizing the number and types of transactions, even the relatively small sized general contracting firm takes part in many daily transactions. Material purchasing, labor payment, equipment purchasing and depreciating, and billings to owners necessitate numerous transactions.

The complexity of discussing typical construction industry financial transactions is increased by the fact that the firm may recognize transactions using one of two alternative accepted accounting methods. That is, the firm may use a *cash method* or an *accrual method*. In addition, several firms and industries have adopted modifications of the cash method and the accrual basis methods of accounting. The cash method is primarily used by small businesses, nonprofit organizations, and for personal records. In the cash method, revenue and expenses are recognized only when cash is actually received or expended. As such, a construction firm would not recognize the expense of purchasing concrete until the invoice was paid in cash. Perhaps because of the small size of many construction firms, but more likely due to the industry's lack of accounting practice sophistication, several construction firms maintain some form of a cash basis of accounting.

For most construction firms, the accrual method is much more adequate and appropriate than the cash method. Better control is obtained and planning is facilitated when the accrual basis is used. In the accrual method of accounting, revenue is considered in the period during which it is earned (i.e., title of goods is transferred or services are performed), even if payment is received in the prior (i.e., prepaid) or following period. Similarly, items of expense are recognized in the period in which they are incurred, regardless of whether they are prepaid or accrued (i.e., incurred in current period but not paid until the following period). Within the accrual method of accounting, there is a modification for the recognition of revenue for long term (i.e., greater than one year in duration) construction projects. This modification or procedure, which is referred to as the *percentage completion method* is discussed in a following section.

The firm has a choice of the cash method or the accrual method (if the firm is not a corporation subject to S.E.C. control it also has a unwise choice of adopting no method). The only constraint in selecting a method is the Internal Revenue's statement that the firm should use a consistent method for financial accounting and for determining its tax liability.[3] However, as will be demonstrated in a following section, there are many exceptions to this statement. Ignoring the tax provisions or benefits, many arguments can be made for the accrual method. Several unexpected financially related construction firm failures can be traced to the lack of an adequate accrual accounting method. Perhaps the only argument for a cash method is its simplicity. However, this argument is often overem-

---

[3]Sommerfield, R., Anderson, H., and Brock, H., *An Introduction to Taxation*, Harcourt Brace Jovanovich, Inc., New York, 1972, pp. 105–116.

phasized in that the number of transactions that require modifications due to the use of an accrual system are few.

Many financial transactions would be recognized by the construction firm at the same point in time and in the same manner independent of the accounting method used. In particular, any transaction that does not involve a prepaid or accrued item would be handled identically in the cash or accrual method. As a means of illustrating typical construction firm transactions and as a means of differentiating between the cash and accrual methods, let us consider typical transactions which are part of the everyday business of the construction firm.

9.3.1 Initial Investment: Contributed Capital

Every firm, be it a construction firm, a small grocery store, or a large automobile company starts with the initial investment of monetary and nonmonetary assets by investors or owners of the firm. Whereas this initial investment may be very simple as to the accounting recognition (e.g., the initial investment of $5,000 by a single investor in his own construction company), the initial transaction can also be very complex. For example, complex partnership investments and corporation stock issues may require several accounting journal entries. The possible issue of stock subscriptions, stock options, convertibles, and treasury stock all require accounting entries and skill beyond that which is discussed in this chapter.

The need for understanding complex corporation stock issues and investment capital is decreased when one considers the construction industry. As discussed in an earlier chapter, few construction firms take the corporation form. On the other hand, the percentage of construction firms taking this form will likely increase in the future.

A large percentage (approximately 80%) of construction firms originate with a single investment of one or two individuals in the firm. This investment may be cash, equipment, or cash and equipment. The cash and equipment are considered as assets of the newly created firm and the investment is recognized by creation of a contributed capital investment account. For example, let us assume that Andy Jackson invests his life savings of $10,000 and his 1974 Ford pickup truck in a newly created general contracting firm. Assuming the truck has a fair market value of $5,000 an estimated remaining life of five years, and is to be depreciated using straight line depreciation (discussed later), the initial accounting entry would be recorded as follows.

Cash	10,000	
Truck (5 years life, straight line)	5,000	
Andy Jackson, proprietor		15,000

It should be noted that the debit entries (those listed first) are equal in amount to the credit entry. Andy Jackson's contributed capital account (referred to as his capital account) is increased when he makes another investment or may be decreased if he decides to make a withdrawal of the invested capital.

Let us assume that instead of Andy Jackson's sole investment, he joined forces with his friend Steve Janko in forming a partnership to start a small construction firm. Andy Jackson's initial contribution is still $10,000 cash, and his $5,000 fair market value truck. Steve Janko's investment is $5,000 cash. Assuming Jackson and Janko are to be credited for their investment, the initial accounting entry would be as follows.

Cash	15,000	
Truck (5 year life, straight line)	5,000	
Andy Jackson		15,000
Steve Janko		5,000

As an alternative to the described partnership agreement, let us assume that Steve Janko has had a college education as an engineer and as such negotiates with Jackson to own a larger share of the business. In particular, let us assume that the partnership agreement is such that Janko is to be credited with 50% of the firm's contributed capital.

It should be noted that Janko only invests 25% of the cash and equipment assets. How then is the accounting entry to be made to recognize a 50% ownership? This can be done by one of two alternative accounting entries. For one, the entry can be made using the *bonus method*. Using the bonus method, Jackson's capital account is reduced and the amount of reduction is added to Janko's account. The total capital remains unchanged. That is, the total capital is $20,000.

If Janko is to be credited for 50% of the total capital, his final capital account balance should be $10,000. However, he only contributes $5,000. As such, Jackson in effect gives up $5,000 of his investment and transfers it to Janko. The entry would be made as follows.

Cash	15,000	
Truck (5 year life, straight line)	5,000	
Andy Jackson		10,000
Steve Janko		10,000

Had Janko contributed more than 50% of the initial capital and he was
to be credited for 50%, Jackson, instead of Janko, would receive the
bonus.

Instead of Jackson offering Janko a bonus, let us assume that in their
agreement they decided that Janko's education was an asset to the firm
and they wanted to treat it as such. This is done by the recognition of
goodwill. In a *goodwill method* an asset account labeled "goodwill" is
debited for the value assigned to Janko's education. In the example in
question, the dollar amount of goodwill to be recognized is determined
by the fact that Janko's total capital account is to be 50% of total capital.
Jackson's capital account remains unaffected at $15,000. Thus, if Janko
is to be credited with an equal amount, goodwill recognized must be
equal to $10,000 and Janko's capital account increased $10,000. The
entry follows.

Cash	15,000	
Truck (5 year, straight line)	5,000	
Goodwill	10,000	
Andy Jackson		15,000
Steve Janko		15,000

Unlike cash which is considered a current asset and the truck which
is considered a fixed asset, the goodwill is an *intangible asset*. Such an
asset has no physical value, but adds to the earning potential of the
firm. Other types of intangible assets include patents and copyrights.
Similar to fixed assets, intangible assets are not to remain indefinitely
on the firm's financial statements. In particular, intangible assets are to
by *amortized* (part of the value written off as an expense each accounting period). Goodwill is to be written off by consistent charges to
an expense account over a period of forty years or less.[4] It should also
be noted that the goodwill method illustrated for initial company organization is somewhat inconsistent with the latest published
A.I.C.P.A. opinions. One of the recent opinions states that goodwill is
to be recognized only when it is purchased. For example, goodwill can
be recognized when a firm pays more than the fair market value for the
assets of another firm. The assigning of goodwill to the "purchase" of
the skills of an individual is a questionable point. In general, the skills
of employees and owners of a firm are not recognized as assets by a
firm. For example, a construction firm with well-trained and experienced management certainly have an "asset" in that they add "value"

---

[4]Accounting Principles Board, AICPA, "Intangible Assets", *Opinion 17*, New York,
August, 1970, p. 339.

to the firm. However, current accounting practice has not accepted *human resource* accounting in total.

The initial entry necessary to recognize the formation of a corporation varies depending on the complexity of the initial stock issuance. The more complex possibilities will not be considered here. A corporation may be closed or it may be open. A *closed corporation* issues stock to a select few individuals. In reality, other than the legal and tax differences, the closed corporation differs very little from the partnership. A firm which has its stock traded in the open market is an *open corporation*. As such, ownership of the firm is constantly changing hands. Because most open corporations are large in size, few construction firms are in fact open corporations. On the other hand, because of the liability and tax benefits of the corporation, an increasing number of construction firms are closed corporations.

Because the accounting transaction investment entries are similar for partnerships and the closed corporation; let us consider the initial investment entries for an open corporation. The initial cash for the firm is raised through the issuance of stock. Types of stock were discussed in an earlier chapter. Generally, common stock is issued for the starting of a corporation. The common stock may be par-value or no par-value stock. *Par-value stock* has a designated dollar "value" associated with it. Normally, the par-value is low and the dollar amount received for the stock exceeds the stated par-value. The amount received in excess of the par-value is referred to as "premium on capital stock" and is recognized separately from the dollar amount of the par-value of the stock. Even if stock is no par-value stock, the stock is normally assigned a stated value. As such, it differs little from par-value stock. The par-value or stated-value of stock has little significance other than it is accounted for separately in the accounting process and some state statutes require a firm to retain the dollar amount of the par-value or stated-value stock. That is, the firm is prohibited from using this dollar amount for paying dividends or buying back issued shares of stock. This dollar amount of required capital to be retained is referred to as *legal capital*.

Ignoring the possibility of stock subscriptions (i.e., when an investor enters into an agreement to purchase and pay for stock at a later date), a typical corporation stock issuance is recognized as follows.

Cash	25,000	
Common Stock (10,000 shares at $2 par-value)		20,000
Premium on common stock		5,000

Most state statutes prohibit the issuance of stock at less than par-value (i.e., at a discount).

Stock subscriptions, authorization of stock not issued, and the issuance of several different classes of par-value stock would require a different entry or entries from the one shown. The reader should refer to an intermediate level accounting book for the handling of these more complex entries. Their occurrences are infrequent in construction industry accounting.

9.3.2 Debt Capital

Not every construction firm obtains monetary and nonmonetary assets by means of contributed capital. The amount of assets required to start a sizeable firm may exceed the amount of available contributed capital from owners of the firm. Even when equity capital can be obtained, the firm may choose to obtain some of its required assets by means of taking on debt. Such a practice can lead to favorable *leverage*, that is, higher earnings to investment can be obtained.

There are essentially three different means of obtaining capital for obtaining the firm's assets. Raising contributed capital and the corresponding accounting entries has been discussed in the previous section. A second means of obtaining capital is through the earnings of the firm. That is, income from operations can be held back by the firm and used for purchase of assets. Income from operations is discussed in a following section. Obviously, this source of capital is not available to the firm immediately upon starting the firm. Contributed capital and capital retained from operations are referred to as owner's equity.

The third means of obtaining capital, the taking on of debt (i.e., borrowing money), provides the typical construction firm with a substantial portion of their initial capital for purchasing assets and for financing their continuing operations.

Purchasing assets on account, signing a note payable, financing of equipment through a lease (discussed in a following section), and issuing bonds are all examples of obtaining assets by means of debt capital. The issuance of bonds as a means of obtaining debt capital is not a common construction industry practice in that this form of raising debt capital is generally available to only large firms. Regardless of whether the construction firm is a proprietorship, a partnership, or a corporation; the required accounting entries for debt capital transactions are the same.

The obtaining of debt capital creates a liability to the firm in that the capital has to be repaid (usually with an interest cost) to the lender. Liabilities are normally classified as being *current liabilities* or *long-term liabilities*. The A.I.C.P.A. defines a current liability as designating an obligation whose liquidation is reasonably expected to require the use of existing resources properly classified as current assets or the creation of other current liabilities.[5] Perhaps more simply stated, liabilities are debts the firm expects to repay within its operating cycle which normally can be taken as one year. Typical current liabilities are as follows.

(1) Accounts payable
(2) Short term notes payable
(3) Advances held as returnable deposits
(4) Taxes
(5) Bonus obligations

Most current liabilities are not normally recognized in a cash accounting method. As such, typical journal entries are absent for accounting for current liabilities when using the cash method.

Because the issuance of bonds is not a common occurrence for the construction firm, only basic entries for this issuance are discussed. Let us assume that in order to expand its operations a relatively large construction firm decides on the issuing of $100,000 of bonds payable in ten years with an annual interest rate of 5%. In other words, the construction firm is willing to pay the purchasers of the bonds $5,000 interest each year and repay the $100,000 face value of the bonds after 10 years. Assuming that the firm was successful in selling the bonds for exactly $100,000, the accounting journal entry necessary in the construction firm's books would be as follows.

Cash	100,000	
Bonds Payable		100,000

The annual interest expense to the construction firm would be recognized by the following entry.

Bond Interest Expense	5,000	
Cash		5,000

The above entries assumed that the firm received exactly $100,000 for the $100,000 face value bonds. More likely than not, the firm would receive something less or more than the $100,000. If the firm's financial status was sound and the current interest rate for marketable securities was lower than 5%, the bond investor would likely be willing to pay more than $100,000 for the bonds. For example, the construction firm

[5]AICPA, *Accounting Research Bulletin, No. 43*, New York, June, 1973.

might receive $105,000 for the bonds. The $5,000 is referred to as a *premium* on the bonds. The fact that the bonds sold at a price greater than the face value results in an effective interest rate (referred to as the *yield*) less than the stated face value interest rate.

More likely than not, the construction firm will receive less than the expected $100,000 assuming that the 5% is the current marketable interest rate. This is because the typical investor views the construction industry as a financially risky investment. Unfortunately, statistics prove the investor correct.

Let us assume that the construction firm receives $95,000 from the issuance of the 5% $100,000 bonds. The $5,000 shortage is referred to as a *discount* on bonds. In effect, the firm is paying a higher interest rate than 5% in that they only receive $95,000 instead of $100,000. This higher interest rate can be calculated using *yield tables.*

Let us assume this latter transaction in regard to the required journal entries. The issuance of the bonds would be recorded as follows.

Cash	95,000	
Discount on Bonds Payable	5,000	
Bonds Payable		100,000

The bond discount account would be amortorized along with the annual interest expense journal entry. Assuming 10 year period of amortorization this would be as follows.

Bond Interest Expense	5,500	
Cash		5,000
Discount on Bonds Payable		500

In effect, the annual interest expense is increased $500. The above entry has been made assuming straight line amortorization of the discount. The accounting entries required for the handling of the premium on bonds would be similar to those made for the discount on bonds.

9.3.3 Accounting for Cash

Cash is considered to be a current asset in that a firm will use its cash throughout its operating cycle. Normally, cash is made available to the firm from initial investment (equity investment or from creditors of debt), or from the income from operations. Less frequent in occurrence is the obtaining of cash from selling one's assets and from selling a portion of the business. Any cash received from operations is debited along with a credit to income. Cash obtained from temporary investment of cash (e.g., savings accounts, short term securities, etc.) is debited along with a credit to interest income. The accounting for income is discussed in a following section.

Accounting for cash normally presents little difficulty. There are no estimates required or valuation problems in that the accounting unit of measure is expressed in the monetary unit. The main difficulty in accounting for cash is to provide a means of controlling cash receipts, payments, and petty cash.

The numerous daily cash transactions that are part of running a construction firm and construction project necessitate the existence of one or more petty cash funds. Items such as small hand tools, paper cups, refreshments, and miscellaneous supplies may be purchased from cash in the petty cash fund. Because of the availability of the cash in this type of fund, there has to be concern in regard to controlling cash payments from such a fund.

Two different systems can be used to control a petty cash fund. One system is referred to as a *fluctuating fund system* whereas the other is referred to as a *nonfluctuating fund system* (also referred to as an *imprest fund*). The initial accounting entry is the same for each of the petty cash systems. Let us assume a firm creates a $500 petty cash fund. The initial accounting entry is as follows.

Petty Cash	500	
Cash		500

The petty cash account, like the cash account, is considered an asset to the firm.

Accounting control and entries for transactions after the initial transaction vary depending on the system used. Generally, when a fluctuating system is used, an individual in control of the fund is required to maintain a petty cash book. Disbursements are entered into a book which is used as a basic record when the fund is replenished. As disbursements are made, an expense account is debited and the petty cash fund is credited. For example, let us assume that a few small tools costing $40 are purchased from the petty cash account. The accounting entry would be as follows.

Small Tools Expense	40	
Petty Cash		40

After a period of time the petty cash fund is replenished by a debit to petty cash and a credit to cash. However, this additional cash is not necessarily equal to the cash disbursements made. It is evident, that when using this approach, the balance in the petty cash account fluctuates.

The nonfluctuation or imprest petty cash system is normally preferred in that it is easier to audit than the fluctuating system. Using the imprest system, disbursements are made from the petty cash fund and recorded and summarized in a petty cash book. No accounting debit or credit is made to adjust the initial petty cash entry unless it is desired to increase or decrease the fund. Instead, after the petty cash book is summarized, a check is drawn to the petty cash fund for the exact amount of the expenses. A journal entry is made that debits the appropriate expense accounts and credits cash. For example, let us assume that during a given time period, the only disbursement from the petty cash fund was the previously described $40 small tools expense. Using the imprest fund system, the required accounting entry would be as follows.

Small Tools Expense	40	
Cash		40

Other petty cash disbursements would be handled in a similar manner. As can be observed, the petty cash fund does not fluctuate.

Regardless of whether the fluctuating or imprest system is used, the firm should immediately investigate any abnormal overages or shortages. Unfortunately, overages can usually be explained whereas shortages may be difficult to pinpoint and correct.

At the end of each month, the firm should reconcile (compare) the actual cash on hand and on deposit in the bank with the balance of cash shown in the accounts. This means of control involves analysis of the monthly bank statement and the cash records maintained by the firm. Even assuming no cash is kept on hand, the cash balance per bank statement and the cash balance per books of the firm will differ for some of the following reasons.

(1) Items already recorded as cash receipts in the books of the company are not yet added to the bank statement. For example, a deposit may be made by the firm in late May and not be recorded by the bank until early June.

(2) Items already added to the bank balance are not added to the balance on the company books. For example, the bank may credit the firm's account for interest on their deposit at the end of May. However, the firm is not aware of the interest until early June.

(3) Items already recorded as cash disbursements on the company books are not deducted by the bank from the bank balance. For example, the firm may have written checks in May but the checks do not clear the bank until sometime in June. These checks are considered as being *outstanding*.

(4) Items already deducted from the bank balance are not deducted from the firm's book balance. For example, the bank's service charge in May may not be recognized by the firm until June.

In order to reconcile the firm's book balance of cash to that of the bank statement adjustments must be made to recognize the above types of transactions. Obviously, if the balance per book does not reconcile with the balance per bank statement after the necessary adjustments are made, the difference should be immediately investigated. It is the reconciliation that alarms the firm to the need to investigate.

The reconciliation of cash per books and cash per bank statement is commonly referred to as a *cash proof*. While several cash proof procedures can be used, the one illustrated in Fig. 9.9 is all encompassing in its treatment of balances and adjustments. The proof of cash illustrated in Fig. 9.9 is for a one month period of time.

As can be observed in the illustration, the proof is made by first listing the balance per bank statement. The first entry would correspond to the balance per statement as of May 1. Next receipts and disbursements for the month of May as listed in the bank statement would be shown. Finally, the balance as of May 31 would be shown.

As indicated earlier, adjustments are necessary in order to reconcile the cash per bank statement to the cash per company books. These adjustments are next made on the cash proof shown in Fig. 9.9. Nega-

Proof of Cash
For the Period Ending May 31, 1975

	Balance May 1	May Receipts	May Disbursements	Balance May 31
Balance per Bank Statement	$22,400	$1,500	$ 650	$23,250
Deposits in Transit:				
Start of Period	1,500	(1,500)		
End of Period		550		550
Outstanding Checks:				
Start of Period	(2,000)		(1,500)	(500)
End of Period	—	—	1,000	(1,000)
Corrected Balances	$21,900	$ 550	$ 150	$22,300
Balance per Company Books	21,900	425	100	22,225
May Service Charge			50	(50)
Note and Interest Collected	—	125	—	125
Corrected Balances	$21,900	$ 550	$ 150	$22,300

Fig. 9.9. Reconciliation of cash.

tive entries are shown in brackets. Let us consider the "outstanding checks" adjustments shown in the cash proof. As indicated in the first column, there was $2,000 checks outstanding on May 1. However, during the month of May, $1,500 of the $2,000 of outstanding checks cleared the firm's bank. As such, $1,500 of disbursements were recorded by the bank in May. However, since we have already adjusted the bank balance for the May 1 outstanding checks in the first column of the cash proof, the $1,500 must be added back in the disbursements column. As such, the $1,500 is listed as a negative disbursement in the disbursement column which acts to reduce the recorded disbursements for the month. The $1,500 is subtracted from the $2,000 initially entered to yield a final column outstanding checks from the start of the period of $500.

In addition to the outstanding checks carried forward from May 1, $1,000 of checks were written in May that had not cleared the bank by May 31. As such, $1,000 is added to the disbursement column as shown and subtracted from the balance in the ending balance column. The end result is that a total of $1,500 ($500 from May 1 outstanding checks and $1,000 from outstanding checks written in May) must be deducted from the ending balance per bank statement in order to reconcile the amount per book.

Other adjustments are made in a manner similar to that for outstanding checks. Having made all of the adjustments, the adjusted cash bank balance should equal the cash book balances. While no differences are shown in the cash proof illustrated, such differences should be traced and corrected. In effect, the cash proof provides a means of discovering mishandling of cash, theft, or fraud.

9.3.4 Accounting for Fixed Assets

The typical construction firm has a substantial share of its contributed capital and debt capital invested in fixed assets. Fixed assets are properties and rights which the business retains more or less permanently for utilization in its operation of performing production. Fixed assets include both tangible assets and intangible assets. Intangible assets such as goodwill, patents, and copyrights are rare in the construction industry. On the other hand, fixed assets such as plant (office building, furniture, etc.), and equipment may make up a large percentage of the construction firm's assets. Construction equipment in particular plays an important role in the production process performed by the typical construction company. Earthmovers, cranes, reuseable forms (e.g., Symons forms), trucks, and mortar mixing equipment are just a few of the types of equipment used by the construction firm. Construction equipment is usually recognized by three different classifications: (1) heavy equipment, (2) miscellaneous tools and equipment, and (3) trucks and autos. The large dollar value associated with such equipment has an important impact on the firm's financial statements. The importance of accounting for equipment in the construction industry is evidenced by the fact that the A.I.C.P.A. has published an audit guide on the subject matter.[6]

The construction firm normally has several options available to it in regard to the use of construction equipment. For one, they may choose to purchase a piece of equipment. As an alternative to purchasing a piece of equipment, the firm may choose to rent or lease it. Several different types of lease agreements can be arranged each of which requires different accounting treatment and each of which has a different impact on the firm's financial statements. Lease agreements and their accounting recognition are discussed in a later part of this section.

Let us assume a construction firm purchases a piece of equipment. The equipment should be recorded at an asset value equivalent to purchase cost plus any shipment or installation costs. Available discounts, whether taken or not, should be deducted from the equipment's invoice cost. For example, let us assume a firm purchases a $40,000 crane and the manufacturer charges an additional $200 for transportation of the equipment. The agreement between the construction firm and the equipment dealer is such that the construction firm will receive a 5% discount on the $40,000 if cash is paid when the crane is delivered. However, the construction firm only pays $10,000 upon delivery with the balance due covered by a note payable which is given to the equipment dealer. The journal entry required to recognize the purchase of the crane is as follows.

Equipment—Crane	38,200	
Allowance for Discount	2,000	
Cash		10,000
Note Payable (8% annual interest)		30,200

Thus, the crane is *capitalized* at $38,200. It should be observed that the potential $2,000 discount has been deducted from the $40,000 invoice cost. The lost discount would be recognized as an expense to the construction firm. The journal entry necessary to recognize the expense is as follows.

[6]*Audits of Construction Contractors*, AICPA, New York, 1965, pp. 26–29.

Discount Lost Expense	2,000	
Allowance for Discount		2,000

Occasionally a construction firm will purchase a major piece of equipment on a deferred payment plan. For example, it may be required to make three annual end of year payments of $37,410 in a purchase agreement for a large earthmoving scraper. During this time the going interest rate was 6%.

To record the scraper at $112,230 (i.e., $37,410× 3) would include in the fixed asset account the interest cost implicit in the contract. Instead, the scraper purchased on a deferred payment plan should be recorded at the equivalent cash price excluding all interest and implicit interest. The interest should be charged to expense and not capitalized as part of the asset.

In order to determine the value at which the asset purchased on a deferred payment plan should be recorded, the present worth of the annual payments has to be determined. The existing interest during the period in which the payments are to be made should be used in determining the present value. For example, for the scraper that was purchased by means of three annual $37,410 end of year payments, a 6% interest rate yields a present value of $100,000. It is this value at which the scraper should be recorded. The annual interest expense is calculated as 6% times the outstanding principle balance to be paid.

Rather than purchase a piece of construction equipment outright, the firm may purchase a piece of equipment by "trading in" an old piece of equipment as part payment for the new equipment. The accounting cost principle requires that the new equipment be valued (i.e., capitalized) as the sum of the fair market value of the old equipment traded in plus any cash given to the seller. Any difference between the book value of the old equipment and its par market value at the date of exchange should be recognized as a loss or gain on the disposition of the equipment.

Let us assume a construction firm trades in an old truck for a new one. The old truck's original cost was $20,000; depreciation to date on the truck is $15,000 (leaving a book value of $5,000). The new truck had a selling price of $25,000. The construction firm traded the old truck and $17,000 cash for the new truck. Since the firm paid $8,000 less cash than the selling price of the new truck, one can assume that the old truck had a fair market value of $8,000. As such, the accounting entry is made as follows.

Truck—New ($17,000 + $8,000)	25,000
Accumulated Depreciation—Old Truck	15,000

Cash		17,000
Truck—Old		20,000
Gain on Exchange of Trucks		3,000

The $3,000 gain is reported on the firm's income statement. Any loss on a similar exchange would be handled in a similar manner. The debit to "Accumulated Depreciation" is required to offset earlier credits to this account. Depreciation accounting entries are discussed in a following section.

It should be noted that the tax law does not recognize a gain or loss when similar assets are exchanged. The accounting entry necessary to be compatible with tax laws would be as follows.

Truck—New	22,000	
Accumulated Depreciation—Old Truck	15,000	
Cash		17,000
Truck—Old		20,000

The difference in the two entries (financial accounting versus tax accounting) is that in the latter entry the new truck is capitalized as the sum of the depreciated value of the old truck plus any cash paid in respect to the exchange.

Because of the type of work which the construction firm performs, it is not unusual for the typical construction firm to construct some of its own plant. This is particularly true in regard to the building of its home office building, temporary branch offices, and material warehouses. Not only is there the potential to build its assets for less cost than if contracted externally, but the construction firm may be able to use would be idle personnel for construction of their own plant.

An accounting problem as to recognizing general overhead arises when a firm constructs their own assets. Two possibilities exist. For one, the construction firm may construct its plant when in fact they are operating at capacity. That is, all of their personnel are gainfully employed. In this situation, clearly the asset constructed should be charged for additional overhead costs and a share of the firm's general overhead.

In the second situation, the firm may use idle personnel to construct the asset (i.e., the plant). The question arises as to whether any of the general overhead should be allocated to the newly constructed asset. Clearly, this general overhead would exist even if the asset were not constructed. Why then should the asset be assigned a portion of these overhead costs? On the other hand, counter arguments can be made for assigning a portion of the overhead to the asset constructed. For one it can be argued that the asset should include overhead, otherwise loss from idle time is overstated. In addition, consistent with the cost principle an allocation is necessary if the true cost of the asset being constructed and the firm's other on-going operations are to be determined. The author favors the allocation of general overhead mainly because of this latter argument. In addition, should the cost of constructing the asset exceed the cost at which it could have been externally contracted, proper accounting would require that the excess cost be written off as a period loss and the asset valued at the cost at which it could be externally contracted.

Current accounting practice does not allow accounting entry recognition of the fair market value of equipment or plant owned by the construction company. For example, a construction firm may have built three central offices in 1960 for a cost of $100,000. In 1974 after depreciation charges have been made against the initial cost, the central office may have a book value of $25,000. It is this value that is reported in the financial statements. However, because of rapidly increasing inflation in the 1960s and early 1970s, the central office may have a current value of $50,000. Many arguments can be made for revaluation of the central office account by "writing up" the asset. However, current practice requires that cost be used as the basis of the asset. Perhaps a continuing high rate of inflation will force the accounting profession to acknowledge the need for *price level adjustments*.

Equipment repairs and maintenance are a normal occurrence when owning construction equipment. The relevant question in regard to accounting for repairs and maintenance is whether such costs should be capitalized as part of the cost of the equipment or expensed as a period cost. In general, only those expenditures that add to the production capacity of the equipment should be capitalized. Costs that are expended to maintain the equipment's production level, or to restore the equipment to its normal production level should be expensed. The end result is that most, if not all, construction equipment repairs and maintenance costs should be expensed rather than capitalized.

9.3.5 Depreciation of Fixed Assets

Fixed assets, including construction equipment, are purchased because of their future revenue generating potential. As such, as the revenue is generated, a portion of the cost of the asset should be periodically matched with the period revenue. This process is referred to as *depreciation accounting*. In particular, depreciation accounting is a system of accounting which aims to distribute the cost of a tangible capital asset, less any salvage, over the estimated useful life of the unit in a systematic and a rational manner. It is a process of allocation, not of valuation.[7]

Note should be made of the fact that depreciation is to be recognized in a systematic and rational manner. Alternative depreciation methods such as the straight line method, the declining balance method, and the sum of the digits method have all been judged to be systematic and rational. It is possible to use one depreciation method for financial accounting and yet another for tax purposes. For example, several firms use the straight line method for financial accounting and the declining balance or sum of the digits method for determining tax liability.

In determining the periodic depreciation charge for a piece of equipment, the initial cost of the equipment, its salvage value, and the equipment's useful life must be determined. As to the useful life it should be noted that construction firms sometimes purchase equipment for a specific project. When the project is completed, the firm disposes of the equipment rather than retain it for future work. When this is the case, the useful life of the equipment to the construction firm is the term of the project—say 18 months—and not the physical life of the equipment which may be eight years. The amount to be depreciated should be the equipment's total cost less its estimated salvage at the time of disposal.

Regardless of which depreciation method is used to depreciate a given piece of equipment, the type of accounting journal entry remains the same. For example, let us assume that using an acceptable depreciation method, a periodic depreciation charge on a given truck is determined as $2,000. The periodic accounting journal entry would be as follows.

Equipment Depreciation Expense	2,000	
Accumulated Depreciation—Truck		2,000

The dollar value of the entry would depend on the cost of the asset, the useful life of the asset, the salvage value, and the depreciation method used.

The firm should use a depreciation method that best matches the utilization of the equipment to the revenue earned. However, in practice, the practicability of a given method overrides the matching concept. Several depreciation methods determine the depreciation charge as a function of time. Others determine the depreciation charge as a

[7]AICPA, *Accounting Terminology Bulletin*, No. 1, New York, August, 1973.

function of asset usage. The more frequently used acceptable depreciation methods are discussed in the following paragraphs.

Straight Line Depreciation. Much construction equipment depreciates either totally as a function of time, or as a function of both time and use. Let us consider the more frequently used time depreciation. The *straight line depreciation* method is the simplest means of depreciating a piece of equipment as a function of time. It is the depreciation method used most widely by construction firms. The equipment is merely depreciated equally over its expected life. It we let P equal the initial cost, n the expected life, and L the salvage value after a life of n periods; then the depreciation charge per time period is as follows.

Depreciation charge per unit time $= (P - L)/n$

Usually n is given in years, so that the depreciation charge per unit time becomes the *annual depreciation charge*. For example, let us assume that the initial cost of a piece of equipment is $12,000. Its estimated salvage value after its expected life of 5 years is $2,000. The annual depreciation charge is calculated as follows.

Annual depreciation charge $= (\$12,000 - \$2,000)/5 = \$2,000$

Sum of the Digits Depreciation. As previously mentioned, a contractor can usually optimize his tax benefits if he can depreciate his equipment such that the equipment is depreciated more in its early years than in its later years. In other words, he would like to depreciate his equipment so that the depreciation charge for the first year (from this point on, we will assume the interval of time to be a year) is more than the depreciation charge of the second year, and so on. One such time depreciation method which does this is referred to as the *sum of the digits depreciation* method. Consider the previous example in which a piece of equipment is purchased with a salvage value of $2,000. Using the sum of the digits depreciation method, we sum all the digits between 0 and n. In this example, n = 5, so the sum of the digits from 0 to 5 equals $1 + 2 + 3 + 4 + 5$, which equals 15. The sum of the digits will always be given by the formula, $n(n + 1)/2$. The depreciation charge for any given year is now found by multiplying $(P - L)$ by the fraction derived from subtracting the depreciation year from n + 1 and dividing the result by the sum of the digits. Calculating the depreciation charge for the first year in our example, it would be as follows.

Depreciation charge first year $= (\$12,000 - \$2,000)(5)/15 = \$3,333.33$

The 5 in the above expression is derived from subtracting 1 from the sum of n + 1. If we let m represent the year for which we are calculating the depreciation charge, then the depreciation charge for that year may be calculated from the following general formula.

Depreciation charge for mth year $= 2(P - L)(n + 1 - m)/(n(n + 1))$

In the example, the depreciation charge for the second year therefore becomes the following.

Depreciation charge for second year
$$= 2\ (\$10,000)\ (5 + 1 - 2)/(5(5 + 1)) = \$2,666.66$$

The depreciation charge for the remaining years may be found in a similar manner. It will be found that each year the depreciation charge decreases from the previous year.

Declining Balance Depreciation. As an alternative to the sum of the digits depreciation method, a construction firm may use the so-called *declining balance depreciation* method for accelerated or fast write off of its construction equipment. Using the declining balance depreciation method, the depreciation charge for a given year is derived by taking a constant percentage of the previous year's nondepreciated balance. This method requires a non-zero salvage value, since theoretically a nondepreciated value of zero would never be reached. The depreciation rate, which is a constant percentage, is found from the following formula.

$$\text{Depreciation rate} = D = 1 - (L/P)^{1/n}$$

In this formula, P is the initial cost, n is the expected life, L is the salvage value after n periods, and D is the constant depreciation rate. Once D is determined, the depreciation charge for a given year is found by multiplying D by the nondepreciated value of the equipment. In the previous example, if P is $12,000, n is 5 years, and L is $2,000, D is calculated as follows.

$$\text{Depreciation rate} = D = 1 - (2,000/12,000)^{1/5} = 0.301$$

Having determined this value, the depreciation charge for the first year is found as follows.

$$\$12,000 \times 0.301 = \$3,612$$

The depreciation charge for the second year is found in a similar manner.

$$(\$12,000 - \$3,612) \times 0.301 = \$2,524.79$$

The depreciation charge for the remaining years may be found in a similar manner. After 5 years, the nondepreciated value is $2,000 which is, of course, equal to the salvage value.

Double Declining Balance. As previously indicated, reducing charge depreciation is acceptable for tax determination. However, the tax law states that the amount of depreciation must not be more than double the amount that would result under the straight line method. As such, a depreciation method referred to as the *double declining balance* method evolved. This method is similar to the declining balance method just discussed except that the depreciation rate is determined as being equal to twice the straight line rate.

The straight line rate used in the previously discussed example was twenty percent (i.e., 1/5 times 100). The double declining balance depreciation rate would be 40%. Assuming a $2,000 salvage, the depreciation charge for the first year would be calculated as follows.

Depreciation charge first year = ($12,000 − $2,000)(.4) = $4,000

Similarly, the depreciation charge the second year would be calculated as follows.

Depreciation charge second year = ($12,000 − $2,000 − $4,000)(.4) = $2,400

Constant Unit Use Charge Depreciation. A construction firm also has several use *depreciation methods* available for depreciating its construction equipment. Even though much of a contractor's equipment depreciates (wears out) with use, contractors have a tendency to depreciate the equipment as a function of time. This is partly because depreciation methods which are a function of use require the contractor to keep close track of the production performed by his equipment. It is suggested that the contractor keep these records. He is thus able to use the more accurate use depreciation methods when they are applicable, and is also aided in his cost control program.

The most basic and realistic use depreciation method is referred to as the *constant unit use charge depreciation* method. In this method, all of the production units produced or performed by a piece of equipment are charged at the same rate. For example, let us assume that we buy an earth-moving piece of construction equipment for $12,000. The manufacturer informs us that the expected life of the equipment is 1,000,000 cubic yards of earth removal. At that time, the equipment's salvage value is estimated to be $2,000. Using the constant unit use charge depreciation method, a depreciation rate or cost per unit of use, is calculated as follows.

Depreciation rate = $D = (P - L)/n$

In the example above, the depreciation rate is calculated as follows.

Depreciation rate $= D$
$$= (\$12{,}000 - \$2{,}000)/(1{,}000{,}000 \text{ cu yd})$$
$$= \$0.01/\text{cu yd}$$

The depreciation charge for the equipment for any given year is then calculated by multiplying the depreciation rate by the number of production units produced or performed in that year. In the example, let us assume that 120,000 cu yd of earth were moved by the equipment in a given year. The depreciation charge for that year is then calculated as follows.

Depreciation charge $= (\$0.01)/(\text{cu yd}) \cdot (120{,}000 \text{ cu yd})$
$$= \$1{,}200$$

The depreciation for other years may be found in a similar manner.

Declining Unit Use Depreciation. By means of use depreciation methods, a construction firm can also accelerate its depreciation of equipment. One such use depreciation method is called the *declining unit use charge* method. In this method, early production units are assigned a higher depreciation rate than later production units. Let us suppose we want to depreciate the first 500,000 cu yd of production in the previous example at twice the rate as the final 500,000 cu yd of expected life of production. We must first determine an equivalent number of production units, by doubling the first 500,000. Thus, we have a total of 2 • (500,000) plus 500,000, or 1,500,000 production units. The depreciation rate for the first 500,000, units is found by dividing (P − L) by 1,500,000 and multiplying the result by 2. This is done as follows.

Depreciation rate (first 500,000 units)
$$= [(\$12,000 - \$2,000)/1,500,000 \text{ cu yd}] \cdot 2 = 0.0133 \text{ cu yd}$$

The depreciation charge for any given year is found by multiplying the production units produced or performed in the year by the respective depreciation rate for those units. In our example, assume that prior to the fourth year, 400,000 cu yd of production have been performed. We are interested in calculating the depreciation charge for the fourth year for which 200,000 cu yd of earth are moved by the equipment. The depreciation charge for the year is found by multiplying 100,000 units (part of the first 500,000 units) by the depreciation rate of $0.0133 per unit, and adding it to the product of 100,000 units (part of the last 500,000 units) and the depreciation rate of $0.00666 per unit. The result is as follows.

Depreciation charge (fourth year)
$$= (100,000) \times (0.0133) + (100,000) \times (0.00666) = \$2,000$$

The depreciation charge for any other year is found in a similar manner.

9.3.6 Accounting for Leases

The large dollar cost associated with the purchase of equipment and the rather speciality characteristics of some types of construction equipment results in the typical construction firm renting or leasing a substantial portion of their equipment used to build projects. In addition to having less initial negative effect on the firm's cash flow (i.e., its liquidity), the renting or leasing of equipment can result in a smaller unit cost of usage when the firm only needs the equipment for a select few operations. On the other hand, if equipment is used rather continuously by the construction firm, the purchasing of the equipment normally results in a much lower cost per unit of usage. However, even when this is the case, the construction firm's cash availability may restrict the firm to renting or leasing a needed piece of equipment.

When equipment is rented, the accounting is relatively simple. The rental cost of the equipment is allocated to particular projects on some reasonable basis such as direct cost of the projects, duration of the projects, equipment time on the projects, or equipment mileage on the projects. The accounting entry to record the allocated cost is made by debiting a project expense account and crediting cash paid for the rental or an account payable if the rental company issues the equipment on credit. Assuming a $2,000 rental cost is paid by a construction firm for the use of a piece of equipment on a single work item, the accounting entry would be as follows.

Project Expense—Equipment Rental	2,000	
Cash		2,000

Unlike purchased equipment, equipment rentals do not appear as an asset on the firm's financial statements. However, substantial rental committments should be disclosed in footnotes to a construction firm's financial statements.

Leasing differs from renting in that leases are normally considered to be for a longer period of time. For example, whereas a construction firm may rent a piece of equipment for a one month duration, a lease agreement for the equipment might run five or ten years. More important than the duration difference between leasing and renting is the fact that leases may in fact be purchases or options to purchase. Such agreements require accounting recognition that differs from that used for recognition of rental agreements.

Under some circumstances, a lease agreement may actually represent an installment purchase of equipment. While the recognition of such an agreement may sometimes be difficult to detect, it is normally characterized by the following circumstances.[8]

   (1) When the lease is made subject to the purchase of the equipment for a nominal sum or for an amount obviously much less than its fair value at the time of purchase.
   (2) When the lease agreement stipulates that the rentals may be applied in part as installments on the purchase price of the equipment.

---

[8]*Audits of Construction Contractors*, AICPA, New York, 1965, p. 27.

(3) When the rentals obviously are not comparable with other rentals for similar equipment so as to create the presumption that portions of such rentals are partial payments under a purchase plan.

Additional means of determining whether an agreement is a lease or an installment purchase should focus on which party is liable for maintaining the equipment and which party bears the risk of ownership. In a true lease (sometimes referred to as an *operating lease*) the owner (i.e., the lessor) retains the usual risk of ownership. His rental receipts are computed to cover the usual ownership cost of depreciation, taxes, insurance, and a profit. The lease is normally readily cancellable by the lessor, and no special equipment ownership is given up by the lessor. On the other hand, some, if not all of these conditions are absent in the installment purchase agreement (which is alternatively referred to as a *financing lease*). For example, the lease is noncancellable, and the costs of maintenance, insurance, taxes, etc. are assumed by the leasee.

The construction firm's accounting recognition of an operating lease are similar to the recognition of a rental agreement. That is, a debit to rent or lease expense and a credit to cash is recognized. The entry is exactly the same as the one previously made for the described rental payment.

If the firm prepays some of the equipment lease expense (as is often required), that portion which is prepaid should be recognized as an asset rather than as an expense in the period paid. For example, let us assume a construction firm initially pays an equipment leasing firm $4,000 for the lease of a piece of equipment, $2,000 of which is to cover the lease cost in the current period. The accounting journal entry would be as follows.

Lease Expense	2,000	
Prepaid Lease Expense	2,000	
Cash		4,000

The $2,000 prepaid lease expense amount would be removed in the following accounting period and an expense recognized.

When an equipment lease agreement is such that it actually is a form of an installment payment purchase, it is preferable to include the equipment among the contractor's assets and to recognize the related indebtedness as a liability. That is, the equipment is to be capitalized and a liability is recognized. This type of recognition is necessary in order to fully disclose the firm's financial position. The accounting entry necessary to capitalize the leased equipment differs depending on whether a straight line amortization or present value amortization is used. Since present value is a more exact method it will be illustrated.

Using the present value method, the accounting entry should debit the equipment account for the present value of the equipment rights and credit a liability to the leasing company. For example, let us assume a construction firm enters into a financing lease whereby it obtains rights to a piece of equipment through five equal end of the year payments of $4,747.93 each. The capitalized amount of the assets should be the total cost paid minus any implied interest costs. Let us assume that the current on-going annual interest rate is 6%. The capitalized value of the equipment would be determined by means of the following calculation.

Present value of = ($4,747.93)   (Present value of a uniform series
equipment rights   for five periods and at 6%)

Present value of = ($4,747.93) (4.2124)
equipment rights

Present value of = $20,000
equipment rights

The accounting entry required to recognize the lease purchase agreement would be as follows.

Equipment—Leasehold	20,000.00	
Discount on Lease Obligation	3,739.65	
Liability—Lease Obligation		23,739.65

The discount represents the cost exceeding the calculated present value cost. It is an interest cost that will be amortized over the period of the lease agreement. Other than the portion of the liability that is due in the current period (i.e., a current liability), the dollar amount of the liability is considered long term.

Additional accounting period entries have to be made to recognize the annual lease payments and to depreciate the asset. However, it should be noted that the periods for which these two different entries are to be made may differ. For example, whereas the lease agreement is to be for five years, the equipment may have a useful life of ten years. As such, depreciation is to be recognized over a ten year period.

Using a present value amortization of the interest payments the accounting entries necessary to recognize the payment of the first rental payment follows.

Liability—Lease Obligation	4,747.93	
Cash		4,747.93

It is also necessary to recognize the interest expense.

Interest Expense   1,200.00
    Discount on Lease Obligation   1,200.00

The interest expense for the accounting period is calculated as 6% times the unpaid balance which for the first period is $20,000. In the following period it would be 6% times the unpaid balance of $16,452.07 or an interest expense of $987.12.

An accounting entry would be necessary to record the depreciation. Assuming a ten year life and straight line depreciation, the accounting entry would be as follows.

Expense—Depreciation Equipment Leasehold   2,000
    Equipment   2,000

Similar entries would be made in following accounting periods.

9.4 Methods of Recognizing Revenue and Expense

Practically all of the accounting journal entries described in the previous sections would be treated similarly in a cash or accrual accounting method. For example, depreciation expense would be recognized identically in both methods. However, if cash was not exchanged in a revenue or expense transaction, the accounting recognition would differ depending on whether the cash or accrual method was used. For example, a purchase of material would not be recognized as an expense in a cash accounting method until the cash was actually paid. That is, no account payable would be recognized in a cash method whereas it would be recognized in an accrual method.

Prepaid or deferred transactions are not recognized in the cash accounting method. For example, in an earlier section a prepaid lease account was recognized when the construction firm paid a $4,000 lease expense of which $2,000 was prepaid. In the cash method of accounting, the entire $4,000 payment would be recognized as a lease expense in the year in which the payment was made. No asset (i.e., the prepaid expense) would be recognized. On the other hand, if a lease payment was due in a given year or accounting period, but the construction firm did not pay the expense until the following year or accounting period, no expense would be recognized in the year due when using the cash method. Using the accrual method, the lease expense would be accrued and recognized in the year it was due.

As one might suspect, a firm can substantially manipulate its revenues and expenses under the cash method by prepaying or deferring payments. On the other hand, since revenues and expenses are recognized when goods are received or services are performed when using the accrual method, less potential for revenue and expense manipulation results when using the accrual accounting method. This is yet another of the reasons for the preference of the accrual versus cash method of accounting. The important difference between the two methods in regard to revenue recognition and net income is illustrated by means of examples in this and the following sections.

9.4.1 Short Duration Projects

Recording income (i.e., revenue minus expenses) on construction contracts of short duration presents few problems. A short duration contract is one in which the construction work performed takes place in a period of time less than a year. When such is the case, the firm does not recognize profits until the project is substantially completed. For example, let us assume that a construction firm starts a four month construction project on February 1, 1975. The project proceeds according to schedule and is completed on May 1, 1975. In preparing its March 1975 quarterly financial statements, revenues and expenses (i.e., cash received for partial performance or paid to material suppliers and labor) are ignored in the statements. Not until the June 31, 1975 quarterly statements are prepared are the revenues and expenses recognized. This is because at that time, the four month project (i.e., a short duration project) is completed.

What if on March 31, 1975 the construction firm could reasonably foresee that the performing of the project was going to result in a loss rather than result in a profit? Consistent with the *conservatism accounting principle,* the best procedure would be to estimate the loss and recognize it in the March 31, 1975 quarterly statement. Assuming an estimated loss of $3,000, the appropriate accounting journal entry would be as follows.

Income Summary	3,000	
Estimated Loss—Job 101		3,000

The estimated loss would be recognized as a current liability. In certain circumstances (i.e., where the loss is not as certain) it may be appropriate to recognize the estimated loss by means of a footnote to the financial statement.

9.4.2 Percentage of Completion and Completed Contract Methods

Many construction projects require more than a year's duration to complete. The increasing complexity and size of building construction and heavy and highway construction projects result in an increasing number of long duration projects. If income is to only be recognized as the project is completed (i.e., as is consistent with previously discussed generally accepted accounting principles), a construction firm's reported income can vary substantially from one year to the next. For example, if a firm is currently engaged in three projects, all of which are three years in duration, the firm will report no income in the first two years. In the third year it will appear that the firm suddenly experienced a "good year" where in reality much of the reported income is in fact "earned" in the prior two years. Thus, the problem of accounting for long term construction projects.

In practice, when engaging in a long duration project, the construction firm regularly bills the project owner (e.g., every two weeks) and receives payment from the owner for its partial performance of the contract. As the construction firm performs work on the owner's project, it obtains a lien on the project. This fact along with the wide variations that can occur when only recognizing revenues and expenses when a project is completed, resulted in the A.I.C.P.A. acknowledging an exception to the accounting principle of recognizing income when the project is completed. In particular, the A.I.C.P.A. suggested two methods of accounting for long term fixed price contracts.[9]

(1) The precentage of completion method—"preferable when estimates of costs to complete and extent of progress towards completion of long term contracts are reasonably dependable."

(2) The completed contract method—"preferable when lack of dependable estimates or inherent hazards cause forecasts to be doubtful."

For purposes of illustrating and contrasting the two methods of recognizing revenue for long duration projects, let us consider the Mica Construction Company which started doing business in January, 1975. The firm's construction activities for the year 1975 are as follows.

---

[9]Ibid., p. 13.

Project	Total Contract Price	Contract Expenditures to Dec 31, 1975	Estimated Additional Cost to Complete	Cash Collections to Dec 31, 1975	Billings to Dec 31, 1975
101	$ 310,000	$187,500	$ 12,500	$155,000	$155,000
102	415,000	195,000	255,000	210,000	249,000
103	350,000	320,000	—	300,000	350,000
104	300,000	16,500	183,500	—	4,000
	$1,375,000	$719,000	$451,000	$665,000	$758,000

The above records have been maintained on the completed contract method. Any work remaining to be done on the contracts is expected to be completed in 1976.

The completed contract method of recognizing revenue is similar to the method for accounting for short duration projects. That is, the method conforms with the concept that income should not be recognized prior to the point of sale. The method requires no estimate of profits earned prior to completion of the contract. This is the advantage of the completed contract method. On the other hand, the method has the disadvantage that income may be distorted from year to year.

When using the completed contract method, all costs incurred by the construction firm during construction are accumulated in a Construction in Process Account. For example, let us assume that the $187,500 expense on project 101 consisted of a single transaction. The Mica Construction Company would recognize this transaction in 1975 by means of the following entry.

Construction in Process—Job 101   187,500
     Cash   187,500

Billings by the construction firm to the project owner are debited to Accounts Receivable (an asset account) and credited to Revenue Billed on Construction Contracts. Assuming the entire $155,000 billing on project 101 was made through a single billing (as is the case of expenses, this would normally be several transactions), the accounting journal entry would be made as follows.

Accounts Receivable   155,000
     Revenue Billed on Construction Contracts—Job 101   155,000

As the cash is received from the project owner, the accounts receivable account is reduced and cash is debited. For project 101, this would be done by the following entry.

| | PROJECT | | | | |
	101	102	103	104	Total
Completed-Contract Method					
Revenue to Report			$350,000		$350,000
Less Costs to be Matched			320,000		320,000
Provision for Contract Loss		$ 35,000			35,000
Net Revenue (Loss)		($ 35,000)	$ 30,000	$	$ (5,000)
Percentage of Completion Method					
Revenue to Report	$290,625	$179,833	$350,000	$24,750	$845,208
Less Costs to be Matched	187,500	195,000	320,000	16,500	719,000
Net Revenue (Loss)	103,125	(15,167)	30,000	8,250	126,208
Less Provision for Full Contract Loss		(19,833)			(19,833)
Net Revenue (Adjusted Loss)	$103,125	($ 35,000)	$ 30,000	$ 8,250	$106,375

Fig. 9.10. Completed contract versus percentage complete revenue.

Cash   155,000
    Accounts Receivable   155,000

No income is recognized prior to the completion of a contract. As such, in the year 1975, Mica Construction Company would recognize a positive income only from project 103. This is shown in Fig. 9.10. The amount of income (sometimes referred to as net income) recognized would be the difference between the revenue billed to the project owner and the expenses incurred by the firm on the project in question. For project 103 this amounts to $350,000 minus $320,000 or $30,000. The actual journal entry required to recognize the income would be made by closing out the Billings and Work in Process accounts as follows.

Revenue Billed on Construction Contracts—Job 103 350,000
    Construction in Process—Job 103   320,000
    Income on Projects—Job 103   30,000

From inspection of Fig. 9.10, it should be noted that a negative income (i.e., a loss) is recognized for project 102 in the year 1975 even though the project remains uncompleted in 1975. This is consistent with the conservatism accounting principle. That is, all reasonable expected losses should be reported. Since the firm estimates that its total cost of completing project 102 is $450,000 (of which they have already expended $195,000), and the total fixed price contract is for $415,000; a $35,000 loss is expected and recognized. However, because the project is not yet completed, the Billings and Work in Process accounts are not closed. Instead, the loss is recognized by the following entry.

Loss on Projects—Job 102   35,000
   Estimated Loss on Construction Projects—Job 102

                                                35,000

The estimated Loss account is recognized in the firm's financial position statement as a current liability. The Loss on Projects is closed to the Income Summary account. In total, the Mica Construction Company would report a $5,000 loss from operations for the year 1975.

As to Mica's financial position statement (i.e., their balance sheet) for the year ended 1975 the accounts receivable, cash received from billings, and the estimated losses from projects would all be recognized in the statement. In addition, the net balance between the Construction in Process (a debit) and Revenue Billed on Construction Contracts (a credit) accounts would be recognized as a current asset (assuming the projects will be completed in the following year) if the difference is a debit, or as a current liability if the difference is a credit. As is shown in Fig. 9.11, there is a total net current liability of $9,000. This results from the surplus billings in excess of cost account for project 102. Project 103 is not recognized in the calculation in that the Billings and Work in Process accounts for this project have been closed.

All of the costs discussed up to this point can be considered as direct costs. It is common practice not to accumulate general and administrative costs (i.e., overhead) as contract costs. However, it is suggested that when using the completed contract method, a better matching of revenues and expenses is obtained if these costs are allocated to individual projects. If this is not done, the firm may have to report a loss (due to general and administrative costs) merely because several projects are in the "Work in Process" stage and none are completed in the accounting period in question.

The *percentage of completion method* is generally the preferable method for recording income on long duration projects. The major advantage of the method is that the method recognizes income on a current basis and as such results in a more regular flow of income. On the other hand, the method has the disadvantage of being dependent on estimates of costs which are subject to uncertainties. The A.I.C.P.A. recommends that the income is to be recognized by determining

(1) The percentage of estimated total income that incurred costs to date bear to estimated total costs after giving effect to estimates of costs to complete based upon most recent information.

(2) The percentage of estimated total income that may be indicated by such other measures of progress toward completion as may be appropriate having due regard to work performed.

In most circumstances, the first means of estimating income to be recognized will prove appropriate. However, for certain types of projects total incurred costs may not be the best measure of income earned. Where a more meaningful allocation of income would result, the second means of estimating income noted allows for a better method. For example, a more appropriate recognition of income may in certain circumstances be based on the percentage of direct labor costs expended to the estimated total direct labor costs for the project.

As in the case of the completed contract method, when using the percentage of completion method, project costs incurred in the construction of a long duration project are accumulated in a Construction in Process account. Interim billings by the construction firm to the project owner are debited to Accounts Receivable and credited to Revenue Billed on Construction Contracts. When cash is received from the project owner, Cash is debited, and Accounts Receivable are credited. As such, expense, billings, and cash receipt transactions are handled identically in the two methods for accounting for long duration projects.

Unlike the completed contract method, the percentage of completion method recognizes income on the basis of the percentage of completion of the project. Let us consider the 1975 construction transaction data previously presented for the Mica Construction Company. In order to determine the amount of income to be recognized for any one project, the actual incurred costs of the project, the total estimated cost of the project and the total contract price must be recognized. Let us consider project 101. To date, costs have been incurred equal to $187,500. Since estimated costs to complete are determined as $12,500, the total estimated cost of project 101 is $200,000. Multiplying the ratio of incurred costs to total estimated cost times the total contract price of $310,000 results in recognition of $290,625 of revenue. From this recognized revenue of $290,625 must be subtracted the $187,500 of expenses to yield recognized reportable income of $103,125. It should be noted that the $103,125 income could also have been calculated by multiplying the ratio of incurred costs to total costs times the calculated total expected profit of $110,000 (the contract price of $310,000 minus the estimated total cost of $200,000). The calculations for determining the income to be reported for each of the four projects are summarized in Fig. 9.10.

As can be observed in Fig. 9.10, the income to be reported for project 103 is the same regardless of whether the completed contract or percentage of completion method is used. This is because the project is started and finished in the year 1975. It should also be observed that while the calculations for project 102 yields a net reportable loss of $15,167, the actual loss reported is adjusted to $35,000. This is to satisfy A.I.C.P.A. recommendations as to reporting the reasonable projected loss in total.

The recognizing of income by means of the percentage of completion method is accomplished by debiting the Construction in Process account and crediting an account entitled Income on Construction in Process. At statement time, the Income on Construction in Process is closed to Income Summary. The Mica Construction Company would recognize the income from project 101 by means of the following journal entry.

Construction in Process—Job 101	103,125	
Income on Construction in Process—Job 101		103,125

At statement time the following journal entry would be made.

Income on Construction in Process—Job 101	103,125	
Income Summary		103,125

When a project is completed during the accounting entry in question, the income journal entry is identical to that used for the completed contract method. That is, the Revenue Billed on Construction Contracts would be debited, and the Construction in Process account credited. The net difference would be income if a credit or a loss if a debit. This income or credit would in turn be closed to income summary.

As was true in the completed contract method, when using the percentage of completion method, the net balance between the Construction in Process and Revenue Billed on Construction accounts is shown on the statement of financial position as a current asset if there is a debit and as a current liability if there is a credit. The calculations for determining the asset or liability for each of the projects is shown in Fig. 9.11. As can be observed from the figure, the dollar amount of billings is the same amount as used in the completed contract method. However, no longer are these compared only to the incurred costs. They are compared to the Construction in Process account which is adjusted to account for period income. For example, the $290,625 Construction in Process amount listed for project 101 includes incurred costs of $187,500 and reported period income of $103,125.

The different financial statement affects of the completed contract and percentage of completion methods can be observed from Figs. 9.10 and 9.11. The statement differences tend to decrease when the construction firm engages in a somewhat steady amount of work. That is, if

	PROJECT			
	101	102	104	Total
Completed Contract				
Contract Expenditures to Dec 31	$187,500	$195,000	$16,500	$399,000
Billings to Dec 31	155,000	249,000	4,000	408,000
1. Costs in Excess of Billings	$ 32,500		$12,500	$ 45,000
2. Billings in Excess of costs		$ 54,000		$ 54,000
Percentage of Completion				
Costs and Estimated Revenue	290,625	179,833	24,750	495,208
Billings to Date	155,000	249,000	4,000	408,000
1. Costs and Estimated Earnings in Excess of Billings	$135,625		$20,750	$156,375
2. Billings in Excess of Costs and Estimated Earnings		69,167		69,167
Add Loss to be Incurred		19,833		19,833
To be Reported as Billings in Excess of Costs and Estimated Earnings		$ 89,000		$ 89,000

Fig. 9.11. Assets and liabilities—completed contract versus percentage of completion.

there is no wide variation in the amount of work completed from one accounting period to the next, the completed contract method approaches the percentage of completion method as to income and financial position results. However, in evaluating the two methods, one has to recognize that the construction industry is not characterized by a constant volume of work. That is, the volume of work performed by most construction firms varies substantially from season to season and from year to year.

The construction firm should recognize the accounting principle of consistency when using the completed contract or the percentage of completion method. This does not mean that the firm must use one of the methods for all of their projects (even though the use of one method simplifies the accounting process). What is necessary is that the firm apply the same accounting treatment to the same set of conditions from one accounting period to another.

9.5 Adjustments and Changes

As indicated in an earlier discussion of the accounting cycle, after accounting journal entries are made, adjusting entries are often needed to recognize unrecorded entries and changes in an accounting method. Along with the required journal entries, a worksheet is used to analyze the required adjustment as to its affect on the financial statements.

The rather unsophisticated accounting practices followed by many firms in the construction industry increase the need to recognize accounting adjusting entries. Many construction firms keep books on a cash basis. In order to satisfy the needs of third parties, it may be necessary to change the firm's books to an accrual basis in order to produce required financial statements.

In order to illustrate required accounting adjusting entries for unrecorded transactions and for a change in accounting methods, let us consider financial data for the Small Construction Company.[10] This company specializes in carpentry and painting. The parttime bookkeeper for the company keeps the records on a cash basis. At year end the bookkeeper prepared the following trial balance.

Small Construction Company
Trial Balance
December 31, 1974

	Debit	Credit
Cash—General	$ 23,600	
Cash—Imprest Payroll	1,000	
Inventory, Jan 1	1,700	
Trucks and Equipment	24,800	
Accum. depr.—Trucks and Equipment		$ 10,100
Suspense		10,350
Retained Earnings		5,450
Capital Stock		5,000
Sales		363,000
Paint and Wood	75,000	
Subcontractors	9,800	
Labor	210,000	
Payroll Taxes	8,500	
Officer and other Salaries	23,000	
Other Expenses	16,500	
	$393,900	$393,900

[10]Anderson, J. W., Lentilhon, R. W., *The CPA Examination*, South-Western Publishing Company, Cincinnati, 1972, pp. 5–14.

The company decided at year end that the financial statements and income tax returns are to be prepared on an accrual basis. The firm is to continue its practice of using the completed contract method. In addition to the trial balance prepared on a cash basis, other relevant information to the preparing of financial statements is as follows.

1) The company's bank reconciliations showed outstanding checks totaling $1,400 for the general cash account and none for the payroll account. The payroll cash account is operated on the imprest basis with $1,000 as the fixed amount. The only other reconciling items arose from the company's method of treating payroll taxes. At the end of each payroll period a check is deposited in the payroll cash account for the amount of the payroll taxes. The employer's portion is expensed when the check to be deposited is drawn. The bookkeeper draws checks on the payroll account to pay the payroll taxes when they are due. The following amounts are on deposit in the payroll cash account.
   (a) $1,100 for December F.I.C.A. taxes
   (b) $2,100 for December Federal Witholding taxes
   (c) $900 for 4th quarter State Unemployment tax
   (d) $800 for 1974 Federal Unemployment tax
In addition, the company has on hand depository receipts totaling $6,300 covering October and November F.I.C.A. and withholding taxes.

(2) The bookkeeper maintains a cost analysis job record. The records for December jobs follow.

Job No.	Status	Contract Price	Paid Billings	Unpaid Billings	Paint & Wood	Direct Labor	Subcontracts Charged
102	Closed	$8,000	$1,800	$6,200	$ 650	$5,100	$700
103	Open	9,800	3,000	1,000	400	3,200	500
104	Closed	9,000	1,700	7,300	1,200	6,700	—
105	Open	6,000	700	1,500	300	1,000	—
106	Closed	4,500	4,500	—	550	2,450	—

No other jobs are ongoing. The amount shown as "Subcontracts Charges" is the subcontractor's billing. For estimating purposes, Small Construction Company treats insurance, payroll taxes, and administrative expenses as period costs.

(3) The physical inventory of paint and wood amounted to $2,100. Prior years experience has been that about one-third of the paint and wood on hand is discarded during the following year.

(4) The company paid the country club expenses of $1,600 for Mr. Small, the company president, in accordance with the approval of the officers. The company also reimbursed him in 1975 for the $600 cost of his country club membership noninterest bearing bond he took when he joined the club. The $600 will be refunded when he leaves the club. These expenditures were charged to Other Expenses. Mr. Small has kept records which show that 40% of his country club expenses related to the business.

(5) To obtain additional working capital for the company, Mr. Small borrowed $10,000 from his life insurance company (a cash loan provision) and turned over the proceeds to the company as a loan. The company does not pay the premiums on the policy. The bookkeeper recorded the transaction in the Suspense account.

(6) The following schedule was taken from the company's income tax return from the previous year. The company's books were in agreement.

Item	Date Acquired	Cost	Prior Depreciation	Life	Depreciation This Year
Truck 1	1/1/70	$ 3,000	$1,500	6 yrs	$ 500
Truck 2	7/1/71	3,600	900	6 yrs	600
Misc Eq	1/1/69	12,000	3,600	10 yrs	1,200
Office Eq	1/1/69	2,000	1,600	10 yrs	200
		$20,600	$7,600		$2,500

Truck I was sold to an employee on July 1 for $350 cash. The proceeds were applied to the purchase of Truck 3, which was invoiced by a dealer at $4,200. The company paid cash for the new truck. The sale of Truck I was placed in Suspense. The new truck has an estimated life of 6 years. All depreciation is computed by the straight line method. The bookkeeper has not recorded depreciation for 1974.

(7) Income taxes are ignored in this example.

Several adjustments are necessary in order to produce the financial records of an accrual basis. Let us consider each of the seven sets of additional information individually.

(1) From the information given, $4,900 of checks have been written from the general cash account to the payroll cash account. Since the balance of the payroll cash account is stated at $1,000 (i.e., the fixed amount in the account), it is apparent that the $4,900 must be entered (i.e., an adjustment) as follows.

Cash—Imprest Payroll	4,900	
Accrued Payroll Taxes		4,900

(2) The bookkeeping has been performed using a cash basis and a completed contract method. To change the financial status of projects to an accrual basis requires several entries. Let us consider then individually.

(a) The subcontractor's job 102 invoice for $700 has not been paid, and the $200 subcontractor's invoice on job 104 has not been received. Since these are liabilities at year end, the following entry is required.

Subcontractors	900	
Accounts Payable		900

This entry is necessary because using the cash basis the entry would not have been made.

(b) Using the cash basis, a sale is recognized only when cash is received. However, when using an accrual basis a sale is recognized when a receivable or cash is recognized. Since $6,200 remains unpaid on the closed job 102 and $7,300 remains unpaid on the closed job 104, these amounts are receivables on Dec. 31. The entry required to adjust to the accrual basis is as follows.

Accounts Receivable	13,500	
Sales		13,500

(c) Jobs 103 and 105 are not yet finished. Using the completed contract method no revenue or expense should be recognized until the jobs are complete. However, as can be observed from the data given, using the cash basis, $3,000 and $700 of revenue have been recognized from jobs 103 and 105 respectively. In addition, $1,000 and $1,500 are billed (i.e., receivables) on jobs 103 and 105. These amounts are uncollected and unrecognized in the cash basis accounting method. As such, the adjusting entry required is as follows.

Sales	3,700	
Accounts Receivables	2,500	
Billings on Jobs in Process		6,200

The Billings on Jobs in Process account is currently absent in the cash basis method. It is a necessary account in the accrual method.

(d) There is no Jobs in Process account. Rather than charge cash payments as expenses, they should be accumulated in the Jobs in Process account (i.e., an asset account) in a completed contract method. The sum of the paid expenses of jobs 103 and 105 (the jobs that are not completed) are $700 and $4200, and $500 for the paint and wood, labor, and subcontractors accounts. The adjusting accrual entry is as follows.

Jobs in Process	5,400	
Paint and Wood		700
Labor		4,200
Subcontractors		500

(3) Of the paint and wood inventory, $2,100, one-third is to be discarded. This leaves an ending inventory of $1,400. Since the trial balance shows an inventory of $1,700, the following adjustment is necessary.

Paint and Wood	300	
Inventory		300

(4) Of the $2,200 expended in connection with Mr. Small's country club membership, $600 represents a noninterest bearing bond to be refunded when membership is terminated. The $600 should be reclassified as follows.

Investment	600	
Other Expenses		600

(5) When the proceeds of the life insurance loan were received, the following entry was made.

Cash—General Account	10,000	
Suspense		10,000

However, Suspense is a "wash" (i.e., nominal) account which is to be closed. This is accomplished as follows.

Suspense	10,000	
Loans Payable—Officers		10,000

(6) Depreciation for the year has not been recorded. The amount is determined as follows.

Asset	Basis	Life	Depreciation
Truck 1	$3,000	6 yrs	$ 250 (½ yr)
Truck 2	3,600	6 yrs	600
Truck 3	4,200	6 yrs	350 (½ yr)
Misc. Eq.	12,000	10 yrs	1,200
Office Eq.	2,000	10 yrs	200
Depreciation Expense			$2,600

Thus, the required depreciation entry is as follows.

Depreciation—Trucks and Eq.   2,600
   Accum. Depr.—Trucks and Eq.   2,600

Examination of the depreciation schedule reveals that depreciation was incorrectly calculated in prior years. This is determined as follows.

Miscellaneous Equipment (acquired 1/1/69)

Cost $12,000/10 yrs	$1,200/yr	
Depreciation for 5 yrs	= 6,000	
Depreciation taken	= 4,800	
Underdepreciation	=	$1,200

Office Equipment (acquired 1/1/69)

Cost $2,000/10 yrs	$ 200/yr	
Depreciation for 5 yrs	= 1,000	
Depreciation taken	= 1,800	
Excess depreciation	=	(800)
Net Underdepreciation	=	$400

The net underdepreciation is adjusted by the following entry.

Correction of Depreciation   400
   Accumulated Depreciation—Trucks
   and Equipment   400

The sale of truck I had been entered as

Cash	350	
Suspense		350

The proper entry to record the sale would have been entered as

Cash	350	
Accumulated Depr.—Trucks and Eq.	2,250	
Loss on Sale of Truck	400	
Trucks and Equipment		3,000

The situation is corrected as follows.

Suspense	350	
Accumulated Depr.—Trucks and Eq.	2,250	
Loss on Sales of Trucks	400	
Trucks and Equipment		3,000

All of the required adjustments are now made. The entries are summarized in the worksheet shown in Fig. 9.12. The worksheet facilitates the producing of financial statements.

From a study of the Small Construction Company accounting entries, it can be observed that the cash method assigns receipts to the period in which cash is received and expenses to the period in which cash is paid. Because of time lags, revenues and expenses determined in this way may not relate to each other, nor to the period to which assigned. The conversion of net income using the cash method to net income using the accrual method can be made by the following schedule.

Net Income,	cash basis
Add:	Accrued income, end of year
	Prepaid expenses, end of year
	Accrued expenses, beginning of year
	Prepaid income, beginning of year
Deduct:	Accrued expenses, end of year
	Prepaid income, end of year
	Accrued income, beginning of year
	Prepaid expenses, beginning of year
Net Income,	accrual basis

9.6 Accounting Errors

The firm that is somewhat unsophisticated as to their accounting practices is likely to make several errors in recording transactions. The

Small Construction Company
Worksheet
For Year Ended Dec 31, 1974

	Trial Balance		Adjusting Entries		Income Statement		Financial Position	
	Dr.	Cr.	Dr.	Cr.	Dr.	Cr.	Dr.	Cr.
Cash	$ 23,600						$23,600	
Cash—Imprest Payroll	1,000		$ 4,900				5,900	
Inventory, Jan 1	1,700			$ 300			1,400	
Trucks & Equip	24,800			3,000			21,800	
Acc Depr— Trucks & Eq		$ 10,100	2,250	3,000				$10,850
Suspense		10,350	10,350					
Correction of Depreciation			400		$ 400			
Retained Earnings		5,450						5,450
Capital Stock		5,000						5,000
Sales		363,000	3,700	13,500		$372,800		
Paint & Wood	75,000		300	700	74,600			
Subcontractors	9,800		900	500	10,200			
Labor	210,000			4,200	205,800			
Payroll Taxes	8,500				8,500			
Officers Sal	23,000				23,000			
Other Expenses	16,500			600	15,900			
Accured Payroll Taxes				4,900				4,900
Accounts Pay able				900				900
Accounts Receiv			16,000				16,000	
Jobs in Progress- Billings				6,200				6,200
Jobs in Progress- Costs			5,400				5,400	
Investments			600				600	
Loan Payable, Officers				10,000				$10,000
Depreciation— Trucks & Equip			2,600		2,600			
Loss of Sale of Truck			400		400			
Net Income					31,400			31,400
	$393,900	$393,900	$47,800	$47,800	$372,800	$372,800	$74,700	$74,700

Fig. 9.12. Worksheet for adjustments.

typical construction firm falls into this category. As an example of an error, a construction firm may enter a transaction as a capital transaction when in fact it should have been treated as an expense transaction. Unless such an error is corrected, the firm's financial statements will be in error.

Somewhat similar to the change from the cash method of accounting to the accrual basis of accounting is a *change in accounting principle*. However, whereas the change of cash to accrual methods is only for changing bookkeeping date, a change in accounting principle may be more permanent. A change in accounting principle may consist of a .

firm's switch from straight line depreciation to declining balance depreciation, the firm's switch from FIFO (first in first out) inventory valuation to LIFO (last in first out) inventory valuation, or the firm's switch from completed contract method to percentage of completion method.

The change of accounting principle normally results in a requirement for a catch-up adjustment entry. The entry should be fully disclosed to reflect the operational affect of the change. On comparative statements, full disclosure and compatibility require that net income and earnings per share data be provided on a pro forma (forecasted) basis assuming retroactive application.

Let us assume that Ace Construction Company has been depreciating its trucks, which cost $200,000, on a straight line basis over a 10 year life with no expected salvage. After the second year the company decided to adopt double declining depreciation in that it would have tax advantages. The change in accounting principle would have the following effect.

Double Declining Balance
Year 1 (200,000 × .2) $40,000
Year 2 (160,000 × .2)   32,000 $72,000
Straight Line Recorded
Years 1 and 2 equal (200,000/10) × 2   40,000
                                                           $32,000

The accounting entry required to recognize the change in accounting principle would be as follows.

Adjustment due to Depreciation Change   32,000
    Accumulated Depreciation   32,000

The adjustment due to the depreciation change would be recognized as an extraordinary item in the firm's income statement for the current year.

A firm may be in error in making one of the required estimates that are part of the accounting process. For example, the firm may underestimate or overestimate the life of a piece of their equipment. Similarly, they might overestimate the collectability of their receivables. One might treat the change in estimate by a retroactive adjustment or treat it by a prospective (future) adjustment. Current accounting practice favors the prospective treatment.

To illustrate a change in estimate, assume that a piece of construction equipment that cost $12,000 with no expected salvage is being depreciated over a 10 year life. However, on the basis of new information after 5 years use, a 15 year life appears to be more accurate. The

change should be handled by prospective entries. In particular, starting
the sixth year, the change would be recognized as follows.

Depreciation recognized to date (10 year life) = 5 × 1,200   = $6,000
Depreciation to be charged over next 10 years = 12,000 − 6,000 = $6,000

The depreciation entry for the sixth year and each of the years, seven
through fifteen, would be as follows.

Depreciation Expense ($6,000/10)	600	
Accumulated Depreciation		600

Perhaps more common in occurrence than a change in accounting
principle or a change in estimate, is an erroneous journal entry. Such
errors must be corrected before issuance of financial statements. While
most errors in journal entries are the result of the construction firm's
lack of a sophisticated accounting system, some errors may be intentional in order to manipulate income or financial position or to conceal
fraud.

When an error is detected, incorrect account balances should be
adjusted to their correct balances and any net adjustment should be
reported as an Adjustment-Correction of Error. This entry should be
closed to retained earnings and reported as a prior period adjustment
(i.e., not appear on the income statement). In respect to comparative
financial statements, incorrect financial data for each period reported
should be corrected for all subsequently discovered errors. When presenting comparative financial statements, the data for each year being
presented should be restated to the correct basis and any required adjustment should be shown as a prior period adjustment of the retained
earnings for the first period being reported.

9.7 Financial Statements

The entire accounting process can be viewed as aimed at the preparation of financial statements. These statements normally include the
statement of financial position (less appropriately referred to as the
balance sheet), the *income statement* (less appropriately referred to as
the profit and loss statement), and the *statement of changes in financial
position* (less appropriately referred to as the funds statement or as the
statement of source and application of funds). In addition, several additional supplementary statements are sometimes prepared. A partial
listing of the additional financial statements follow.

(1) Amounts Due on Contracts
(2) Contracts in Process
(3) Joint Venture Operations
(4) Selling, General, and Administrative Expenses
(5) Statement of Contracts Completed
(6) Consolidated Statements

While creditors and investors may be interested in these additional statements or schedules, the statements and schedules mainly serve an internal purpose for the company. Because they are more significant, both as to internal and external purposes, only the statement of financial position, the income statement, and the statement of changes in financial position are discussed in this section.

Typical formats of the three financial statements were presented in Figs. 9.6–9.8. As was discussed in an earlier section, the actual form of presentation of each of the statements varies significantly in practice. Each industry is somewhat unique as to the types of accounts that are used and therefore included in the financial statements. Regardless of the accounts used by a specific industry, the accounts can be identified as to broadly defined accounting classifications. These classifications provide the basis for the preparation and presentation of the financial statements.

9.7.1 Statement of Financial Position

The statement of financial position reports on the basic economic equation of the firm. This equation is as follows.

$$\text{Assets} = \text{Creditor's Equity} + \text{Owner's Equity}$$

While individual types of accounts may vary from one firm to the next, the basic economic equation holds true for each and every firm. For example, the types of owner's equity accounts differ for the individual proprietor and the corporation. However, each type of firm has equity accounts which have the affect of balancing the asset and creditor's equity portion of the economic equation.

The creditor's equity segment of the basic economic equation for a firm is more commonly referred to as the liabilities of the firm. When the firm is a corporation the owner's equity segment is commonly referred to as stockholder's equity. A fourth category referred to as "deferred credits" sometimes appears in the basic economic equation. However, if possible, its use should be avoided. Because of the infrequency of the need for a deferred credit (an example would be the premium on bonds payable) it will not be considered in this chapter.

The broad based economic equation is further subdivided into classifications that provide the means of analyzing, interpreting, and comparing the financial statements with past statements and statements of other firms. Although the classifications vary somewhat from one firm to the next depending on the type of firm, the following classifications are typical.

Assets: (1) Current assets
(2) Investments and funds
(3) Fixed assets—tangible
(4) Fixed assets—intangible
(5) Other assets
(6) Deferred charges

Liabilities: (1) Current liabilities
(2) Long term liabilities

Owner's Equity: (1) Contributed capital
(a) Capital stock
(b) Contributions in excess of par
(2) Retained earnings
(a) Appropriated
(b) Unappropriated

Most of the account classifications are self-explanatory. For example, current assets are those that are readily available and likely to be used in performing the firm's operations in the current accounting period. "Other assets" are those assets which do not fit the other asset classifications. In particular, a receivable from one of the firm's officers, and a company office which is currently not being used in the firm's production process fit into the "other asset" category. Deferred charges represent debit balances derived from expenditures but involving a future benefit. They are similar to prepaid expenses except for the fact that the future benefits extend beyond a year's time. A construction firm's *organizational costs* can be treated as a deferred charge (i.e., an asset) rather than being expensed in the year in which they occur. Deferred charges are eventually matched to revenue and expensed.

Constructo Construction Company
Statement of Financial Position
December 31, 1975

ASSETS			LIABILITIES AND CAPITAL		
Current Assets:			Current Liabilities:		
Cash		$ 95,400	Note Payable		$ 21,000
Accounts Receivable			Accounts Payable		18,500
Due on Contracts	$ 21,500		Withheld from Employees		4,500
Claims for Approved Change Orders	13,400		Billings in Excess of Costs and Est. Earnings		28,500
Other	5,100	40,000	Accrued Taxes		1,500
Costs and Estimated Earnings in Excess of Billings on Uncompleted Contracts		128,100	Total Current Liabilities		74,000
Inventory of materials		21,000	Capital Stock and Retained Earn:		
Investment in Joint Ventures		53,500	Common Stock, 2500 shares authorized 100 par, 2106 shares issued		210,600
Prepaid Expenses		5,000	Retained Earnings		234,400
Total Current Assets		343,000	Total Liabilities & Capital		$519,000
Plant, Property & Equip		155,000			
Other Assets		21,000			
Total Assets		$519,000			

Fig. 9.13. Statement of financial position—construction firm.

The difference between appropriated retained earnings and unappropriated retained earnings lies in whether the retained earnings are restricted or not restricted as to being available for payment of dividends and other uses. In particular, some retained earnings may be restricted in that the firm's bond agreement with creditors. The creditors may restrict the payment of dividends in order to assure the creditors that retained earnings are available for bond interest and principle payments.

A typical construction firm's statement of financial position is shown in Fig. 9.13. As can be observed from the statement, several accounts unique to the construction industry are part of the statement. For example, "claims for approved change orders" is a current asset account somewhat unique to the construction industry. In effect, it is a type of receivable. As previously discussed, when the costs of projects in progress exceed the billings, the difference is shown as a current asset. It should be noted that a liability is also shown for billings in excess of costs. The showing of both entries may seem contradictory. However, they are both shown because they are from dissimilar types of projects. When such is the case, they should not be netted. The actual calculation of the amounts would likely be shown by means of a note to the financial statement or a supporting schedule. A schedule would likely also be prepared to support the amount listed for plant, property, and equipment.

While the amounts shown in the financial position statement shown in Fig. 9.13 are for a given point in time (i.e., in effect a snapshot of the firm's financial position), comparative financial position statements are sometimes prepared. This is done by showing the financial status of each account listed at the current point in time and at some past point in time such as one year prior. Such statements aid the reader in his analysis of the statement.

9.7.2 Income Statement

The income statement is merely the summation of the firm's revenues and expenses for a given period in time. The relevant period of time is normally a quarter of a year or an entire year. However, when in need of a bank loan, a firm may be required to prepare an income statement for a period of time as short as a month.

The income statement has grown in significance over the past few years. Whereas creditors and investors of prior years placed their emphasis on the analysis of the firm's financial position statement, the income statement has played an increasingly significant role. Today's investors are primarily concerned with a firm's ability to continually increase their reported annual operating and net income.

As discussed in an earlier section, and as is true in regard to the financial position statement, the form and individual accounts included in the income statement vary in practice. Some statements may report all revenue (operating and nonoperating) first followed by a listing of all expenses, whereas other statements may first list operating revenue and operating expenses followed by nonoperating revenues and expenses. In addition, some statements may provide a combined income statement and retained earnings statement whereas in other-cases the income statement may be presented independently of the retained earnings statement. The income statement purpose remains the same regardless of the form of the statement. The statement is to yield the net income for the firm for a given period of time. In addition, if the firm is a corporation, a calculation yielding the net income earned per share of company stock (indicative of the firm's rate of return on investments) is made and the *earnings per share* (E.P.S.) is reported on the income statement.

Constructo Construction Company
Income Statement
For the Year End December 30, 1975

Billings to Owners Under Completed Contracts	$5,150,400
Direct Contract Costs	4,526,300
	624,100
Less—Provision for Losses on Uncompleted Contracts	138,000
Operating Income	486,100
Other Income:	
Share of Income from Joint Ventures	51,400
Income from Equipment	8,400
Gain on Sale of Equipment	21,000
Total Income	566,900
Indirect Costs and Administrative Expenses	282,000
Federal Taxes on Operating Income	124,000
Federal Taxes on Extraordinary Income	21,000
Net Income for the Year	$ 139,900
E.P.S. on Operating Income (100,000 shares)	1.19
E.P.S. on Extraordinary Income (100,000 shares)	.21
E.P.S. on Net Income (100,000 shares)	1.40

Fig. 9.14. Income statement—construction firm.

Typical construction industry accounts summarized in an income statement can be observed from Fig. 9.14. The statement has been made using the completed contract method. As discussed in an earlier section, the accounts and the dollar amounts to be reported in the income statement differ depending on whether the percentage of completion or completed contract method is used for recognizing revenue.

In addition to the identification of the form of the income statements and the types of accounts that are part of the statement, two other aspects of the statement should be noted. For one, it should be observed that operating income is identified separately from extraordinary income. The two incomes make up net income. In addition, proper accounting (i.e., *interstatement* tax recognition) requires that those taxes relevant to ordinary income be identified with ordinary income, and those taxes relevant to extraordinary income be identified with extraordinary income.

Operating income is somewhat self explanatory. It is that income related to the normal income producing function of the firm. In the case of the construction firm it is primarily the income received from building projects. Extraordinary income is of a character significantly different from the typical business activity income of the firm. It has a material effect on income and its occurrence is not expected to recur frequently. The construction firm's selling of part of their central office, or condemnation of part of their branch offices would be considered as extraordinary items on the firm's income statement.

The separation of operating income and extraordinary income is important in that a better analysis of the firm can be made. In particular, most of the attention is drawn towards the trend in operating income in that extraordinary items while strongly influencing net income are viewed as occurring only once. In many cases there is a fine line between what is an operating income item and an extraordinary income item. The situation is made even more complex by the existence of *prior period adjustments*. A prior period adjustment is something that relates to prior periods and as such is excluded in the determination of net income for the current period. Such an item is recognized in the retained earnings statement only. Examples of prior period adjustments (which are rare in occurrence) include nonrecurring adjustments in income taxes and accounting errors resulting from erroneously entered transactions.

If shares of stock make up the contributed capital of the firm (as is true in the case of the corporation) yet another important aspect of the income statement should be noted. A recent A.I.C.P.A. opinion requires that several calculations of earnings per share of stock (E.P.S.) be shown on the firm's income statement. In particular, the E.P.S. is to be calculated and shown for income before extraordinary items (i.e., operating income), for extraordinary items, and for net income. In addition, if the firm has existing stock options outstanding, or has issued bonds or preferred stock that are convertible to common shares of stock, each of the three previously identified E.P.S. amounts should be shown for both outstanding stock, and for the fully diluted effect of the stock options, etc. As such, six different E.P.S. amounts can and should appear on the income statement when this is the case. Such a practice is in agreement with the full disclosure generally accepted accounting principle. It should be noted that even when the firm is not a corporation, differentiating between operating income, extraordinary income, rate of return from operating income, and rate of return from net income all aid in the analysis and evaluation of financial operations. This, of course, is the purpose of the income statement.

9.7.3 Statement of Changes in Financial Position

Not as widely published or recognized as the financial position or income statement, but of increasing significance and frequency is the statement of changes in financial position. The statement is viewed essential to the fair reporting of the causes of the changes in the financial position (i.e., the balance sheet) from one period to the next. While the income statement reports changes as a result of operations, it does not reflect all of the financial changes between two consecutive accounting periods. As such, the statement of changes in financial position has grown in acceptance and importance as to potential investors and creditors.

A recent A.I.C.P.A. opinion has made the statement of changes in financial position a mandatory statement for firms required by the S.E.C. to publish statements. The firm only has latitude as to the form of statement it presents. In particular, the statement of changes in financial position can be prepared on a *working capital basis* or on a *cash basis*. Regardless of which basis is used, the preparation of the statement of changes in financial position is less straightforward to prepare than the income statement or the financial position statement. Whereas the income statement and statement of financial position are merely the representation of summed accounts, the statement of changes in financial position requires the analysis of transactions. The statement of changes in financial position has three specific purposes. These are as follows.

(1) To report on all the financing and investing transactions of the firm.
(2) To report on the generation and application of funds (either on a working capital or cash basis).
(3) To report the causes of all of the changes in financial position during the period.

Similar to the income statement, the statement represents a period of time.

As indicated earlier, the statement of changes in financial position can be prepared on a working capital or cash basis. Whereas the working capital basis reports on changes in working capital, the cash basis reports only on changes in cash. The difference between current assets and current liabilities represents net available working capital. If working capital is increased, it is said to be *generated*. If it is decreased, it is said to be *applied*.

The cash basis is more informative and more in line with the needs of the construction industry. The statement of changes in financial position prepared on a cash basis is very useful in the cash planning and cash control that are necessary ingredients of operating a construction firm. The cash basis statement focuses on the critical financing strengths and weaknesses of the firm. Because of its frequent use by the construction industry and because of its superiority, only the cash basis prepared statement of changes in financial position will be discussed in detail in this section. However, in order to illustrate the difference between the two methods, let us consider some example transactions and their treatment using each of the two bases. The transactions and their affect on working capital and cash follow.

Transaction			Cash	Working Capital
1. Sell a Fixed Asset:				
Cash	5,000		5,000	5,000
Note Rec.—Short Term	4,000			4,000
Note Rec.—Long Term	10,000			
Accumulated Depr.	11,000			
Fixed Asset		28,000		
Gain		2,000		
Total Generated			5,000	9,000
2. Borrow from Bank:				
Cash	20,000		20,000	20,000
Note Payable—Short Term		10,000		−10,000
Note Payable—Long Term		10,000		
Total Generated			20,000	10,000
3. Purchase Asset:				
Fixed Asset	30,000			
Cash		10,000	10,000	10,000
Note Payable—Short Term		5,000		5,000
Note Payable—Long Term		15,000		
Total Applied			10,000	15,000
4. Depreciate Equipment:				
Depreciation Expense	10,000		0	
Accumulated Depreciation		10,000		0
Total Applied			0	0

5. Pay Off Debt:

Account Payable—Short Term	10,000			−10,000
Account Payable—Long Term	15,000			
Cash		25,000	25,000	25,000
Total Applied			25,000	15,000

Other than the noticing of the different affects of the transactions on working capital and cash, two other points should be noted. For one transaction one indicated a gain from the selling of an asset. While this gain is recognized in the calculation of income, it does not create working capital or cash. Secondly, inspection of transaction four indicates the depreciation expense (which is used in the calculation of net income) does not use working capital or cash. These latter two facts are sometimes used as a means of calculating the changes in working capital from operating income. In particular, the changes in working capital from net income (i.e., excluding extraordinary items) is calculated as follows.

Net Income	xxx
Plus—Depreciation	xxx
Minus—Gain on Sale of Fixed Asset	xxx
Working Capital Generated by Net Income	xxx

The point to be made is that depreciation is an expense that does not reduce net working capital (or cash) and an accounting gain from the sale of an asset does not increase net working capital (or cash).

Let us now turn our attention solely to the statement of changes in financial position prepared on a cash basis. A statement of changes in financial position prepared on a cash basis is shown in Fig. 9.15. The statement satisfies the minimum disclosure requirements of the A.I.C.P.A. As can be observed, the statement starts by reporting the cash generated from income before extraordinary items. However, whereas only depreciation has to be usually added back to the income when the working capital basis is used, other items such as inventory and receivables also have to be added back to income when the cash basis is used. Having reported cash generated from operations exclusive of extraordinary items, the statement goes on to report cash generated from the extraordinary items. Cash applied is then reported and a total increase or decrease in change in cash for the period is reported. Finally, while not affecting cash inflow or outflow, transactions that

Constructo Construction Company
Statement of Changes in Financial Position—Cash Basis
For the Year Ended December 31, 1975

Cash Generated:		
Income before Extraordinary Items		$ 35,000
Add Items not affecting Cash:		
Inventory Increase	$(7,000)	
Trade Receivables Decrease	2,000	
Depreciation Expense	2,000	(3,000)
Total Cash Generated by Operations Exclusive of Extraordinary Items		32,000
Extraordinary Items Generating Cash:		
Permanent Investments Sold		38,000
Other Sources of Cash:		
Bonds Payable Sold		10,000
Total Cash Generated		$ 80,000
Cash Applied:		
Land Purchased	28,000	
Notes—Short Term Paid	31,000	
Total Cash Applied		59,000
Increase in Cash for the Period		$ 21,000
Financing and Investing Activities Not Affecting Cash:		
Building Acquired, Gave Long Term Mortgage		125,000
Total		$125,000

Fig. 9.15. Statement of changes in financial position—construction firm.

involve financing and investing activities of the firm that do not affect cash are reported. This is done consistent with the more recent expanded purpose of the statement in changes in financial position.

9.8 Summary

Perhaps of all the types of business skills, the construction industry is least sophisticated in its financial accounting practices. This is extremely unfortunate when one considers the importance of financial accounting to the construction industry. While financial accounting is aimed at the producing of financial statements, it also proves useful in the control of costs, and in the short and long term decision making of the firm.

The financial accounting cycle can be viewed as consisting of journalizing, posting, adjusting, summarizing (i.e., a trial balance), closing, and producing of statements. Occasionally the cycle also includes the reversing of entries and the correction of errors. This cycle along with generally accepted accounting principles (G.A.A.P.) provide the framework of financial accounting. Through the use of this framework, the preparation of an income statement, a statement of financial position, and a statement of changes in financial position are made possible.

The construction industry while sharing many of the same accounting practices and principles of other industries, requires the use of some unique accounting principles and practices. For example, special attention is given to the fact that the ordinary construction project often takes a long duration to complete. This fact has resulted in acceptance of an unique means of recognizing revenue (i.e., the percentage of completion method). Similarly, special attention and accounting practices result because of the typical construction firm's high dependence on construction equipment and leasing.

While being a deserving topic in itself, financial accounting is not totally independent of such subject areas as law, cost accounting, or taxes. These subject areas have been discussed elsewhere.

Case 9.1. Closet Construction Company: Decision to Sell a Business

Mr. H. Closet is the sole proprietor of a medium-sized plumbing and heating business. Owing to the increasing amount of government contract work in his business territory and the fact that the federal government requires that union scale wages be paid on all government work, Closet is being pressured to unionize his shop. Sensing Closet's distaste for unions and knowing that he is near the age of retirement, a syndicate promoter, the Ulm Company, has extended a $100,000 cash offer for his business.

Closet, however, sees a large amount of business coming his way if he unionizes and receives the government contracts. He decides that if he does stay in business, he will definitely sell out in eight years. His investment in current assets (cash, inventory, accounts receivable) will be expanded by $24,000 because of the increased volume of business. His equipment will not be in very good condition eight years hence. He therefore expects to sell the business at the end of the eighth year for $40,000.

Closet estimates that the government contract work will result in a $200,000 increase in yearly sales. Nongovernment sales will remain constant at $400,000 a year. Direct material costs are proportional to sales. His direct labor costs are proportional to sales but will increase by 10% for all labor because of higher unionized wages. Variable overhead is assumed to vary with sales, and annual fixed overhead will total $60,000. Straight line depreciation will increase from $8,000 per year to $10,000 per year, because new equipment must be purchased for $16,000. All fixed assets will be fully depreciated at the end of eight years. Selling and administrative expenses will remain at $17,000. Disregard any tax effects.

CLOSET CONSTRUCTION COMPANY
Income Statement
(Last Year)

Sales		$400,000
Cost of goods sold:		
Direct materials	$125,000	
Direct Labor	175,000	
Variable overhead	30,000	
Fixed overhead	54,000	384,000
Gross Margin		16,000
Selling and administrative expense, fixed		17,000*
Net Income (loss)		$(1,000)

*Includes a $10,000 salary paid to Mr. Closet.

(1) Prepare an income statement, assuming that there will be $200,000 of government contract work and that all costs will vary as stated above. This statement will be applicable to any of the next eight years.

(2) Assume that his minimum desired rate of return is 8% and that Closet considers his annual net cash flow as his $10,000 salary plus any cash flow from operations. Should Closet sell his business now, or continue in business for another eight years as a union shop? If he sold out, Closet would retire and not work elsewhere. Assume that all additional investments in the business by Closet will be made immediately.

(3) Discuss the limitations of the analysis that influenced your recommendation.

Case 9.2. Heavy Construction Company: Projected Statements

Heavy Construction Company specializes in the construction of heavy and highway projects. Because of the large scale nature of two upcoming projects and because of the need to purchase new equipment, the owners of the firm have determined that they need cash budgets and projected income statements for calender years 1975, 1976, and 1977.

Heavy Company uses the completed contract method of accounting whereby construction costs are capitalized (considered an asset) until the contract is completed. Since all general and administration expenses can be identified with a particular contract, they also are capitalized (work in progress) until the contract is completed.

Heavy's December 31, 1974 balance sheet is as follows.

Assets		Liabilities & Net Worth	
Cash	$ 72,000	Loans Payable	$ —
Due on contracts	—	Accrued Construction costs	612,4
Costs of uncompleted contracts in excess of billings	—	Accrued income tax payable	65,00
Plant and equipment	$2,800,000	Common stock ($10 par)	500,00
Less accumulated depreciation	129,600	Paid in capital	100,00
Total	$2,742,400	Retained earnings	1,465,00
		Total	$2,742,4

Two contracts will be started in 1975—Contract A and Contract B. Contract A and Contract B are expected to be completed in December 1976 and December 1977, respectively. No other contracts will be started until after contracts A and B are completed. All other outstanding contracts had been completed in 1974.

Total estimated revenue for Contract A is $2,000,000 and for Contract B is $1,500,000. The estimated cash collections per year are as follows.

	1975	1976	1977
Contract A	$ 800,000	$1,200,000	—
Contract B	300,000	450,000	$750,000
	$1,100,000	$1,650,000	$750,000

Estimated construction costs to be incurred are estimated as follows.

	Contract A	Contract B
1975	$ 720,000	$ 250,000
1976	1,000,000	400,000
1977	—	650,000
	$1,720,000	$1,300,000

Depreciation expense is included in these estimated construction costs. For 1975, 10% of the estimated construction costs represents depreciation expense. For 1976 and 1977, 15% of the estimated construction costs represent depreciation expense. The cash portion of these estimated construction costs is paid as follows: 70% in the year incurred and 30% in the following year.

Total general and administrative expenses (not included in construction costs) consist of a fixed portion each year for each contract, and a variable portion which is a function of cash collected each year. For the two prior years, cash collected and total general and administrative expenses (based on one contract in each year) were as follows.

	Cash Collected	Total general & administrative expense
1974	$1,350,000	$27,250
1973	1,180,000	24,700

The general and administrative expenses all represent cash expenses and are paid in the year incurred.

Dividends are expected to be distributed as follows.

1975 Stock—10% of common stock outstanding
1976 Stock split—2 for 1
1977 Cash—$1.00 per share
    Heavy Company will acquire a new asset in 1976 for $700,000 and plans to pay for it that year. When the cash balance falls below $70,000, Heavy Company obtains short term loans in multiples of $10,000. The interest rate is 10% per year.

    You are to prepare projected income statements for the years 1976 and 1977. Assume the firm's effective tax rate is 40%. Also prepare cash budgets for the years 1975, 1976, and 1977. The preparation of such budgets is discussed in Chapter 7.

Case 9.3. Option Construction Company: Alternative Methods of Revenue Recognition

    The owners of the Option Construction Company have consulted you to aid them in determining how they should report income from their long term contracts. It is trying to choose between the percentage of completion and completed contract method. In particular the firm would like to know the difference in taxable income for 1975 for the two methods.

    This is the firm's first year of operation. Construction activities for the year ended December 31, 1975 are as follows.

Project	Total Contract Price	Billings Thru Dec. 31, 1975	Cash Collections Thru Dec. 31, 1975	Contract Costs Incurred Thru Dec. 31, 1975	Estimated Additional Costs to Complete Contracts
A	$ 520,000	$ 350,000	310,000	$ 424,000	$ 106,000
B	670,000	210,000	210,000	126,000	504,000
C	475,000	475,000	395,000	315,000	—
D	200,000	70,000	50,000	112,750	92,250
E	460,000	400,000	400,000	370,000	30,000
	$2,325,000	$1,505,000	$1,365,000	$1,347,750	$732,250

All the contracts are with different clients. Any work remaining to be done is expected to be completed in 1976.

In order to be able to determine the difference in reportable 1975 income for tax purposes, prepare income (or loss) schedules using the percentage of completion method and the completed contract method. Assume that selling, general, and administrative expenses for 1975 for Option Company were $65,000.

Appendix A

Interest Tables

The time value of money is often an important factor to consider in choosing one of several alternatives. The value of money at a particular point in time may be found through the use of interest formulas. The values of these formulas are a function of time (n), and the interest rate (i) affecting the money over the defined time period. If the interest rate is constant over the time period n, the value of a particular interest formula may be found by substituting the values of n and i into the formula. Each table which follows assumes a fixed interest rate, i, as given above the table. The values of 6 different interest formulas are given in each table as a function of n. The 6 interest formulas given are single payment compound amount, single payment present worth, sinking fund factor, capital recovery factor, uniform series compound amount, and uniform series present worth.

4 per cent Compound Interest Factors

	SINGLE PAYMENT		UNIFORM SERIES				
	Compound Amount Factor caf'	Present Worth Factor pwf'	Sinking Fund Factor sff	Capital Recovery Factor crf	Compound Amount Factor caf	Present Worth Factor pwf	
n	Given P To find S $(1+i)^n$	Given S To find P $\dfrac{1}{(1+i)^n}$	Given S To find R $\dfrac{i}{(1+i)^n-1}$	Given P To find R $\dfrac{i(1+i)^n}{(1+i)^n-1}$	Given R To find S $\dfrac{(1+i)^n-1}{i}$	Given R To find P $\dfrac{(1+i)^n-1}{i(1+i)^n}$	n
1	1.040	0.9615	1.00000	1.04000	1.000	0.962	1
2	1.082	0.9246	0.49020	0.53020	2.040	1.886	2
3	1.125	0.8890	0.32035	0.36035	3.122	2.775	3
4	1.170	0.8548	0.23549	0.27549	4.246	3.630	4
5	1.217	0.8219	0.18463	0.22463	5.416	4.452	5
6	1.265	0.7903	0.15076	0.19076	6.633	5.242	6
7	1.316	0.7599	0.12661	0.16661	7.898	6.002	7
8	1.369	0.7307	0.10853	0.14853	9.214	6.733	8
9	1.423	0.7026	0.09449	0.13449	10.583	7.435	9
10	1.480	0.6756	0.08329	0.12329	12.006	8.111	10
11	1.539	0.6496	0.07415	0.11415	13.486	8.760	11
12	1.601	0.6246	0.06655	0.10655	15.026	9.385	12
13	1.665	0.6006	0.06014	0.10014	16.627	9.986	13
14	1.732	0.5775	0.05467	0.09467	18.292	10.563	14
15	1.801	0.5553	0.04994	0.08994	20.024	11.118	15
16	1.873	0.5339	0.04582	0.08582	21.825	11.652	16
17	1.948	0.5134	0.04220	0.08220	23.698	12.166	17
18	2.026	0.4936	0.03899	0.07899	25.645	12.659	18
19	2.107	0.4746	0.03614	0.07614	27.671	13.134	19
20	2.191	0.4564	0.03358	0.07358	29.778	13.590	20
21	2.279	0.4388	0.03128	0.07128	31.969	14.029	21
22	2.370	0.4220	0.02920	0.06920	34.248	14.451	22
23	2.465	0.4057	0.02731	0.06731	36.618	14.857	23
24	2.563	0.3901	0.02559	0.06559	39.083	15.247	24
25	2.666	0.3751	0.02401	0.06401	41.646	15.622	25
26	2.772	0.3607	0.02257	0.06257	44.312	15.983	26
27	2.883	0.3468	0.02124	0.06124	47.084	16.330	27
28	2.999	0.3335	0.02001	0.06001	49.968	16.663	28
29	3.119	0.3207	0.01888	0.05888	52.966	16.984	29
30	3.243	0.3083	0.01783	0.05783	56.085	17.292	30
31	3.373	0.2965	0.01686	0.05686	59.328	17.588	31
32	3.508	0.2851	0.01595	0.05595	62.701	17.874	32
33	3.648	0.2741	0.01510	0.05510	66.210	18.148	33
34	3.794	0.2636	0.01431	0.05431	69.858	18.411	34
35	3.946	0.2534	0.01358	0.05358	73.652	18.665	35
40	4.801	0.2083	0.01052	0.05052	95.026	19.793	40
45	5.841	0.1712	0.00826	0.04826	121.029	20.720	45
50	7.107	0.1407	0.00655	0.04655	152.667	21.482	50
55	8.646	0.1157	0.00523	0.04523	191.159	22.109	55
60	10.520	0.0951	0.00420	0.04420	237.991	22.623	60
65	12.799	0.0781	0.00339	0.04339	294.968	23.047	65
70	15.572	0.0642	0.00275	0.04275	364.290	23.395	70
75	18.945	0.0528	0.00223	0.04223	448.631	23.680	75
80	23.050	0.0434	0.00181	0.04181	551.245	23.915	80
85	28.044	0.0357	0.00148	0.04148	676.090	24.109	85
90	34.119	0.0293	0.00121	0.04121	827.983	24.267	90
95	41.511	0.0241	0.00099	0.04099	1012.785	24.398	95
100	50.505	0.0198	0.00081	0.04081	1237.624	24.505	100

4½ per cent Compound Interest Factors

	SINGLE PAYMENT		UNIFORM SERIES				
	Compound Amount Factor caf'	Present Worth Factor pwf'	Sinking Fund Factor sff	Capital Recovery Factor crf	Compound Amount Factor caf	Present Worth Factor pwf	
n	Given P To find S $(1+i)^n$	Given S To find P $\dfrac{1}{(1+i)^n}$	Given S To find R $\dfrac{i}{(1+i)^n-1}$	Given P To find R $\dfrac{i(1+i)^n}{(1+i)^n-1}$	Given R To find S $\dfrac{(1+i)^n-1}{i}$	Given R To find P $\dfrac{(1+i)^n-1}{i(1+i)^n}$	n
1	1.045	0.9569	1.00000	1.04500	1.000	0.957	1
2	1.092	0.9157	0.48900	0.53400	2.045	1.873	2
3	1.141	0.8763	0.31877	0.36377	3.137	2.749	3
4	1.193	0.8386	0.23374	0.27874	4.278	3.588	4
5	1.246	0.8025	0.18279	0.22779	5.471	4.390	5
6	1.302	0.7679	0.14888	0.19388	6.717	5.158	6
7	1.361	0.7348	0.12470	0.16970	8.019	5.893	7
8	1.422	0.7032	0.10661	0.15161	9.380	6.596	8
9	1.486	0.6729	0.09257	0.13757	10.802	7.269	9
10	1.553	0.6439	0.08138	0.12638	12.288	7.913	10
11	1.623	0.6162	0.07225	0.11725	13.841	8.529	11
12	1.696	0.5897	0.06467	0.10967	15.464	9.119	12
13	1.772	0.5643	0.05828	0.10328	17.160	9.683	13
14	1.852	0.5400	0.05282	0.09782	18.932	10.223	14
15	1.935	0.5167	0.04811	0.09311	20.784	10.740	15
16	2.022	0.4945	0.04402	0.08902	22.719	11.234	16
17	2.113	0.4732	0.04042	0.08542	24.742	11.707	17
18	2.208	0.4528	0.03724	0.08224	26.855	12.160	18
19	2.308	0.4333	0.03441	0.07941	29.064	12.593	19
20	2.412	0.4146	0.03188	0.07688	31.371	13.008	20
21	2.520	0.3968	0.02960	0.07460	33.783	13.405	21
22	2.634	0.3797	0.02755	0.07255	36.303	13.784	22
23	2.752	0.3634	0.02568	0.07068	38.937	14.148	23
24	2.876	0.3477	0.02399	0.06899	41.689	14.495	24
25	3.005	0.3327	0.02244	0.06744	44.565	14.828	25
26	3.141	0.3184	0.02102	0.06602	47.571	15.147	26
27	3.282	0.3047	0.01972	0.06472	50.711	15.451	27
28	3.430	0.2916	0.01852	0.06352	53.993	15.743	28
29	3.584	0.2790	0.01741	0.06241	57.423	16.022	29
30	3.745	0.2670	0.01639	0.06139	61.007	16.289	30
31	3.914	0.2555	0.01544	0.06044	64.752	16.544	31
32	4.090	0.2445	0.01456	0.05956	68.666	16.789	32
33	4.274	0.2340	0.01374	0.05874	72.756	17.023	33
34	4.466	0.2239	0.01298	0.05798	77.030	17.247	34
35	4.667	0.2143	0.01227	0.05727	81.497	17.471	35
40	5.816	0.1719	0.00934	0.05434	107.030	18.402	40
45	7.248	0.1380	0.00720	0.05220	138.850	19.156	45
50	9.033	0.1107	0.00560	0.05060	178.503	19.762	50
55	11.256	0.0888	0.00439	0.04939	227.918	20.248	55
60	14.027	0.0713	0.00345	0.04845	289.498	20.638	60
65	17.481	0.0572	0.00273	0.04773	366.238	20.951	65
70	21.784	0.0459	0.00217	0.04717	461.870	21.202	70
75	27.147	0.0368	0.00172	0.04672	581.044	21.404	75
80	33.830	0.0296	0.00137	0.04637	729.558	21.565	80
85	42.158	0.0237	0.00109	0.04609	914.632	21.695	85
90	52.537	0.0190	0.00087	0.04587	1145.269	21.799	90
95	65.471	0.0153	0.00070	0.04570	1432.684	21.883	95
100	81.589	0.0123	0.00056	0.04556	1790.856	21.950	100

5 per cent Compound Interest Factors

	SINGLE PAYMENT		UNIFORM SERIES				
	Compound Amount Factor caf'	Present Worth Factor pwf'	Sinking Fund Factor sff	Capital Recovery Factor crf	Compound Amount Factor caf	Present Worth Factor pwf	
n	Given P To find S $(1+i)^n$	Given S To find P $\dfrac{1}{(1+i)^n}$	Given S To find R $\dfrac{i}{(1+i)^n-1}$	Given P To find R $\dfrac{i(1+i)^n}{(1+i)^n-1}$	Given R To find S $\dfrac{(1+i)^n-1}{i}$	Given R To find P $\dfrac{(1+i)^n-1}{i(1+i)^n}$	n
1	1.050	0.9524	1.00000	1.05000	1.000	0.952	1
2	1.103	0.9070	0.48780	0.53780	2.050	1.859	2
3	1.158	0.8638	0.31721	0.36721	3.153	2.723	3
4	1.216	0.8227	0.23201	0.28201	4.310	3.546	4
5	1.276	0.7835	0.18097	0.23097	5.526	4.329	5
6	1.340	0.7462	0.14702	0.19702	6.802	5.076	6
7	1.407	0.7107	0.12282	0.17282	8.142	5.786	7
8	1.477	0.6768	0.10472	0.15472	9.549	6.463	8
9	1.551	0.6446	0.09069	0.14069	11.027	7.108	9
10	1.629	0.6139	0.07950	0.12950	12.578	7.722	10
11	1.710	0.5847	0.07039	0.12039	14.207	8.306	11
12	1.796	0.5568	0.06283	0.11283	15.917	8.863	12
13	1.886	0.5303	0.05646	0.10646	17.713	9.394	13
14	1.980	0.5051	0.05102	0.10102	19.599	9.899	14
15	2.079	0.4810	0.04634	0.09634	21.579	10.380	15
16	2.183	0.4581	0.04227	0.09227	23.657	10.838	16
17	2.292	0.4363	0.03870	0.08870	25.840	11.274	17
18	2.407	0.4155	0.03555	0.08555	28.132	11.690	18
19	2.527	0.3957	0.03275	0.08275	30.539	12.085	19
20	2.653	0.3769	0.03024	0.08024	33.066	12.462	20
21	2.786	0.3589	0.02800	0.07800	35.719	12.821	21
22	2.925	0.3418	0.02597	0.07597	38.505	13.163	22
23	3.072	0.3256	0.02414	0.07414	41.430	13.489	23
24	3.225	0.3101	0.02247	0.07247	44.502	13.799	24
25	3.386	0.2953	0.02095	0.07095	47.727	14.094	25
26	3.556	0.2812	0.01956	0.06956	51.113	14.375	26
27	3.733	0.2678	0.01829	0.06829	54.669	14.643	27
28	3.920	0.2551	0.01712	0.06712	58.403	14.898	28
29	4.116	0.2429	0.01605	0.06605	62.323	15.141	29
30	4.322	0.2314	0.01505	0.06505	66.439	15.372	30
31	4.538	0.2204	0.01413	0.06413	70.761	15.593	31
32	4.765	0.2099	0.01328	0.06328	75.299	15.803	32
33	5.003	0.1999	0.01249	0.06249	80.064	16.003	33
34	5.253	0.1904	0.01176	0.06176	85.067	16.193	34
35	5.516	0.1813	0.01107	0.06107	90.320	16.374	35
40	7.040	0.1420	0.00828	0.05828	120.800	17.159	40
45	8.985	0.1113	0.00626	0.05626	159.700	17.774	45
50	11.467	0.0872	0.00478	0.05478	209.348	18.256	50
55	14.636	0.0683	0.00367	0.05367	272.713	18.633	55
60	18.679	0.0535	0.00283	0.05283	353.584	18.929	60
65	23.840	0.0419	0.00219	0.05219	456.798	19.161	65
70	30.426	0.0329	0.00170	0.05170	588.529	19.343	70
75	38.833	0.0258	0.00132	0.05132	756.654	19.485	75
80	49.561	0.0202	0.00103	0.05103	971.229	19.596	80
85	63.254	0.0158	0.00080	0.05080	1245.087	19.684	85
90	80.730	0.0124	0.00063	0.05063	1594.607	19.752	90
95	103.035	0.0097	0.00049	0.05049	2040.694	19.806	95
100	131.501	0.0076	0.00038	0.05038	2610.025	19.848	100

5½ per cent Compound Interest Factors

	SINGLE PAYMENT		UNIFORM SERIES				
	Compound Amount Factor caf'	Present Worth Factor pwf'	Sinking Fund Factor sff	Capital Recovery Factor crf	Compound Amount Factor caf	Present Worth Factor pwf	
n	Given P To find S $(1+i)^n$	Given S To find P $\dfrac{1}{(1+i)^n}$	Given S To find R $\dfrac{i}{(1+i)^n-1}$	Given P To find R $\dfrac{i(1+i)^n}{(1+i)^n-1}$	Given R To find S $\dfrac{(1+i)^n-1}{i}$	Given R To find P $\dfrac{(1+i)^n-1}{i(1+i)^n}$	n
1	1.055	0.9479	1.00000	1.05500	1.000	0.948	1
2	1.113	0.8985	0.48662	0.54162	2.055	1.846	2
3	1.174	0.8516	0.31565	0.37065	3.168	2.698	3
4	1.239	0.8072	0.23029	0.28529	4.342	3.505	4
5	1.307	0.7651	0.17918	0.23418	5.581	4.270	5
6	1.379	0.7252	0.14518	0.20018	6.888	4.996	6
7	1.455	0.6874	0.12096	0.17596	8.267	5.683	7
8	1.535	0.6516	0.10286	0.15786	9.722	6.335	8
9	1.619	0.6176	0.08884	0.14384	11.256	6.952	9
10	1.708	0.5854	0.07767	0.13267	12.875	7.538	10
11	1.802	0.5549	0.06857	0.12357	14.583	8.093	11
12	1.901	0.5260	0.06103	0.11603	16.386	8.619	12
13	2.006	0.4986	0.05468	0.10968	18.287	9.117	13
14	2.116	0.4726	0.04928	0.10428	20.293	9.590	14
15	2.232	0.4479	0.04463	0.09963	22.409	10.038	15
16	2.355	0.4246	0.04058	0.09558	24.641	10.462	16
17	2.485	0.4024	0.03704	0.09204	26.996	10.865	17
18	2.621	0.3815	0.03392	0.08892	29.481	11.246	18
19	2.766	0.3616	0.03115	0.08615	32.103	11.608	19
20	2.918	0.3427	0.02868	0.08368	34.868	11.950	20
21	3.078	0.3249	0.02646	0.08146	37.786	12.275	21
22	3.248	0.3079	0.02447	0.07947	40.864	12.583	22
23	3.426	0.2919	0.02267	0.07767	44.112	12.875	23
24	3.615	0.2767	0.02104	0.07604	47.538	13.152	24
25	3.813	0.2622	0.01955	0.07455	51.153	13.414	25
26	4.023	0.2486	0.01819	0.07319	54.966	13.662	26
27	4.244	0.2356	0.01695	0.07195	58.989	13.898	27
28	4.478	0.2233	0.01581	0.07081	63.234	14.121	28
29	4.724	0.2117	0.01477	0.06977	67.711	14.333	29
30	4.984	0.2006	0.01381	0.06881	72.435	14.534	30
31	5.258	0.1902	0.01292	0.06792	77.419	14.724	31
32	5.547	0.1803	0.01210	0.06710	82.677	14.904	32
33	5.852	0.1709	0.01133	0.06633	88.225	15.075	33
34	6.174	0.1620	0.01063	0.06563	94.077	15.237	34
35	6.514	0.1535	0.00997	0.06497	100.251	15.391	35
40	8.513	0.1175	0.00732	0.06232	136.606	16.046	40
45	11.127	0.0899	0.00543	0.06043	184.119	16.548	45
50	14.542	0.0688	0.00406	0.05906	246.217	16.932	50
55	19.006	0.0526	0.00305	0.05805	327.377	17.225	55
60	24.840	0.0403	0.00231	0.05731	433.450	17.450	60
65	32.465	0.0308	0.00175	0.05675	572.083	17.622	65
70	42.430	0.0236	0.00133	0.05633	753.271	17.753	70
75	55.454	0.0180	0.00101	0.05601	990.076	17.854	75
80	72.476	0.0138	0.00077	0.05577	1299.571	17.931	80
85	94.724	0.0106	0.00059	0.05559	1704.069	17.990	85
90	123.800	0.0081	0.00045	0.05545	2232.731	18.035	90
95	161.802	0.0062	0.00034	0.05534	2923.671	18.069	95
100	211.469	0.0047	0.00026	0.05526	3826.702	18.096	100

6 per cent Compound Interest Factors

| | SINGLE PAYMENT | | UNIFORM SERIES | | | | |
| | Compound Amount Factor caf′ | Present Worth Factor pwf′ | Sinking Fund Factor sff | Capital Recovery Factor crf | Compound Amount Factor caf | Present Worth Factor pwf | |
n	Given P To find S $(1+i)^n$	Given S To find P $\dfrac{1}{(1+i)^n}$	Given S To find R $\dfrac{i}{(1+i)^n-1}$	Given P To find R $\dfrac{i(1+i)^n}{(1+i)^n-1}$	Given R To find S $\dfrac{(1+i)^n-1}{i}$	Given R To find P $\dfrac{(1+i)^n-1}{i(1+i)^n}$	n
1	1.060	0.9434	1.00000	1.06000	1.000	0.943	1
2	1.124	0.8900	0.48544	0.54544	2.060	1.833	2
3	1.191	0.8396	0.31411	0.37411	3.184	2.673	3
4	1.262	0.7921	0.22859	0.28859	4.375	3.465	4
5	1.338	0.7473	0.17740	0.23740	5.637	4.212	5
6	1.419	0.7050	0.14336	0.20336	6.975	4.917	6
7	1.504	0.6651	0.11914	0.17914	8.394	5.582	7
8	1.594	0.6274	0.10104	0.16104	9.897	6.210	8
9	1.689	0.5919	0.08702	0.14702	11.491	6.802	9
10	1.791	0.5584	0.07587	0.13587	13.181	7.360	10
11	1.898	0.5268	0.06679	0.12679	14.972	7.887	11
12	2.012	0.4970	0.05928	0.11928	16.870	8.384	12
13	2.133	0.4688	0.05296	0.11296	18.882	8.853	13
14	2.261	0.4423	0.04758	0.10758	21.015	9.295	14
15	2.397	0.4173	0.04296	0.10296	23.276	9.712	15
16	2.540	0.3936	0.03895	0.09895	25.673	10.106	16
17	2.693	0.3714	0.03544	0.09544	28.213	10.477	17
18	2.854	0.3503	0.03236	0.09236	30.906	10.828	18
19	3.026	0.3305	0.02962	0.08962	33.760	11.158	19
20	3.207	0.3118	0.02718	0.08718	36.786	11.470	20
21	3.400	0.2942	0.02500	0.08500	39.993	11.764	21
22	3.604	0.2775	0.02305	0.08305	43.392	12.042	22
23	3.820	0.2618	0.02128	0.08128	46.996	12.303	23
24	4.049	0.2470	0.01968	0.07968	50.816	12.550	24
25	4.292	0.2330	0.01823	0.07823	54.865	12.783	25
26	4.549	0.2198	0.01690	0.07690	59.156	13.003	26
27	4.822	0.2074	0.01570	0.07570	63.706	13.211	27
28	5.112	0.1956	0.01459	0.07459	68.528	13.406	28
29	5.418	0.1846	0.01358	0.07358	73.640	13.591	29
30	5.743	0.1741	0.01265	0.07265	79.058	13.765	30
31	6.088	0.1643	0.01179	0.07179	84.802	13.929	31
32	6.453	0.1550	0.01100	0.07100	90.890	14.084	32
33	6.841	0.1462	0.01027	0.07027	97.343	14.230	33
34	7.251	0.1379	0.00960	0.06960	104.184	14.368	34
35	7.686	0.1301	0.00897	0.06987	111.435	14.498	35
40	10.286	0.0972	0.00646	0.06646	154.762	15.046	40
45	13.765	0.0727	0.00470	0.06470	212.744	15.456	45
50	18.420	0.0543	0.00344	0.06344	290.336	15.762	50
55	24.650	0.0406	0.00254	0.06254	394.172	15.991	55
60	32.988	0.0303	0.00188	0.06188	533.128	16.161	60
65	44.145	0.0227	0.00139	0.06139	719.083	16.289	65
70	59.076	0.0169	0.00103	0.06103	967.932	16.385	70
75	79.057	0.0126	0.00077	0.06077	1300.949	16.456	75
80	105.796	0.0095	0.00057	0.06057	1746.600	16.509	80
85	141.579	0.0071	0.00043	0.06043	2342.982	16.549	85
90	189.465	0.0053	0.00032	0.06032	3141.075	16.579	90
95	253.546	0.0039	0.00024	0.06024	4209.104	16.601	95
100	339.302	0.0029	0.00018	0.06018	5638.368	16.618	100

7 per cent Compound Interest Factors

	SINGLE PAYMENT		UNIFORM SERIES				
	Compound Amount Factor caf′	Present Worth Factor pwf′	Sinking Fund Factor sff	Capital Recovery Factor crf	Compound Amount Factor caf	Present Worth Factor pwf	
n	Given P To find S $(1+i)^n$	Given S To find P $\dfrac{1}{(1+i)^n}$	Given S To find R $\dfrac{i}{(1+i)^n-1}$	Given P To find R $\dfrac{i(1+i)^n}{(1+i)^n-1}$	Given R To find S $\dfrac{(1+i)^n-1}{i}$	Given R To find P $\dfrac{(1+i)^n-1}{i(1+i)^n}$	n
1	1.070	0.9346	1.00000	1.07000	1.000	0.935	1
2	1.145	0.8734	0.48309	0.55309	2.070	1.808	2
3	1.225	0.8163	0.31105	0.38105	3.215	2.624	3
4	1.311	0.7629	0.22523	0.29523	4.440	3.387	4
5	1.403	0.7130	0.17389	0.24389	5.751	4.100	5
6	1.501	0.6663	0.13980	0.20980	7.153	4.767	6
7	1.606	0.6227	0.11555	0.18555	8.654	5.389	7
8	1.718	0.5820	0.09747	0.16747	10.260	5.971	8
9	1.838	0.5439	0.08349	0.15349	11.978	6.515	9
10	1.967	0.5083	0.07238	0.14238	13.816	7.024	10
11	2.105	0.4751	0.06336	0.13336	15.784	7.499	11
12	2.252	0.4440	0.05590	0.12590	17.888	7.943	12
13	2.410	0.4150	0.04965	0.11965	20.141	8.358	13
14	2.579	0.3878	0.04434	0.11434	22.550	8.745	14
15	2.759	0.3624	0.03979	0.10979	25.129	9.108	15
16	2.952	0.3387	0.03586	0.10586	27.888	9.447	16
17	3.159	0.3166	0.03243	0.10243	30.840	9.763	17
18	3.380	0.2959	0.02941	0.09941	33.999	10.059	18
19	3.617	0.2765	0.02675	0.09675	37.379	10.336	19
20	3.870	0.2584	0.02439	0.09439	40.995	10.594	20
21	4.141	0.2415	0.02229	0.09229	44.865	10.836	21
22	4.430	0.2257	0.02041	0.09041	49.006	11.061	22
23	4.741	0.2109	0.01871	0.08871	53.436	11.272	23
24	5.072	0.1971	0.01719	0.08719	58.177	11.469	24
25	5.427	0.1842	0.01581	0.08581	63.249	11.654	25
26	5.807	0.1722	0.01456	0.08456	68.676	11.826	26
27	6.214	0.1609	0.01343	0.08343	74.484	11.987	27
28	6.649	0.1504	0.01239	0.08239	80.698	12.137	28
29	7.114	0.1406	0.01145	0.08145	87.347	12.278	29
30	7.612	0.1314	0.01059	0.08059	94.461	12.409	30
31	8.145	0.1228	0.00980	0.07980	102.073	12.532	31
32	8.715	0.1147	0.00907	0.07907	110.218	12.647	32
33	9.325	0.1072	0.00841	0.07841	118.933	12.754	33
34	9.978	0.1002	0.00780	0.07780	128.259	12.854	34
35	10.677	0.0937	0.00723	0.07723	138.237	12.948	35
40	14.974	0.0668	0.00501	0.07501	199.635	13.332	40
45	21.002	0.0476	0.00350	0.07350	285.749	13.606	45
50	29.457	0.0339	0.00246	0.07246	406.529	13.801	50
55	41.315	0.0242	0.00174	0.07174	575.929	13.940	55
60	57.946	0.0173	0.00123	0.07123	813.520	14.039	60
65	81.273	0.0123	0.00087	0.07087	1146.755	14.110	65
70	113.989	0.0088	0.00062	0.07062	1614.134	14.160	70
75	159.876	0.0063	0.00044	0.07044	2269.657	14.196	75
80	224.234	0.0045	0.00031	0.07031	3189.063	14.222	80
85	314.500	0.0032	0.00022	0.07022	4478.576	14.240	85
90	441.103	0.0023	0.00016	0.07016	6287.185	14.253	90
95	618.670	0.0016	0.00011	0.07011	8823.854	14.263	95
100	867.716	0.0012	0.00008	0.07008	12381.662	14.269	100

8 per cent Compound Interest Factors

	SINGLE PAYMENT		UNIFORM SERIES				
	Compound Amount Factor caf′	Present Worth Factor pwf′	Sinking Fund Factor sff	Capital Recovery Factor crf	Compound Amount Factor caf	Present Worth Factor pwf	
n	Given P To find S $(1+i)^n$	Given S To find P $\dfrac{1}{(1+i)^n}$	Given S To find R $\dfrac{i}{(1+i)^n-1}$	Given P To find R $\dfrac{i(1+i)^n}{(1+i)^n-1}$	Given R To find S $\dfrac{(1+i)^n-1}{i}$	Given R To find P $\dfrac{(1+i)^n-1}{i(1+i)^n}$	n
1	1.080	0.9259	1.00000	1.08000	1.000	0.926	1
2	1.166	0.8573	0.48077	0.56077	2.080	1.783	2
3	1.260	0.7938	0.30803	0.38803	3.246	2.577	3
4	1.360	0.7350	0.22192	0.30192	4.506	3.312	4
5	1.469	0.6806	0.17046	0.25046	5.867	3.993	5
6	1.587	0.6302	0.13632	0.21632	7.336	4.623	6
7	1.714	0.5835	0.11207	0.19207	8.923	5.206	7
8	1.851	0.5403	0.09401	0.17401	10.637	5.747	8
9	1.999	0.5002	0.08008	0.16008	12.488	6.247	9
10	2.159	0.4632	0.06903	0.14903	14.487	6.710	10
11	2.332	0.4289	0.06008	0.14008	16.645	7.139	11
12	2.518	0.3971	0.05270	0.13270	18.977	7.536	12
13	2.720	0.3677	0.04652	0.12652	21.495	7.904	13
14	2.937	0.3405	0.04130	0.12130	24.215	8.244	14
15	3.172	0.3152	0.03683	0.11683	27.152	8.559	15
16	3.426	0.2919	0.03298	0.11298	30.324	8.851	16
17	3.700	0.2703	0.02963	0.10963	33.750	9.122	17
18	3.996	0.2502	0.02670	0.10670	37.450	9.372	18
19	4.316	0.2317	0.02413	0.10413	41.446	9.604	19
20	4.661	0.2145	0.02185	0.10185	45.762	9.818	20
21	5.034	0.1987	0.01983	0.09983	50.423	10.017	21
22	5.437	0.1839	0.01803	0.09803	55.457	10.201	22
23	5.871	0.1703	0.01642	0.09642	60.893	10.371	23
24	6.341	0.1577	0.01498	0.09498	66.765	10.529	24
25	6.848	0.1460	0.01368	0.09368	73.106	10.675	25
26	7.396	0.1352	0.01251	0.09251	79.954	10.810	26
27	7.988	0.1252	0.01145	0.09145	87.351	10.935	27
28	8.627	0.1159	0.01049	0.09049	95.339	11.051	28
29	9.317	0.1073	0.00962	0.08962	103.966	11.158	29
30	10.063	0.0994	0.00883	0.08883	113.283	11.258	30
31	10.868	0.0920	0.00811	0.08811	123.346	11.350	31
32	11.737	0.0852	0.00745	0.08745	134.214	11.435	32
33	12.676	0.0789	0.00685	0.08685	145.951	11.514	33
34	13.690	0.0730	0.00630	0.08630	158.627	11.587	34
35	14.785	0.0676	0.00580	0.08580	172.317	11.655	35
40	21.725	0.0460	0.00386	0.08386	259.057	11.925	40
45	31.920	0.0313	0.00259	0.08259	386.506	12.108	45
50	46.902	0.0213	0.00174	0.08174	573.770	12.233	50
55	68.914	0.0145	0.00118	0.08118	848.923	12.319	55
60	101.257	0.0099	0.00080	0.08080	1253.213	12.377	60
65	148.780	0.0067	0.00054	0.08054	1847.248	12.416	65
70	218.606	0.0046	0.00037	0.08037	2720.080	12.443	70
75	321.205	0.0031	0.00025	0.08025	4002.557	12.461	75
80	471.955	0.0021	0.00017	0.08017	5886.935	12.474	80
85	693.456	0.0014	0.00012	0.08012	8655.706	12.482	85
90	1018.915	0.0010	0.00008	0.08008	12723.939	12.488	90
95	1497.121	0.0007	0.00005	0.08005	18701.507	12.492	95
100	2199.761	0.0005	0.00004	0.08004	27484.516	12.494	100

10 per cent Compound Interest Factors

	SINGLE PAYMENT		UNIFORM SERIES				
	Compound Amount Factor caf'	Present Worth Factor pwf'	Sinking Fund Factor sff	Capital Recovery Factor crf	Compound Amount Factor caf	Present Worth Factor pwf	
n	Given P To find S $(1+i)^n$	Given S To find P $\dfrac{1}{(1+i)^n}$	Given S To find R $\dfrac{i}{(1+i)^n-1}$	Given P To find R $\dfrac{i(1+i)^n}{(1+i)^n-1}$	Given R To find S $\dfrac{(1+i)^n-1}{i}$	Given R To find P $\dfrac{(1+i)^n-1}{i(1+i)^n}$	n
1	1.100	0.9091	1.00000	1.10000	1.000	0.909	1
2	1.210	0.8264	0.47619	0.57619	2.100	1.736	2
3	1.331	0.7513	0.30211	0.40211	3.310	2.487	3
4	1.464	0.6830	0.21547	0.31547	4.641	3.170	4
5	1.611	0.6209	0.16380	0.26380	6.105	3.791	5
6	1.772	0.5645	0.12961	0.22961	7.716	4.355	6
7	1.949	0.5132	0.10541	0.20541	9.487	4.868	7
8	2.144	0.4665	0.08744	0.18744	11.436	5.335	8
9	2.358	0.4241	0.07364	0.17364	13.579	5.759	9
10	2.594	0.3855	0.06275	0.16275	15.937	6.144	10
11	2.853	0.3505	0.05396	0.15396	18.531	6.495	11
12	3.138	0.3186	0.04676	0.14676	21.384	6.814	12
13	3.452	0.2897	0.04078	0.14078	24.523	7.103	13
14	3.797	0.2633	0.03575	0.13575	27.975	7.367	14
15	4.177	0.2394	0.03147	0.13147	31.772	7.706	15
16	4.595	0.2176	0.02782	0.12782	35.950	7.824	16
17	5.054	0.1978	0.02466	0.12466	40.545	8.022	17
18	5.560	0.1799	0.02193	0.12193	45.599	8.201	18
19	6.116	0.1635	0.01955	0.11955	51.159	8.365	19
20	6.727	0.1486	0.01746	0.11746	57.275	8.514	20
21	7.400	0.1351	0.01562	0.11562	64.002	8.649	21
22	8.140	0.1228	0.01401	0.11401	71.403	8.772	22
23	8.954	0.1117	0.01257	0.11257	79.543	8.883	23
24	9.850	0.1015	0.01130	0.11130	88.497	8.985	24
25	10.835	0.0923	0.01017	0.11017	98.347	9.077	25
26	11.918	0.0839	0.00916	0.10916	109.182	9.161	26
27	13.110	0.0763	0.00826	0.10826	121.100	9.237	27
28	14.421	0.0693	0.00745	0.10745	134.210	9.307	28
29	15.863	0.0630	0.00673	0.10673	148.631	9.370	29
30	17.449	0.0573	0.00608	0.10608	164.494	9.427	30
31	19.194	0.0521	0.00550	0.10550	181.943	9.479	31
32	21.114	0.0474	0.00497	0.10497	201.138	9.526	32
33	23.225	0.0431	0.00450	0.10450	222.252	9.569	33
34	25.548	0.0391	0.00407	0.10407	245.477	9.609	34
35	28.102	0.0356	0.00369	0.10369	271.024	9.644	35
40	45.259	0.0221	0.00226	0.10226	442.593	9.779	40
45	72.890	0.0137	0.00139	0.10139	718.905	9.863	45
50	117.391	0.0085	0.00086	0.10086	1163.909	9.915	50
55	189.059	0.0053	0.00053	0.10053	1880.591	9.947	55
60	304.482	0.0033	0.00033	0.10033	3034.816	9.967	60
65	490.371	0.0020	0.00020	0.10020	4893.707	9.980	65
70	789.747	0.0013	0.00013	0.10013	7887.470	9.987	70
75	1271.895	0.0008	0.00008	0.10008	12708.954	9.992	75
80	2048.400	0.0005	0.00005	0.10005	20474.002	9.995	80
85	3298.969	0.0003	0.00003	0.10003	32979.690	9.997	85
90	5313.023	0.0002	0.00002	0.10002	53120.226	9.998	90
95	8556.676	0.0001	0.00001	0.10001	85556.760	9.999	95
100	13780.612	0.0001	0.00001	0.10001	137796.123	9.999	100

15 per cent Compound Interest Factors

	SINGLE PAYMENT		UNIFORM SERIES			
	Compound Amount Factor caf'	Present Worth Factor pwf'	Sinking Fund Factor sff	Capital Recovery Factor crf	Compound Amount Factor caf	Present Worth Factor pwf
n	Given P To find S $(1+i)^n$	Given S To find P $\dfrac{1}{(1+i)^n}$	Given S To find R $\dfrac{i}{(1+i)^n-1}$	Given P To find R $\dfrac{i(1+i)^n}{(1+i)^n-1}$	Given R To find S $\dfrac{(1+i)^n-1}{i}$	Given R To find P $\dfrac{(1+i)^n-1}{i(1+i)^n}$
1	1.150	0.8696	1.00000	1.15000	1.000	0.870
2	1.322	0.7561	0.46512	0.61512	2.150	1.626
3	1.521	0.6575	0.28798	0.43798	3.472	2.283
4	1.749	0.5718	0.20027	0.35027	4.993	2.855
5	2.011	0.4972	0.14832	0.29832	6.742	3.352
6	2.313	0.4323	0.11424	0.26424	8.754	3.784
7	2.660	0.3759	0.09036	0.24036	11.067	4.160
8	3.059	0.3269	0.07285	0.22285	13.727	4.487
9	3.518	0.2843	0.05957	0.20957	16.786	4.772
10	4.046	0.2472	0.04925	0.19925	20.304	5.019
11	4.652	0.2149	0.04107	0.19107	24.349	5.234
12	5.350	0.1869	0.03448	0.18448	29.002	5.421
13	6.153	0.1625	0.02911	0.17911	34.352	5.583
14	7.076	0.1413	0.02469	0.17469	40.505	5.724
15	8.137	0.1229	0.02102	0.17102	47.580	5.847
16	9.358	0.1069	0.01795	0.16795	55.717	5.954
17	10.761	0.0929	0.01537	0.16537	65.075	6.047
18	12.375	0.0808	0.01319	0.16319	75.836	6.128
19	14.232	0.0703	0.01134	0.16134	88.212	6.198
20	16.367	0.0611	0.00976	0.15976	102.444	6.259
21	18.822	0.0531	0.00842	0.15842	118.810	6.312
22	21.645	0.0462	0.00727	0.15727	137.632	6.359
23	24.891	0.0402	0.00628	0.15628	159.276	6.399
24	28.625	0.0349	0.00543	0.15543	184.168	6.434
25	32.919	0.0304	0.00470	0.15470	212.793	6.464
26	37.857	0.0264	0.00407	0.15407	245.712	6.491
27	43.535	0.0230	0.00353	0.15353	283.569	6.514
28	50.066	0.0200	0.00306	0.15306	327.104	6.534
29	57.575	0.0174	0.00265	0.15265	377.170	6.551
30	66.212	0.0151	0.00230	0.15230	434.745	6.566
35	133.176	0.0075	0.00113	0.15113	881.170	6.617
40	267.864	0.0037	0.00056	0.15056	1779.090	6.642
45	538.769	0.0019	0.00028	0.15028	3585.128	6.654
50	1083.657	0.0009	0.00014	0.15014	7217.716	6.661
55	2179.622	0.0005	0.00007	0.15007	14524.148	6.664
60	4383.999	0.0002	0.00003	0.15003	29219.992	6.665
65	8817.787	0.0001	0.00002	0.15002	58778.583	6.666

20 per cent Compound Interest Factors

	SINGLE PAYMENT		UNIFORM SERIES			
	Compound Amount Factor caf'	Present Worth Factor pwf'	Sinking Fund Factor sff	Capital Recovery Factor crf	Compound Amount Factor caf	Present Worth Factor pwf
n	Given P To find S $(1+i)^n$	Given S To find P $\dfrac{1}{(1+i)^n}$	Given S To find R $\dfrac{i}{(1+i)^n-1}$	Given P To find R $\dfrac{i(1+i)^n}{(1+i)^n-1}$	Given R To find S $\dfrac{(1+i)^n-1}{i}$	Given R To find P $\dfrac{(1+i)^n-1}{i(1+i)^n}$
1	1.200	0.8333	1.00000	1.20000	1.000	0.833
2	1.440	0.6944	0.45455	0.65455	2.200	1.528
3	1.728	0.5787	0.27473	0.47473	3.640	2.106
4	2.074	0.4823	0.18629	0.38629	5.368	2.589
5	2.488	0.4019	0.13438	0.33438	7.442	2.991
6	2.986	0.3349	0.10071	0.30071	9.930	3.326
7	3.583	0.2791	0.07742	0.27742	12.916	3.605
8	4.300	0.2326	0.06061	0.26061	16.499	3.837
9	5.160	0.1938	0.04808	0.24808	20.799	4.031
10	6.192	0.1615	0.03852	0.23852	25.959	4.192
11	7.430	0.1346	0.03110	0.23110	32.150	4.327
12	8.916	0.1122	0.02526	0.22526	39.581	4.439
13	10.699	0.0935	0.02062	0.22062	48.497	4.533
14	12.839	0.0779	0.01689	0.21689	59.196	4.611
15	15.407	0.0649	0.01388	0.21388	72.035	4.675
16	18.488	0.0541	0.01144	0.21144	87.442	4.730
17	22.186	0.0451	0.00944	0.20944	105.931	4.775
18	26.623	0.0376	0.00781	0.20781	128.117	4.812
19	31.948	0.0313	0.00646	0.20646	154.740	4.843
20	38.338	0.0261	0.00536	0.20536	186.688	4.870
21	46.005	0.0217	0.00444	0.20444	225.026	4.891
22	55.206	0.0181	0.00369	0.20369	271.031	4.909
23	66.247	0.0151	0.00307	0.20307	326.237	4.925
24	79.497	0.0126	0.00255	0.20255	392.484	4.937
25	95.396	0.0105	0.00212	0.20212	471.981	4.948
26	114.475	0.0087	0.00176	0.20176	567.377	4.956
27	137.371	0.0073	0.00147	0.20147	681.853	4.964
28	164.845	0.0061	0.00122	0.20122	819.223	4.970
29	197.814	0.0051	0.00102	0.20102	984.068	4.975
30	237.376	0.0042	0.00085	0.20085	1181.882	4.979
35	590.668	0.0017	0.00034	0.20034	2948.341	4.992
40	1469.772	0.0007	0.00014	0.20014	7343.858	4.997
45	3657.262	0.0003	0.00005	0.20005	18281.310	4.999
50	9100.438	0.0001	0.00002	0.20002	45497.191	4.999

25 per cent Compound Interest Factors

	SINGLE PAYMENT		UNIFORM SERIES			
	Compound Amount Factor caf'	Present Worth Factor pwf'	Sinking Fund Factor sff	Capital Recovery Factor crf	Compound Amount Factor caf	Present Worth Factor pwf
n	Given P To find S $(1+i)^n$	Given S To find P $\dfrac{1}{(1+i)^n}$	Given S To find R $\dfrac{i}{(1+i)^n-1}$	Given P To find R $\dfrac{i(1+i)^n}{(1+i)^n-1}$	Given R To find S $\dfrac{(1+i)^n-1}{i}$	Given R To find P $\dfrac{(1+i)^n-1}{i(1+i)^n}$
1	1.250	0.8000	1.00000	1.25000	1.000	0.800
2	1.562	0.6400	0.44444	0.69444	2.250	1.440
3	1.953	0.5120	0.26230	0.51230	3.812	1.952
4	2.441	0.4096	0.17344	0.42344	5.766	2.362
5	3.052	0.3277	0.12185	0.37185	8.207	2.689
6	3.815	0.2621	0.08882	0.33882	11.259	2.951
7	4.768	0.2097	0.06634	0.31634	15.073	3.161
8	5.960	0.1678	0.05040	0.30040	19.842	3.329
9	7.451	0.1342	0.03876	0.28876	25.802	3.463
10	9.313	0.1074	0.03007	0.28007	33.253	3.571
11	11.642	0.0859	0.02349	0.27349	42.566	3.656
12	14.552	0.0687	0.01845	0.26845	54.208	3.725
13	18.190	0.0550	0.01454	0.26454	68.760	3.780
14	22.737	0.0440	0.01150	0.26150	86.949	3.824
15	28.422	0.0352	0.00912	0.25912	109.687	3.859
16	35.527	0.0281	0.00724	0.25724	138.109	3.887
17	44.409	0.0225	0.00576	0.25576	173.636	3.910
18	55.511	0.0180	0.00459	0.25459	218.045	3.928
19	69.389	0.0144	0.00366	0.25366	273.556	3.942
20	86.736	0.0115	0.00292	0.25292	342.945	3.954
21	108.420	0.0092	0.00233	0.25233	429.681	3.963
22	135.525	0.0074	0.00186	0.25186	538.101	3.970
23	169.407	0.0059	0.00148	0.25148	673.626	3.976
24	211.758	0.0047	0.00119	0.25119	843.033	3.981
25	264.698	0.0038	0.00095	0.25095	1054.791	3.985
26	330.872	0.0030	0.00076	0.25076	1319.489	3.988
27	413.590	0.0024	0.00061	0.25061	1650.361	3.990
28	516.988	0.0019	0.00048	0.25048	2063.952	3.992
29	646.235	0.0015	0.00039	0.25039	2580.939	3.994
30	807.794	0.0012	0.00031	0.25031	3227.174	3.995
35	2465.190	0.0004	0.00010	0.25010	9856.761	3.998
40	7523.164	0.0001	0.00003	0.25003	30088.655	3.999

30 per cent Compound Interest Factors

n	SINGLE PAYMENT		UNIFORM SERIES			
	Compound Amount Factor caf'	Present Worth Factor pwf'	Sinking Fund Factor sff	Capital Recovery Factor crf	Compound Amount Factor caf	Present Worth Factor pwf
	Given P To find S $(1+i)^n$	Given S To find P $\dfrac{1}{(1+i)^n}$	Given S To find R $\dfrac{i}{(1+i)^n-1}$	Given P To find R $\dfrac{i(1+i)^n}{(1+i)^n-1}$	Given R To find S $\dfrac{(1+i)^n-1}{i}$	Given R To find P $\dfrac{(1+i)^n-1}{i(1+i)^n}$
1	1.300	0.7692	1.00000	1.30000	1.000	0.769
2	1.690	0.5917	0.43478	0.73478	2.300	1.361
3	2.197	0.4552	0.25063	0.55063	3.990	1.816
4	2.856	0.3501	0.16163	0.46163	6.187	2.166
5	3.713	0.2693	0.11058	0.41058	9.043	2.436
6	4.827	0.2072	0.07839	0.37839	12.756	2.643
7	6.275	0.1594	0.05687	0.35687	17.583	2.802
8	8.157	0.1226	0.04192	0.34192	23.858	2.925
9	10.604	0.0943	0.03124	0.33124	32.015	3.019
10	13.786	0.0725	0.02346	0.32346	42.619	3.092
11	17.922	0.0558	0.01773	0.31773	56.405	3.147
12	23.298	0.0429	0.01345	0.31345	74.327	3.190
13	30.288	0.0330	0.01024	0.31024	97.625	3.223
14	39.374	0.0254	0.00782	0.30782	127.913	3.249
15	51.186	0.0195	0.00598	0.30598	167.286	3.268
16	66.542	0.0150	0.00458	0.30458	218.472	3.283
17	86.504	0.0116	0.00351	0.30351	285.014	3.295
18	112.455	0.0089	0.00269	0.30269	371.518	3.304
19	146.192	0.0068	0.00207	0.30207	483.973	3.311
20	190.050	0.0053	0.00159	0.30159	630.165	3.316
21	247.065	0.0040	0.00122	0.30122	820.215	3.320
22	321.184	0.0031	0.00094	0.30094	1067.280	3.323
23	417.539	0.0024	0.00072	0.30072	1388.464	3.325
24	542.801	0.0018	0.00055	0.30055	1806.003	3.327
25	705.641	0.0014	0.00043	0.30043	2348.803	3.329
26	917.333	0.0011	0.00033	0.30033	3054.444	3.330
27	1192.533	0.0008	0.00025	0.30025	3971.778	3.331
28	1550.293	0.0006	0.00019	0.30019	5164.311	3.331
29	2015.381	0.0005	0.00015	0.30015	6714.604	3.332
30	2619.996	0.0004	0.00011	0.30011	8729.985	3.332
35	9727.860	0.0001	0.00003	0.30003	32422.868	3.333

Index

Absolute liability, 109, 118
Absorption costing, 278–281
Accelerated
    payment, 131, 159
    tax, 323
Accounting
    adjustments, 377–381
    changes, 377, 386–387
    cost, see Cost accounting
    cycle, 332–344
    error, 263, 384–387
    financial, 229–230, 331–397
    fixed assets, 356–360
    responsibility, 233–234
    transactions, 344–369
Accrual method, 345–346, 369–
    370, 378–384
Acts of God, 123
Advertisement, 90–92
Agent, 133
AICPA, 331–332, 353, 357, 371,
    374–376, 393–394, 396
Amortize, 158, 348, 367–368
Annual cost method, 315–318
Annuities, 307–309
Assignment, 118
Associated General Contractors,
    90, 92
Attractive nuisance, 109
Audit, 235–236, 331, 338, 357
Authority, 9–10, 46

Average investment method,
    296–298, 312
Badge system, 253
Balance sheet, see Financial posi-
    tion statement
Bank, 235, 331
Bank reconciliation, 354–356
Behavior approach, 2–4
Bid strategy, 81–89
Bill of exchange, see Draft
Bird dogging, 90, 92
Bonding capacity, 19–20
Bonds, 21, 166–170, 351–352
Bonus method, 347–348
Bookkeeping, 243, 260–264
Breach of contract, 108, 110,
    117–118, 121–125
Budget, 7, 269, 273, 281–289
Building codes, 181
Business
    failure, 1
    management, 2–5
Call privilege, 167
Capital
    asset, 295
    budgeting, 295–326
    gain, 325–326
Cash
    flow, 55, 57, 59, 145, 232,
        281–289, 323, 365

Cash (continued)
  method, 345–346, 351,
    369–370, 378–384
  proof, 354–356
Cashier's check, 130
Certified check, 130
Certified Public Accountant, 235,
  331
Change in financial position,
  341–344, 387, 394–397
Change order, 124
Checks, 126, 128–130
Civil Rights Act, 134–135
Clique, 199–200
Columnar format, 270, 273
Commercial
  construction, 16–18
  paper, 126–134
Communication, 39, 72, 188–193
Compensating balance, 153
Competition, 79–89
Competitive bid, 70, 89, 94, 265
Completed contract method, 59,
  371–377
Computer, 233
Conservative principle, 337, 370,
  373, 377
Consistency principle, 336
Construction firm
  size 19–20
  types, 15–24
Construction loan, 57
Construction management,
  23–24
Construction manager, 20
Contract
  agreement, 112–115
  bilateral, 111
  competent parties, 116–118
  cost plus, 111, 113
  exchange, 120–121
  expressed, 111

implied, 111
legal subject matter, 118–
  121
quasi, 111
separate-but-equal, 136
termination, 121–126
unilateral, 111–112
valid, 110
void, 110
voidable, 110, 114–116, 118
Contract law, see Law
Contributed capital, 346–350
Controller, 9, 45
Controlling, 5–6, 8–9, 40, 273
Conversion privilege, 167
Corporation
  formation, 35
  liability, 37–38
  statements, 234–235
  stock, 36
  tax, 35–37
Cost
  accounting, 9, 40, 229–290
  budget, 242
  committed, 279
  control, 229
  conversion, 242
  direct, 238, 241, 270
  fixed, 236–238
  function, 238
  historical, 242
  labor, 248–254, 261–263
  material, 244–248, 263–264
  object, 236–239, 265
  overhead, 254–260
  period, 236, 278
  prime, 242
  principle, 335–336
  product, 236, 240
  replacement, 336
  standard, 243
  unit, 236, 239–240

variable, 236–238
Credit line, 57, 153
Current ratio, 59–60, 159

Damages
    compensatory, 124
    mitigate, 124–125
    nominal, 124
    punitive, 124
Davis Bacon Act, 134
Debenture, 168
Debt, 50, 53, 56–57, 165–170
Debt capital, 350–352
Decision making
    centralized, 9, 41
    decentralized, 9, 41
    experience, 10
    experimentation, 10
    follow-the-leader, 10
    intuition, 10
    marginal analysis, 10–11
    systems approach, 11
Deferred charge, 389
Departmentation, 7
Depreciation, 297, 315, 321–324,
    360–365
Design-Build, 20, 22–23
Developer, 20, 22, 34. 57
Direct costing, 278–281
Directing, 5–6, 8, 183–188
Discounted cash flow, 309–315
Disaffirm, 116
Distribution, 69
Document flowcharting, 260–
    264
Dodge Service, 90
Draft, 126, 132–133
Draw account, 145
Dun and Bradstreet, 58, 62
Duress, 115
Dynamic programming, 93

Earning power, 48–53
Earnings per share, 391, 393
Economic analysis, 164
Embezzlement, 106
Endorsement
    co-maker, 153
    guarantor, 126, 153
    types, 126
Equipment
    accounting, 357–360
    depreciation, 321, 360–365
    financing, 160–164
    usage, 17
Equity, 50, 56–57, 165, 170–173
Estimating, 233
Exception principle, 336
Expected profit, 82–89
External relations, 23, 70–71,
    92–95

Failures, see Business failure
Fayol, Henri, 3
Federal Trade Securities Act, 170
Feedback, 193
Felony, 106
Financial
    accounting, 279, 331–397
    analysis, 58–63
    leverage, 48, 50–53, 350
    liquidity, 53, 365
    ratios, 58–63, 155
    risk, 53, 57
    structure, 48–58
Financial position statement,
    56–57, 60, 158, 333, 340–
    344, 387–391
Financing, see Funding
First year depreciation, 323–324
Fixing bids, 106, 109
Forebearance, 120
Forecasting, 6
Forgery, 107, 130

Fraud, 115, 122, 130
Full disclosure principle, 335
Function
    line, 45
    staff, 45
Functional approach, 2–5
Funding, 143–173

General contractor, 20–21
Goodwill method, 348
Grapevine, 191
Growth
    horizontal, 44–45, 55
    planned, 71, 76, 143, 279,
        282–283
    vertical, 45
Guarantor, see Endorsement

Hawthorne plant studies, 2
Heavy and highway construc-
    tion, 16–18, 295

Immediate profit, 81–89
Imprest fund, 354
Incidental beneficiary, 117
Income
    non-passive, 37
    passive, 39
    statement, 60–61, 158, 279,
        340–344, 387, 391–393
Indenture, 166
Independent contractor, 133
Indictment, 106
Industrialized building, 279, 281
Information system, 47, 233–234,
    260
Insolvency, 168, 171
Installment purchase, 366–367
Intangible asset, 348
Interest
    amount, 51, 53
    debt, 168–169

formulas, 300–309
points, 163
Investment
    banker, 170–171, 173
    tax credit, 324–325
Invoice, 263

Job order costing, 265–270
Joint venture, 24, 33–35, 117
Journal, 337–339

Labor
    groups, 198–202, 221–222
    unions, 4, 134–135, 181–
        183, 197–198, 272
Law
    administrative, 105–106
    common, 103
    constitutional, 104
    contract, 104, 110–126
    criminal, 104–108
    employment, 134–135
    private, 104, 108
    public, 104
    statute, 103
    tort, 104, 108–109, 125
Leadership
    authoritarian, 183–184, 187
    democratic, 184, 187
    free rein, 184, 187
    participative, 184
    qualities, 3, 8, 183–188
Learning curve, 181
Lease,
    accounting, 57, 357, 365–
        369
    commitment, 324
    financing, 165, 367–368
    operating, 367
    purchase, 324
    tax, 321–322

Leaseback, 161–162
Ledger, 339–340, 343
Legal capital, 349
Leverage, see Financial leverage
License, 26, 35–36, 107, 116, 118
Lien, 125–126, 371
Limited partnership, 24, 33–35
Liquidity, see Financial liquidity
Loan
        participation, 157
        short term, 150–156

Managerial grid, 186–188
Manufacturing industry, 70
Margin, 49
Marketing, 69–97
Marketing research, 72–76
Marshaling of assets, 31, 33
Matching principle, 335
Materiality, 336–337
McGregor, Douglass, 194, 196
Mechanic's lien, see Lien
Method, 7
Method Productivity Delay
        Model, 211–220
Misdemeanor, 106–107
Monopoly, 78–79
Monthly billings, 147
Motion analysis, 208–211
Motivation, 8, 180, 193–198, 204,
        220–223

National Labor Relations Act, 105
Negotiated bid, 70, 89, 94
Novation, 118

Offset, 151–152
Open shop, 107
Option contract, 112–113
Ordinary annuity, see Annuities
Ordinary terms, 147
Organizational

chart, 7, 41–42
chain structive, 41–47
circular structure, 41–42,
        47–49
structure, 7–8, 39–49, 71,
        190, 204
Organizing, 5–7, 39
Originating house, 170
OSHA, 108
Overhead, 17, 19–20, 269, 274,
        278, 374
Overtime, 237, 241

Parol evidence, 115
Partnership
        authority, 30
        formation, 27
        income, 27–29
        liability, 30–31
        liquidation, 31–33
        tax, 28–30
Par value, 168, 349
Payback method, 298–300, 312
Payroll, 251–254, 260–264
Percentage completion method,
        59, 337, 371–377
Perfect competition, 78–79
Personnel management, 179–223
Petty cash, 353–354
Phased construction, 23
Piece work, 197
Placing, 95–96
Planning, 5–6, 69, 71–76, 181,
        233
Policy, 6
Posting, 339–340
Preemptive right, 171
Prepayments, 131
Present worth, 169, 310, 318–
        320, 358, 368
Pricing, 69, 71, 77–89
Prime rate, 155, 164, 319

Privity of contract, 136
Procedure, 6–7
Process
    chart, 210
    costing, 265–266
Procurement, 45, 271
Productivity
    construction, 179–183
    delays, 212–213
    models, 205–223
Profit
    margin, 63, 231
    ratios, 62
    volume curve, 77
Profit and loss statement,
    see Income statement
Promissory notes, 126, 130–132
Promoting, 69, 71, 89–95
Proprietorship, 24–26
Prospective, 171

Quantitative approach, see Sys-
    tems approach
Quick ratio, 60–61

Rate of return, 49, 53, 296–298,
    309–315
Ratify, 116
Real Estate Investment Trust, 22
Reasonable man, 109, 113–114,
    123
Receivables, 54–55, 61
Relevant range, 237
Rescind, 115, 121
Residential construction, 16–18
Responsibility, 9, 46
Restitution, 116
Retainage, 145, 285
Retention, 54–55
Revenue principle, 334–335
Reversing entries, 343

Revoke, 113

Sales, see Marketing
Sales volume, 77
Salvage value, 297, 317–318, 361
SBA, 145, 157, 160, 164
Scientific approach, 3–4
Securities and Exchange
    Commission, 35, 235, 331,
    345, 394
Security, 151
Selling, see Promoting
Semantics, 189
Serial bond, 166
Service industry, 70
Sight draft, see Draft
Sinking fund, 166
Spec builder, 20–22, 57
Specialization, 40
Standard, 7–8
    cost, 269–278
    time, 206–207
Statute of frauds, 110–111
Sterotype, 192
Stock
    closed, 36
    common, 171–172
    open, 36
    preemptive right, 36
    preferred, 171–172
    rights, 171
    treasury, 172
Stop payment order, 129–130
Subchapter S corporation, 24,
    38–39
Subcontractor, 19–21, 133–135
Substantial completion, 122, 285,
    335
Supervision, see Leadership
Supplier intersale, 148
Sureties, 58
Systems approach, 3–5

Tax, 36–37, 52–53, 168–170,
   240–241, 243, 315, 320–
   321, 324–326, 332, 345,
   359, 386, 392
Tax option corporation, see
   Subchapter S corporation
Taylor, Frederick, 2–3, 208
Theory X, 8, 193–198, 221
Theory Y, 8, 193–198
Therblig, 209–210
Time
   draft, see Draft
   lapse, 213
   motion studies, 272
   study, 206–207
   value of money, 295–326
Timekeeper, 246–254, 266
Trade
   credit, 146–150, 157
   discount, 149–150
Trade acceptance, 132

Treasurer, 45
Trial balance, 340–341
Turnover, 49

Underwrite, 171
Uniform Commercial Code, 127,
   129
Uniform Partnership Act, 27
Unions, see Labor unions
Usury, 119–120

Variances, 269–278

Wall Street Journal, 76, 91
Working capital, 59, 143, 155, 170
Work-in-progress, 266, 281
Workmen's compensation, 135
Work sampling, 207–208
Worksheet, 340–342, 384–385

Yield, 166–169, 352